DEEP WOODS
FRONTIER

GREAT LAKES BOOKS

Philip P. Mason, Editor
Department of History, Wayne State University

Dr. Charles K. Hyde, Associate Editor
Department of History, Wayne State University

DEEP WOODS FRONTIER

A History of Logging in Northern Michigan

THEODORE J. KARAMANSKI

 WAYNE STATE UNIVERSITY PRESS   Detroit

Library of Congress Cataloging-in-Publication Data
Karamanski, Theodore J., 1953–
  Deep woods frontier : a history of logging in northern Michigan / Theodore J. Karamanski.—Great Lakes Books ed.
    p. cm.—(Great Lakes books)
  Bibliography: p.
  Includes index.
  ISBN 0-8143-2048-1 (alk. paper).—ISBN 0-8143-2049-X (pbk. : alk. paper)
  1. Logging—Michigan—Upper Peninsula—History. I. Title. II. Series.
SD538.2.M5K37   1989
634.9′82′097749—dc19   88–32320
                                                                            CIP

ISBN-13: 978-0-8143-2049-5
ISBN-10: 0-8143-2049-X

FOR EILEEN
MY BEST FRIEND AND DEAREST COLLEAGUE

CONTENTS

ILLUSTRATIONS

Photographs following page 123.

MAPS

PREFACE

The Upper Peninsula of Michigan holds a special place in the imagination of many midwesterners. Its vast forests and expansive lakeshores show what the landscape of the entire Great Lakes region was like before cities and industry. When I was growing up in Chicago, the Upper Peninsula always seemed like a frontier region. It was as far north as could be driven in one day from the metropolitan areas of Chicago, Detroit, or Milwaukee. It was at the farthest reaches of the region Chicago was in, yet the Upper Peninsula's austere beauty and resource wealth was much more akin to the wilderness of the Canadian shield, which stretched from Lake Superior to the Arctic Ocean. The Upper Peninsula seemed to be the United States' share of the taiga—a land my imagination populated with fur traders, Indians, and lumberjacks. Historical study has been a way for me to create a more accurate image of the northern frontier. Yet this book is in some ways a product of the enduring romance of the north woods.

Youthful images and professional opportunities merged in 1982 when I was employed by the USDA Forest Service to evaluate the sites of several abandoned lumber camps in northern Michigan. As I walked over the remains of once busy bunkhouses covered by second growth forest and talked with the gray-haired men who worked there, the idea to write this book took root. I would like to thank the supervisors and staff of the Hiawatha and Ottawa national forests for the opportunity to begin research on this book through a series of cultural resource location and evaluation projects. The cultural resource professionals and paraprofessionals in each of the ranger districts, especially Rebecca Dinsmore and David Schmidt in the Ottawa National Forest, were of great assistance. John Franzen of the Hiawatha National Forest helped conceive these projects and was an active ally in locating records and informants. I also would like to acknowledge the help of Dr. Janet Brashler, now of the Monongahela National Forest, who shared her enthusiasm for the cultural history of Michigan and the potential for its study. Without the assistance of the USDA Forest Service and its staff this book would not have been written.

Deep Woods Frontier is a local history. Much of the material in this study was available only because of the hard work and dedication of several local history societies in northern Michigan. The following groups provided vital information: the Delta County Historical Society, Ontonagon Historical Society, Alger County Historical Society, Schoolcraft County Historical Society, Luce County Historical Society, and the Iron County Museum. Among the most helpful individuals were: James Carter, Hoyt Avery, Sheldon Cobb, Gene Worth, Robert Schemlling, Rudi Jehn, Faye Swanberg, Frances Merton, William Taylor, Bert Simmions, Harvey Barret, Malcolm McIver, and Mrs. Alan Mercier. Special thanks must go to the great storehouse of Upper Peninsula history, the John M. Longyear Research Library of the Marquette County Historical Society. In particular let me thank Rachel Crary and Marcy Houlmont for their help over the past four years. I would also like to thank Stuart Sunblad of the Cleveland-Cliffs Iron Corporation, Fred Peterson of the Longyear Realty Corporation, and John Force of the Keweenaw Land Association for helping me consult their timber records. James Kaysen of Cedarburg, Wisconsin, shared his files on logging railroads.

Research was similarly assisted by the staffs of the Michigan Historical Collections in Ann Arbor; the Burton Historical Collection in the Detroit Public Library; the State Library in Lansing, Michigan; Clarke Historical Library in Mount Pleasant, Michigan; the Baylis Library in Sault Sainte Marie, Michigan; the Michigan State University Archives in East Lansing; Michigan Technological University Special Collections Department; the Lilly Library in Bloomington, Indiana; the Federal Archives and Records Center in Chicago; the Chicago Historical Society, the Newberry Library; the Center for Research Libraries in Chicago; the Northwestern Library in Evanston, Illinois; and Cudahy Library at Loyola University. I would like to thank David Krippen at the Ford Archives. Special acknowledgment is due Leroy Barnett, archivist at the States Archives of Michigan, for the wonderful advice and assistance he offered me throughout this project.

Closer to home I would like to acknowledge several colleagues at Loyola University. Robert McCluggage has been a continuing source of insights and bibliographic leads. My departmental chairmen, first Walter Gray and more recently Joseph Gagliano, have supported my desire to integrate public history work with scholarly research. Thomas J. Bennett of the Research Service Department has been helpful with many project proposals and a 1985 summer research grant. Research assistants William Irvine, John Vogel, and Melinda Campbell worked on the project. Joel Mendes and Gerald Morin did an excellent job helping me gather oral history accounts of the lumber industry and investigate forest ghost towns. My associate at the Mid-American Research Center, David J. Keene, was—as always—a valued partner in fieldwork. Sharon Linger typed the manuscript and offered useful suggestions. I would also like to thank Joanne Grossman for her assistance in preparing the index.

Finally, I would like to thank the people who lived the story of *Deep Woods Frontier* and shared their memoirs: John Brotherton, Robert Radcliffe, Bertha Harding, Kenneth Mallmenn, Percy LaRock, Charles Taylor, Francis Furlong, John Anguilm, Everette Colegrove, Lawrence Boucha, Louis Verch, Wanio Turin, Simon Brozoznowski, Edward Glocke, Oscar Greenlund, James Stark, Wes Camps, Paul Malovrh, Robert Anderson, George Corrigan, Edward Erickson, Anthony Andreski, Bess Elliot, and Thomas Nordine.

INTRODUCTION

"What will I find if I continue north from here?" The speaker was a short man wearing a felt hat set low on his head to shield him from the setting sun. His name was Cleng Peerson, and his words were tainted by a strong Norwegian accent. In front of him was a bronzed and hardy fur trader, Solomon Juneau. The pathetic cluster of huts about them was all there was of the city of Milwaukee in 1833. The fur trader thought over the man's question. Perhaps he pictured the expansive forests and giant lakes of the north country. What would the traveler find to the north? Juneau wryly replied, "Nothing but woods, to the world's end."[1]

Juneau's response may be folklore, but it reflects the awesome reality of the Great Lakes wilderness. Explorers, fur traders, and early settlers were greeted by the sight of a vast green canopy covering the earth. To the west of Lake Michigan lay Wisconsin's forests, to the east Michigan's belts of hardwood and pine. To fur traders at the growing settlement of Chicago and to downstate prairie farmers, these were the "north woods"—a land of roving Indian hunters, sparkling rivers, and most of all, tall timber. North of Wisconsin and beyond lower Michigan's forests lay the Upper Peninsula. Surrounded on three sides by inland seas, the Upper Peninsula was the remote deep woods frontier. Here the vast forest that stretched north from Solomon Juneau's cabin finally ceased, on the rocky shores of Lake Superior.

Dense forests were only one of the Upper Peninsula's many natural resources. Over time, the exploitation of iron ore, copper, even silver, have molded the landscape. Agriculture and some manufacturing have helped develop the dark peninsula. Yet since the 1830s, exploitation of the deep woods consistently has been a vital feature of life in the area. The forests of the Upper Peninsula are an excellent historical laboratory for exploring the effects of logging on the social and natural environments. This is a history of how the logging industry colonized the Upper Peninsula of Michigan, the environmental consequences of this exploitation, and the degree to which the loggers were forced to adjust to an altered environment. It is the story of the relationship between individuals, industry, and the environment.

The logging industry in the Upper Peninsula followed a pattern experienced throughout the upper Great Lakes region. Changes in the environments that were being exploited and the introduction of new technologies of exploitation created three historical watersheds not unlike Lewis Mumford's stages of industrial growth.[2] The first period was the water-pine era, between 1835 and 1900, when loggers concentrated on exploiting pine or other softwood species. The harvested logs were shipped and processed for market by technologies employing wind and waterpower. By 1900 to at least 1935, railroads were vital to the exploitation of hardwood forests. The rail-hardwood era—though beginning sooner in some parts of the region—yielded to the gasoline-pulpwood era during the Depression of the 1930s. During this final period, pulpwood became the principal product of a specialized forest products industry. Trucks, chain saws, and other internal combustion equipment dominated the cutting and transportation of resources. Each of these periods uniquely affected the social life, spatial arrangement, natural environment, and business structure of the logging towns that made up the deep woods frontier.

Though economics sometimes serves as a backdrop for events considered, this is not an economic history of logging in northern Michigan. Nor is this strictly a social history, an environmental history, or an exercise in historical geography. It is instead a story of individuals, business, and a remote section of the upper Great Lakes region that deals comprehensively with a neglected chapter in regional history.

THE SETTING

The Upper Peninsula of Michigan is composed of 16,453 square miles of diverse terrain. It stretches for more than 260 miles east to west, and from north to south is just over 100 miles wide. Its area is larger than that of the combined states of Massachusetts, Connecticut, and Delaware. The Great Lakes have been very important in the region's history and geography. Lake Superior forms the Upper Peninsula's northern border; to the south lies Lake Michigan and southeast Lake Huron. Deep bays, natural harbors, and the Sault Sainte Marie Canal have made the Upper Peninsula's hundreds of miles of coastline important to commercial development.

The terrain of the western Upper Peninsula is much more rugged than that of the eastern counties. The Porcupine Mountains and the

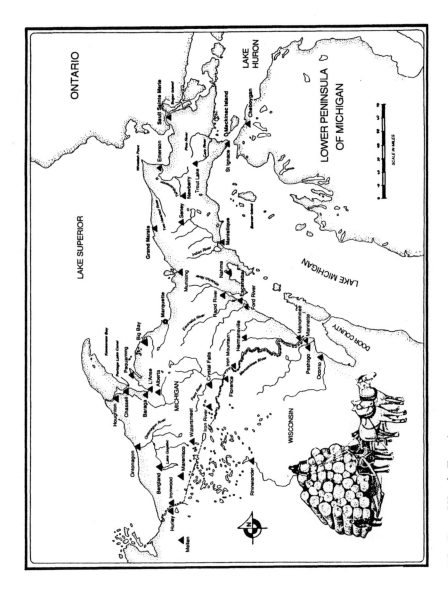

The Deep Woods Frontier

Huron Mountains, which shadow the south shore of Lake Superior, are the two most prominent upland areas in the Upper Peninsula. All of the western region has undulating ridges and valleys. The hills of the Keweenaw Peninsula once were rich in copper ore. Cities sprouted and then withered as the copper country experienced the boom-bust cycle typical of mineral regions. The same pattern has been experienced along the three principal iron ranges of the western Upper Peninsula. The Gogebic Range, which stretches from far western Michigan into Wisconsin, and the Menominee Range to the southeast were both opened in the late nineteenth century only to almost completely close about 100 years later. The earliest of the iron ranges is the Marquette Range, which was opened in 1845 and remains an important source of iron ore today.

The topographic relief of the Upper Peninsula gradually falls off farther east. The counties of Alger, Schoolcraft, Luce, Chippewa, and Mackinac are geologically distinctive from the western region; the uplands of the west are underlain by Precambrian rock, while the eastern counties rest on Paleozoic formations. As a result, rock outcroppings are less common in the east and the landscape is marked by long monotonous stretches of flat land. Marshes and swamps are an important feature in the east. The lack of mineral wealth in this area has meant that agriculture and, especially, logging have been vital to the local economy.[3]

The element of continuity between the Upper Peninsula's eastern and western counties is the forest. In 1941, after more than 100 years of logging, close to ninety percent of the area was still covered by trees. That surviving forest was different from the original forest that became part of Michigan in 1834. The primeval forest of the Upper Peninsula was dominated by hardwood species, such as sugar maple, yellow birch, elm, hemlock, and basswood. Spruce-fir species were typically found on the margins of interior swamps and along the rocky shores of the Great Lakes. Stands of pine favored sandy soils. Towered over by the white pine—the most sought-after of the early timber types—the pineries of the Upper Peninsula made up only fifteen percent of the total forest area. Swamp conifers, such as black spruce, tamarack, and cedar were most common in the great swamps of the eastern Upper Peninsula.[4]

Since the early nineteenth century, the forest landscape of the Upper Peninsula has awed explorers and travelers. Henry Rowe Schoolcraft, who explored the lower Ontonagon River in 1820, was apprehensive of the "heavy forest":

> One cannot help fancying that he has gone to the ends of the earth, and beyond the boundaries apppointed for the residence of man. Every object tells us that it is a region alike unfavorable to the productions of the animal and

vegetable kingdom; and we shudder in casting our eyes over the frightful wreck of trees, and the confused groups of falling-in banks and shattered stones. Yet we have only to ascend these bluffs to behold hills more rugged and elevated; and dark hemlock forests, and yawning gulfs more dreary, and more forbidding to the eye.[5]

What for Schoolcraft was a menacing tangle of trees and copper hunting prospectors "a comparatively useless pine forest" to be burned off to reveal veins of ore, was a resource of more enduring value than metal ore.[6] It would take a particular type of explorer to appreciate the potential of the forest and to transform its verdant setting into a scene of industry. It would take a man able to assess the lumber market, calculate transportation costs, estimate the standing board feet in the forest, and then risk all that his calculations were correct and his luck would hold long enough to establish a pioneer business in the wilderness. That man was a logger.

PART 1

THE PINE ERA

1

THE PASSING OF THE FUR FRONTIER

The first businessmen in the Great Lakes region were fur traders. Like the loggers who followed them, fur traders were involved in a seasonal exploitation of natural resources. Their operations were plagued by limited capital, poor transportation, and vicious competition.[1] Because of these similarities fur traders were important in making logging part of the regional economy. Not only did fur traders establish many of the settlements that blossomed into logging ports, but as pioneer businessmen, fur traders began several important logging ventures. The fur trading firm of Conant and Mack founded one of the early logging establishments in the Detroit area. Rix Robinson, an agent of the American Fur Company, was cofounder of the Grand Haven Company, which as early as 1853 had one hundred thousand dollars invested in a western Michigan logging operation. The first sawmill built in the timber-rich Saginaw Bay area was built by two fur traders, Ephraim and Gardner Williams, who were farsighted enough to see the area's potential.[2] All along the lakeshores of Wisconsin and Michigan, fur traders broke the ground on which loggers later profited handsomely.

In the Upper Peninsula, fur traders fulfilled the same purpose. Their pioneering operations focused attention and capital on those areas of greatest logging potential. This was particularly true for the Sault Sainte Marie and Menominee River regions. Here fur traders began rolling back the deep woods frontier.

Sault Sainte Marie was one of the crossroads of the voyageurs' highway that linked Montreal with a continent-spanning network of trading posts. Unlike Lakes Michigan, Huron, and Erie, whose waves flow smoothly together to form one waterway, Lake Superior is at a higher elevation. To join the other lakes, its waters must tumble down broad and rocky falls on the Saint Marys River. Since the seventeenth century, when French explorers and fur traders first reached Lake Superior, Sault Sainte Marie was a vital break point on the inland water route. As early as 1668, the French Jesuit priest and explorer, Jacques Marquette, had a mission at Sault Sainte Marie. Later several small farms and trading posts were founded there. Unfortunately, the Treaty of Paris in 1783 wrenched apart the growing fur trade community. The south bank of the Saint Marys River became American territory; the land to the north was administered by the British as part of their Canadian possessions.

After the War of 1812 cleared up any doubts about the permanence of the border, the American Fur Company made Sault Sainte Marie its most important post in the Lake Superior country. The company was the invention of John Jacob Astor, a German immigrant who so shrewdly traded furs that he became one of the wealthiest men in the early republic. The American Fur Company, which was held together by a patchwork of lesser partners and employees on the frontier, was the first successful continentwide business in the United States. Although the North West Company, Astor's rival on the Canadian side of the border, had a small sawmill in operation as early as the 1780s, the American Fur Company did not show any interest in logging until 1822 when the United States Army began construction of a fort at the Sault. To speed contruction, the army erected a sawmill near the fort. Soldiers dug out a raceway for the mill by cutting through the sandstone and clay along the bank. The mill was operated by a water-powered turbine. A contemporary thought that "the sawmill is a very good one and performs its labor with very great dispatch. . . . In operation it performs 140 strokes per minute."[3] The mill was the first in the Upper Peninsula and it marked the first tentative steps toward an important industry.

After Fort Brady (as the Sault post was named) was completed, the army continued to maintain the mill. When fire destroyed the mill house in 1826, it was quickly rebuilt. Later the raceway was deepened to float boats of trade goods around most of the falls. The sawmill was operated through a four-year lease between the army and local businessmen.[4] Originally, the American Fur Company had little interest in leasing the mill; their concern was solely with the pelts of beaver and marten. But by 1834 the structure and orientation of the company began to change. The Astor family withdrew from the firm. Perhaps the wily old merchant sensed that the salad days of the Great Lakes fur trade were over. Certainly competition was increasing and reports that the "fur trade is dull—the Indians do not hunt" from posts like Sault Sainte Marie became more and more common.[5] Despite such warnings Ramsay Crooks, the new head of the American Fur Company, was optimistic about the future. He planned to restore the fur trade by defeating competitors in head-to-head contests. He also saw future profits in new activities such as commercial fishing and the marketing of flour, which would allow the company to profit from the growing agricultural settlements of the Midwest.[6]

Crooks's plans directly affected the Sault Sainte Marie sawmill. The mill could supply boards for the construction of schooners and wooden barrels necessary to operate a successful commercial fishery on Lake Superior. During the fall and winter of 1834 while Crooks planned the lakes fisheries, the sawmill also figured in his scheme to eliminate fur trade competitors. The army leased the mill to John Hulbert, the principal American rival for furs at the Sault. Hulbert's four-year lease with the army ran out in 1835. Although Hulbert had the right to renew his lease on the mill, he hoped to improve the terms of his agreement with the government. The mill was almost ten years old and hardly a model of efficiency. The merchant planned first to refuse the offer of renewal, then renegotiate the lease to his advantage. No one in the small community of Sault Sainte Marie had shown the slightest interest in the old works. The strategy would have been safe, perhaps even smart, if it had not been for Gabriel Franchere, the American Fur Company agent. He somehow divined Hulbert's plan and rushed the news to Crooks, who, in turn, quietly informed the army of the company's intention of engaging the sawmill at the original terms. When the quartermaster at Fort Brady accepted Hulbert's refusal, Hulbert was shocked to discover that he had lost an important annex of his business to his rivals. The American Fur Company found itself in the lumber business.[7]

The sawmill did not thrive under the fur company's management. Crooks was anxious to keep expenditures to a minimum. When the millrace needed repair, he maneuvered to get the army to do the work.[8] At the Sault, the fur traders did sponsor some logging work. To construct a storehouse and to build a schooner, they sent axmen into the forest. The cutting area was five miles from town. The timber was cut and squared by ax in the forest, after which it was drawn to town, over the snow, by horse and oxen.[9] But the American Fur Company also shipped nine thousand feet of pine board from Detroit to the Sault that same year.[10] Therefore, the mill would seem to have been of little utility by 1839. Yet the mill was deemed important enough by the army for it to oppose a state-sponsored scheme to build a canal around the falls. The commandant at Fort Brady demanded that canal construction not disrupt the millrace. Because of this opposition, and a surprising lack of resolution by the state and its contractors, the first attempt to build a canal on the American side of the falls collapsed. The dispute was unfortunate because the old sawmill ceased being worthy of argument. In its run-down condition, it faded from historical view.[11]

By 1842 the American Fur Company also began to fade from the Sault

Sainte Marie scene. The venerable old firm was overwhelmed by more vigorous rivals on the frontier and it was forced into bankruptcy. This left many of the company's former agents free to embark on their own enterprises. The most successful on Lake Superior was Pierre B. Barbeau. He deserted the sinking ship of the American Fur Company two months before its end and established his own general store and fur trading post at the Sault. His timing was propitious. The Lake Superior copper boom began the next year. Hundreds of prospectors, armed with little more than government reports of copper deposits in the Keweenaw Peninsula, passed through the Sault. Barbeau prospered by selling them food, clothing, prospecting equipment, and other items. On the heels of this horde came the iron hunters. Iron ore was discovered in the hills southwest of present-day Marquette, Michigan. Each year the number of people passing through the Sault for the mining country increased. Steamships plied the shoreline between Copper Harbor, Marquette, and Sault Sainte Marie. Between 1840 and 1850 the population of the Upper Peninsula jumped from thirteen hundred to nearly six thousand.[12]

Such a dramatic increase in population did not bode well for the future of Barbeau's fur trade business, but it did point the way to new opportunities. Miners anxious to develop mineral properties spurned the massive pine and hardwood forests that surrounded them and ordered lumber from Barbeau. The fur trader's only access to lumber was from his suppliers in Detroit, who bought boatloads of boards from mill owners on Lake Saint Clair. So keen was the demand for boards in the early years of the rush that cargoes were sometimes intercepted by rival prospectors.[13] It was ludicrous, as well as expensive, to import lumber to the Upper Peninsula. What was needed was another mill. Barbeau's business affairs were complex enough already but he was willing to assist his son-in-law, James P. Pendill, to undertake the project. Sometime between 1846 and 1849 Pendill erected a mill twenty-five miles west of Sault Sainte Marie, on Whitefish Bay.

Pendill's sawmill is one of the few early mills in northern Michigan for which some detailed records have survived. The mill was built along the bank of a creek flowing into Whitefish Bay. A raceway was carved out of the creek and water powered the mill. Originally Pendill appears to have put in one of the new muley saws to cut the wood, though he experienced frequent breakdowns from the temperamental saw. In 1858 he ordered his subordinates to replace the muley with an "old fashioned sash" saw.[14] The mill sold lumber to build an Indian mission at nearby Naomikong Point. Builders in the Sault and elsewhere along the south shore of Lake Superior ordered Pendill's lumber. Barbeau not only kept the mill supplied but arranged for the sale of its products. Timber was cut near the mill site and hauled by double-oxen sleighs. Pendill employed a small crew of eight men, who worked in the woods during the winter and at the mill during the spring. On a good day the mill could saw between twenty-five hundred and three thousand feet.[15] As at many frontier establishments, cash was desperately short. One winter, forest operations were threatened by the death of several oxen. Unable to buy new draft animals, the mill manager was forced to rent oxen from the Indian mission. The rental fee was paid in lumber. Food supplies were also bartered from nearby farmers.[16] Pendill seems to have lived at the mill with his family until 1855 when he landed at Marquette with a load of lumber and built the grand three-storied Tremont House hotel.

The mill was then leased to would-be lumbermen. However, the high cost of supplies, the limited local market, and a lack of capital conspired to defeat the lessees. James H. Anthony, one of the latter tenants, gradually spent more time fishing, trading furs, and making maple sugar.[17] The sawmill fell into disrepair and Pendill merely leased the property as a fishing station. The opening of the first Sault Sainte Marie Canal in 1855 offered Pendill and Barbeau the opportunity to market northern Michigan pine in Detroit and Chicago. But neither man was committed to an experiment in the lumber business. Instead, they concentrated their investments on commercial fishing and real estate.[18] Meanwhile, other small sawmills were erected to serve the budding mining towns on Lake Superior's south shore. As early as 1844 William G. Boswell operated a sawmill at the mouth of Falls River near L'Anse. In 1852 this mill was planning to saw three hundred thousand feet of lumber, most of it for sale elsewhere on the lake.[19] At Ontonagon that same year, Capt. John G. Parker set up a small steam mill.[20] But commercial logging in the Lake Superior country was a premature enterprise in the 1850s. Prospectors and fur traders could, for a short time yet, call the region their own.

THE FUR TRADE AND MENOMINEE RIVER LOGGING

The Menominee River was one of the most important waterways in the history of northern Michigan. Size alone made its potential magnificent. Its waters drained four thousand square miles. Fed by many smaller streams, the fingers of the Menominee River reached from the shores of Green Bay on Lake Michigan to within twelve miles of Lake Superior.[21] Despite dangerous rapids and falls, the river was an excellent route to the interior of the western Upper Peninsula. It is only natural that such a strategic waterway as the Menominee River, like the Sault Sainte Marie rapids, would attract the attention of the early fur traders and become the scene of early commercial logging.

William Farnsworth began logging on the Menominee River drainage. Like Pierre B. Barbeau, he was a disgruntled American Fur Company trader who went into the fur business for himself. Unlike Barbeau, he was a bold man who would brook no opposition. When he first began trading on the Menominee River, the American Fur Company tried to drive him out of business by inciting the local Indians to seize his goods. However, Farnsworth held them at bay and at last forced them to flee when he boldly threatened to touch a lighted candle to a keg of gunpowder. Even so, the trade returns along the river were meager. To augment that everdecreasing source of profit, Farnsworth turned to logging. In 1831 he and a Detroit-based partner, Charles R. Brush, received a permit to build a sawmill near the mouth of the river, on a site that was then Indian land. Their venture did not prosper. Brush, who seems to have been forced on Farnsworth by Lewis Cass, governor of the Michigan Territory, was a useless partner.[22] To hold down costs, they engaged loggers on terms typically used by fur traders to hire voyageurs. One man, for example, signed a yearly contract that was payable not in cash but in "clothing, and such other merchandise as his necessities shall require." Even such low labor costs when joined to the cost of mill construction and the high price of cargo transport could not keep the mill from going into debt. When Farnsworth could not meet his increasing financial losses, the mill was seized by the sheriff of the territory and sold at auction.[23]

Although Farnsworth had failed as a lumberman, his dream of exploiting the Menominee's forest resources was shared by others. His mill changed hands several times (once for the mundane fee of eighteen barrels of whitefish), yet no one could make it pay. Farnsworth's former millwright, Charles McLeod, tried operating his own mill twelve miles upriver near rapids. Even though McLeod cut free timber off the public domain, he could not turn a profit, and after five years closed the mill. More than one man was ruined trying to launch the logging frontier on the Menominee River.

Dr. Jonathon C. Hall is an example. He was a successful physician who inexplicably left his home in Ithaca, New York, for health reasons. With a small fortune and the capital of his partner, Horace Jerome of Ohio, Hall bought the old Farnsworth mill. For several years they operated at the old mill site; but its dam was so ruined by the 1845 spring flood that they decided to build a new, modern facility. Hall had by this time committed himself completely to the lumber business. He invested ten thousand dollars in the sawmill and owned over forty thousand dollars in total property at the Michigan site. His work force included forty men, who divided their time between mill work and forest operations. Yet the good doctor's efforts were rewarded by a steady stream of frustrations.

He quarreled with John Kittson, who had a trading post on the Upper Menominee River. When Kittson found that Hall's waterpower dam obstructed his passage upstream, he attacked the dam with a band of engagés and Indians. The rupture in the retaining wall played havoc with Hall's cutting schedule. Legal action proved fruitless when Michigan officials wanted Hall to pay for the cost of capturing and transporting Kittson for trial in Mackinac. Such frustrations were all the more nerving because after all that Hall invested in his logging venture it proved to be only marginally profitable—and that in the prosperous years of the early 1850s. The Panic of 1857 knocked Hall off his feet. All his capital was invested in the mill and its operations; he had no reserves to weather a depression. By 1860 he was completely ruined.[24]

Although Hall had lost his entire fortune in the Menominee venture, he had laid the foundation for successful logging in the Upper Peninsula. His only consolation was that his health improved markedly.

Nor was Hall the only lumberman to go bust during the panic. After 1857, lumber prices plummeted in the Great Lakes region. Mills were closed; partnerships dissolved. The political crisis over secession further depressed the market. Only the most resourceful and fortunate loggers could hold their business together. One such man was Isaac Stephenson.

2

MIGRATION OF THE LUMBERMEN

A harsh, cold wind skimmed over the ice of Green Bay sweeping the snow into drifts that threatened to shutter windows and close off the weak light of a winter afternoon. It was February 1867. There was little activity and no excitement in the mills; warehouses and offices that lined the riverfronts of the twin cities of Menominee and Marinette, save for a meeting under way in a store on the Wisconsin side of the river. Gathered in the poorly heated room were the most important merchants and lumbermen in the area. Harrison Ludington, Nelson Ludington, Isaac Stephenson, and his brother Robert represented the Nelson Ludington Company, a giant logging concern that produced close to eighteen million board feet of lumber each year.[1] Samuel Stephenson spoke for Kirby, Carpenter and Company, one of the largest owners of pinelands in Michigan. Also present were Augustus C. Brown and Jesse Spaulding, veteran lumbermen involved with the Menominee River Lumber Company.[2] The problem faced by the lumber barons was less threatening than the stark profit margins and low prices Jonathan Hall and William Farnsworth were forced to endure. Ten years and a Civil War more than doubled the price of lumber. The infant enterprise of former fur traders had become a booming business employing thousands of workers and supporting several giant companies. The lumber barons gathered that day did not discuss economic survival; instead the topic was how to survive the perils of prosperity.

Isaac Stephenson did most of the talking. He noted that "within less than a score of years" lumber production along the Menominee River shot up "from one hundred million to approximately seven hundred million feet" . . . more mills were erected, older mills were enlarged, and on the lower reaches of the river and along the bay shore, the lumber area steadily expanded." To feed those mills, forest operations employed a small army of woodchoppers. Each spring, Stephenson reminded the lumbermen, the Menominee River was chocked with "millions of feet of pine and hemlock logs, which sometimes extended from bank to bank for miles." All loggers operating on the Menominee River faced the problem of driving their logs to the lakeshore. Driving logs—releasing loose timber into a river so that it could be floated to a downstream mill—was begun about 1813 in upstate New York and spread quickly throughout the Northeast. But when many individual loggers operated on the same river, chaos could result. Loggers were careful to strike each log with an iron hammer that left a distinctive mark. Like the branding of cattle, this differentiated one man's logs from another's. Yet the log marks did nothing to prevent timber from being mixed up, and if an unscrupulous party supervised the sorting process, much timber could be stolen. Bitter rivals could sabotage another's entire operation by preventing the logs from making it downriver. Water levels could be adjusted at dams so that thousands of feet of timber would be hung up in shallows, or logs could be diverted downstream past the mill sites. To end this sort of cold war, Stephenson suggested that one central organization—to which all the major operators would subscribe—be founded to supervise driving on the river. They had seen such "boom" companies operate successfully in the East; all present agreed and the Menominee River Boom Company was formed.[3]

The boom company, which brought some order to the busy banks of the Menominee River, was an idea imported from New England. The eastern logging states of Maine, New York, Pennsylvania, as well as the Canadian colonies of Quebec and New Brunswick, were vital in the direction and organization of logging in northern Michigan. The men present that cold February day in Marinette were a case in point. Isaac Stephenson and his brothers Samuel and Robert hailed from New Brunswick and moved to Michigan after several seasons of logging in Maine. Nelson and Harrison Ludington were born in upstate New York. Augustus Brown cut his teeth logging in the Empire State. Brown's associate, Jesse Spaulding, was a logger in Pennsylvania before becoming one of the wealthiest Chicago lumber merchants.[4] The other big lumbermen on the river also were from eastern logging states: William Goodman (Pennsylvania), Daniel Wells (Maine), Frederick Carney (New Brunswick), Andrew Merryman (Maine), and Andrew Stephenson (New Brunswick).[5] Naturally the terminology used by these men in the East became part of the logging "lingo" of the Great Lakes loggers. Large logging camps were described not by the number of men working there but after the Maine fashion of how many teams of oxen were employed. An average size camp would be a "two-team" outfit. A camp bunkhouse or shanty was often described as "a state of Maine." Much of the equipment, such as the broadax, the "go-devil," and the scrivener's scale, which were necessary to take a log from stump to mill, originated in Maine.[6] The amateurish efforts of James Pendill and the fur traders at the Sault may have pointed the way to commercial logging, but it was veteran lumbermen who supplied the capital and know-how to establish an industry.

Among the most important of the pioneer eastern loggers was Jefferson Sinclair of Maine. In the Pine Tree State, he was one of the most successful businessmen in the forest. To a youthful admirer he was the "Napoleon of lumbering," a title he earned because of the expert manner in which he directed his extensive logging operations. His camps were scattered over the vast pine forests along the Saint John River, the Penobscot River, and their many tributaries. Sinclair built the boom on the Penobscot River at Old Town, Maine, which brought order to logging on that stream, and he supervised the first large-scale drive on the Saint John River.[7] In 1845 Sinclair sold his business interests in Maine and immigrated west to the Great Lakes region. His organizational skills figured in the growth of the then infant logging business of northern Michigan.

Moving a family and transferring a business cross-country was formidable for Sinclair. Four years before, he had made an extensive scouting trip of the western states and purchased a tract of farmland near Racine, Wisconsin. But the distance between Maine and Lake Michigan seemed much greater when Sinclair set out with two concord buggies, all his furniture, logging equipment, his family, and their retainers. Their journey took them by steamship, railroad, and canal boat—all before they even reached the Great Lakes. Finally at Buffalo the party boarded the large lake steamer *Empire*. The steamer was buffeted by November gales across three lakes. More than once Sinclair and his family thought their journey would end disastrously in those cold waters. With "no small measure of satisfaction" the Sinclairs stepped ashore in Milwaukee.[8]

After settling his family in their new home, Sinclair threw himself once more into the business of logging. From his brother-in-law, J. B. Smith, he purchased an interest in a sawmill in the Upper Peninsula. Smith had controlled the mill for about four years. It had been built in 1838 by Donald McLeod, a Green Bay logger. Smith purchased it in 1842 and expanded its capabilities by building a second mill. But Smith did not have the background nor were the circumstances right for his operation to flourish. Smith's mills were modern enough, though he lacked the capital and forest experience necessary to make them pay. Experience was something in which Jefferson Sinclair was rich. He also had the capital to purchase lands when they became available, and he was keen to investigate his brother-in-law's operation.[9]

Early in 1846 Sinclair set out for the mill. It was at the mouth of the

Escanaba River on the north shore of Green Bay. The journey from Milwaukee to Escanaba was arduous. Traveling by sleigh on the ice of the lake, Sinclair skirted the fringes of the forested wilderness. Nor was there much to greet him when he arrived at the river. Smith's establishment consisted only of the mills, a boardinghouse, and a few outbuildings, but it was enough to impress the New Englander. Sinclair also saw pioneer mills on the nearby Whitefish, Ford, and Cedar rivers. These primitive operations, combined with others on the Menominee River and at Green Bay, were probably worth less than fifty thousand dollars in real value.[10] Yet Sinclair could see that in potential they were each worth millions. Returning to Milwaukee, Sinclair sought a partner with whom he could fully develop the Escanaba River's logging potential. He was, by the standards of that day, a wealthy man, but he needed a partner with even greater access to capital if the venture was going to succeed.

Sinclair found his partner at the City Hotel in Milwaukee. Daniel Wells, the inn's proprietor, was also from Maine and had been one of Sinclair's earliest acquaintances in the Midwest. Wells was the son of a Maine cotton manufacturer, and he had already profited handsomely from real estate speculation in Wisconsin. He brought to the partnership not just money but a feel for land purchases and a knowledge of business in the lakes states. Together, Sinclair and Wells bought complete control of the Escanaba mill site. They also bought and refitted the schooner *Nancy Dousman*, which would carry lumber from the Upper Peninsula to the towns at the lower end of the lake.[11]

That fall, the schooner was sent north to Escanaba with supplies and personnel for the mill. Among the loggers was a group of Maine woodsmen, whose skills at logging would be important in the partnership's success. One of those strong young men was Isaac Stephenson. He was born in 1829, the son of a Scotch-Irish logging foreman, near Maugerville, New Brunswick. Young Isaac began lumbering at the tender age of eleven working as a camp cook. After the death of his mother, the family immigrated to Maine, and the boy began working in logging camps along the Saint John River. Here he met Jefferson Sinclair. The businessman took a fatherly interest in young Isaac. After consulting with the boy's family, Sinclair brought Isaac into his household and educated him in letters and lumbering. Isaac Stephenson accompanied the Sinclair family westward in 1845. A year later, as he journeyed north on the *Nancy Dousman*, young Stephenson prepared himself for the biggest challenge of his seventeen years. For the first time he would go into the woods not as a lowly cookee or chore boy, but as a woodsman. Considering the shortage of skilled woodsmen in the Lake Michigan frontier, Stephenson had only to learn his trade well to guarantee his future.[12]

When he arrived at the mill site, Stephenson was sent to a logging camp about twenty-five miles up the Escanaba River. The camp was built near several stands of tall pine trees. The high transportation costs faced by Sinclair and Wells, who had to ship to northern Michigan all the food for man and beast and return with cargoes of bulky lumber, impelled the partners to harvest only the best trees. Among the most valuable pine were the tall, slim trees that could be converted into ship masts. Navies in Europe and America had long regarded such trees as a strategic resource. Masts were also vital to the growing merchant fleet of the Great Lakes. It took skilled woodsmen to outmaneuver a giant tree and a six-oxen team through the forest. Most lumberjacks had difficulty handling more than two oxen at a time. For a time, Sinclair and Wells enjoyed a monopoly of the Lake Michigan mast trade because of their access to Maine woodsmen. Stephenson, in particular, excelled at this task. His oxen team hauled 150 masts out of the woods that first winter. The finest one was 107 feet long and only twelve inches thick at the butt.[13]

For several years Isaac Stephenson lived the life of a lumberjack. He hauled timber logs in the winter and worked on spring log drives when warm weather ended forest operations. The camps of Sinclair and Wells were set up much like logging shanties of Maine. Even years later Stephenson could vividly recall camp life:

> We were up for breakfast at five o'clock and off to work before day light and did not return until dark. . . . The rations upon which we thrived were, to say the least, meager, and there was not enough variety to tempt even a normal appetite. As there were no farms in the vicinity to rely upon, the supply of vegetables was small. We were rarely able to obtain any at all. For five and one-half months during one winter we did not see a vegetable and were given fresh meat only once. Camp fare consisted of the inevitable pork and beans, bread, and tea which we sweetened with Porto Rico molasses in lieu of sugar. Occasionally we had a little butter and dried apples but so infrequently that they seemed a luxury. . . .

The men worked six days a week. On Sundays they stayed in their log shanty and repaired their tools and clothing.[14]

Among young Stephenson's most important tasks was "cruising," or locating stands of tall pine trees. The Sinclair and Wells operation on the Escanaba River was beyond the range of the Deputy United States Surveyors, who were required to map a region before the General Land Office could offer specific tracts for sale. Bold loggers, such as Sinclair and Wells, and their neighbors along Bay De Noc, Darius Clark who had a mill on the Rapid River and Edward Light on the Sturgeon River, built their establishments on land they claimed but did not own.[15] Federal regulations allowed them to file preemption claims on unsurveyed land. The claim secured the pioneer the right to use the land until it was offered for sale and gave them the first option to buy the land at the minimum price of $1.25. This generous legislation, intended for struggling farm families, not aspiring capitalists, in part explains the attraction that the northern reaches of Green Bay and Bay De Noc held for loggers. They could gain access to forestlands without any initial cash outlay. The smart loggers, however, knew that eventually their success would rest on forest ownership. Capitalists like Sinclair and Wells used their early presence in the field to send young men like Isaac Stephenson into the verdant forest and locate the best logging prospects.

Stephenson spent many weeks scouting the banks of the rivers that flowed out of the Upper Peninsula into Lake Michigan. At the time, there were no roads in the region, only game paths and a few Indian trails. Stephenson looked for mature stands of pine near smooth flowing rivers. Timber located away from water transportation would be too costly to harvest. When the first lands in the region were offered for sale in July 1848, Stephenson accompanied Jefferson Sinclair and Daniel Wells to the Sault Sainte Marie land office to purchase their claims. In the years that followed, Stephenson became a regular visitor to the land office. In the name of his employers he secured some of the most valuable logging sites along Green Bay including the future sites of Escanaba, Nahma, and Ford River, Michigan.[16]

Many other loggers in the region were neither as savvy nor as scrupulous. Preemption claims continued to be filed by loggers unwilling to pay for access to timber. They would loot a tract of land of its merchantable trees and then abandon the claim. The understaffed government land offices could do little to isolate the bogus pioneer from the genuine article. By 1849 the Commissioner of the General Land Office noted with disgust that "not three in a hundred" preemption claims on forest lands resulted in an eventual purchase. Some loggers did not even bother to file a preemption claim but merely cut timber off government land. Lamely, the United States government upgraded the stealing of timber from public lands to a penal offense. However, such laws without enforcement had little effect deterring timber thieves.[17] In fact, land office officials were sometimes in league with dishonest lumbermen. Isaac Stephenson, who was often engaged in the arduous task of locating pinelands, claimed:

> It was the rule rather than the exception that the explorer who had undergone privation and hardship to find timber, when he came to enter it at the land office was met with the statement of the recorder that it had already been entered. This, of course, was not true. The recorder had a list of willing

"dummies" always at hand who were put down as the purchasers of the property which was afterward sold at a neat profit to himself and his co-conspirators who supplied the money.[18]

Timber-stealing remained a problem in the logging industry throughout the nineteenth century

Looting the public domain did provide loggers with short-term profits, but it was not the basis for a long-term lumber business. For such a venture three ingredients were necessary: capital, timberlands, and logging expertise. Profits could definitely be made by simply bankrolling a logging venture or speculating in timberland or even specializing in forest operations. But the businessmen who grew to dominate the forests of the Upper Peninsula were those who fused money, timber, and expertise into an efficient, comprehensive lumber company. Isaac Stephenson, like several other eastern-born loggers, prepared throughout the 1850s to forge such a business.

Stephenson's career as a logger advanced at a frantic pace. At the tender age of nineteen, he was made superintendent of logging operations for Sinclair and Wells. With a solid grasp of good logging technique, "a strong arm and a heavy fist" he maintained discipline and accomplished the winter's work. After two years of working in this capacity, Stephenson and a partner, Maine logger David Langley, established their own contract logging firm. Still associated closely with his mentor Jefferson Sinclair, Stephenson agreed to put in logs at a fixed price per thousand feet. This was riskier than operating as superintendent for the partnership. Stephenson was personally responsible for paying his lumberjacks' salaries and footing the cost of camp and logging supplies. If he failed to cut enough timber, because of illness among his crew or poor weather conditions, he might be unable to recoup his costs. Yet Stephenson prospered as a contractor; each season he turned a larger profit. His fortunes were clearly in the ascendancy. Lumbermen all along Lake Michigan's north shore approached him with offers of employment or partnership. But Stephenson was not anxious to break his association with Jefferson Sinclair.

Only after Stephenson matured, married, and mastered the logging business did he tire of Jefferson Sinclair's paternal engagement in his business affairs. In 1854 he broke with the older man and took charge of logging operations for the partnership of Mason and Holt.[19] The two men were among the first loggers to exploit the Whitefish River, an excellent logging river whose fingers reached deep into the interior.[20] Mason was a millwright and capable of operating the firm's sawmill on Little Bay De Noc. Holt was a Chicago lumber merchant who could skillfully market their product. But neither man knew forest operations well enough to supervise the actual logging. Stephenson supplied the practical expertise the partners needed. The cooperative venture was successful for four years. During that time, Stephenson grew prosperous enough to try to purchase a controlling interest in the firm. But when Mason tried to saddle the young man with an unreasonable contract, Stephenson not only withdrew his offer but quit the service of Mason and Holt.[21]

No sooner did one opportunity close than another opened. In 1858 Isaac Stephenson became part owner of the N. Ludington Company. That firm was successor to the old Sinclair and Wells partnership for whom Stephenson had labored so long. In 1851 Sinclair and Wells joined with Milwaukee businessmen Harrison and Nelson Ludington to form the company. At first, the company had that magic mixture of capital, markets, and logging expertise that guaranteed success. Harrison Ludington and Daniel Wells were the money men. Nelson Ludington knew the lumber market and oversaw the partners' Chicago lumberyard.[22] Jefferson Sinclair, with his Maine contacts and field experience, guaranteed efficient forest operations. The company's balance was upset in June 1855 when Jefferson Sinclair withdrew from business. He suffered from melancholia and in four months took his own life. For the last time, Sinclair's actions shaped Stephenson's life. The N. Ludington Company tried to do without a skilled logger among its owners. But the Panic of 1857 threw the partners into a desperate strait. In May of the following year, Stephenson joined the firm as a junior partner.[23]

Stephenson's first task was to revive the N. Ludington Company mill at the little town of Marinette, on the Wisconsin side of the Menominee River. The Ludington brothers had correctly forecast that the Menominee was potentially a magnificent logging stream. However, they could not forecast the Panic of 1857, which sent businesses across the United States into a tailspin. The rival sawmills of Dr. Jonathan Hall and the newly formed New York Lumber Company were forced into bankruptcy.[24] The Ludington mill was also forced to suspend operations. Stephenson, acting as his own millwright, cleared out the cobwebs from the mill, hired a crew, and started the saws humming.

Isaac Stephenson respected his new partners' business acumen but as he later somewhat harshly put it: "Neither of the Ludingtons nor Daniel Wells, who remained in partnership with them, had the slightest knowledge of the practical side of lumbering."[25] This meant that the young woodsman would have a free hand directing not only the Marinette mill but also forest operations. He chose the locations of his logging camps, which gradually were placed deeper and deeper into the interior. The Menominee River was like a highway for Stephenson, and its many tributaries served as access roads to remote stands of pine. He knew this section of the Wisconsin-Michigan frontier from his days as a timber cruiser for Jefferson Sinclair. When he went into the back country, he was greeted by the sight of " . . . great forests that stretched away on all sides. . . . " He was certain that the Menominee River country constituted " . . . the greatest timber-producing region in America."[26] At Stephenson's urging, the N. Ludington Company purchased much of Sinclair's former timber holdings.[27] Stephenson himself made several personal purchases of pinelands, an investment from which he would profit handsomely.

The price that the N. Ludington Company was forced to pay for timberlands increased steadily during the 1860s. Competition for pinelands increased as more loggers grasped the significance of the Menominee River's four thousand square-mile drainage. The twin cities of Menominee, Michigan, and Marinette, Wisconsin, became the focus for the first giant logging operations in the Upper Peninsula. Isaac Stephenson encouraged his two brothers, whom he had earlier urged to come west and who had been contract loggers in the Bay De Noc area, to move to Menominee where greater opportunity existed. They quickly found work with their brother's rivals.

Stephenson's most durable competitor was the Menominee River Lumber Company. This firm received its start in 1860 after a group of Pennsylvania and New York capitalists had invested eight thousand dollars to build a modern steam mill at Marinette. But the New York Lumber Company, as it was named, ran neither its forest nor mill operations efficiently. The Panic of 1857 swept aside the original owner, and Jesse Spaulding, a Chicago lumberman, who had cut his teeth on the Pennsylvania logging frontier, stepped in with his own organization. The Menominee River Lumber Company was headed by experienced lumbermen. Besides Spaulding, the firm's partners included other veteran lumbermen: Philetus Sawyer, who was fast on his way to becoming the wealthiest logger in the Wolf River logging district; and Otis Johnson and Francis Stockbridge, who were owners of the Saugatuck Lumber Company in lower Michigan and pineland speculators throughout the Upper Peninsula. They hired Augustus Brown, a veteran logger, to manage their mill. Yet the firm struggled financially for its first four years, barely escaping bankruptcy.[28]

In 1859 Isaac's brother, Samuel Stephenson, bought an interest in a small mill operated by Abner Kirby on a sandbar in the Menominee River. Like his brother, Samuel had control over the practical tasks of logging and milling. The company's modest means were greatly expanded in 1861 when Augustus and William Carpenter joined the business, eventually incorporating under the title Kirby-Carpenter Company. The Carpenter brothers operated a small lumberyard in Monroe, Wisconsin. The merger gave them access to the timber supplies they needed to enter the Chicago market.[29]

Two later but notable arrivals on the Menominee logging frontier were the Hamilton and Merryman Company and the H. Witbeck Company. The former was created in 1868 by two pairs of brothers. Irenus and Woodman Hamilton were Fond du Lac, Wisconsin, businessmen with twelve years experience in the lumber business. They joined with Andrew Merryman, who with his brother, R. C. Merryman, had emigrated from Maine to Fond du Lac where they too established a lumber business. The Merrymans and Hamiltons were able to pool a formidable amount of capital. Andrew Merryman, the most experienced woodsman in the group, journeyed up the Menominee River to scout good pinelands. He bought an old cabin from the Indians and worked at cruising for months. Living on salt pork and hardtack and battling mosquitoes and swamps, he was able to evaluate a considerable amount of wilderness. On the basis of his reports, the partners purchased sixty-two thousand acres of prime forestlands.

The H. Witbeck Company was one of the most aggressive of the Marinette lumber firms. It was founded in 1869 by Daniel Wells, Jr., son of Jefferson Sinclair's old partner, John H. Witbeck, and Frederick Carney. Witbeck was a New York-born blacksmith who moved west at the age of twenty and forged a successful lumber business in Chicago.[30] His partner, Frederick Carney, was a Canadian-born logger who had ten years experience in Michigan, harvesting pine on contract.[31]

The Menominee River's leading loggers had several critical things in common. Each firm represented a union of logging experience, timberlands, knowledge of the lumber market, and capital. Their ability to integrate these diverse components made them immensely successful. The woodland wisdom of Isaac or Samuel Stephenson, Frederick Carney, Andrew Merryman, or Augustus Brown would have had little range for expression if it were not for the money provided by Daniel Wells, Woodman Hamilton, Harrison Ludington, and Francis Stockbridge, as well as the marketing experience of Nelson Ludington, Anthony Van Schaik, Ireanus Hamilton, John Witbeck, and Augustus Carpenter.

Yet even with the integration of all the vital tasks of lumbering, the leading firms of the Menominee River struggled through the first years of the 1860s. The economy of the Midwest was only just beginning to recover from the Panic of 1857 when the election of Abraham Lincoln and the secession crisis that followed brought a return to hard times. The price of lumber suffered a fifty percent drop in the vital Chicago market as fighting began between the North and South. For the Menominee mills to flourish, it would be necessary to wait until the Chicago lumber market recovered.[32]

As early as 1848 Chicago's lumbermen had handled more than sixty million board feet per year.[33] As the pineries of Wisconsin and Michigan grew, the city improved its transportation system. The Illinois and Michigan Canal gave Lake Michigan lumber easy access to the markets of the Mississippi Valley. Railroad connections linked the lumberyards on the Chicago River to buyers throughout the country. By the eve of the Civil War, Chicago was the world's greatest lumber port.[34] The war eventually created a boom that transformed the already dynamic city even further. Immigrants from Ireland, the German states, and the East Coast poured into Chicago, nearly tripling the population during the 1860s. Even when the end of the war brought an end to the national business boom, Chicago's markets continued to seethe with activity.[35]

This meant prosperity for the Lake Michigan logging community. Lumber that could only fetch $6.75 per thousand feet in 1861 leaped to the undreamed of price of $23 per thousand feet by 1864. Lumbermen like Isaac Stephenson who had invested in forestlands for a dollar an acre suddenly looked like geniuses. Loggers and mill operators throughout the region strained to expand production. During the 1864 season alone, the port of Chicago recorded the arrival of more than half a billion feet of pine, along with vast quantities of shingles, lath, and pickets.[36] The banks of the Chicago River, where the yards and warehouses of the lumber merchants spread for great distances, were impregnated with the sweet smell of cut wood. Historian James Pactor, who visited the city in 1867, was impressed to find that "the harbor is choked with arriving timber vessels; timber trains snort over the prairie in every direction."[37]

It was vital for the logger on the Menominee River to have close communication with the Chicago market. Because most of the pine was harvested during the winter and transported to the mill in the spring, not until the summer and fall was the lumber ready for sale. By that time the lumberman had already borne the cost of stumpage, logging, milling, and labor—he had to be assured a market for the product. Successful loggers, such as the N. Ludington Company, Kirby-Carpenter Company, and the Hamilton & Merryman Company, maintained lumber-yards in the Windy City. These yards were managed by a partner responsible for marketing the wood. He also was vital in forecasting the lumber market and advising the chief of forest operations on the extent of logging that was advisable. The Chicago partner also ordered the equipment and supplies needed to carry out logging.

During the Civil War boom and the year that immediately followed, the Chicago partners clamored for more lumber. All the major loggers at this time had switched to steam-powered mills and could increase their cut. The real pressure fell on the loggers. By 1865 the readily accessible pine along the Menominee River and the Lake Michigan shore had been cut. It was necessary to push farther up the main stream and its many branches to reach rich stands of pine or hemlock. To harvest a vast amount of pine required a huge labor force in the forest. Companies such as Kirby-Carpenter dispatched as many as five hundred men upriver.[38] But as operations pushed deeper into the interior, the cost of transporting the lumber to the lakeshore mills increased. Dams had to be built along the waterway to ensure the proper flow of water. Such dams were expensive and their regulation caused many conflicts among the loggers. The solution to this problem was the formation of the Menominee River Boom Company.[39]

The decision by the major lumbermen at the Menominee to meet with Isaac Stephenson on that cold February afternoon in 1867 marked the coming of age of the Menominee River logging district. By pooling their capital and forming a separate company to handle the problem of dam building and log driving, the major lumbermen could reduce their individual costs. More important, a risky aspect of logging would now be properly organized so that disasters such as floods, which could drive millions of feet of logs into Lake Michigan, were much less of a threat. Lumbermen could plan their increasingly complex business, which included marketing, transportation, land management, milling, and logging, with greater confidence.

Isaac Stephenson, as vice president of the boom company, took charge of bringing the idea into effect. It was no small task. He built forty dams along the Menominee River and its tributaries. Dams already in place were bought from their builders and became the property of the boom company. Stephenson also oversaw the removal of boulders and the blasting of shoals that hung up logs sent downstream. Near the mouth of the river, Stephenson supervised the building of an elaborate network of cribs and piers that anchored the log channel used to sort and shift the logs to their proper owner.[40] In its first year of operation, the company handled sixty million feet of logs.[41]

The company began its busy season in the spring when melting snow began to slow forest operations. It sent a log scaler upriver to measure how many feet of logs each company was putting in the river. As the ice broke up on the Menominee, the boom company's river drivers went to the head of the waterway. The company handled all logs in the main river. Logs on the banks of tributaries were driven to the main river by their owner's lumberjacks, but under the supervision of the boom company. The most important task of the boom company was the management of water levels. Too much water put undue pressure on downstream dams and the boom at the mouth of the river. The bursting of a dam or boom could result in the loss of millions of feet of logs. Too little water could result in logs grounding on rocks and perhaps causing a logjam. When the "drive" neared the river's mouth, it was necessary to divide the logs among their owners. Logs whose markings were obscured by bruises were turned over to the boom company which sold them at an auction. The net returns from these stray logs would then be distributed to the lumber companies on a basis of how many logs they had put into the river.[42]

The establishment of the Menominee River Boom Company was not unique. The Michigan legislature enacted a general statute for the formation of boom companies in 1864.[43] In a short time, lumbermen working on the Muskegon, Tittabawassee, Cass, Cheboygan, and Manistee rivers formed cooperative joint stock companies to handle the problem of log transportation. Menominee River loggers were merely responding to the same conditions that influenced the industry throughout the Great Lakes region. What makes Isaac Stephenson and the lumbermen of the Menominee significant is that they pioneered the establishment of large integrated lumber companies in the Upper Peninsula of Michigan. The formation of the boom company was the final step necessary to open the region's most important waterway to commercial logging.

THE DEVELOPMENT OF COMMERCIAL LOGGING
ON THE NORTH SHORE OF LAKE MICHIGAN

Eastern lumbermen were also dominant in the development of other logging centers on the Lake Michigan shore. Manistique developed into an important lumber port in the post-Civil War period. Its development began when New York lumbermen Abijah Weston and Alanson Fox purchased that town's leading, but nontheles struggling, business, the Chicago Lumber Company. Under their guidance the Chicago Lumber Company became one of the giants of Michigan logging history. The men were experienced lumbermen used to operating on a grand scale. They were partners in the firm of Fox, Weston & Bronson, one of the most important lumbering houses in New York. When they agreed to expand their empire to Michigan, they spared no expense. Between 1869 and 1870 they bought 140,000 acres of timberlands along the Wisconsin-Michigan border. This was merely a speculation. For actual logging operations, they agreed to concentrate on the Manistique River drainage. An initial purchase of 50,000 acres served as a base.[44] This was gradually expanded upon. When the company finally closed its doors, its holdings had grown to more than 160,000 acres.[45] They expanded the capabilities of the Chicago Lumber Company mill and organized a second company, the Weston Lumber Company, to operate another mill in town. Despite the separate names, the Chicago and Weston lumber companies were in practice the same firm. They had the same owners, board of directors, and management. In 1884 they built a third mill in the town also operated under the name of the Weston Lumber Company.[46]

The Chicago Lumber Company's production was awesome. Its mills averaged a combined cut of seventy-five to eighty million feet per year.[47] It was not unusual for the Chicago Lumber Company to operate nine logging camps per season, and this was besides the many contract loggers who worked for the company. When the mill employers of the Chicago and Weston plants were counted, Alanson Fox and Abijah Weston were responsible for between twelve hundred and fifteen hundred employees. They even operated their own fleet of steamships, barges, and sailing schooners.[48] Rival lumbermen followed Fox and Weston to the Manistique area. The neighboring towns of Thompson and South Manistique were born as mill locations. The partnership of Hall & Buell was bold enough to begin milling right in Manistique itself. When the combined cuts of all these lumbermen flowed down the Manistique River in the spring, it usually amounted to about 150 million feet of logs.[49] For twenty miles on either side of the town the shore of Lake Michigan was covered with sawdust from the busy mills.[50]

Weston and Fox dominated not merely the lumber industry of Manistique but the town's entire economic life. Nearly all the land in the town site belonged to either one or both of the Chicago Lumber Company's principal owners. The town stores, boardinghouses, funeral parlor, and cemetery were company property. It is little wonder that the Chicago Lumber Company thought it was in a position to dictate social behavior. Alanson Fox was a devout Baptist. His father, who founded the family lumber business, was a minister of that denomination. As a prominent layman, Fox believed it was his duty to shape moral behavior in the communities in which he worked.[51] For many years he prevented the establishment of saloons in Manistique. Such "dives" were the hallmark of any mill town. But the Chicago Lumber Company's lock on most property in the town allowed Fox to keep Manistique relatively sober. All leases or title transfers in the town carried a proviso forbidding the sale of intoxicating liquors. For a while Fox's moral program was a success. But he eventually ran afoul with a fellow New Yorker.

In the early 1880s, as Manistique's reputation as a logging center spread, a former New York saloon keeper, Daniel Heffron, approached the Chicago Lumber Company and tried to buy a lot near the sawmill. The company would have gladly obliged Heffron, but he backed out of the purchase when he saw the proviso restricting liquor sales. Undaunted, Heffron canvassed Manistique residents until he found someone who had nothing to do with the Chicago Lumber Company and owned a small block of land in the town. In this manner Heffron opened Manistique's first saloon. The company did not lose gracefully and watched Heffron's establishment like a hawk, prepared to close him down for the slightest infraction. But he did not miss a trick, and despite the surveillance and Sunday sermons, Heffron did a land-office business. Cunningly, he subdivided his block and sold lots to other dealers in nefarious goods. Soon Manistique had a "sin strip" complete with billiard halls and bars. Eventually twenty-nine saloons were established in the little town.[52]

Nahma and Saint Ignace also became seats of significant logging operations. Vermont-born George Farnsworth built Nahma, and another granite-stater, Francis Stockbridge, guided Saint Ignace's leading lumber operation. Farnsworth built his fortune first through the Oconto Company in Wisconsin, and not until 1881 did he expand operations to the Upper Peninsula. To do so, he founded a second firm, the Bay De Noquet Company. With 125 acres of forestland along the Sturgeon River and a steam-powered mill at its mouth, Farnsworth made Nahma a busy lumber port.[53] Saint Ignace, just across the straits from lower Michigan, became the headquarters for the Mackinac Lumber Company. Headed by Stockbridge and his partner of many years, Otis Johnson, the Mackinac Lumber Company cut white pine at a feverish pace. Nonetheless, their holdings were so extensive that they were not exhausted until seventeen years later. Lumber from the Saint Ignace sawmill later went to build the famous Grand Hotel on nearby Mackinac Island, a project sponsored by Stockbridge.[54]

Between 1875 and 1892, the Mackinac Lumber Company cut more than 200 million feet of lumber.[55] Such a production figure would have astounded men such as Jonathan Hall who pioneered logging on the Upper Peninsula's Lake Michigan shore. Yet compared with the hauls being recorded on the Menominee or Manistique rivers, it was nothing to note. By the 1890s the scale of pine lumber production in the region had reached its zenith. Government statisticians decried the vast amount of timber that had been cut in the Upper Peninsula in so short a time. But most lumbermen looked to the future, confident that, as one of their number explained, "The pine forest had no bounds."[56]

LAKE SUPERIOR LOGGING MATURES

A critical factor in the expansion of the logging frontier into the Upper Peninsula was the development of the area's transportation system. It was an easy matter for mid-nineteenth-century lumbermen to exploit the northern shore of Lake Michigan, but if the vast forests of the Lake Superior region and the interior were to be exploited, problems of access and egress had to be overcome. Where natural waterways did not offer easy transport, internal improvement in the form of canals and railroads were required.

The principal obstacle to the commercial development of the Lake Superior country was the falls at Sault Sainte Marie, which prevented direct commerce with the lower lakes. This shipping bottleneck pinched capitalists intent on exploiting the rich copper and iron ore resources of the western Upper Peninsula; in lobbying for a passage around the falls, they unwittingly laid the foundation for commercial logging in the region.

The state of Michigan had tried to build a canal around the Sault as early as 1839. Efforts to get federal financial support for the project failed until the copper and iron booms demonstrated the area's strategic importance. As it was, Congress dragged its feet on a canal bill until August 1852. But when it finally acted it did so generously. Congress offered 750,000 acres of federal land in Michigan to the company that could build locks and a canal linking Lakes Huron and Superior. Seizing the opportunity to win the land bounty was Charles T. Harvey. He formed the Saint Mary's Falls Ship Canal Company by uniting Michigan and New York capitalists. Two years of hard labor, difficult engineering, and almost a million dollars finally produced a canal in June 1855. Harvey and his partners claimed a virtual real estate empire in Michigan, including 140,000 acres of prime pinelands in the Upper Peninsula. Both the large grant and the canal itself stimulated speculation and exploitation of lumber in the Upper Peninsula.[57]

Canal construction stimulated the demand for lumber in the Sault Sainte Marie area. Within two years of the canal's completion, the Sault had two mills competing for local trade and shipping boards south to urban markets. Although the canal failed to lead immediately to lumbering on the scale of the Menominee River or Bay De Noc, the waterway did make the Upper Peninsula's Superior shore attractive to Canadian lumber dealers.

In 1854 the United States and the British North American provinces agreed to the Reciprocity Treaty. Under this historic trade agreement, the natural products (such as fish and grain) and the unmanufactured raw material (such as iron ore and lumber) of both countries could move across the border without tariffs. Reciprocity stimulated the lumber industry along the international border. Artificial political barrers were lifted, and lumbermen were free to follow the natural trade patterns and waterways that linked Maine with New Brunswick, upstate New York with Ontario, and the Upper Peninsula of Michigan with Georgian Bay and western Ontario. Among the host of American lumbermen who established operations in Canada during the reciprocity era was the Weston family, which later developed Manistique as a lumber center. For many Maine and New York lumbermen, Canada was a stopping place in their "cut and get out" migration from the East to the Lake Superior country.[58] But the exploitation of forest products worked both ways. Canadian lumbermen also used reciprocity to skim the cream off the eastern Upper Peninsula's pine forests. American lumbermen harvested sawlogs in the Canadian forest, which were then cut into boards for export to the American market. In contrast, Canadian lumbermen operating in northern Michigan cut "squared" timber, which was destined not for the sawmill but for reexport to Great Britain and the ship-building industry.

The squared timber trade was the earliest form of commercial logging in Canada. Before the American Revolution, Canada's forests were valued chiefly for the fur-bearing animals they sheltered. When the new republic was formed to the south, however, Canada became the Royal Navy's chief source of timber for masts and spars. But the long logs eligible for masts, often ninety feet or more in length, were difficult to remove from the forest. Woodsmen trimmed them before transport. This trimming, or squaring, process was a challenge to the skill of the men wielding the broadax. Armed only with their ax and a chalk line, they could trim the bark and transform a tree into a square mast with lines so smooth that they looked as if they had been mechanically planed. The speed and accuracy of the axmen amazed many urbanites. One observer noted, "His axe swished through and bit into the timber with such rhythm and speed that it resembled the vane of a windmill whirling in a brisk breeze."[59]

The squared timber business had a distinctly French-Canadian flavor. The finest hewers and choppers were Quebecois woodsmen. The principal entry port of the squared timber trade was Quebec City. From its crowded timber coves along the Saint Lawrence River, two types of squared timber were shipped to Britain. The large timbers went directly to shipbuilders for masts; smaller logs, known as a "balk" or "stock," only about forty to sixty feet long, would be shipped to British sawmills for lumber production.[60]

Hewing squared timber was as wasteful as it was difficult. When the axman completed his artistry and the squared timber was hauled to water, the forest was left littered with the debris of the chopping. The top of the tree, what lumberjacks called the "crown," was axed off and discarded, although if it were trimmed and sent to a sawmill it could produce several hundred feet of high-quality board. Similarly, the butt end of the log was discarded; the squaring process meant the squandering of hundreds of feet of quality board from each tree. This does not even take into account the smaller pine or hardwood trees cut down and left to rot by the choppers because they were in the way of removing the giant logs. One squared timber operation in the Upper Peninsula produced 202,000 feet of pine, but in its wake the Canadians left 600,000 feet of potential lumber lying on the forest floor.[61] The crime of this practice was not merely the incredible waste of the region's best trees but the damage that was done to future forest growth. The exceptional amount of debris left by squared timber logging created the worst type of fire hazard.

Stimulated by the twin incentives of the Sault Sainte Marie Canal and the Reciprocity Treaty, Michigan loggers working on contracts with Canadian merchants and Canadian loggers operating independently began to exploit the rich pine forests that were accessible from Lake Superior's south shore. From Whitefish Bay to Grand Island, the forest echoed for the first time with the ring of cold steel on virgin timber. The details of few of these operations have passed into the historical record.

George Dawson is perhaps the best-known of the northern Michigan squared timber loggers. He began to exploit the logging opportunities of the region during the 1860s. Using his brother, Thomas Dawson, as a partner and Sault Sainte Marie as his base, he was in excellent position to serve Canadian log merchants. His most important client was the Kingston, Ontario, firm of Calvin and Breck, who were major timber rafters on the Saint Lawrence River for three generations. An 1871 agreement between the logger and the shipping firm reveals Dawson's heavy reliance on the Kingston merchant's capital and connections. Calvin and Breck agreed to advance the Dawson brothers sixteen thousand dollars to buy between eight and nine thousand acres of land south of Lake Superior. The land would be owned by the Canadians, who would then sell the Dawsons the rights to log the tracts and would share in the profits from the operation.[62] The Canadian company also provided Dawson with the skilled Canadian axmen needed to square the timber. Dawson set the axmen's wages in Michigan although the Canadian firm made the payments to the families of the lumberjacks from a joint account.[63]

For eight years Dawson and the firm of Calvin and Breck operated together in the Upper Peninsula. They gradually expanded their land purchases, with Dawson using his knowledge of the region's forest to scout the best tracts. Their logging operation extended as far west as Grand Marais but was mostly concentrated along the Two Hearted River.[64]

Dawson usually employed twenty to twenty-five men, who were divided into four- or five-man gangs. They spent from October to January cutting and shaping the pine. At the end of the year many of the

French-Canadian choppers would leave for home; a skeleton crew completed the cutting and remained in camp until spring. When the ice was out, Dawson would blast a passage through the rocky Two Hearted River rapids and float the pine to the lakeshore for shipment to Canada.[65]

Isolation was a feature of logging camp life throughout the history of lumbering in northern Michigan. But the operations of the early squared timber choppers were particularly remote. Dawson tried to bring in the supplies he needed by water before winter. Once snow began, a trip to "civilization" at Sault Sainte Marie entailed a major journey along the frozen lakeshore. Business affairs had often forced Dawson to make the dangerous winter trek. Just how dangerous winter travel could be was demonstrated in January 1879. Several French-Canadian choppers whose contracts had expired set off for Sault Sainte Marie. They followed the shoreline until they reached Whitefish Bay, on whose frozen surface they set out. A blizzard quickly came up, and the crossing was transformed from a long walk to a frozen nightmare. By the barest of margins, the men were able to stagger into town. They were all frostbitten and required medical attention. One of the choppers was so badly exposed he died.[66]

To brave such conditions required a hardy constitution and considerable physical strength. Dawson's foreman, Dave Ranson, boasted of both. Born in Perth, Ontario, he first went into the woods at the age of thirteen. Camp food must have agreed with him because when he began work for Dawson in 1868, he stood six feet two inches and weighed 225 pounds. Dawson wanted a man of Ranson's physique as foreman to discourage challenges to authority. He also had an affection for the young but experienced woodsmen. After engaging Ranson, Dawson took him to a hotel for dinner. Before entering the restaurant, he took Ranson aside and advised: "Now, young man, don't be bashful. . . . Have all you want to eat." But after seeing the logger quickly devour several entrées, Dawson was shocked. He sat back and exclaimed, "Dave, I'll never tell you that again." But once Ranson was in the woods he proved worth his weight in prime-cut steaks. He was a skillful river driver, an expert oxen teamster, and a competent leader of the "red sash brigade," as residents of the Upper Peninsula referred to Dawson's French-Canadian choppers.[67]

Dave Ranson eventually became one of the eastern Upper Peninsula's most notable loggers. His mentor, George Dawson, remained in the squared timber business at least until July 1879, when his agreement with Calvin and Breck came to an end.[68] But by no means did this mean the squared timber trade was over in the region.

The Reciprocity Treaty with Canada expired in 1866. Yet many of the channels of commerce opened under its auspices continued to flourish. Well into the 1880s, Canadian timber buyers continued to contract for squared timber. But as time wore on, the process became increasingly viewed with a critical eye. In October 1876 an irate lumberman from Sault Sainte Marie complained to the *Northwestern Lumberman* that an Ontario-based company's operations were "a very destructive one to our forests." He went on to insinuate that the squared timber loggers were to blame for the rapid decrease in the region's forests.[69] In 1879 a landowner who charged trespassing by squared timber makers demanded special compensation because trimming the wood left so much combustible material on the ground that the lands were "almost worthless."[70] Some British merchants responded to these complaints from northern Michigan and elsewhere by changing their specifications from squared timber to "waney" pine, which preserved at least a portion of the tree trunk's natural curve, or wane. However, even this modest modification was largely a result of fear of declining giant pine forests, more than concern for sound forestry. In the end it was the decline of the resource base that brought to a close the squared timber trade. By the late 1890s the massive timbers popular among Canadian buyers were scarce in the Upper Peninsula, and an important chapter in the logging industry was closed.[71]

One of the reasons that squared timber loggers were squeezed out of northern Michigan was the increase in lumbering along the south shore of Lake Superior in the post-Civil War period. Giant steam-powered mills rose at points such as Emerson, Bay Mills, and Sault Sainte Marie. They represented a multimillion dollar investment in a region that only a generation before had been a wilderness.

3

THE IRON ROAD TO THE INTERIOR

In July 1889 Charles F. Street proudly surveyed the village he had created. In less than a year, the spot he had selected on a map had been transformed from one dense woodland to a bustling little community boasting electricity, more than twenty houses, and a waterworks. Most important of all, in Street's eyes, was a large sawmill equipped with three band saws and adjacent planing, lath, and shingle mills. It took Street only a short time to see that the promise he had made to his partners to build "one of the most complete outfits in northern Michigan" had been fulfilled.[1] All that remained was to harvest the pine and transform the logs into lumber. To effect this, Street conferred with Finley Morrison, his experienced superintendent. They discussed the forest operations, which would eventually entail six separate logging camps employing 350 men and would produce 25 million feet of pine.[2]

Street remained at his village only a short time; he was anxious to get back to his Chicago lumberyard and report the progress he had seen to his partners. Before he left, it was decided to name the village Interior, after the Interior Lumber Company, the group Street represented. The name reflected a distinctive fact about the town. It was on the banks of the Ontonagon River, but it was far from either the shore of Lake Superior or Lake Michigan. Previously, the successful sawmills in northern Michigan were near a deep water port. But three decades of intensive exploitation had reduced the readily accessible pine near the lakeshore or along major rivers. At the same time, railroads, encouraged by state land grants and the expanding mineral industry, were laid out through the interior of the Upper Peninsula. During the late 1880s and throughout the 1890s, the railroad was important in making logging practical on northern Michigan's inland plains and along its rugged western flank. The Interior Lumber Company was one of a handful of enterprises that pioneered the use of rail connections to make the final assault on the pine of the Upper Peninsula.

The first railroads in the Upper Peninsula, the Iron Mountain Railroad (1857) and the Peninsula Railroad (1864), were built to connect the rich iron mines of the Marquette Range with Lakes Superior and Michigan. In 1872 the Chicago & Northwestern Railway reached the Upper Peninsula city of Escanaba and effected a junction with the Peninsula Railroad. In 1881 the mineral district was linked to the eastern Upper Peninsula when the Detroit, Mackinac, and Marquette Railway was completed. A car ferry at Saint Ignace gave this railroad access to the expanding steel network of the Lower Peninsula. By 1888 the Upper Peninsula had a fairly sophisticated transportation system with the addition of the Duluth, South Shore and Atlantic Railroad (D.S.S.&A), which linked Sault Sainte Marie with Montreal; the Milwaukee Road, which reached northward from Wisconsin to the D.S.S.& A. tracks at Champion, Michigan; and the Chicago & Northwestern, which extended its track westward from Iron River to the Gogebic Iron Range on the Michigan-Wisconsin border.[3]

Charles F. Street was quick to appreciate the opportunities created by this transportation system. No sooner had the Chicago & Northwestern laid down the steel on their western extension then the Chicago lumberman organized the Interior Lumber Company.[4] He secured its future with the remarkable purchase of an estimated 500 million feet of pine trees.[5] This vast store he ordered cut at a frantic pace. During one fifty-six-day period in 1891, the Interior Lumber Company mill averaged more than 179,000 feet of lumber per day, not to mention shingle production.[6] In Chicago, Street was in communication with lumberyards across the country. Although he would sometimes ship lumber from Interior to his Chicago yard for retail sale, he was often successful at marketing it directly to eastern buyers. In 1889, for example, he sold his firm's entire cut to New York lumbermen and shipped the lumber directly from the Interior mill.[7]

Other lumbermen were quick to imitate Street's success. In the area around the town of Watersmeet, a group of sawmill settlements was established. Logging spur lines radiated from this and other forest towns. A new pattern of exploitation was taking root in the north country; a technology more sophisticated than the broadax and crosscut saw promised to accelerate the rate of exploitation.

The building of the Detroit, Mackinac, and Marquette Railroad opened the interior of the eastern Upper Peninsula to logging and created a window of opportunity for Robert Dollar, one of the most colorful lumbermen in the region. Shortly after the railroad was completed, in December 1881, Dollar and three partners purchased more than sixty thousand acres of forest.[8] The railroad operators were anxious to sell to Dollar. They had heavy debts from construction (and eventually would file for bankruptcy). But the state of Michigan rewarded them with a grant of 1,300,000 acres. With so much land they were willing to sell for the bargain price of $1.75 per acre. Dollar had personally scouted the lands in Luce, Chippewa, and Schoolcraft counties, and knew they were first-class white pine.[9]

Dollar had not always been such a high rolling businessman. He was a Scotch-born immigrant to Canada who began work in the lumber industry in 1861 as a chore boy. He received ten dollars a month for cleaning dishes, serving food, and chopping firewood seven days a week. It did not take him long to realize that "if I were going to move in this world I must have some education, and therefore [I] started to write and figure on birch bark." His part-time studies soon won him a promotion to camp clerk. By the age of twenty-two, he was foreman of his own camp in the Quebec forest.[10] His rise to business success was not unchecked by failure. After saving enough money to begin his own logging business, he was bankrupted by faulty decisions and the Panic of 1873. For several years, he worked only to clear the debts of this unfortunate experience.

Like most lumbermen, Dollar endured harsh conditions in the wilderness. On one occasion he marched for three days through the forest with only a single piece of bread to eat. Like the proverbial frugal Scotsman, he ate only a part of his bread each day while his companions hungrily devoured their portion the first evening of the journey.[11] In 1876 he nearly died on the ice of Georgian Bay. He led four wagons loaded with provisions and hay across the bay to relieve several of his camps that were short of supplies. It was slow going because the March thaw made the lake ice weak and dangerous. When the party was out of the sight of land, a tremendous gale blew up. Dollar ordered the wagons to halt and drew them in a circle. According to his chart, he was less than a mile from an island. Taking an ax, he set off in the gale to locate it as a refuge for the men and horses. But after struggling for only a quarter mile, he realized it was a hopeless effort and he headed back to the wagons. The wind by this time was fierce. It was nearly impossible to stand against it. Dollar staggered along, slipping on the ice and being literally blown into cold ponds of water. For hours he wandered across the ice, hopelessly lost. One slip on the ice broke his hand. His clothes, soaked, gradually turned as hard as a suit of frozen armor. Near death, he fell to the ice time and time again. The final time he struck the back of his head and lost consciousness. Robert Dollar should have died then and there. He was in the advanced stages of hypothermia, suffering from multiple bruises, and lay unconscious on the frozen lake. But after a while he awoke, shook the snow off his face, and looked around. Luck was with him. Through the blizzard he could make out the dark outline of trees—land was nearby. He staggered into the woods, cut some brush for kindling, and prepared to make the fire that could save his life. He had a box of matches in his pocket. His raw, frozen fingers tried to pry open the iced-over cloth. When the pocket finally yielded, he opened the matchbox to find only two matches. Dollar later recalled: "I took great precautions to make sure they would not misfire. I got behind a perpendicular rock out of the wind, and everything ready, [I] was pleased beyond measure when the first match started the fire." He spent the night thawing out his clothes. The next morning he rejoined the wagons and continued on to his camps.[12]

Five years after this adventure, Dollar was in the Upper Peninsula. He was cruising for tracts of giant white pine. Twenty miles south of Lake Superior, in what is now Schoolcraft County, Dollar found some of "the finest timber I ever saw." The pine trees there consistently measured eighteen feet in circumference.[13] This was the stumpage that Dollar secured in 1881 from the Detroit, Mackinac, and Marquette Railroad. It became the basis for the American Lumber Company. He selected a sawmill site east of the town of Newberry, on the banks of the Tahquamenon River. The town that grew up there was named Dollarville after its founder.[14]

Dollar made maximum use of the Upper Peninsula's crude railroad network. Besides responsibilities for the American Lumber Company's operations at Dollarville, he also supervised personally sponsored outfits on the Laughing Whitefish River, the Autrain River, the Two Hearted River, and, later on, the Dead River and the Peshekee River. He was able to inspect the development of logging activities at these diverse localities and still maintain a residence in Marquette, Michigan, by using the Detroit, Mackinac, and Marquette Railroad. To try to direct such extensive operations meant a heavy travel schedule, but the potential profits were also considerable. Robert Dollar's diary for this period records his unceasing travels and understandable concern about the weather:

Tuesday, January 1, 1884—Cloudy. Left home at 8:30 and went to Dollarville. Six inches snow in Marquette, twelve inches at Dollarville.

Wednesday, January 2, 1884—Fine and cold. Got to Grand Marais at 6:00 P.M.

Thursday, January 3, 1884—Very bad storm, snow & wind. Went to camp at Hurricane River and back to camp. Stormed fearfully.

Friday, January 4, 1884—Very cold and stormy. Was in woods all day, Found good timber.

Saturday, January 5, 1884—Cold and still stormy. Snow on skidways 25 inches—roads heavy. Camp to Grand Marais tonight.

Sunday, January 6, 1884—Cold and very stormy. Roads heavy. Got to

Dollarville at 7:00 P.M. Over two feet snow part of the way and at R.R. only one foot.

Monday, January 7, 1884—Cloudy and cold. Got home tonight at 8:00 P.M.

On the trip, he covered close to 250 miles, 170 by rail. It was a typical work schedule for Dollar during the seven years he logged in northern Michigan. He rarely took two days off in a row and was seldom in one place for more than a day. Without the railroad service between Marquette and Saint Ignace, he would have had to curtail his activities.[15] As it was, the train was his second home. In 1887 alone, he traveled more than 29,000 miles by rail and covered close to a thousand by horseback.[16]

Although Dollar was an active rail traveler and the Detroit, Mackinac, and Marquette gave him access to the interior pine plains of northern Michigan, he remained to a considerable extent an old-time lumberman in his orientation. Water was the time-honored medium for moving logs, and it was on lakes and rivers that Dollar moved most of his logs. Logging camps on the Autrain or the Laughing Whitefish rivers might be supplied by rail, but the logs were driven down to the lakeshore and then rafted to market. Dollar was a major participant in the rafting of Upper Peninsula logs. He logged extensively along the Two Hearted and lower Tahquamenon rivers. Each spring he would have the logs boomed at the rivers' mouth and arranged into rafts for Saginaw Bay lumber companies.[17]

Even the Dollarville mill beside the rail line was dependent on water transportation. Logs were driven down the upper Tahquamenon to the mill site. Some were immediately processed into sawed lumber. The largest logs, however, were loaded on railcars and shipped to Saint Ignace where they were either formed into rafts or loaded onto schooners for shipment east.[18] When the pine stands along the upper Tahquamenon were thinned, Dollar still kept the mill supplied by water. Because it was impossible to drive logs up the river from the still abundant pine forests of the lower Tahquamenon, Dollar approached the problem another way. His men built a stern-wheeled steamboat and they used it to tow small rafts of lumber up the river to the mill.[19] The effort, which seems to have been successful, reveals Dollar's commitment to water transport. He never contemplated building a rail spur to harvest the lumber.[20]

One reason for Dollar's reluctance to invest in the expensive technology of rail transportation was his fluid business situation. He was constantly scouting, purchasing, and selling tracts of timber. His partnerships and agreements were short term and changed from year to year. In July 1883, after two years as manager, Dollar resigned from the American Lumber Company. The move cost him his hefty annual salary of ten thousand dollars, but it did not slow the pace of his travels or business dealings.[21] He entered into contracts with the Kingston, Ontario, firm of Calvin and Breck, who had earlier got Upper Peninsula pine from George Dawson. For the Canadian trade, he provided squared timber that was shipped to Great Britain. Later he agreed to cut timber for Francis Palms, the Detroit money man who bought the Dollarville mill and controlled the Peninsula Land Company. The latter firm supervised the thousands of acres of land the state legislature had granted to the Detroit, Mackinac, and Marquette Railroad. This made Palms the largest pineland dealer in Michigan. To handle the extra work lumbering for Palms, Dollar brought his half-brothers William and Joseph into business.[22] For the lumber Dollar cut on his personal account, he often traveled to Tonawanda, New York, or Chicago to arrange marketing.

By 1887 Dollar began to reflect on the "amount of hustling it was taking to keep my business going." Each year, giant pine was becoming harder and harder to find, and his profits were also declining. At the same time, the severe cold of the Lake Superior winter began to sap the strength of the forty-three-year-old lumberman.[23] He began to cut back on his winter schedule, spending less time in the lumber camps and more time in warmer climates. One trip took him to California where he saw the giant redwood trees. The biggest trees in the world revitalized his spirits, and within a year he decided to sell off his Michigan investments and move to the Golden Coast.[24] Robert Dollar gradually withdrew from lumbering and made his fortune in California as a shipping magnate. But his career as a lumberman in Michigan had laid the foundation for the exploitation of the interior pine plains of the eastern Upper Peninsula.

Hard on Dollar's heels when he moved into the interior was another self-made timber king, Russell Alger. Like Dollar, Alger specialized in cutting giant pine and cedar for masts and spars. From his base at Harrisville on lower Michigan's Lake Huron shore, Alger sent great rafts of long timber to Lake Erie shipbuilders and sawmills. Alger and his partners controlled more than fifty thousand acres of forestlands in Alpena County. In 1881 their annual cut exceeded sixty million board feet; at such a rate even their abundant lands would be exhausted in a few years. They needed a new source of timber. To effect that expansion, Alger reorganized his company into Alger-Smith and Company. With partners Revand D. Hawley and Martin S. Smith and several others, Russell Alger also formed the Manistique Lumber Company in 1882. The firm was capitalized at three million dollars, and it purchased fifty thousand acres of timberland in the Schoolcraft County area of the Upper Peninsula.[25]

Because Alger bought this land as a timber reserve, it was not immediately developed. He did cosponsor a subsidiary company to improve the Manistique River for log driving, although no large-scale logging was commenced. Only after 1889, when Alger-Smith's lower Michigan operations declined, was more attention paid to the Upper Peninsula lands. Alger proposed to use the Detroit, Mackinac, and Marquette Railroad to transport long timber cut on the headwaters of the Manistique River to Saint Ignace. There he proposed to boom the logs and assemble them in rafts for transport to market.[26] But the cost of rail transport and rafting may have cut too deeply into Alger's profits, because shortly thereafter Alger-Smith and Company signed a contract with the Chicago Lumber Company of Manistique by which the latter firm agreed to saw the timber into lumber. The finished lumber was then ready for shipment on Lake Michigan lumber schooners to markets throughout the region. By contracting with the Manistique River Improvement Company to drive its logs to Lake Michigan and allowing the Chicago Lumber Company to saw the timber, the Alger-Smith and Company, one of the biggest lumber companies in Michigan, kept a low profile in the Upper Peninsula.[27]

Yet Russell Alexander Alger was not the type of person to stand offstage very long. He had his share of humility and hardship as a young boy and wanted no more of it. He was born in 1836, the son of a failed Ohio agriculturalist. When he was twelve, his parents, weakened by fever and hardship, died. Russell tried to assume responsibility for the household of his three siblings, but it was too much for a boy of his years; the family was broken up, each child being "turned out" to a relative. He worked for several years as a farm laborer, using any spare time for schooling and sending extra money to his sisters. Russell had nursed plans for attending college, but could not raise the necessary money. He did become a schoolteacher for two years, before reading law under the direction of two Akron, Ohio, lawyers. Although he passed his examination for the bar, Russell Alger did not last long in the legal profession. He found indoor office work tedious and bad for his health. He sought outdoor activity and challenging work. Russell went to Michigan where he heard that a man, if he were bold and hardworking, could make a fortune in the forests.[28]

In 1860 Alger and a partner founded a shingle mill in Grand Rapids, Michigan. At first the business prospered and Alger felt secure enough to get married. But gradually he was undercut by the political events that would bring the Civil War and change his life. In 1861, because of the secession crisis, the lumber market collapsed and with it Alger's business. To pay off creditors, he took work as a sawyer. The war was an escape from this dreary life and a chance to prove himself once more. He raised a company of cavalry and was appointed captain in the Michigan volunteers. He compiled an admirable service record, fighting in some of the war's most terrible engagements, notably at Gettysburg. At war's end, he was commissioned a brevet brigadier general. His political prominence was enchanced by personal friendships with Generals George Armstrong Custer and Philip Sheridan, and an acquaintance with Abraham Lincoln. He returned from the war in late 1864, anxious to put his newly acquired command skills to work in a more profitable way.[29]

He moved his family to Detroit where he engaged in a wide range of business affairs. Using old army friends, he invested in oil lands, sawmills, even a brick company. The latter enterprise failed but as part of it Alger acquired control over several barges and a schooner. He stumbled into the shipping business and in six months made a small fortune shipping lumber on the lakes. Through this connection he reentered the lumber business in a big way. He bought up government timberland in north central Michigan, generally paying no more than $1.25 per acre. By personally scouting the lands in advance and supervising the logging, Alger built his reputation as a careful but successful lumberman. But he was not so careful as to ignore innovations that could expand his business. In 1876 he became one of the first Michigan lumberman who built their own railroad to remove logs from the forest. His decision to buy and later harvest his extensive pinelands in the Upper Peninsula was also bold.[30]

Most of the Alger-Smith timberlands were grouped around a whistle-stop town on the Detroit, Mackinac, and Marquette Railroad known as Seney. Alger had tried using the Manistique River to drive the logs south to Lake Michigan, and he tried using the railroad to ship the logs to Saint Ignace for rafting; both plans had worked fairly well while most of the timber was near either the railroad or the tributaries of the Manistique River. But by the late 1880s this easily accessed pine had been largely exploited. If Alger was going to exploit most of his holdings, he would need a different method. The logical resolution of the problem was to do what he had done earlier in lower Michigan: build his own railroad into the isolated forest.

Work on the railroad began in 1886 and a year later the line was linked to the trunk route at Seney. Alger named the operation the Manistique Railway because most of its early hauling was done for the Manistique Lumber Company, a subsidiary of Alger-Smith. But woodsmen throughout the Upper Peninsula always playfully referred to the line as the "Myrtle Navy Railroad," after the brand of the crew's favorite chewing tobacco. By 1893 the track was extended north to Grand Marais on Lake Superior. Alger and his partners made the quiet fishing village their Upper Peninsula headquarters. A dormant mill was enlarged to hold two new band saws and a circular saw. Ship traffic into Grand Marais harbor increased fourfold almost overnight. In one day, twenty-two ships arrived, dropping off supplies and loading finished lumber. The Manistique Railway brought millions of feet of logs out of the forest, as over five hundred lumberjacks, armed with crosscut saws, worked throughout the year. In a few short years Alger's fast maturing operations made Grand Marais one of the dynamic lumbering centers of the Upper Peninsula.[31]

While the general's operations in northern Michigan matured, he became more involved in national politics. Alger had served as governor of Michigan from 1884 to 1887, and in 1888 he was a leading candidate for the Republican presidential nomination. He remained a major figure in Republican politics until his death. He served as William McKinley's secretary of war during the Spanish-American War.[32]

Alger made much of the rags-to-riches nature of his career during political campaigns. Like many candidates, he wanted to appear as a friend of the workingman. During his gubernatorial campaign, he stopped to inspect some of his lumberjacks driving logs on the Fox River. After watching the men labor in ice-cold water on a bitter spring morning, Alger asked the lumberjacks how much they were paid. One of the men answered, "A dollar and seventy-five cents a day and chuck when we are near enough to the wanigan to eat." Alger was surprised by the meager amount and shouted to his foreman: "That's not enough for such work. Raise them." The foreman promptly raised the men's salary but shortly after Alger departed, wages were again cut back. While addressing a crowd of lumberjacks in Seney, Alger's appeal for working-class votes was interrupted by a drunken blacksmith who said: "You're a damned liar, you pay the lowest wages in this whole damned country." That the man was employed by Alger-Smith lent force to his remarks and the embarrassed general beat a hasty retreat. Nonetheless, Alger received overwhelming voter support in the Upper Peninsula during his political career, and it was that support that eventually swept him into the State House.[33] An ironic twist to Alger's politicking among his disgruntled workers came in 1901 when a former section hand on the Manistique Railway assassinated the president of the United States, William McKinley.

By that time, Alger-Smith was already looking away from Michigan for its timber future. The Manistique Railway allowed Alger's various lumber subsidiaries to exploit the pine forests of Schoolcraft, Alger, and Luce counties at an accelerated pace. During peak logging periods, the mills at Grand Marais operated twenty-four hours per day, sawing millions of feet of pine and exhausting Alger-Smiths's twenty-two thousand acres of pine and forty-six thousand acres of hemlock.[34] Such rapid depletion of Michigan forests did not concern Alger; if he did not cut the pine, someone else would have. To secure his own future, Alger bought a million dollars worth of pine in Alabama and established a logging company in Florida. However, most of the equipment and many of the men working near Seney and Grand Marais were transferred to the next stop in the migratory progression of the Great Lakes lumber industry, Minnesota. By 1902 Alger-Smith owned five million feet of timber near Duluth and employed seventeen hundred men.[35] The transfer of Alger-Smith to Minnesota pulled the plug holding people and business in the little town of Grand Marais. At its peak, three thousand people lived in the lakeshore village; seventeen thousand passengers a year traveled the Manistique Railway that linked the town to the outside world. But after Alger-Smith tore up the track on the line in 1911, the town withered to a tenth of its former size. The outlying countryside was similarly devastated. The vast pine plains that the railroad had opened to logging were reduced to desolate slashings that bred fires, which further degraded the area's future by ruining the soil.[36] The railroad that made the logging possible was also moved to Minnesota where a similar pattern was followed.

A good example of the significance of railroad trunk lines in developing the pine forests of the western Upper Peninsula is the Milwaukee, Lake Shore and Western Railway. Eventually this line was absorbed by the Milwaukee Road, but at first it pioneered in developing the forest resources of Houghton and Ontonagon counties. Three separate lumber towns, Pori, Frost, and Sidnaw, grew up along its final section between Lake Superior and the Soo Line. Each were small company towns with not more than two hundred people, founded by lumbermen drawn to the area by the prospect of cheap pinelands and reasonable shipping rates.[37] However, the most significant contribution of the line was the linking of the port of Ontonagon with the rail system of the lower states. This paved the way for the massive logging activities of the Diamond Match Company, the single biggest timber cutter in the Upper Peninsula.

The Diamond Match Company was one of the first great monopolies of late-nineteenth-century American enterprise. The Machiavelli behind the corporation was Ohio C. Barber. By joining the largest match manufacturers in the United States into a single firm, Barber cornered between eighty-five and ninety-five percent of the market. He eliminated scores of smaller competitors by controlling patents on new equipment and by dominating distributors.[38] After securing a virtual monopoly on the sale of his product, Barber turned to integrating all phases of production. Like his contemporary, John D. Rockefeller, Barber wanted to secure his sources of supply. In September 1882 the

Diamond Match Company bought control of the Ontonagon Lumber Company and the Sisson and Lilley proprietorship, which pioneered commercial logging in Ontonagon. This was part of a general plan to purchase timberlands as they became available. But when the corporation's board visited Ontonagon County two months later, it fell under the spell of the region's vast tracts of pine. Here was all the pine they would need for years to come. Plans for linking the town by rail were in the works; it seemed to be the ideal time and place for a major investment.[39]

To select still more lands, Barber sent to Ontonagon a team of people headed by W. Wallace Warner. Their task was to consolidate Diamond Match's already considerable forestlands with more purchases. Warner, acting as if he already owned the county, virtually took over the register of deeds office. His assistants monopolized every tract book, deed record, and file trying to create their own abstract file for the county. The clerk, unable to conduct anything like normal business, finally was forced to have Warner and his horde evicted from the premises. Monopolies were seldom accorded such treatment in those days, especially at the hands of backwoods public officials. Diamond Match's counsel brought suit against the county, demanding special access to public records. But the Michigan Supreme Court noted that the Match King was incorporated in the state of Delaware and not domestic to Michigan but was a "private foreign corporation" not entitled to unique privileges in Michigan.[40] The incident did not deter Diamond Match from continuing to invest in the area, eventually to the tune of one million dollars, but it did inaugurate what proved to be a rocky relationship between the monopoly and the county.[41]

The Diamond Match Company moved methodically to develop its huge holdings in northern Michigan. The Ontonagon River was a wild, muddy stream with many impediments to river driving. Earlier loggers had operated a boom company, which had done much to clear the stream, but several dams were still needed before large-scale logging could commence. Expert river drivers were brought in to handle the task and logging began in a modest way.[42] All the early lumber sawed in the mills was shipped by water. Although Ontonagon had a railroad running twenty miles to the town of Rockland as early as 1882, it was not for nearly another ten years that it had full service to the nation's rail system. This curtailed the scale and focus of Diamond Match's operations. Because most of its match factories were located on waterways, schooners from Ontonagon could supply them with wood.[43] The trouble was that a single Diamond Match plant required six million feet of timber annually, and there were a total of eight plants around the country. The limited number of ships and barges owned by the company and the brief shipping season on Lake Superior meant that, until Ontonagon got rail service, the Diamond Match Company could not fully integrate logging with match production.[44]

Once Ontonagon was linked to Milwaukee by rail, the Diamond Match Company's operations greatly expanded. The sawmills operated around the clock, lighted by an electric generating plant. Between 250 and 400 men worked in the mills, depending on the season. When operating at capacity, as they did for much of the early 1890s, the mills could produce as much as seventy million feet of lumber per year. To make use of the new rail service, the company also built a factory for the manufacture of wooden boxes in Ontonagon.[45] Besides supplying the match factories, the lumbering branch of the monopoly became an aggressive marketer of forest products in its own right. In 1891, for example, the Diamond Match Company sold twenty-five million feet of Michigan lumber to a single Wausau, Wisconsin, customer.[46]

Although the ability to ship lumber enabled the Diamond Match Company to expand its lumbering operations, railroads also lowered the cost of the actual logging. The best pine in the Ontonagon country was twenty-eight miles south of the city along the south branch of the Ontonagon River and its tributaries. The completion of the Duluth, South Shore and Atlantic Railway in 1888 brought rail service to the southern tier of Ontonagon County. Where the rails crossed the Ontonagon River, a small but wild town named Ewen grew up. Ewen and the neighboring community of Matchwood became service centers for the lumber camps operating in their vicinity. Ready access to supplies made it cheaper to maintain camps deep in the woods.[47]

The high-water mark of pine logging in northern Michigan came in the 1894-95 logging season. Forest fires, caused by a dry summer but spurred by the debris from Diamond Match's own logging, ravaged the woods of southern Ontonagon County. The fast-burning fire did not consume the pine forests, but the trees were badly scorched by the blaze. If the wood was harvested immediately, it could still be made into first-class board. But if logging was delayed the scorched trees would fall prey to the worms and insects that feasted on deadwood. There was no alternative for the Diamond Match Company but to cut as much of the damaged timber as possible.[48]

Bad news travels swiftly. The office of John H. Comstock, head of the company's lumber department, was quickly jammed with loggers. Only days after the fire, they began to apply for contracts to cut timber on the burned land. It was impractical for the Diamond Match Company itself to hire and supervise the thousands of lumberjacks needed for the task ahead, so it made good sense to hire these small-scale loggers known as "jobbers" to undertake a portion of the work. Jobbers from around the country wrote to Comstock. His mailbox was choked with 250 applications. From this throng, Comstock selected the twenty-one most reliable woodsmen and let contracts to cut a total of 120 million feet of pine. Comstock then met with Robert E. Stephenson, head of Diamond Match's forest operations, and they planned the winter's campaign for the company lumberjacks. They were careful to save the best logging "chances," those closest to water and transportation, for the Diamond Match camps. Stephenson was instructed to cut a minimum of thirty-five million feet of scorched pine.[49]

Never before had such a tremendous cut been planned by one company. Six thousand lumberjacks, a small army, labored through the winter butchering timber. Thirteen million feet of pine per week fell in the wake of their cross-cut saws. A total of twelve hundred horses, brought from farms in far-off Iowa and southern Wisconsin, hauled the mountain of wood from the cuttings to the banks of the Ontonagon River.[50] Stephenson and his staff of supervisors were run ragged shuttling sleighs of hay, oats, beans, and bacon from depot to camp to keep the men and beasts working at full strength. Through the winter, the piles of logs on the river landings grew into foothills. By spring, they had reached Bunyanesque proportions. One hundred eighty-five million feet of pine were scaled at the side of the Ontonagon River. The people of Ontonagon, the lumberjacks, and especially O. C. Barber were proud and boastful. A reporter for the *Ontonagon Herald* stated that he had witnessed "the greatest lumbering operations ever carried on in the known world by one firm." It was estimated that if all the logs were loaded on railroad flatcars, it would take a train more than 250 miles long to carry the haul.[51]

But the company did not plan to remove the timber by train. The program outlined by Comstock called for the logs to be pushed into the Ontonagon River and driven downstream to the waiting mills on Lake Superior. It was at this point that the ambitious appetite of the Diamond Match Company ran afoul of the restrictions of nineteenth-century technology and the obstacles of the serpentine Ontonagon River. Mammoth logjams occurred all along the course of the drive. Further delays were endured at the dams along the stream. Normally, the task of sluicing the logs through the chute on the dam caused little worry. In an hour, skilled river men could slide between a half and a full million feet of logs downstream. But the tremendous haul of logs involved in the 1895 spring drive produced inevitable delays. Each delay meant less water in the river, and the Diamond Match Company needed all the water it could get to work its logs through the gorges and shallows of the Ontonagon. The whole vexing process came to a halt at Grand Rapids. Here the river makes a sudden turn to the west. The swift flowing water is divided by an island as it falls over rocks. The bend, the island, and the rocks all made Grand Rapids a major obstacle for 180 million feet of pine. Through skill and hard work, the river drivers wrestled the first part of the drive past the obstacle but the lion's share of the logs, hung up by low water, became jammed. Once the pile of logs began to mount, there was no clearing the stream. For the remainder of 1895 and all through the spring and summer of 1896, the Ontonagon River remained choked at Grand Rapids.[52]

The problem was not critical. Enough lumber got through in 1895 to keep the mills running at capacity. Grand Rapids was only eight miles south of the mills, so it functioned as a remote holding boom for the mill. Several thousand feet of logs could be cleared each day and sent downriver. But because of the jam on the river, and the tremendous backlog from the year before, the Diamond Match Company cut only three million new feet of pine in 1896, quite a contrast from the year before. Finally in 1897 the jam was finally cleared and all the logs were delivered to the lakeshore.

Despite the logjam on the river, residents of Ontonagon were optimistic about the future of their town as a lumber center. The giant cut of 1894–95 was seen as proof of the town's strength as a lumbering center rather than as evidence of a declining resource base. After all, had not the Diamond Match Company itself demonstrated its faith by investing in Ontonagon? Many residents lived in company houses, shopped at the company-owned store, and most of the workingmen were employed in the Match King's plants.[53] The town's relations with the company may have begun a bit roughly, with the dispute in the county recorder's office, but things, at least to people in 1896, seemed to have worked out fine.

Ontonagon residents shared their faith in the future of lumbering with the residents of Menominee, Manistique, Grand Marais, and other lumber towns in the Upper Peninsula. Menominee residents were proud that the more than twenty mills in or near their town produced one-half billion board feet of lumber each year.[54] Manistique residents were fond of pointing to their busy harbor and telling visitors of the millions of feet of lumber they shipped to eastern ports.[55] When railroads brought three hundred thousand feet of logs into Grand Marais each day and schooners sailed away with one and a half million feet of lumber in their holds, most Grand Marais residents saw the process as progress.[56] Ontonagon residents were no different from other Upper Peninsula people, at least until the fatal fire of 1896. Just one year after they had so self-satisfiedly hosted the "world's greatest logging operation," their town was in ashes and they were forced to consider what their future would be after the pine was gone.

The Ontonagon fire of August 1896 marked the beginning of the end of the reign of white pine as monarch of the northern Michigan forest. Like the decline in pine production, fire struck the village of Ontonagon only after many warnings had gone unheeded. For weeks before the blaze, townspeople had awakened each morning to the smell of burning wood and the sight of white clouds of smoke in the distance. The swamps west of the town had been dried by the summer sun and periodically became the scene of smoldering fires. There seemed no cause for alarm because such fires had always proved harmless. But Tuesday, August 28, was different from other days. A brisk breeze from the southwest pushed the fire toward the fences of the Diamond Match Company. A few men were sent out to dig fire trenches. They seemed to have the matter in hand when, about noon, the breeze suddenly picked up and the west side of town was engulfed in flames.[57]

Everyone took the fire seriously now. The men were sent rushing from the two giant mills to try to save the lumberyard. It was futile; the fire had gained too much strength. In short order, the central business district was enveloped in flames and smoke. The breeze carried burning brands of wood flying through the air, enabling the fire to spread quickly from block to block. For the people of the town, there was no longer any question of fighting the fire; the priority became escape. An eyewitness remembered:

> Every person in the lower end of town who could get by the flames went in the direction [of the neighboring towns] of Greenland and Rockland and others sought refuge on the beach and in the boats. About this time, between 3 and 4 o'clock, the wind changed to the northwest and began a race for life. The wind had attained a velocity of seventy-five miles per hour, huge banks of smoke hid the sun from view, the air was filled with firebrands and the terror-stricken people dropped everything they had and ran for their lives. No person can describe the wild scene at this juncture. Many of the poor people saw houses catching fire ahead of them and terror stricken they hardly knew what to do. They realized, however, that their only alternative was to keep ahead of the monster tidal wave of flame which was pursuing them and on they went some in wagons but most of them on foot. Horses were lashed into a mad gallop and men, women and children ran like wild. . . . No power on earth could stem that sheet of flames.

People standing a half mile away from the fire could not face the heat of the blaze. Approximately 340 buildings were reduced to ashes; more then two thousand people were without homes or possessions.[58]

The editor of the *Ontonagon Herald* reflected the determination of the townspeople to rebuild when he wrote: "There are too many resources here to be abandoned and so we say to our citizens, cheer up, pull off your coats and go to work." The Diamond Match Company, however, agreed with one-half of that sentiment. It was not prepared to abandon the remaining stands of Ontonagon pine it controlled, nor was it prepared to rebuild its many mills and plants. The fire had come at an embarrassing moment for the company. A battle for control of corporate stock had made it imperative for the board of directors to raise capital. Value of Diamond Match stock tumbled when it was learned that all that remained of the Ontonagon complex was the charred sawdust burner. The board decided the best way to remedy the situation was to take the $410,000 due the company from its insurace company and apply it to the corporate debt. The remaining timber would be cut, floated to Ontonagon, and then sent by rail to the Diamond Match mill at Green Bay, Wisconsin, for milling.[59]

To the people of Ontonagon, this was an unexpected blow when they could least afford it. As winter approached, hundreds were still homeless, living in tents on the edge of a charred town. They needed their jobs back, but the company had exported those jobs to Green Bay where the dearth of Wisconsin pine had made mill workers happy to accept the Michigan logs. In anger, the townspeople watched as a few men worked pulling logs out of the river and onto flatcars for shipment south. The county of Ontonagon retaliated by increasing its assessment of the company's property by fifty percent.[60] For a time the shipment of timber to Green Bay was held up by a tax warrant. But the company protested and took the county to court. Ontonagon and the Diamond Match Company ended their relationship the way it began in 1882—in a legal dispute. There were, however, several significant differences. Now the pine was cut, the village was in ashes, and the people learned what the Michigan State Supreme Court had meant when it referred to the Diamond Match Company as a "private foreign corporation."[61]

Ontonagon's unhappy fate presaged the future of other northern boom communities built on pine. During the late 1890s, the amount of pine logs coming down the Menominee, Tahquamenon, and Manistique rivers declined. At Saint Ignace, Whitefish Bay, and the mouth of the Two Hearted River, where once vast log booms were assembled, pine logs became scarce. By 1897 even the town of Interior, one of the late-developing pine towns, was in decline. The mill owners had cut the remainder of the timberland, and rather than purchase more real estate, elected to collect their profits. The mill was closed, the equipment sold, and the town was left for the forest to reclaim.[62]

Some communities, like Interior, withered and died without pine lumber. Others found new life in the exploitation of the region's yet largely untapped stands of hardwood.

4

THE PROCESS AND PATTERN
OF PINE LOGGING

On a fall day in 1947, workmen renovating Memorial Hospital in Manistique discovered strange markings on some lumber they were removing. Local newspapers picked up the story and readers wrote letters speculating about the marks. Some people believed they were Chippewa Indian symbols; others thought they were like hieroglyphics; most people in Manistique did not know what they were. An old lumberman, William Crowe, was shocked that anyone would regard these marks as mysterious. "I supposed everyone was familiar," Crowe wrote, "with the system of log marking used in the old pine lumber days." All logs driven by water were marked by a corporate symbol. But in less than fifty years, the residents of even an old lumber town had forgotten many of the prosaic details of the pine era.[1] Those details had died with the lumbermen who lived that early history; by 1947 log marks were no longer important in the logging industry. During the primary phase of logging in the Upper Peninsula, a distinctive land-use pattern appeared in the forest. It was based on the abundance of softwood, particularly pine, and the utility of the wood, wind, and water-power technology of the nineteenth century. The timber type and technology used at this time reveals significant features of the pine logging frontier.

TECHNOLOGY OF PINE LOGGING:
FOREST OPERATIONS

The operations of a lumber company can be divided into three phases: forest operations, transportation to the mill, and sawing logs into board. Each of these required a distinctive application of technology.

There has always been a primitive simplicity to forest operations. During all eras of logging in the Upper Peninsula, forest operations usually took place in a seasonal context that saw logging camps established in the fall, timber cut in the winter, and logs transported in the spring. The foundation for this sequence was laid during the pine era. When considering the technological factors of logging, continuity is also at least as important a theme as the effects of changing material culture on the conduct of the industry. Tools introduced in the primary phase of logging—the ax, crosscut saw, and pickaroon—remained standard elements in the logger's arsenal until the very recent past. For these reasons, pine logging was significant long after the last of the giant pine had been cut.

When lumbermen first focused on the forests of the Upper Peninsula in the 1840s, timber was felled by skilled axmen, or "choppers." A crew of four men worked at the task. Two axmen would attack the tree, carefully felling it parallel to the skid road by which the log would be removed. When the tree fell to earth, "with a swishing crescendo culminating in a crash," two men, "swampers," would trim the limbs from the tree and cut away the bark from one side.[2] White pine logs required little trimming; however, the bark had to be partly cut away to leave at least one smooth surface for the teamster who would haul the log to a landing area. These short hauls, in the early years only a few hundred yards long, were accomplished by means of a travois, or "go-devil"—a simple hardwood frame that lifted the log partly off the ground. This frame was harnessed to a team of draft animals, and the pine was dragged to the riverbank or lakeshore.[3]

Isaac Stephenson, who was among the pioneer woodsmen of the Upper Peninsula, contended that for most lumber companies, "the difference between success and failure oftentimes depends upon the ingenuity displayed in the harvesting of the timber." Because it was here that so many lumber companies made or lost their fortunes, there was considerable innovation in the tools and techniques used in the forest.[4] By 1880 the system used by the first pine loggers had been significantly reformed. The most important change was how the ax was used. It was no longer the principal felling instrument. Woodsmen still used the ax to chop away the pine's bark, but once a good cut was made, the ax gave way to the crosscut saw. Two men working with a six- to seven-foot long saw could cut down a tree much quicker than the most skilled choppers.[5] A pair of sawyers could fell as many as fifteen trees a day and "buck," or divide, these trees into as many as seventy-five twenty-foot logs.[6]

The method of getting logs to the landing was also improved. Early lumbermen relied on hastily cut travois or skid roads. These were not really roads but pathways from which major obstacles such as trees or boulders were removed. As the pine adjacent to the banks of streams or on the lakeshore became scarce, lumbermen went deeper into the forest and they needed better roads. Systematic lumber operations, which removed large quantities of softwood rather than selectively gathering the tallest pine for ship masts, also required better roads. Later pine loggers laid out carefully cleared and banked roads. Through the heart of every logging operation were several main roads, about twenty yards wide, usually laid out on level ground, preferably along a creek bottom. From these main roads, a system of branch roads stretched out, as one lumberman remembered, "like the limbs of a tree, covering the land to be logged with a network of thoroughfares, all of which led into the main camp." These secondary roads were much narrower, about eight to ten feet wide. But like the main road they were carefully leveled. Roots were chopped away; depressions filled; rocks removed. John Nelligan, who moved from New Brunswick to the forests of the Upper Peninsula, contended: "In the rapid and efficient construction of roads, no body of men on earth can excel a skilled logging crew." The final step in preparing the roads for logging would come early in winter when water was sprinkled over the snow-covered surface to create a base of ice for easy hauling.[7]

With the emergence of ice roads, the travois and the ponderous oxen, which had been the favorite draft animal, retreated from the scene. Sleds drawn by horses operated on the ice roads. Horses were easier to work as teams than oxen.[8] The large breeds of horses favored by lumbermen (a horse would often weigh about one thousand pounds) could haul much heavier loads than oxen. A two-oxen team would seldom pull more than one thousand feet of pine per load.[9] In contrast, a team of horses working in the Menominee River valley in 1891 hauled a load scaled at more than twenty-one thousand feet.[10] The greatest load ever hauled in the Upper Peninsula was assembled in February 1893. Ontonagon County lumberjacks brought together just over thirty-six thousand board feet of white pine—a total of fifty logs. The load was held onto the sled by two thousand pounds of chain. This mammoth load was not sent to the sawmill; it was meant to be part of the Michigan exhibit at the Columbian Exposition in Chicago. Nonetheless, a team of horses weighing a total of thirty-five hundred pounds did manage to pull the full sleigh eighty yards.[11] Although such loads were exceptional, more pulling power, better sleds, and ice roads enabled lumbermen to efficiently move the increasing number of logs felled by the crosscut saw to landings, even though they were operating farther and farther from the waterways.

As the pine era progressed, more and more of its tools were manufactured or were produced by craft specialists. When Isaac Stephenson went into the forests of northern Michigan as a young man, he could boast, "I could build a bateau, make all of the tools used for river driving, ox yokes, and sleighs, shoe oxen and horses and exercise generally the functions of a blacksmith, carpenter or millwright. . . ." Lumberjacks in the 1850s and 1860s had to depend on their own ingenuity because of the remoteness and isolation of their work environment and the primitiveness of their technology. A travois, an ax handle, or a pike were tools made by early lumberjacks largely from materials available in the forest. Yet by the end of the pine period, it was rare to find men with such skills. Specialists were more common. To build or repair tools, a camp required a blacksmith to work with metal and a "wood butcher," or handyman, who mounted the iron work on wood. Others specialized as sawyers, top loaders, boatman, and so forth. At the end of the pine era, Stephenson reflected on the specialization of skills by writing that "even the 'boss' himself" could not carry out the many tasks of which a pioneer lumberjack was capable.[12]

TECHNOLOGY OF PINE LOGGING: WATER TRANSPORTATION

The most distinctive technological features of the pine era revolved around the use of water as a transportation medium. River drives provide a quintessential illustration of the importance of waterways to early lumbermen. When the first mills were built in the Upper Peninsula, transportation often was not a problem. Fine pine logs were sometimes found adjacent to the mill site. Pendill's Mill on Whitefish Bay was supplied with logs skidded by oxen from the nearby cuttings.[13] Lumbermen, however, soon exhausted the pine that stood near their lakeshore mills. As early as 1851 loggers on the Escanaba River had camps built far into the interior, to within thirty miles of Lake Superior.[14] Pioneer loggers on the Whitefish, Sturgeon, and Manistique rivers also were forced to undertake forest operations far from the lakeshore during the 1850s.[15] The log drive quickly became the indispensable mechanism by which logs harvested from a distance forest could be cheaply brought to the millpond.

At least since the Middle Ages, lumbermen had made use of rivers and their current to transport logs. The first log drives in America saw colonial contractors floating masts for the Royal Navy.[16] This was no innovation; water was and remains the preferred medium for the transportation of all large, bulky staples. The log drive as it was used in northern Michigan was introduced by Empire State lumbermen in 1813, on the headwaters of the Hudson River. Instead of forming their logs into rafts, as was usually done, several lumbermen let them float freely downstream to be sorted out at the mill.[17] What made the log drive unique was how an entire river was integrated with moving logs. Small tributaries were dammed to regulate the flow of water into the river; lakes at the head of the river were similarly dammed and transformed into reservoirs. When it was necessary to prevent jams, obstacles in the riverbed were removed and the stream might be rechanneled, all to facilitate the log drive.[18] All lumbermen who cut logs along a river were forced to cooperate with one another to some extent. This is where log marks originated. Each log was struck by a hammer that left an imprint of a company's symbol, thereby distinguishing it from the logs of a competitor. At the mouth of the river, booms, like those Isaac Stephenson had organized on the Menominee River, caught and sorted the logs.

The log drives of the Upper Peninsula inspired some of the most colorful fictional images of the region. The tales of Stewart Edward White and William Davenport Hulbert celebrated the courage and daring of "the riverman," who in the face of danger and with life in the balance, remained nonplussed and "changeless as Egyptian sphinx."[19] The historical lumberjacks of the Upper Peninsula stoically took in stride the very real dangers of breaking a logjam or working at the brink of rapids. Yet what stood out from their experience were not feats of daring (such as Hulbert's fictional hero logrolling for his life at the brink of Tahquamenon Falls) but long days of hard, cold work.[20] Isaac Stephenson, who supervised log drives on the Escanaba River during the 1860s, blandly described the work as "more or less dangerous" than timber cutting. He and his men had "to work waist deep in the icy waters to keep the stream of logs moving." After four hours of such work, Stephenson remembered "our flesh was blue and our teeth [were] chattering as if we had the ague."[21] Charles Schaible, a young Ohio farm boy on his first drive down the Whitefish River, was more impressed. He remembered: "It was an awful sight to see, we had to walk in the water up to our waste to keep as many logs in line as we could and the water had lots of ice cakes floating in it and was very cold but the old hands walked right out in and never said a word."[22] Despite the cold water and often thirty-degree temperature, Stephenson contended that he had fewer sick men on the river drive than in camp.[23]

Although Stephenson, who at mid-century was a strong young man, strapping and self-assured, may have indulged in a touch of bravado when he said the cold, wet work did the men "more good than harm," the river drivers do seem to have been remarkably hardy. Young Schaible, who after one day of work thought he would surely take sick, eventually thrived on the danger and excitement of the drive. He later recalled: "You do not mind the cold or cold water, you get too interested to mind the cold, what would kill a man another time does not efect [*sic*] him on the drive. . . . "[24] Yet lumbermen recognized the harsh conditions of the drive and were careful to select only the best and strongest jacks for the task. As a resident of Iron River, Michigan, recalled: "It was work for he-men."[25] Perhaps, but they were "he-men" clad in heavy wool clothing and fortified with the best logging food. A Chicago Lumber Company river driver recalled:

> On the river they feed you better. You had to take your lunch out in a pack on your back and you had to carry your own lunch in that. They used to feed you ham and eggs and such stuff as that where in the old lumber camps it was sow belly, red horse or corn beef, which made it more attractive for the man or men who were working on the river drive.[26]

River drivers were also paid more than mere woods workers. But with the good food and higher pay came greater risks.

An early Upper Peninsula logger recalled: "Death constantly walked by the side of the men on the river and it made frequent appearances in the most casual and unexpected ways. It was so casual that it was treated almost callously. . . . A drowning man did not even slow up the work . . . the drive had to go on."[27] A fatal step, a little too much haste, or incompetence could cost the "river pigs" their lives. The June 1888 issue of the *Northwestern Lumberman* reported the death of a Bay De Noquet Company lumberjack on the Sturgeon River:

> Three bends above Eighteen Mile Creek, a man named Ed, whose other name the men couldn't learn, slipped off the log, fell into the water and was rolled right under. He couldn't swim, and in any case, there would have been little hope of saving him, as he had probably been knocked senseless by the rolling, grinding logs. The boys on the drive met by the side of the river and contributed each a little toward his burial. So Ed was buried about a mile from Nahma, in a little overgrown cemetery which might have been used by the Jesuit Fathers a century ago. Possibly, such is the irony of circumstance, this is the only notice that the death of poor Ed, the log driver, will ever receive. So be it. It is Kismet, and however melancholy, is inevitable in the lives of emperors or lumbermen.[28]

Yet it was the ever present danger of death or injury that elevated the task of river driving from being merely frigid drudgery to the subject of romantic tales.

Log drives usually were conducted in the spring. The thaw ended forest operations as ice roads melted and swelled the streams with the extra water needed to move a large amount of logs. Most Upper Peninsula rivers lacked the consistent flow of the Wisconsin or Saint Croix rivers, in which logs could be floated in almost any season. However, at least one stream in the region, the Indian River, allowed loggers the option of driving logs into the late fall and early winter. The headwaters of the Indian were a series of small lakes whose levels could be manipulated to provide enough water to carry logs far downstream. Harvey Crookson Saunders, foreman for the Chicago Lumber Company, supervised one such drive in the winter of 1904.

The loggers were forced to resort to a winter drive because there had been a shortage of snow that winter. A lack of winter snow threatened to curtail the amount of logs the Indian River could move in the spring. Forest operations were also disrupted. The ice roads by which logs were brought to the river landing could not be used until after Christmas, and only then after the men carried snow onto the roads. A result of this was a tremendous amount of cut lumber piling up along the skid roads. The Chicago Lumber Company knew it faced a major challenge moving all their cut logs to the river before the spring. To ease the burden, the loggers tried to immediately drive out those logs they had near the river. The weather was mild enough to keep the Indian River open, although it was still dangerously cold for the river drivers. Saunders later remembered how carefully he and his men prepared their mufti for the drive: "We got rubbers with as high tops as possible with heel plates, sharp spikes and we got them as large as possible so there would be room for extra socks. We cut and shaped the plates so that they would cover the entire sole of rubber as calked as river boots would be. We then fastened them to the rubber boots with copper rivets."[29]

The weak flow in the Indian River that December meant that even with the water in the reservoir lakes, the dam operators could only guarantee a six-hour flood each day. The working day for river drivers were twelve to fourteen hours, so the water limitations and short hours of daylight meant that the river men only had to work a half day. The cold temperature confounded their work by creating small islands of frozen sand and ice on which logs were hung up and jams began. But the lumberjacks, thrilled to be making $2.70 per day, twice their regular pay, worked feverishly. They covered a respectable nine miles the first day and kept up that pace for a month. Finally, near the end of January, three days of temperature between fifteen and twenty degrees below zero closed the river completely, ending the drive until spring.[30]

Special logging dams were part of the technology that made river driving possible in most of the Upper Peninsula. Lumbermen had few requirements for a stream to be used for logging. The streambed had to be wide enough and straight enough to allow the free passage of large logs. High banks were considered another asset, because they would confine the flow and prevent logs from being carried into the flooded forest where they would be lost. When streams did not fully meet these meager requirements, loggers improvised. They did not hesitate to straighten oxbows and dynamite obstacles to allow for the free flow of logs. But dams, which guaranteed the water necessary to float timber, were the most important tool available to the lumbermen. They also represented a major cost of logging. They were largely built of timber available at the site with cheap labor but nonetheless they were expensive. A dam with sluiceways for logs to pass through might cost as much as two thousand dollars.[31]

The heavy burden of dam building can be illustrated by the operations of the Bay De Noquet Company. In September 1883 the company sent several veteran loggers up the Sturgeon River to plan forest operations for the coming season. The men selected the locations of camps to be built, laid out sleigh roads, and selected the locations of any new dams. They also noted where crib work was needed to prevent log jams and inspected existing dams for signs of stress. Select lumberjacks were then sent upriver to accomplish the recommended tasks. The Bay De Noquet Company account books for that month alone indicate that twenty-seven hundred dollars was spent working on seven Sturgeon River dams. The most expensive of these dams was the "East Branch Dam" on the upper river, which cost more than thirteen hundred dollars. This outlay, which came only two years after the company built several new dams on the river, represented an expense greater than the labor costs of a large logging camp for most of the winter.[32]

Cost was a minor drawback to river driving in comparison with the problems of shrinkage and the conflicts with other loggers that arose from sharing a river. The two problems were related. Shrinkage was the difference between the amount of logs scaled in the forest and the amount of logs measured at the boom after the drive. Naturally some logs were going to be lost during even the best run drive, but there was also the potential of timber theft. Russell Alger believed he was the victim of such theft during the early 1890s. His logs were cut deep in the interior and originally driven to Lake Michigan to be manufactured in the mills of the Chicago Lumber Company. To prevent disputes on the river, all drives on the Manistique River were supervised by the Manistique River Improvement Company, a wholly owned subsidiary of the Chicago Lumber Company. After several years of finding a discrepancy between the amount of logs Alger had put into the river and the amount of lumber credited to his account by the Chicago Lumber Company, the general sent several trusted men to investigate the situation in Manistique. They discovered a large amount of Alger logs in the millpond of a competitor, the North Shore Lumber Company. Because it was the Improvement Company's job to prevent such theft, Alger stopped sending his logs down river and began shipping them to a port he could control, Grand Marais.[33]

Not all disputes among river drivers involved theft. In 1896 the Fence River Logging Company and the proprietorship of Hamilton & Merryman waged a virtual war over driving arrangements on the Fence River, a tributary of the Menominee. Hamilton & Merryman operated a pair of logging dams along the upper river; the Fence River Logging Company built two dams on the lower river. Fists began to fly when each planned to drive its logs at the same time. Both loggers closed the gates of their dams to build up a sufficient head of water. But the upper dams so reduced the flow of water below that the Fence River Logging Company could not move its cut. Rather than wait for Hamilton & Merryman's logs to move downstream, and drive the logs together, the Fence River men moved to destroy the upper dams. There must have been a history of bad blood between the companies because Hamilton & Merryman had posted a twenty-five-man guard at the dam. A battle royal ensued when the two groups of rivermen met. The Fence River lumberjacks enjoyed a two-to-one superiority, and after many right hooks, angry jabs, and no doubt several bites, they brushed their way past the guards and tore away the gates of the dam. The sudden flood of water broke apart both upper dams and played havoc with Hamilton & Merryman's drive. The partners threatened to have all sixty Fence River lumberjacks thrown in jail. But in the end, it only brought suit for four thousand dollars to replace its dams.[34]

Some lumbermen were just as quick to resort to violence as the much storied woodworkers that labored for them. The Ford River Lumber Company once tried to bill the Harmon Lumber Company for the cost of driving some of its logs to the lakeshore. The Harmon logs had been stranded at the headwaters a year before, and Harmon made no effort to retrieve them the next spring. The foreman of the Ford River Company thought he had done right by bringing them down with his logs, but he wanted to be relieved of the extra costs he incurred. He met the Harmon representative in the abandoned milltown of Metropolitan. The Harmon man lured him into a small room, shut the door, and threatened, "Cancel that bill in a hurry or I'll pound hell out of you!" The Harmon logger may have only been bluffing, but the foreman took no chances and tore up the bill. Several years later he was intimidated by the same logger into driving the other man's logs at a reduced price just to be spared another confrontation. River driving was not a branch of the lumber industry for the timid.[35]

An even more serious problem with the technology of the river drive was natural shrinkage. Often as much as ten percent of the logs pushed into the river would be lost by natural means.[36] The Holt Lumber Company, which took over the Diamond Match timberlands in Ontonagon County, lost only six percent of the logs it drove on the Ontonagon River between 1902 and 1905. But that resulted in the loss of more than ten thousand logs.[37] Attempts were made to recover this valuable timber. But the woodsman the Holt Lumber Company sent down the Ontonagon River could only salvage 186 logs.[38] Many of the logs that could not be recovered had become "deadheads," the term river men used for sunken logs. Other logs were carried deep into the forest by high water, only to be stranded as the level of the river dropped. Deadheads could be refloated years later and still be made into fine lumber. Water did little damage to quality pine. The rivermen working the tail end of the drive tried to retrieve as many stranded logs as possible. But as the water retreated, the giant pine logs became unwieldy. Such logs were often left behind to rot. However, logs long thought lost to shrinkage would sometimes turn up later in the boom. In 1897 two logs passed through the Menominee River boom twenty years after they were cut and stamped.[39] Another nightmare for the lumberman were dry winters, which would not only foul forest operations but affect spring river drives. Shallow rivers like the Indian or the Ontonagon were more susceptible to low-water problems than the better driving streams like the Menominee and Manistique, but it was something all lumbermen feared. The worst example of this was between 1895 and 1897 when almost 150 million feet of pine were tied up on the Ontonagon.[40]

Log rafting was another important technological adaption of water as a transportation medium. The feasibility of enclosing many logs in a boom and towing it a long distance was proven in 1885. That summer, three million feet of logs were towed from the mouth of the Two Hearted River to Bay City. The boom even survived one of the worst storms of the year on Lake Huron without losing a single log. The experiment was particularly noteworthy because it cost only seventy cents per thousand feet for the entire journey. For the ten years that followed, rafting became popular on Lake Superior and Lake Huron. The size of rafts towed increased when lumbermen learned that larger booms withstood storms better than the smaller ones. Storms did occasionally succeed in wrecking raft booms, but, if the tugboat skipper continued to circle the logs with his line of boom sticks, the loss of logs could be controlled.[41]

Interest in long-distance rafting was particularly strong among the owners of the giant sawmills of Saginaw Bay. In the 1880s they began to suffer a shortage of pine. For fifty years the Tittabawassee River and its tributaries had supplied all the white pine lumbermen could handle. When those forestlands were exhausted and the annual cuts began to decline, lumbermen had to make new plans. Some gave up hope in the Saginaw and moved to sell their mills while they were still worth something. Others planned to disassemble their plants and have them rebuilt, at considerable expense, at a new location. But there were 112 separate sawmills in the Saginaw area; not all could sell out or relocate. Some of them turned to rafting as a desperate measure to supply their mills.[42] In 1888 forty million feet of logs came down from Lake Superior to the mills of Saginaw.[43] A full quarter of all the lumber made there came from the north.[44]

Several established Upper Peninsula lumber companies, although they possessed sawmills of their own, tried to profit from Saginaw's log famine by rafting their timber to the hungry mills. The most notable of these was the Mackinac Lumber Company of Saint Ignace. The company had better access to Lake Huron than most of its northern Michigan rivals. Beginning in 1888 the company sent huge rafts of pine and cedar south. The profits from its first attempts were not very flattering, but the company stuck with the experiment.[45] In 1889 the company went so far as to shut down its mill at Saint Ignace and sent almost seven million feet of timber to be sawed and marketed at Bay City.[46]

Rafts of softwoods from northern Michigan were sent to sawmills throughout the Great Lakes region. Tonawanda, New York; Cleveland, Detroit, and Saginaw were all able to keep plants operating and workers employed with resources shipped from the Upper Peninsula's forests. The West Bay, Michigan, firm of Mosher & Fisher was a major proponent of log rafting. After successfully rafting millions of feet of pine to its mill, it began to approach mill owners in other dying lumber ports, promising "an interminable lease on life" through rafting. Muskegon lumbermen were seduced by this promise until October 1887 when a storm on Lake Superior scattered a huge raft of Mosher & Fisher logs.[47] Such periodic disasters dampened enthusiasm for rafting.

Like river driving, rafting also often left the lumbermen awash with legal problems. In 1886 the Mackinac Lumber Company was hit by a daring gang of log rustlers. They stole across the Straits of Mackinac and pirated a huge raft of cedar and pine. Before the company caught on to the theft, the logs had been sold to a third party.[48] More common were legal difficulties caused by transporting large rafts of pine through the narrow Saint Marys River. In 1890 the steamer *Joliet* was forced aground when a giant raft filled the entire channel. A second ship, when faced with the same choice, pushed ahead, tearing the boom and scattering the logs. Damage to the *Joliet*, which was aground for two days, was estimated at thirty thousand dollars. The bill for repairs and losses was placed at the lumberman's door. Two years later, a log raft closed the Keweenaw Peninsula's Portage Lake Canal for three days. Nor were these isolated incidents. The Lake Carriers' Association demanded a Congressional investigation of the dangers of log rafting. They secured an Army Corps of Engineers hearing, which led to punitive recommendations regulating where rafting was permitted, boom styles, and raft size. But Lake Superior lumbermen were not without their clout. Gen. Russell Alger, one of the principal users of rafting, used his power in the Republican party to kill a House bill giving the proposed regulations force of law. With such a powerful enemy, rafting restrictions had no hope.[49] Yet the problems presented by rafting remained, and the rafting of Lake Superior pine through the Saint Marys River gradually declined in the late 1890s.[50]

Rafts were also assembled to transport logs across interior lakes. The Chicago Lumber Company employed a paddlewheel steamer to pull its boom of pine across the calm expanse of Indian Lake.[51] The lake was one of the largest in the Upper Peninsula and presented an obstacle to all loggers on the Indian River. In 1875 two independent loggers, Eben James and Cornelius Ruggles, challenged the Chicago Lumber Company's hold on the Manistique drainage by purchasing timberland along the Indian River. There was no way the company would cooperate with the two new men and they could not afford to buy their own tug to cross the lake. They used a poor man's technology instead. They secured a winch to their raft and attached to it a cable and anchor. The anchor was taken by a rowboat out ahead of the raft and dropped below. The winch would then pull the log raft as far as the anchor and the process would be repeated. In this way the logs could be inched across the lake. The Chicago Lumber Company itself later used a similar device on Skeels Lake on the Upper Indian River.[52]

Winches were also used to help loggers operating on hilly terrain. In 1891 the Nestor Logging Company used a power winch. The company's main ice road had to traverse a steep hill almost fifteen hundred feet high. No matter how the road was laid out, an incline of about twenty percent had to be negotiated. Ordinarily, hills could be overcome by adding an extra team to each sleigh as it climbed the slope, but this grade was too steep. Peter Cameron, the Nestor foreman, who was known to his men as "one of the greatest hustlers on the river," refused to be daunted. With the aid of a Baraga lumberjack, he tore a page out of the book of Rocky Mountain loggers and set up a steam donkey. It was like the Dobler donkey steam engine patented in 1882, which functioned as a power winch. Pacific loggers used it to haul individual logs.[53] Cameron stationed his winch at the top of the hill. When one of his sleighs reached the foot of the hill, a wire cable was attached and the winch pulled the logs to the top of the hill in seven minutes. Without this device, seven more miles of ice roads would have been needed to avoid the hill.[54]

Log chutes were another technological adaptation to get timber from hilly terrain to water. Like power winches, chutes were used frequently in the Rocky Mountains, but the system was pioneered in Pennsylvania during the early nineteenth century.[55] In the Upper Peninsula, log chutes were employed along the Ontonagon River and on the south shore of Lake Superior. There were basically two types of log chutes: the earth slide and the timber slide. The earth slide was a crudely made furrow in soft soil, which kept a log pointed downhill. The timber slide consisted of a chute made of parallel logs supported by cross skids. The logs were debarked and sometimes greased. Both types of chutes worked best during the winter when they could be iced. In 1903 the Holt Lumber Company used both a power winch and a log chute to cut the last of the Diamond Match pinelands.[56] When the Alger-Smith Lumber Company cut the pine off the Kingston Plains, the logs were hauled to the Grand Sable Dunes and then thrust several hundred feet down a log chute to the cold waters of Lake Superior.[57]

The single piece of pine era technology that has been least appreciated by historians is the lumber schooner. Most of the pine that stood in the Upper Peninsula's forests left in the holds of sail-powered schooners. The Great Lakes lumber industry and the schooner grew up together. When the industry expanded during the Civil War era, so too did schooner traffic. By 1868 there were 1,857 vessels operating on the Great Lakes. Lake steamers had already assumed control over the passenger trade and were on their way to becoming the principal grain carriers as well. But schooners held on through the 1880s as the favored means of shipping boards and shingles from nothern Michigan mills to the vast lumberyards along the Chicago River.[58] In 1884 alone, more than eight thousand cargoes of softwood, mostly pine lumber and cedar shingles, were registered at Chicago. Although schooners could not handle large cargoes, they were ideally suited to the lumber trade. They were cheaply built and inexpensive to operate. Special triangular "raffee" sails were designed by Great Lakes mariners so that the ships could be operated with a small crew. The schooners were also fitted with a device known as a centerboard, a retractable keel that made the craft easier to navigate windward. The centerboard and the shallow draft of the schooner proved handy when the ships entered the unimproved harbors of the Upper Peninsula. There seldom were navigation markers and almost never tugs to aid the schooner's approach to a wharf. Yet a captain boldly approached his berth under sail while the crew cannily used the centerboard as an underwater brake to stop the ship.[59]

Some early lumber companies, such as Sinclair and Wells and the Ford River Company, owned and operated their own schooners. But most of the cargoes, even for these companies, were carried by independently owned schooners. As early as 1849, three or four schooners called at Flat Rock (now Escanaba) each week during the sawing season.[60] Most of the vessels were owned by their captains, who negotiated carrying charges from the deck. Some early schooners were owned by ambitious warehouse operators, who would outfit several vessels and enter the shipping business. Isaac Stephenson fell under the spell of the tall-masted schooners. The first wages he earned lumbering in Michigan went to buy a half interest in a schooner. But only days later the ship capsized in a storm and was lost. Stephenson later remembered, "At no time during these early voyages did it seem that we were free from threatened danger." Yet for Stephenson that was part of the romance of the lakes "which had an element of danger sufficient to stimulate a young man's passion for adventure." As soon as he could, Stephenson bought another schooner, which he captained for nine voyages before forsaking the mast. It was a career short on financial reward and long on danger.[61]

Stephenson maintained an active interest in the maritime dimensions of lumbering. While director of the N. Ludington Company, he became directly involved in the problem of lumber transportation. He had barges specially built for the lumber trade. The largest could hold a million feet of lumber. By 1873 Stephenson could persuade three other Menominee lumbermen to join him in establishing a barge company. They operated a fleet of fifteen barges, which allowed them to always have five barges unloading in Chicago, five in transit on the lake, and five more taking on lumber in Menominee.[62] The barges proved profitable partly because of their large carrying capacity and partly because the frugal Stephenson equipped the tugs to burn wood slabs, an inexpensive by-product of milling.[63]

Following Stephenson's example, other northern Michigan lumbermen experimented with the towing of lumber barges. However, because most small-scale lumbermen could not afford to buy the newly designed lumber barges, they improvised. Aged schooners were re-caulked, demasted, and given the inglorious task of being towed from port to port. Another innovation of the post-Civil War era was the "rabbit" barge, a specially designed freighter equipped with its own steam-powered, screw-driven propeller.[64] But the schooner only grudgingly gave up its prominence in the lumber trade. As late as 1890 the 488 schooners on Lake Michigan still accounted for almost forty percent of the shipping on the lake. The shipment of pine and cedar from the Upper Peninsula kept schooner traffic alive on Lake Michigan long after the great white sails faded from Lakes Huron and Erie. Well into the twentieth century, schooner dockings at Marinette, Wisconsin, outnumbered steamer arrivals almost two to one.[65] The remnants of the fleet lingered after the pine was gone, carrying pulpwood, lath, Christmas trees, or even potatoes from the withering lumber ports of the north to the railroad centers of the south.

THE TECHNOLOGY OF PINE LOGGING: SAWMILLS

The focus of attention for all log transport was the sawmill. The appetite of the sawmill dictated the pace of forest operations, river drives, and schooner dockings. The technology of milling had to meet the improvements of transportation and forest operations to bring about any significant growth in lumber production. The sawmill was generally (forgive the expression) at the cutting edge of technological innovations in the lumber industry. The sawmill was not strictly part of the logging business, but the evolution of milling does help illuminate the role of logging in the lumber business.

The first sawmills in the Upper Peninsula were water-powered. Pioneer lumbermen looked for locations that promised not only access to quality pine but also potential waterpower sites. Seldom were such sites available at the very mouth of a river. A good waterpower site had a steady flow of fast water. For this reason many of the early mills on the Escanaba, Ford, and Sturgeon rivers were located upstream, often as much as a mile from the lake.[66] The first mill on the Whitefish River was a full four miles from Bay De Noc.[67] Rapids or small waterfalls were favored locations for lumbermen to lay out the mill, build a dam, and dig a millrace. The fast water entered the mill house through a wooden sluice, poured over the waterwheel, and powered the saw blades.

Originally, lumbermen favored the sash saw as their cutting mechanism. The sash saw was a single blade mounted vertically on a wooden frame.[68] It was a simple, easy-to-operate mechanism that was important in developing the colonial frontier. Some lumbermen favored the sash saw because they lacked skilled sawyers. The major criticism of the sash saw was the slow rate at which it produced boards. One way to increase its production was to place three or four more blades on the frame, creating a gang saw. During the 1850s, lumbermen began to install muley saws in their northern Michigan mills. The muley saw was an American invention designed to further speed the milling process. It used a vertical saw blade like that in the sash saw but without the cumbersome wooden frame that made the sash saw slow.[69]

The major technological leap in mill technology was the application of the steam engine. The increased power of steam mills made the gang and muley saws cut even faster. A steam-powered muley saw produced three hundred strokes per minute.[70] During the 1850s, most lumbermen serious about commercial logging in the north began to adopt the steam engine. It represented a greater capital outlay, but it also liberated the mill owner from the vagaries of climate and water level.

Steam power made the cumbersome gang saw a much favored piece of equipment. Among large pine operators, the gang saw was easily the most popular saw. Some mills used circular saws, which were the fastest single-blade saws available, able to cut between three and four feet per minute.[71] Yet because circular saws had only one blade, and that blade had a tendency to cut unevenly at high speeds, it was not universally popular. Still it was not unusual for a large mill to have one circular saw to slab (trim the rounded sides) off logs that would then be transformed into boards by the gang saw. The problem with both the gang and circular saw was the amount of sawdust they produced. Every large mill had a large silolike structure that functioned as a sawdust burner. A circular saw would turn 312 feet of wood into sawdust for every thousand feet of inch boards it created. Gang saws were only slightly more efficient. Nothing was done about this waste while trees were plentiful. Only after the best pine had been stripped from the eastern states and lower Michigan's forests were in decline was a new technology presented to mill owners. By 1886 the band saw, a narrow band of steel teeth passing over two wheels, was perfected. It quickly became the standard in the industry.[72]

The band saw was accepted by most lumbermen, if only because it saved them money by wasting less wood. There were those who distrusted the new technique. Some lumbermen thought gang saws produced a smoother, better-looking board. Among the holdouts was Abijah Weston, the stodgy president of the Chicago Lumber Company and its sister concern, the Weston Lumber Company. As late as 1898, the giant mills of the two companies were still operating with waterpower. The idea of using band saws to replace the gang saws Weston had personally installed in the mills left the old man cold. Yet his partners were anxious to modernize and they pressured Weston to accompany them on an inspection tour of the Hall & Buell Company mill at South Manistique. It was a model of modern logging. Logs were brought in by train and mechanically fed into the mill where a steam-powered double band saw transformed the logs into board. Efficiency alone impressed the minority stockholders but they were also concerned about squandered profits. Using Hall & Buell's figures, they estimated how much extra board they would have produced with a band saw. They arrived at a staggering amount. In 1890's dollars, they had sawed ninety-three thousand dollars worth of pine into sawdust. Yet Weston was unimpressed. He liked his wasteful old gang saws and would not have his lumber "cut by lightning."[73]

The mill owners along the Menominee River were not as pigheaded. As early as 1887, all the big mills had adopted the band saw.[74] The Delta Lumber Company of Thompson, Michigan, adopted it in the early 1880s when it still was regarded as experimental by many lumbermen.[75] Even the Chicago Lumber Company eventually installed a band saw, but not until the twentieth century and the departure of Abijah Weston.[76] By that time, pine logging was in its decline and a new era of logging was underway.

FOREST RESOURCES AND THE PINE ERA

Pine was the principal timber type exploited during the primary phase of logging in northern Michigan. Lumbermen from the East who immigrated to the Lake Superior country described themselves as "following the pine." Old men looking back on the era of abundance referred to the region as "a white pine empire"; the period was wistfully known as "when pine was king." An aged lumberjack of the 1940s articulated the special place of pine in the minds of all Upper Peninsula woodsmen when he said, "I like pine . . . I don't know why; I just like pine timber."[77]

The first lumbermen in the Upper Peninsula liked pine for two very good reasons. Softwoods such as pine were buoyant and could therefore be easily floated on rivers and lakes. For men operating on the frontier with limited cash, the ability to move bulky logs by water was very important. The second reason for pine's popularity relates to the lumber market. The abundance of pine, first in the eastern states and later in lower Michigan, created a market for pine boards in the construction industry. Pine was a light, yet strong wood that could be easily worked yet was still inexpensive. The balloon frame construction style invented in Chicago in 1839 fueled the demand for dimensioned pine boards.[78]

But as the nation's appetite for cheap pine from Saginaw or Green Bay grew, the accessible pine forests shrunk. By the 1880s some midwestern lumbermen were justly anxious about the future of pine logging. Trade journal editorials proclaimed "the beginning of the end is already here."[79] Some lumbermen began to investigate southern pinelands; others like Russell Alger predicted that the West Coast would be the center of the industry.[80] Some Saginaw Bay lumbermen tried to keep their mills operating by investing in Georgian Bay pinelands. But when the Canadians raised the export tariff on unmanufactured timber, the idea of rafting Canadian logs seemed less attractive.[81] The pine forests of the Upper Peninsula were so highly valued because they were only reaching their peak of production when most of the Midwest's softwood forests were in decline. Northern Michigan, and to an extent northern Minnesota, held out hope for the future.

It was largely a false hope. The Upper Peninsula did not have the forest resources necessary to significantly delay the decline of pine logging. Although there were several large plains of pine forest, where Norway and white pine trees rose in dense stands more than 100 feet above the ground, such areas were not as common as they were in lower Michigan or along the Wisconsin River. The Upper Peninsula lies at the northern edge of the deciduous forest and the southern limit of the boreal forest. Therefore, its timberlands were dominated by northern hardwoods, such as sugar maple, paper birch, and basswood, and by swamp forests species, such as spruce, tamarack, and cedar. Because the region can support such diverse forest types, pure stands of individual timber are not common. Lumbermen looking for pine, save for on the pine plains, usually found it intermixed with mature hardwood trees or amid boreal forest. Intensive pine logging could not be long sustained by such an environment.[82]

Although pine logging began in the Upper Peninsula during the 1830s, it was not until the 1880s, when lower Michigan and Wisconsin logging began to decline, that the region became a vital source of production. In 1881, for example, only 140 million feet of pine was produced by the seven western counties. Over the next decade, however, the pace quickened and each year the cut became larger. By 1892 the haul had risen to 400 million feet of pine annually. But that was the zenith for the area. The Upper Peninsula's limited pine forests were quickly picked clean. In 1909 Michigan officials were surprised to see that the pine cut for the region had shrunk to a mere 11 million feet.[83]

As the amount of standing pine began to decline in the Upper Peninsula, the lumberman's task became more difficult. Unable to harvest the pure pine of the plains, loggers were forced into the swamp forest where white pine grew amid stands of fir and spruce. Logging costs were higher in such terrain and the harvest was thinner. Mills found themselves accepting second-rate logs that earlier would have been left to rot. Jack pine, which lumbermen weaned on white or Norway pine referred to as a "weed tree," became an increasingly more significant part of the haul.[84] Cedar and hemlock also became important. Like pine, they could be floated to market (although hemlock had to be debarked before it could be put in the river). Cedar was considered of little value in the lake states until it was adopted by railroads for ties. Isaac Stephenson claims to have pointed out cedar's decay-resisting qualities to William B. Ogden. The advice was not wasted on Ogden, first mayor of Chicago and president of the Chicago and North Western Railway. Against the advice of those who thought cedar too soft to last long, the timber was tried and it quickly became the standard element for rail ties.[85] The tremendous expansion of American rail lines in the late nineteenth century made cedar ties a staple produce of the northern forest. Two other inventions, barbed wire and the telegraph, created a further demand for cedar as posts and poles. Pine and cedar were also favored woods for making roofing shingles and paving blocks for streets. The streets of Chicago and most Lake Michigan towns were once paved with slabs of pine or cedar. Occasionally, large white pine would still make its appearance in the sawmills of the early twentieth century. Some were even larger than the virgin pine of past decades. They came from hardwood forests and were isolated interlopers. When they were cut there were no more.[85]

Pine logging had a detrimental effect on the forest of northern Michigan. There has been a tendency to criticize the wasteful methods of pine loggers, and with some justice. Yet lumbermen entered the dense woods of the Upper Peninsula frontier with a crude technological arsenal and virtually nothing in the way of restraining regulations. It was a difficult task, exploiting the frontier forests, one that cost the lives and fortunes of the unlucky or reckless. It should be understood that the virgin forests of the Upper Peninsula did not contain only mature trees. Instead, there was a considerable percentage of old growth, rotted and unsuitable for lumber. Younger trees were often not worth the cost of cutting and transportation. When the sawyers found giant rotted pine trees, they let them lie where they fell. The rotted trunks and the branches from healthy timber littered the forest floor after logging was completed. It would usually take seven years for that debris to decay.[87] But rarely did the natural process occur. The deadwood became tinder dry and within a year or two of logging, the cutover lands were a breeding ground for fire.

Fire hastened the decline of pine as the prized product of the northern forests. The forest fires of the Upper Peninsula did not result in the spectacular death tolls of the Peshtigo fire, which decimated parts of northeast Wisconsin, or Minnesota's Hinckley fire; yet they did much to mold the current forest resource situation in the region. The worst fires of the pine era were in 1891, 1894, and 1896. The western Upper Peninsula was particularly hard fit by fire in those years. The 1894 blaze occurred just two days after the famed blaze that destroyed Hinckley, Minnesota, and it did not receive much notice in the national press. But the fire burned across half of the peninsula. The entire population of Norway, Michigan, had to be organized into bucket brigades to keep the town from being consumed. All through the backwoods, homesteaders bundled their belongings and made ready to flee if the fire spread in their direction. The smoke hung in heavy clouds and the intense heat was stifling. The Chicago and North Western Railway suspended operations as its ties caught fire and rails warped.[88] One engineer on another line tried to run the gauntlet through the blazing forest. He paid for this daring with his life when the train drove "into a cloud of smoke and fire, the engine overturned, and he was dashed into eternity." The load of logs the train was carrying added further fuel to the fire.[89]

The 1896 fires were even worse. Not only were thousands of acres of forest scorched, but the towns of Ontonagon and L'Anse were burned. Both towns quickly rebuilt. With the ashes of the old town still smoldering in the background, L'Anse saloon keepers did a brisk business in the street using packing cases as a bar.[90] Such a quick recovery was possible because forest fires were a short-term stimulus for local economies. Although scorched pine was not as valuable as fresh wood, fire-ravaged forests still could be put to use if they were cut immediately. In the wake of forest fires, timber owners scrambled over one another to hire logging jobbers to quickly cut their pine. This gave rise to the suspicion that not all fires were accidental but that they were set by arsonists with an interest in seeing heavy logging activity.[91]

By the 1890s Upper Peninsula lumbermen found themselves caught in a vicious cycle of their own unwitting design. The prices in the lumber markets were generally favorable. Large hauls of pine, however, tended to depress its market value. This was unfortunate because northern Michigan and Minnesota were the last bastions of the white pine frontier. With that timber type becoming dearer and dearer as each year passed, the smart businessman would hold on to his pinelands until production fell off and prices rose. Yet the more pine that was cut, the greater the frequency of forest fires. After each fire, logging had to be increased to harvest the damaged logs before they became riddled with worms. Logging practice was not reformed, so each such salvage operation left further slashings on the forest floor to breed new fires that would spread to virgin tracts. The threat and effect of fire were significant in discouraging any type of conservation, even if it did make good business sense.[92]

Forest fires hurried the pace of logging in the Upper Peninsula. It is true that millions of feet of standing timber were destroyed. But direct fire loss does not seem to have been a major problem for most lumber companies. A United States Census Bureau study of forest fire damage in the lake states revealed that between 1880 and 1890 only 166 logging companies out of 883 surveyed reported losses of standing timber to fire.[93] Although the lumbermen of northern Michigan faced their worst fires after 1890, the report does point to the real tragedy. It was not so much the timber that was destroyed by repeated forest fires, but the habitat that supported pine growth. The humus was burned from the ground and the soil was degraded to such an extent it could no longer support pine timber.[94] Pine was particularly vulnerable to this damage because pine stands admitted little sunlight to the forest floor. The soil in such forests was perpetually moist and encouraged the growth of carpets of moss, often a foot thick. When the giant trees were removed, the moss was left exposed to the sun. It became dry and susceptible to burning. When this ground cover was destroyed, the soil lost much of its ability to retain the moisture needed for vigorous tree growth.[95]

Commercial lumbermen were not the only users of the northern Michigan forests during the nineteenth century, nor were softwoods the only timber exploited. Homesteaders, miners, and charcoal producers also exploited the deep woods frontier.

Homesteaders were pioneer agriculturalists who established backwoods farms, sometimes by the provision of the 1862 Homestead Act, by preemption, or simple real estate purchase. The normal progression of frontier development was for the agriculturalist to succeed the lumbermen and farm the cut-over land; this happened in areas of lower Michigan, New York, and Pennsylvania. But there were many families drawn to the Upper Peninsula in the nineteenth century by opportunities in mining or logging who also established pioneer farms. Their concern was clearing land and planting crops. Trees, particularly hardwood (for which there was little local market), were merely in the way. When they were cut down, they were hauled into piles and burned.[96]

Many early homesteaders were less interested in building a future farm than they were in getting free title to potentially valuable government land. Real estate speculation always went hand in hand with frontier development. Just how lucrative even modest-scale homestead speculation could be is illustrated by an Ontonagon County farmer. A homesteader filed a claim on rich pinelands. His claim must have been surrounded by corporate holdings because after only several years, he was offered sixteen thousand dollars for his 160 acres by a lumberman. Many a homesteader would have leaped to such an offer, but the farmer refused. He was "happy and contented as a lark" on the five cleared acres he shared with his wife, children, cow, pigs, and chickens.[97]

A considerable number of homesteaders had less devotion to farming. In 1890 several "pioneers" tried to file homestead claims on the village of Ontonagon's lakefront. They argued that the beach had been created by the retreating lake and was not on the original town plat. The most common way for phony homesteaders to get rich quick was to locate claims on good pineland and then sell out to the lumber companies nearby. The trouble with this approach was that few of these "tenderfeet" were good judges of timberlands. They might spend five years meeting the government requirements for "proving up" their claim, expecting a large cash sum for their effort. But when professional landlookers investigated the rotted and scattered timber on their holdings, they would learn that the land was "hardly worth buying and in many instances not worth the time and money spent in locating and proving upon it."[98]

The only manufacturers in the Upper Peninsula who paid any real interest in hardwood forests before the 1890s were the charcoal-iron producers. Hardwoods were ideal for making the charcoal needed to transform iron ore into iron bars. There were fifteen such companies in Marquette County, the real headquarters of the industry. Marquette County furnaces had the advantage of being near the iron ore, and the county's forests at first supported enough hardwood to provide the charcoal needed. But with individual plants requiring forty thousand cords of wood annually, it was not long before many furnaces were short of fuel and forced to close. Hardwoods were not as easy to transport as pine, and few producers generated profits great enough to haul fuel from any great distance. One solution was to relocate furnaces closer to the hardwood forests. An example of one such operation is the Jackson Iron Company's Fayette Furnace, on the west shore of Bay De Noc's Garden Peninsula. Iron was shipped by rail to Escanaba, then loaded on scows for transport to Fayette's natural harbor. What justified these efforts was more than twenty thousand acres of hardwood. Thirty charcoal kilns at Fayette devoured more than eighteen hundred cords of that wood, per load, when they were operated at capacity.[99]

During the 1870s and 1880s, charcoal ironworks were established throughout the Upper Peninsula. Escanaba, Menominee, Manistique, and Saint Ignace received furnaces and became centers of hardwood consumption. Alger County became a major producer of charcoal. In 1885 one contractor alone agreed to provide a hundred thousand bushels of charcoal per month to a local furnace. Most of these operations were only marginal. When hardwood was abundant near the furnace, they prospered; but as local supplies became exhausted, the furnaces closed. Charocal iron producers needed the introduction of rail technology to expand their area of exploitation. That would happen, but in the twentieth century.[100]

Iron mines also were important consumers of forest products during the pine era. The Upper Peninsula's iron and copper mines were all subsurface mines, and required large amounts of wood to "shore up" underground shafts and adits. At first, the favored wood for mine timbers was white pine.[101] The Calumet & Hecla Mining Company, the Oliver Iron Mining Company (later U.S. Steel), and Cleveland-Cliffs Company were among the largest timberland owners in northern Michigan. The copper king, Calumet & Hecla, was extensively involved in pine logging. Among its many holdings were more than thirty thousand acres in Chippewa County. Its principal mill was at Shelldrake, a sawdust town on Whitefish Bay. Such extensive timber holdings made good sense for the mining company because of its heavy dependence on wood. The Penn Iron Mining Company alone purchased four million feet of timber in 1891. Nor was that unusual. The Aragon Mine in Norway, Michigan, annually used five million feet.[102] But as pine became more scarce and rose in value, mining engineers experimented with other timber types. By 1900 hemlock was the favored wood, although birch, maple, and even cedar were occasionally used.[103]

As the nineteenth century gave way to the twentieth, the forests of the Upper Peninsula were still ripe with potential for an aggressive lumberman. But the crowning jewel of the deep woods, the lofty white pine forests, had been badly ravaged. Northern Michigan would continue to yield fortunes in forest products, but the logger would have to seek a much more diversified range of timber types. White pine was dethroned and there were no monarchs in the forest to take its place.

SPATIAL DIMENSIONS OF THE PINE ERA

The technological limitations and the timber type orientation of the first loggers combined to create a distinct pattern of land use during the pine era. This pattern is best illustrated by the changing relationship between production points, such as mills or logging camps, and transportation systems, such as lakes, rivers, or railroads. The spatial arrangement of logging during the pine era was not static; it varied from place to place, because of local topography, as well as over time, as the industry evolved technologically. Yet a pattern may be said to exist because of the enduring significance of water transportation to pine logging.

Pine era spatial organization and its evolution can best be explained by example and graphics. Almost any early logging district could serve this purpose, but attention will be focused on the Whitefish River in Delta County, Michigan. The first spatial stage of pine logging is illustrated by Darius Clark's operations on the river in 1847. Clark was a skilled millwright, who rejected the opportunity to take comfortable employment in lower Michigan or Wisconsin where skilled men were in demand, and struggled instead to build his own logging enterprise. His first efforts were concentrated on the Escanaba River where he worked with John and Joseph Smith who operated the first two mills at that place. But by 1845 he moved up the shore of Little Bay De Noc to the Whitefish River.[104] The best site for an overshot water-powered mill was four miles from the Whitefish's mouth, where the river had begun to narrow and the current was swift. The site was also adjacent to quality pine on the west bank of the river. Clark's logging crew was housed at his mill site. A logging road was built from the Whitefish through the pine timber. Felled logs were skidded along the road, probably by oxen, to the riverbank. During winter the Whitefish froze hard enough that the logs could be easily hauled to the mill yard. The mill began to cut lumber in the spring and operated into the early summer until all the backlog was sawed. The Whitefish River was too shallow even for the versatile lumber schooners to pick up cargoes from Clark's mill site, so he built a lumber loading pier at the mouth of the river. Lumber produced by the mill was sent down the river, probably by shallow draft bateau, to the pier.[105]

Clark's operation reveals the typical spatial pattern of early pine logging through several features. He harvested logs near the mill site, which was chosen because of its waterpower capabilities, and he used water to get his product to market. This arrangement was followed with slight variation by the first loggers on the Sturgeon, Ford, and Escanaba rivers as well as at Pendill's Mill on Lake Superior.

Later, pine loggers could not count on having easy access to logs, nor could even the pioneer lumbermen continue to log near their mill sites after their first seasons. By moving upstream, lumbermen opened up a much larger resource base. This later stage of development on the Whitefish River can best be illustrated by the operations of the Jerry Madden Shingle Company in 1899. The company was based across the bay from the Whitefish River in the town of Rapid River. It was a much more flexible location than Clark's early mill site. Rapid River was serviced both by lake vessels and the Soo Line Railway. The firm was owned by Jerry Madden, a veteran logger, and Adam Schaible, an Ohio farmer who taught himself the business of milling logs. The best of the pine in the Whitefish drainage had been cut years before. But pockets of small pine could still be found. It did not pay to make such wood into lumber, but it was well suited for the manufacture of roofing shingles.[106]

In the fall of 1899 Madden and Schaible determined to log a track of land adjacent to Pole Creek, a tributary of the Whitefish. Eight wagons loaded with supplies and building materials followed by forty men were sent into the forest that October. They walked about forty miles up the Whitefish valley on a rough wagon road. For the first several hours, they passed nothing but cutover lands; the last ten miles of the journey were through cool, dark woods. After seventeen hours on the trail, the tired men reached Pole Creek. The next day some of the men began building the logging camp; others began laying out sleigh roads. The task took almost a month, but when they were through, snow had begun to fall and logging could begin. The camp operated until April 3, when the ice roads finally got too soft to bear a load. The men then went into town for their pay and pleasure.

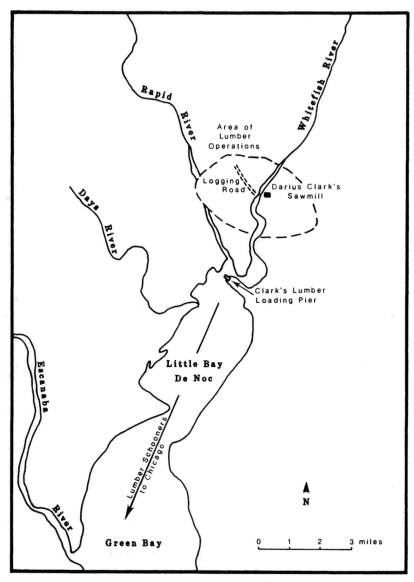

Spatial Arrangement of the Logging Industry in the Early Pine Era
Source: U.S. Land Survey, 1847

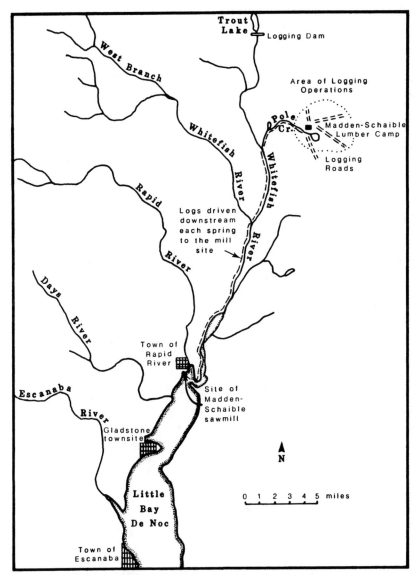

Spatial Arrangement of the Logging Industry in the Pine Era
Source: Charles F. Schiable, *I Was Interested* (Cincinnati: privately printed, 1972)

A week later, the best of the lumberjacks again went upriver to run the drive. The logs had been banked on Pole Creek. A dam on that stream provided the extra water needed to push the mass of logs the two-mile length of the creek. Driving was easier on the comparatively broad Whitefish. But even on the main river, dams were needed to manipulate the water level. The most important dam was at Trout Lake, the source of the river. It took nearly three weeks to drive the river. The Madden—Schaible men cooperated with other loggers, the most important of which was the Garth Lumber and Shingle Company, who had a mill near the mouth of the river. When the logs reached Little Bay De Noc, the Madden—Schaible men formed them into a raft, which was towed to the mill at Rapid River. The logs were made into shingles at the steam-powered mill and shipped to market by rail or schooner.[107]

The log drive was the most significant feature of the pine era spatial pattern. Even lumbermen lured into the interior by the railroad transportation system continued to rely on river drives. When the Chicago and North Western railroad extended its line across the western Upper Peninsula, the partnership of Atwater & Fair built a mill in Marenisco, where the Presque Isle River crossed the track. The Presque Isle became Atwater & Fair's highway in and out of the pineries. Similarly, the Interior Lumber Company was serviced by a rail spur off the Chicago and North Western, yet the logs reached the mill by log drives on the Ontonagon and Tamarack rivers. The buoyancy of pine generally saved pine loggers the cost of having to use railroad technology to move logs from the forest to the mill. That would come later when the harvesting of hardwood brought a new spatial pattern to the forest.

5

THE SOCIAL ENVIRONMENT OF
PINE LOGGING

Thomas Nestor was a gambler. He regularly wagered years of work, sacrifice, and savings that he would successfully complete a logging job. He gambled in 1874 when he invested twenty-three years of earnings in a sawmill. By working at his accounts long into the night and acting as his own chief sawyer, he made the investment pay. Three years later he put those winnings "into the pot" when with two partners he bought seven million feet of pine in a remote region of lower Michigan. Many lumbermen thought it was a bad choice. After all, there were no driveable streams near the tract; but Nestor again won his gamble by building one of the first logging railroads to bring the logs to his mill. However, the biggest gamble Thomas Nestor ever made was in 1881 when he sold all his investments and property in lower Michigan and sank the entire bundle into a logging venture in the western Upper Peninsula. The pineland was superb and the mill at Baraga was efficient and fast, but half of Nestor's holdings were located on the Ontonagon River—a 25-mile log drive and a 140-mile raft journey from the mill. Even for a veteran lumberman, Nestor's investment was a large wager against heavy odds.

Isaac Stephenson, Jefferson Sinclair, Robert Dollar, and even Russell Alger were all gamblers to the extent that they regularly let their fortunes hang in the balance. Many times in their career a forest fire, a dry winter, a shipwreck, or a drop in the lumber market could have ruined them. Isaac Stephenson spoke for many early lumbermen when he reminded industry critics of frontier era hardships:

> The meager returns were scarcely worth the struggle of blazing a way into the forest and risking the dangers that confronted the pioneer. Where some succeeded many failed, and if the opportunities of the time were contemplated face to face and not through the perspective of more than a half century, I doubt very much whether many of the present generation could have been induced to take their chances confronted by such disconcerting odds.[1]

That is not to say that early lumbermen were reckless. Isaac Stephenson was well known among his contemporaries for his cautious approach to investment opportunities. Another pioneer lumberman found his colleague reluctant to pursue nonlogging business interests, even when profits seemed assured.[2] The lumberman operated in a chancy business subject to the caprices of nature, yet it was a business that rewarded boldness, hard work, and ingenuity. Within its confines, the lumberman was willing to gamble.

The social environment of the pine logging era was molded by the questing, risk-taking spirit of a frontier region. Fortunes could be won or lost. In June 1892 lumberman John C. Brown was bankrupt. In years past he had been the biggest single logger on the Lake Superior shore. That very season he employed between eight hundred and a thousand men, but even after he sold his lumber, he was three quarters of a million dollars in debt.[3] Others found fortunes. The careers of Robert Dollar and Russell Alger read like Horatio Alger chronicles. The twin gospels of hard work and success were important in the early history of Upper Peninsula logging. The career of Thomas Nestor reveals the prospects and pitfalls that prospective fortune hunters faced.

Thomas Nestor was born in the poverty of County Mayo, Ireland, in 1833. When he was twelve years old, the already bleak north country landscape was further devastated by the potato famine. The Nestor family tried to hold on to their home in the village of Achille, but by the time the famine entered its third year, they were destitute and desperate. The family took passage to Canada. After a long sea voyage, they passed by the desolate cholera quarantine camps on Grosse Ile where thousands of Irish immigrants suffered in misery, and entered Canada. Nestor's father kept the family in British North America only long enough to earn the money that would take them to the United States. By the end of 1847 the Nestor family was settled in the "thumb" region of Michigan, Sanilac County. Nestor's father took up the blacksmith trade and in just a few years the family bought a farm. Lumbering was the principal industry in the region, and it was not long before Thomas Nestor, his brothers, and their father were working in the forest.[4]

The way of the pine yielded a mixed harvest to the Nestor family. Thomas easily found work and soon won the well-paying job of head sawyer. But in 1864 his father was killed when a falling tree crushed his body. In the years that followed, Thomas Nestor gradually moved from the ranks of the workingman into the coterie of Saginaw Bay lumbermen. His brothers, John and Timothy, also became lumbermen; they moved to the Upper Peninsula in the late 1870s.[5] Thomas himself was attracted to the prospects of the area, and in 1881 he sold his interests in the Saginaw district and headed north.[6]

He headquartered his operations at Baraga, a small hamlet at the bottom of Keweenaw Bay. The site was strategic because at the time it was the westernmost Upper Peninsula port with rail access to the Chicago market. The district adjacent to Baraga had abundant mature pine forests. But, for some reason, Nestor purchased much of his pine along the Ontonagon and Sturgeon rivers (Baraga County), which entailed considerable water transportation to get logs to his mill. He was forced to purchase two steam barges to undertake the task and when they proved insufficient, he had three more built. Further complications resulted when some of the first timber Nestor cut turned out to be largely rotten. From all external appearances, the trees were magnificent Norway and white pine. But when the saw cut through the bark, the wood fragmented. Much of it was not worth the price of transporting. Nestor was outraged; he accused the Michigan Land and Iron Company from whom he bought the land of not dealing in good faith. However, in the end he blamed himself for not personally looking over the tract, rather than trust the land company's estimates.[7]

Nestor's Upper Peninsula venture was plagued by a similar succession of unforeseen difficulties. Some of the problems stemmed from the garrulous Irishman's personal style; others were simple bad luck. He tried to work through those nagging issues, confident that the region held the promise of a brilliant future. Every penny of spare capital his logging generated, Nestor put back into the operation. Eventually his lands and plant entailed a three-million-dollar investment.[8]

That investment was always balanced precariously on the edge of risk. During the summer of 1885 he planned to lay out a railroad branch line that would have given him easy access to the best of his sixty thousand acres of forest. The move was temporarily blocked when an option on lands that Nestor needed for the right-of-way was bought by another party. Nestor was stunned to learn that the purchase was made by another lumberman who had no previous interest in the area and with whom Nestor had discussed his plans in colleague fashion. The misplaced confidence cost Nestor lost time and more money.[9] Nestor himself was not adverse to hardnosed, if not downright unscrupulous, tactics when he was pushed to the wall. After the Michigan Land and Iron Company had sold him rotten tracts of pine, he dealt with the company very carefully. He looked over all tracts for possible defects and was willing to sit for hours in the company's office trying to break the agent's real estate price by pure persistence. That agent finally wrote to his superiors in frustration: "I am tired of Mr. Nestor's style of doing business; he treats this company as if it was a small country store where he expected to dicker and beat down the price of every article purchased."[10] On another occasion, Nestor found himself short on capital and decided to save the cost of driving logs on the Ontonagon River. He ordered his men to dump the winter's cut into the river and then sent them all home. When the Diamond Match Company river drivers came downstream with their log drive, their progress was blocked by Nestor's logs. The match company demanded that Nestor drive his logs down to the lakeshore, but he refused, stating that he had plenty of logs at his mill already and that he wanted his logs left in the river until the next season. With Nestor slyly protesting that he did not want his logs moved, the disgruntled Diamond Match men were forced to drive his logs free of charge to the lakeshore in order to get their own logs to Ontonagon.[11]

Thomas Nestor's career in logging did not end the way novelist Stewart E. White would have written it or the way a Horatio Alger hero would have lived it. His final frustration came in 1899 when squatters began to settle on his land. The Michigan Land Forfeiture Bill had called into question unearned land grants, and the holdings of the Michigan Land and Iron Company were highly suspect. Before waiting for the government to rule on the validity of the grant, real estate speculators masquerading as homesteaders laid claim to large tracts of land that had once been owned by the company. Local courts would not support Nestor's title to the land because it came from a disputed owner. Even though he had camps built and roads laid out, he was prevented, for a time, from even logging on his lands. To make matters worse, his own brother, Timothy, was working against his interests. Timothy was the past mayor of Marquette, Michigan, and an ambitious politician, He wanted revenge on the Michigan Land and Iron Company for selling him poor timberlands, and he tried to broaden his political base by championing the alleged homesteaders in their battle against corporate interests. Timothy Nestor was playing another game as well. He headed a group of investors that tried to claim the Portage Lake Canal Company's land grant. Their arguments were specious at best, but they had strong political support in Lansing.[12] The prospect that Timothy Nestor's complex gambit might ruin his brother did not seem to bother him in the least. Demoralized by this unpleasant affair and anxious about the future, Thomas Nestor threw himself into his work. He concentrated his logging activities on the Ontonagon lands where his title was not challenged. He personally inspected the operation of his logging camps and that May led the river drivers bringing the logs down to the lakeshore. The harsh conditions of the drive must have broken his health because only days after the task was concluded, he became ill and died. He was fifty-seven years old, owned millions of dollars of stumpage and logging equipment, but had only a few dollars of cash to his name.[13]

Thomas Nestor's chronicle of frustration was no isolated case. The Upper Peninsula was as rich and promising as any nineteenth-century frontier area, and it also had the volatile qualities of any unregulated region. Fortunes were won and lost; towns rose and fell in less than a generation. There was an unrestrained quality to the pine era that made all prospects seem possible. Small men made great plans, and damn anyone who blocked their way. As much as loggers cooperated with one another through boom companies and harbor improvements, they also struggled with one another by fair and foul means, anxious to seize any advantage.

Conflicts over river drives were common. The 1896 battle royal on the Fence River was not unique. Only a year earlier John Nelligan had been forced to post armed guards on his driving dams after a competitor dynamited a dam and nearly ruined the entire drive.[14] In 1886 loggers using the Whitefish River had their drive partly disrupted by saboteurs who opened the booms at the mouth of the stream. To prevent the further loss of logs, each operator detailed armed guards to patrol the boom.[15]

When river drives took place on the narrow confines of tributaries or headwaters, there was opportunity for mischief. On the Upper Manistique River and its feeders, the Chicago Lumber Company and its principal Manistique area rivals, the Hall & Buell Company and the Delta Lumber Company, waged cold war every spring. The cost could be high. In 1887 Hall & Buell so crowded the river with its logs that one of its rivals was left with its entire year's cut sitting on the riverbank. To be unable to get logs to the waiting mill was a lumberman's nightmare, but in this case troubles gave way to tragedy. A forest fire broke out that summer and the entire haul was burned at the landings. The incident made the "walking bosses" who supervised the drives for the rival companies mindful of the high cost of being bullied or outsmarted.

Established loggers responded particularly sharp to new operators in their area. Lumbermen, particularly the first ones in an area, liked to look on the river valley in which they operated as their private preserve. They used their size and established facilities to try to drive new rivals from the field. The large logging companies contemptuously referred to small competitors as "haywire outfits," because their second-rate equipment was often held together by no more than wire and a prayer. A successful tactic to disrupt a new competitor was to raid his camp. The new logger's crew was promised higher wages or better food if they went over to the other side.[16] A new operator was also vulnerable in river driving. A well-established firm that operated its own dams could, contrary to custom and law, manipulate water levels so that the smaller operator never got the logs to market. During a drive on a tributary of the Menominee River in the 1890s, a rookie operator tried to forestall that type of treatment by having his lumberjacks put their logs into the river just ahead of the main drive. This guaranteed him enough water to move downstream and forced the other lumbermen to help move his logs. But the veterans still had the last laugh. When they reached the rookie's boom, their men ignored his protests, brushed aside his river drivers, and sluiced the logs down to the main boom where they could be easily stolen by other loggers.[17]

New entrants into the field of pine logging were greeted unenthusiastically because they destabilized the business. Through most of the nineteenth century, pine lumber prices were low and capital for new businesses was dear. What credit was available was generally short term. Banks in the region extended loans only over the logging season; when the spring drive was completed, they were anxious for repayment. These factors made it important that costs be held down and the logger plan for immediate profit.[18] A new logger on a river could drive up labor costs. More important, he was a competitor for timberlands. After the established logger built his mill and improved the river for driving, he still needed to secure his resource base. Some of the early loggers made only limited initial pineland purchases and cut considerable timber off adjacent holdings. A competitor disrupted this profitable arrangement and might even bid up the price of lands sold by the large land-grant companies such as the Saint Mary's Ship Canal Company.

To an extent, the government set the tone for the aggressive but irresponsible pace of exploitation during the pine era. Federal land policy was designed to encourage agricultural settlement. This policy was applied without modification to the upper Great Lakes region, where the environment favored forests, not farms. Many forest acres were bought for the base price of $1.25 per acre. Rather than encourage the gradual development of forest industries through timber reservations, the federal government pursued a headlong policy of transferring title to private hands. This was done at first to encourage the development of transportation systems that would aid settlement. Between 1852 and 1866 Congress granted 1.9 million acres for the building of wagon roads, railroads, and canals in the Upper Peninsula—almost one-fifth of the entire region was given away in this manner. Another massive real estate transfer happened because of the Federal Swampland Grant in 1850. All federal lands in Michigan that were swampy or poorly drained, including vast sections of pine and cedar forest, were turned over to the state. Michigan was supposed to use the proceeds from selling those lands to undertake reclamation and drainage projects. This rarely happened. Most land was sold at the base price to raise money for education. Purchasers were required to undertake drainage, but because this was not enforced the provision was duly ignored. In 1881 the state gave 1.3 million swampland acres as a land grant for the Detroit, Mackinac, and Marquette Railway.

Thousands more acres were given away in smaller amounts through agricultural scrips, military bounties, timber and stone entries, and homestead claims.[19]

The purpose of this major transition to private ownership was to encourage the exploitation of the Upper Peninsula and to that extent the policy was successful. The forests were crisscrossed by rail lines along which mines, towns, and mills sprouted. Capitalists made fortunes by shipping ore and lumber to build the cities of the industrial lower Midwest, while immigrant families found work in their plants, and homes in the Upper Peninsula. But the rapid development of the region came at the cost of natural resources that never could be replaced—iron, copper, and pine.

It was not merely the accelerated pace of development that made government policy ill-advised as the inefficient way it was supervised. Many early lumbermen did not purchase the pinelands they cut. It was common knowledge in pioneer lumber towns who was cutting on public land. An 1857 editorial in the *Lake Superior Journal* all but named the parties and their locations. However, local law enforcement was frustrated by a lack of manpower and the great distances between early settlements. The first lumber communities along Bay De Noc, for example, were administered for many years from Mackinac Island, more than 150 miles away. During the winter, when logging took place, an inspection tour of the pineries would have entailed a hazardous dogsled trip just to reach the scene of action.[20] Although there were government agents who were paid to "look the other way," it was easy enough to avoid even the vigilant employees.[21] One lumberman, Peter DeMay, is said to have made a living cutting illegal timber. He kept his lumberjacks alert for strangers in the woods by telling them that if government agents arrived, they all would be sent to jail. So fearful were some of the men that they would stampede at the mention of a government agent. DeMay took advantage of that near the end of one season by panicking his men to fleeing the camp. Some were afraid to come back for their wages and DeMay pocketed the difference. When he tried the trick in later years, the men were wise and said they would stay and let DeMay be taken to jail. But he never was.[22] The story may be folklore but it underlines the boldness of pine loggers.

Lumbermen were no more scrupulous about cutting pine off private lands. The practice of cutting a "round forty" is a prominent part of all north woods yarns. But it is a fact that loggers regularly cut trees over the line marking their property. This was partly because the locating of property lines was difficult deep in wilderness terrain. But that was part of the lumbermen's trade, and accurate lines were run quick enough if they suspected that someone else might have cut some of their trees.

Upper Peninsula courts were kept busy with trespass cases. Large land-owners such as the Keweenaw Land Association maintained their own surveyors, or land-lookers, to investigate such cases and accurately assess damage. After 1880, when there was a major increase in the price of Upper Peninsula pinelands, lumbermen became far more sensitive to trespasses. Greater care was taken in locating lines and looking for violations. Still, when the head of the Ford River Lumber Company in 1885 said his company "never paid a dollar for trespass," the editor of the *Escanaba Iron Port* remarked that it was very much an exception to the rule.[23]

A story popular among Delta County residents during the 1880s touched on the issue of timber theft. A young boy sat outside a jail in a lumber town. His clothes were dirty, his hair disheveled, and his eyes were red from crying. A well-dressed lad, only a year or two older, saw the crying boy and stopped to give him sympathy.

> "What's the matter, bub?" "Oh," said the tattered one, "my father is in jail." "What is he in jail for?" inquired the swell. "Last night we had no fire and it was so cold; so he went to the lumberyard and stole some pieces of board and they caught him and locked him up," answered the epitome of misery. "Oh, well, don't cry," said the young aristocrat, encouragingly. "He'll come out all right. My father stole a hundred million feet of lumber, and they sent him to Congress!"[24]

On other occasions strong emotions were raised by the blatant activities of timber thieves. One newspaperman threatened: "These gentlemen hold their heads high in Chicago and Milwaukee as capitalists, bankers, etc. and yet their wealth is made in defiance of the laws of this State . . . perhaps the privilege of reflecting on the subject in the state prison for two or three years would aid these gentlemen in being honest hereafter."[25]

Lumbermen were not the worst or only timber thieves in the Upper Peninsula. Nearly as often as a lumberman was guilty of trespass were they put upon themselves. The great landowners in the region, like the Michigan Land and Iron Company or the Peninsula Land Company, were hardly the easiest people to deal with. When the Michigan Land and Iron Company discovered that about a third of the timber they sold to a logger was rotten and not worth the trouble of even transporting, it immediately made plans to unload the rest of its holdings in the area on another logger.[26] Nor were some of the land companies, as Thomas Nestor discovered, adverse to selling stumpage to which they held disputed title. In 1889 Henry M. Atkinson, director of the Metropolitan Lumber Company, purchased 250 million feet of standing pine from the Portage

Lake Ship Canal Company. The history of that company and its grant is one of the most complex in Michigan history. What is important is that the Canal Company's title to some of the four hundred thousand acres it was granted was called into question in March 1889. A mere ten minutes before the expiration of President Grover Cleveland's term, he signed the Michigan Land Forfeiture Bill. This act restored to federal control land grants to construction companies that did not complete their projects. The Portage Lake Ship Canal grant was not clearly included or excluded from the provisions of the act. They had completed their project but there were irregularities under investigation concerning the grant.[27] Unwilling to wait for a federal ruling, real estate speculators and legitimate homesteaders began to file homestead claims on the Canal Company's land. Most claims were for pinelands, poor for farming but worth a healthy price on the lumber market. Before the extent of the controversy was realized, the Metropolitan Lumber Company built a new mill with four band saws and a town with more than forty houses amid the contested land. Once this investment was made, there was nothing for the lumber company to do but cut logs or file for bankruptcy.

A result was a violent dispute between the Metropolitan Lumber Company and the speculator-homesteaders. During the summer of 1890, the company began to log on the disputed land. A logging railroad linked the cutting area with the mill five miles away. When the loggers tried to haul their logs to the track, gunshots rang out. One by one, the draft horses pulling the sleigh stumbled and fell dead in their tracks. Those shots were the opening volleys of an unnerving guerrilla war.

Sometimes sabotage was the homesteaders' weapon. A favorite trick was to drive steel spikes into logs loaded for shipment to the mill. When such a log was run through the band saw, it would destroy the blades and could possibly kill the sawyer. The loggers were very vulnerable to such tactics. Ice roads could be easily ruined by scattering hot ash over their surface, and logging dams were fair game as well; a few well-placed ax blows and a several-thousand-dollar investment was ruined. Legitimate homesteaders who were serious about developing a farm on their claim were among the most impassioned antagonists. They needed the pine on their land to pay for livestock purchases and farm equipment. One bold woman laid her body in the middle of an ice road to prevent a team of horses from removing logs from her claim. Newspapers, faced with regular reports of the repetition of the horse-shooting incident referred to it as the homesteaders "old pastime." However, for the lumberjacks caught in this cross fire, it was a terrifying experience. Looking down at his horses, shot clearly through the head, one lumberman had to admit "the homesteaders are damned good shots."[28]

The violence was not all on the homesteaders' part. Local residents alleged that a homesteader who claimed the very tract that the Metropolitan Lumber Company mill occupied was murdered. His body was found lying face down in a three-inch-deep puddle. The coroner determined the cause of death to be drowning.[29]

Most of the violence in the dispute centered on James Eagen, alias Jim Sommers. In the folklore of the Menominee Range towns, Sommers was a heroic loner who championed the cause of the downtrodden small farmers. He was celebrated for being a crack shot with a lever-action rifle and despite having lived outside the law, he had a rough sense of justice and "a feeling for the underdog."[30] In reality, Sommers was a hotheaded whoremaster from lower Michigan who operated mean saloons and cheap brothels in several northern Michigan mill towns. He had little control over his violent temper and that proved his undoing in Schoolcraft County, where he was based for several years. He nearly beat to death a man named Jack Horn and was driven from Manistique by a citizen's posse. Even Seney, reputed to be the most reprehensible lumber town, wanted nothing to do with him. The Crystal Falls *Diamond Drill* referred to Sommers as "one of the most despicable and widely known toughs in the Upper Peninsula."[31]

Whatever Sommer's motivation for involving himself in the dispute, it surely was not humanitarian. He probably had an interest in a bogus pine claim. Sommers was credited with devising the homesteader's strategy of harassing the Metropolitan Lumber Company by shooting their draft animals, in keeping with his reputation as a marksman. On one occasion he is said to have become so enraged with a Metropolitan Lumber Company employee that Sommers shot his tongue off.[32] But like most Sommers stories the real incident proved more tawdry. Sommers frequented Kate Harrington's saloon in the little town of Atkinson. One evening he entered the bar, anxious for a spree but short of cash. He tried to borrow ten dollars from the bartender, John Ross. When Ross refused, Sommers broke into a rage. He took his Winchester and "began to shoot carelessly about the room . . . One of the deadly misses struck the floor between the feet of Ross, the second one came uncomfortably close to the head of another bystander, and the third took effect in the head of Jerry Mahoney, who sat in a chair, asleep. . . . The bullet entered Mahoney's head near his ear, passing through his head and cutting off his tongue."[33] The shooting made Sommers a fugitive again. After getting food and money from his homestead friends, he eluded a manhunt and fled the Upper Peninsula.[34]

The bitter dispute did not end with Sommer's departure. Armed land claimants still held that they would shoot anyone entering their land. Woodsmen sent by lumber companies to mark out property lines were particularly vulnerable. One land-looker discharged a gun trap that had been set in the brush to shoot anyone tracing a particular section line. The bullet missed the man, passing between his legs. But he got the distinct idea he was not wanted.[35] Finally in 1896 the Department of the Interior ruled that homesteads founded before May 1888 were valid, but that the speculative claims filed after the Metropolitan Lumber Company purchased its timber from the Canal Company were disallowed. Homesteaders who tried to continue their armed opposition to the lumber company found themselves without public support and they ended in jail. Nonetheless, the dispute lingered on in the courts well into the twentieth century.[36]

THE LUMBERJACK OF LEGEND AND LIFE

In June 1947 Wilfred Nevue boarded the morning train from Iron Mountain to the small Upper Peninsula town of Champion. In the smoking car, some men were talking. One of the men said he was an old-timer in the area and told lurid tales of the old pine lumberjacks. Nevue had been a lumberjack during the last days of pine logging in the Huron Mountains, and he knew that the stories the man was telling might have been entertaining—but they were not true. Nevue turned to the man and asked, "What about Clowry [a small hamlet with a big legend]?" "Oh boy," the man answered, "that was awful! There were about thirty saloons and every one had prostitutes living upstairs. There were fights in the streets and all over the place." Nevue cut in, "I lived about four miles from Clowry. All I ever saw was a little depot and a section house—and that is all that ever was there."[37]

The legendary image of north woods loggers is of "a hell-roaring band of booted men" with a "Bunyanesque capacity for liquor, brawling, and women."[38] "A Michigan lumberjack could no more work without whiskey . . . then he could without salt pork and beans . . . Liquor and bawdy houses were synonymous with lumber camps and ore mines."[39] The Upper Peninsula has been identified as the home of Paul Bunyan, the giant logger, and his blue ox Babe. Stanley Newton's tales even locate Bunyan's birthplace in the great Tahquamenon Swamp.[40] The salacious stories and colorful folklore have obscured the true nature of woods workers during the pine era. They were neither prodigious heroes nor drunken brawlers whose raw sensual appetites required sexual satiation each spring. They were simple, tough, hardworking men no more prone to ribald sexual misconduct or to drink than other workers on isolated frontiers.

Modern concepts of work and recreation interfere with understanding nineteenth-century lumberjacks. Industrial discipline came slowly and unevenly to the workplace. Throughout the industrializing of America, older rural life-styles clashed with modern concepts of efficiency, social control, and decorum. Upper Peninsula lumberjacks were part of a distinct industrial subculture that does not seem to have fully shared the Victorian values of the urban and commercial elite.[41] Mill owners, newspaper editors, and shopkeepers in northern Michigan towns shared in varying degrees such values as hard work, individualism, religious duty, sexual control, punctuality, and sobriety. Pine era lumberjacks were not against—merely out of step with—Victorian values. They relished hard work, but often pursued it irregularly—when they were out of money. They lived spartan lives most the year, but indulged themselves with gusto on rare opportunities. The restlessness of many jacks prevented them from putting down roots and kept them moving from camp to camp.

The tension caused by this gap in values can be seen in the very first commercial lumber operation in the Upper Peninsula. During the 1840s, the Sinclair and Wells complex was the most extensive logging venture in the Northwest. Their supervisory staff was middle-class young men from New England, but their work force was largely German and Swedish immigrants.[42] The differences between supervisors and mill hands were aggravated by the mill's isolation for four to five months every year. Henry Judkins, a young man from Maine, had charge of the Flat Rock Mill site during the winter of 1848–49. He felt that "my place is in everything betwixt the men hired and Sinclair and Wells to see that Justice is done on both sides, it falls on me to make all settlements with the men and be the head man in the whole establishment."[43] Judkins had a crew of about eighty mill hands, many of whom he had little sympathy with. "Every vice is no stranger to some of them, I am or have been able to stand my ground with any of them. . . . But was strongly threatened by a foreigner at one time."[44] Isaac Stephenson, who supervised forest operations that winter, also bore the heavy responsibilities of supervision for the first time. He believed that he had "very little trouble" with his men, who "worked willingly and well and were not given to dissension," although his authority was sometimes challenged. Stephenson did not hesitate to use "a strong arm and a heavy fist"[45] when he found shortcomings in a man's work and the jack was recalcitrant.

Many lumberjacks seem to have had rural backgrounds. The timing of logging dovetailed nicely with the farmer's work regime. Just as farm work was slowing down, the logging season would get under way. For cash-poor farmers in Wisconsin or the Upper Peninsula, logging camps were an opportunity for cash employment. Some lumberjacks were itinerant laborers who would harvest grain in August and work on railroad construction gangs or in sawmills during the rest of the summer. Strikes or economic recessions occasionally closed Upper Peninsula mines, and logging became a source of employment for many former miners.[46]

The decline of the New Brunswick pineries at mid-century coincided with the rise of northern Michigan's logging frontier. French-Canadian axmen from the Ottawa Valley also came to the Upper Peninsula. Canadians were particularly important to the squared timber logger who needed men experienced in trimming logs for the British market. Out of 267 lumberjacks working in Harrison Township, Schoolcraft County, in 1900, more than one third were Canadian-born. Similar percentages are borne out by samples of logging camp populations in the 1870s and 1880s. Many Canadian lumberjacks were merely seasonal residents of the Upper Peninsula; after the spring drive, they would recross the border to their homes.[47]

During the years before and just after the Civil War, Irish and German immigrants were the principal European-born lumberjacks, along with some Scots and Swedes, reflecting immigration patterns. Scandinavians increased in number as the nineteenth century wore on, as did the Finns who were recruited for the region by mine labor agents. By 1900 there were eighteen thousand Finns in the Upper Peninsula and more than twenty thousand Scandinavians. Only in the last years of the pine era did eastern and southern Europeans make their way into the woods.[48]

It took a shrewd manager to keep such a diverse group working as a disciplined crew. French-Canadians were known as colorful and daring loggers who dressed brightly in red toques and gaudy sashes, and excelled at river driving—the most dangerous logging chore.[49] Isaac Stephenson found Germans dependable in the forest, describing them as having "unflagging energy" and being "steadier than laborers of any other nationality."[50] Scandinavians also were good river drivers, and the Irish excelled as teamsters.[51]

The ethnic mixture in the camps required some concessions by the lumbermen in charge. Although poplar was abundant, logging camps were seldom built with it because according to French-Canadian custom Christ's crucifix was made of poplar and using the tree for building was bad luck.[52] A camp of Austrians, who did not eat meat daily in Europe, refused to work without meat now that they were in the United States. A Delta County logging camp was laid low when the German boss tried to reward the crew with an old-world style feast of sauerkraut and fresh spareribs. About eleven o'clock that night, the lumberjacks began to dash for the outhouse. Before long, the entire camp needed to use the little two-seat outhouse. Most could not wait in line and used the two-foot snowdrifts. The next time German food was served, the men were much more cautious.[53]

European rivalries occasionally led to explosive social situations. Logger John Nelligan learned this when he joined a party of his river men fresh from a trying drive relaxing with whiskey and beer chasers. The good-natured mood was shattered when an Ulsterman asked a fiddler to play "The Protestant Boys."

> It was an unhappy suggestion. "The Protestant Boys" is a song of the Orangemen and there were several good Irish-Catholics in the crowd. Hell broke loose automatically. Two brothers named John and James Enright swore by all the powers of Heaven and earth there would be no "Protestant Boys" played there that night and they proceeded to clean the place out. A good many of those present, including the poor fiddler (who was French-Canadian), didn't know what it was all about, but that didn't prevent them all from participating in a good fight. In a short time, the place looked like a cross between a hospital and a morgue. The Enright boys were the victors, for no strain of "The Protestant Boys" was heard on the evening air that night.[54]

Such spontaneous fights may have prompted the universal logging camp rule against any talking at the dinner table.

In popular imagery, lumberjacks, fights, and liquor are all linked. Yet by all accounts the lumberjack refrained from drinking and fighting most of the year. A lumberjack who worked in the Huron Mountains of Marquette County remembered that "alcoholic liquors were nearly always prohibited in camps. . . . If a lumberjack went back to camp from a binge or escapade, he sometimes brought with him a bottle of whiskey but that did not last long and thinned out among the crew, its effects were negligible . . . what is more important, the foreman frequently confiscated the bottle with its contents."[55] Bay De Noquet Company officials tried to prevent men from bringing liquor into their camps.[56] When Charles Schiable went into the woods in 1899, some of the men brought a bottle of whiskey to drink on the long hike into camp. But that was the last bottle seen that winter.[57] George Orr, who directed the forest operations of the Chicago Lumber Company, had a standing order that any lumberjack caught with liquor in camp would be immediately fired.[58] Drinking was more prevalent in other nineteenth-century workplaces. In 1869 an anonymous locomotive engineer stated that railway workers "instinctively cultivate a disposition for reckless and excitable habits. . . . During their trips, the fever of excitement was kept up by the influence of strong drink."[59] A New York cigar manufacturer complained that his workers "come down to the shop in the morning; roll a few cigars and then go to a beer saloon."[60] Coopers would often stop work at noon on Saturday and open a barrel of beer right in the shop.[61] The remote location of most logging camps made access to alcohol difficult; when lumberjacks worked closer to saloons, drunkenness seems to have increased.[62] In the spring when the camps broke up, or after the river drive, most lumberjacks went to saloons. Like cowboys after a cattle drive or sailors fresh from a long voyage, lumberjacks were "eager for freedom and ready for a good time."[63] A lumberjack in Rapid River in 1899 found that:

> The town was full of men and every saloon was packed and I never saw men act like they did, they were like wild men nearly all were drunk or half drunk, they all had lots of money and [were] getting rid of it fast. I walked around the town to see the sights, the sidewalks were crowded and some were singing[,] others were trying to dance and some of them got into a fight. . . . Most of the men did not hang around for long, a lot of the men were good men and did not spend their money but left for their homes as soon as they could get a train out, but many got drunk and soon got rid of their money.[64]

This scene was repeated each spring in such pine towns as Emerson, Masonville, Ontonagon, Menominee, and Manistique.

The most notorious towns were Seney, Ewen, Hurley, and Florence. "It was at the break-up of the lumber camps when the spring drives on the rivers began, that Seney acquired the reputation which made it possible . . . to ask the railway agent in neighboring towns for a ticket to hell and be sure of being understood as wanting to go to Seney," a former resident recalled.[65] At one time, Seney had nineteen saloons dispensing whiskey and beer. They were crude places, "tinsel-bedecked and saw-dust floored."[66] They relieved the lumberjacks from a winter of spartan living. When the drinking was well under way, the fighting would begin. Fists, teeth, calked boots, and sometimes knives went into action. A Seney merchant claimed: "The Marquis of Queensbury, who developed the regulations of our man-to-man fighting practice, would have found much to criticize as a witness of a typical fight of lumberjacks. He would have seen some real fights. He would have seen no mixing in, or interference, from the sidelines. . . . When the battle was over, the winner would shout, 'I am a bad man in a small town' or 'I am a wolf,' 'a bear,' or some wild animal."[67] Tim Kane, the foreman of one of the Manistique Lumber Company's camps, was murdered outside a Seney bar when one of his lumberjacks accused him of stealing wages from the men. It was a ludicrous accusation, but both men were well-liquored and began to quarrel. Because it was Christmas Eve, the saloon's patrons separated the two men and evicted the lumberjack from the bar. Kane tried to pursue the lumberjack and was fatally stabbed with a jackknife. Most fights ended with a visit by the local physician who closed the gashes and cleaned sawdust and sand out of their wounds. When deaths did result from alcohol, it was usually because drunken jacks in for a Christmas spree, passed out in the snow on their way back to camp or fell asleep on the railroad tracks. Some saloon owners would throw out unconscious jacks. Only a hardy constitution or vigilant town sheriff could save a man so treated.[68]

The most celebrated incident in Seney was the feud between Dan Dunn and the Hartcourt brothers. Dan Dunn was a pimp and saloon owner with a reputation for murder and skullduggery across upper and lower Michigan. His saloon and bordello in Seney did a lively business, yet he resented the competition of the four Hartcourt brothers—Jim, Steve, Luke, and Tom—who also operated a saloon. For years, hard words and threats passed between Dunn and the Hartcourts. The feud came to a head in June 1891 when Steve Hartcourt entered Dunn's saloon and offered to buy a drink for all the men present. Dunn refused to serve Steve or any other Hartcourt. Angry words followed, and then Dunn smashed a bottle of whiskey on Hartcourt's head. While his opponent staggered, Dunn pulled a revolver from beneath the bar and shot Hartcourt through the jaw. The young man staggered back and tried to pull a gun from his pocket, but it was wrapped in a bandanna. By the time he raised the weapon, Dunn had fired again, hitting Hartcourt in the side. Hartcourt got off one shot at Dunn, but it struck the bar. Steve Hartcourt was brought home where his mother nursed him for two days before he died. Dunn was arrested, but at the preliminary hearing in Manistique he was discharged on the grounds of self-defense. Rumors that Dunn had several Schoolcraft County officials in his pay seemed proven by the verdict. The remaining Hartcourt brothers met Dunn at the rail junction town of Trout Lake, where Dunn was having a drink in a saloon. As soon as he saw the Hartcourts enter the room, he reached for his gun, but Jim Hartcourt was faster. His four bullets ended Dunn's life. Jim Hartcourt later served three years in prison for his deed, but to many people in Seney, he was a hero.[69]

Neither the Hartcourts or Dunn were lumberjacks. Woodsmen did not often resort to guns to settle their disputes. Few lumberjacks owned handguns or could use them effectively. In 1891, near Matchwood, Michigan, a drunken lumberjack named Billie Bondell, upset with the services at a bordello, decided to "clear the house." He produced a thirty-eight caliber revolver and began chasing the scantily clad women and their panicked customers out into the snow. One lumberjack, Peter McQuire, refused to run and tried to disarm Bondell, but the young man fired a shot directly into McQuire's forehead. A normal man would have been dead. But the hardheaded Irishman was merely stunned. The bullet had only plowed a furrow up his forehead and through his scalp.[70]

Typical of the tawdry tragedies was an incident in Ewen, Michigan. The shootist was Joseph Thomas, a nineteen-year-old lumberjack employed by the Nestor Lumber Company. After two months in the woods, the boy left camp and went into town to collect his pay. With a load of cash, he made the rounds from saloon to saloon, several times getting into fights and brandishing a revolver. After one such altercation, a friend of his, Thomas Downey, went out to calm him down. But the lad was in a rage and he fired three times at his friend. The first two shots flew past his head. The third, however, tore into his chest, killing him within minutes. The townspeople, who had done nothing up to this time, chased Thomas intending to lynch him. They cornered him in the forest and only the arrival of the sheriff prevented vigilante justice.[71]

Ewen was as rough a town as any in the pineries. The town sprang from a humble seed. Its first building was a broken-down boxcar, cut in half, which served as the town's rail depot. Homes and saloons and more saloons followed. The town's location at the intersection of the Ontonagon River and the Duluth, South Shore & Atlantic Railway made it a convenient supply center for loggers operating in southern Ontonagon County. By 1891 the town had six hundred residents, fifteen saloons, and on the outskirts several bordellos.[72]. County officials at first tried to keep the town clean. There were raids against the "houses of ill fame," and the proprietors and inmates were vigorously prosecuted.[73] Fire ravaged the town in 1893, burning most of it. The rebirth of the town also rekindled the vice traffic. A pimp and saloon keeper from Wisconsin named LeClaire moved into Ewen. Gambling dens and bordellos operated in the heart of town. LeClaire's prostitutes openly solicited in the streets; in the saloons he had a group of "bum prizefighters" who fronted as waiters but in reality shook down drunken lumberjacks. These toughs were accused of several robberies, but evidence was always lacking. The "respectable citizens" of Ewen were alleged to have to "submit to the most glaring atrocities," but there seems to have been some connivance between LeClaire and the local authorities.[74] Ewen declined as a vice center after 1895 when logging in the area peaked. LeClaire and other toughs moved on to Hurley, Wisconsin, where the pickings were richer.

Seney and Ewen were among the few pine logging communities to support a considerable saloon, gambling, and prostitution racket. Most towns could count on only a flourish of business in the spring. But Seney and Ewen were amid very intensive logging districts, and the towns served as vital supply and administration centers. In 1892, for example, there were thirty-one logging camps within five miles of Ewen. This meant that close to two thousand men were no more than a few hours walk of the town's earthy pleasures. A lumberjack bored with the usual Sunday regimen of washing clothes could hike into Ewen and Seney and blow off steam and still stagger back to camp before day's end. Yet as soon as the number of camps around the towns began to decline, the prostitutes and gamblers pulled out and the number of saloons declined.

The capitals of vice and dissipation for the pine era logger in the north country were two Wisconsin towns, Florence and Hurley. Both towns are near the state line and drew lumberjacks from both states. What allowed these towns to endure as saloon centers was their location on the iron range. Hurley was founded in 1884 by the Northern Chief Iron Company, and it quickly grew into one of the most important towns on the Gogebic Range.[75] Florence, 100 miles southwest, was platted in 1880 by promoters of mineral interest on the Menominee Range.[76] Iron mines gave the towns a large population of young males who could support many saloons. Thirsty lumberjacks helped sustain these dives, but without the mines neither Hurley nor Florence would have built their gaudy reputation.

"Florence . . . of the early eighties," recalled one of the founders of the town, "was a metropolis of vice. There was gambling on the main streets, outdoors in clement weather and unscreened indoors when driven in by cold and storm. Prostitution was just as bold. Its red passion garbings paraded every prominent place in town."[77] John Nelligan, who operated logging camps near the town for many years, remembered Florence as "one of the toughest towns in the north woods. Every other house was a saloon, a house of prostitution, or a gambling hall, and usually all three under one roof. There was no semblance of law and order. The single street was nothing but a mudhole flanked with plank sidewalks and unsafe to venture into at night."[78] Nelligan may have embellished his memories, yet it is a fact that the town boasted twenty-seven saloons by 1883.[79]

The most spectacular dive in Florence was the saloon and brothel of "Old Man" Mudge. He was a mysterious, smooth-talking man who was rumored to have been a minister in lower Michigan or Ohio. Severe rheumatism gave him a crabbed and sinister appearance. Legends built up around him. He was reputed to be one of the most notorious white slavers in the north country. His brothel was said to be filled with trapdoors, secret tunnels, and a macabre chamber of horrors used to break young captives to his will. Great political powers were attributed to Mudge, and he used those connections to keep his chain of brothels free from legal interference.[80] What is known for a fact is that Mudge was a well-dressed man who played the violin and sang for his guests. He operated a colorful house, the doors of which were never locked and whose rooms were usually humming with the sound of music and the revels of jubilant lumberjacks.[81]

Old Man Mudge's partner in crime was his daughter Mina. By all accounts she was a handsome woman. Nelligan remembered her as "one of the most beautiful girls on the range."[82] A resident of Florence with a more Victorian moral caste described her as "glossed over by a fine animal figure, a rubescent complexion, semi-pug nose, lurking grey eyes, sensual lips, and sharpish chin. Her lips were the clew to passion, and eyes and chin betokened the cruelty of a she-hyena." When her father's health finally broke, Mina Mudge operated the brothel on her own, first at their Florence saloon, later, after the town became more respectable, on the outskirts of the forest. The move was necessitated by a "regulator" organization in Florence that struggled to cleanse the town of its rowdies. Led by a young minister and a crusading newspaper editor, the "good citizens" of Florence attacked the most obnoxious of the vice peddlers. The movement temporarily calmed Florence down and won fame for the newspaper editor, Chase S. Osborn. He eventually entered politics and was elected governor of Michigan in 1910.[83] By that time, Mina Mudge closed her brothel and opened a restaurant in Milwaukee.[84]

As seedy as Florence's reputation was during the 1890s, Hurley was clearly the worse of the two. Wisconsin lumberjacks, when asked to name the three worst places, often responded by saying, "Hayward, Hurley, and Hell." If one equated rotgut alcohol, gambling, and prostitution with hell, Hurley qualified. The town's principal avenue, Silver Street, was lined with saloons that peddled all manner of pleasures. Mining companies controlled the neighboring Michigan town of Ironwood and in the interest of efficiency tried to keep their community clean. But they could do nothing in Hurley. The saloon trade early became an important part of the local business community, and bar owners consistently secured the tacit support of the authorities. A miner who worked in Hurley in 1890 remembered it as "the toughest town imaginable. Silver Street had more than fifty saloons with gambling dens, pimps, bawdy houses, and prostitutes everywhere."[85]

But Hurley was not so tough that it could not show compassion. The premier social event of the 1890 season was the funeral of Lotta Morgan, one of the most popular women on Silver Street. She was a high-class prostitute whose generous clients allowed her to buy the most gracious gowns and glittering jewelry. One of them, however, wanted more than even Lotta was prepared to give. On the night of April 11 she was lured into the alley behind Crocker's Saloon and shot. Her assailant then hacked off a section of her scalp with an ax before fleeing. The saloon keepers determined to give Lotta a grand funeral. She was laid in state at the Hurley Opera House before a packed house. Some of the mourners were fresh from the bar and a bit rowdy. When everyone was asked to sing Lotta's favorite hymn, some of them shouted, "Bet on the red" and "Keno." But the minister quieted them and assured the audience that Lotta's favorite hymn was "Where Is My Girl Tonight." The only thing that dampened the day was the Reverend C. C. Todd's righteous sermon, which asked: "Do you wish prosperity or business at such a price as this? Do you want dollars to come to your place stamped with women's honor, stamped with women's blood?" After the service a cortege was organized. Lotta Morgan was escorted to her final resting place and the saloons reopened for a busy trade.[86]

The funeral proved to be so much fun that a week later it was decided to have an encore. There had been no new victims, so a saloon keeper offered his recently deceased dog. The mutt, Curley, Jr., was then laid in state and the ceremony was repeated—without the awkward presence of the minister. The "decent" people of Hurley were disgusted by the affair but the sporting set had a grand time.[87] After the party, however, they became bored with grand funerals, and several months later, when another prostitute was found dead behind a Hurley saloon, no one paid much attention and the "body was carted off" unceremoniously.[88]

Hurley, Florence, Seney, and towns of that stripe served as bases for pimps, prostitutes, and saloon keepers from which they could branch out to other boomtowns. Among the large towns of the Upper Peninsula, Escanaba may have been such a base. Its Ludington Street bristled with saloons where lumberjacks rubbed elbows with railroad men, miners, and schooner crews. At one point, there were ninety-four saloons in Escanaba, one to every thirty-five men. Occasionally crusades were launched by the *Escanaba Journal* to restrict the "lawless liquor dealers," but these efforts enjoyed only temporary success during the pine era.[89] When one town drove out its vice peddlers, they merely moved on to the neighboring burg. Sidnaw indicates of the speed with which they moved into boomtowns. Here pine logging began in 1890; yet as early as 1891, the town had five saloons.[90] Tamarack was even worse; its first five buildings were saloons.[91]

Gamblers on the Upper Peninsula pine frontier were particularly mobile. Silver Street and Hurley seem to have been a stable, safe haven out of which they would forage. Gamblers from there settled in Ewen, during that town's lawless stage. "Tin horn gamblers" was the derisive term used to describe the professionals who were attracted to mill towns each spring. In 1889 and 1890 several professionals set up gambling rooms in Ontonagon. Crap tables and roulette were popular with the Diamond Match loggers. The gamblers stayed in business until the fall, when the camps opened again. The "tin horns" then went south to Chicago.[92] When the spring drive was through, even small towns like Rapid River were attractive to gamblers. A young woodsman noted: "There were all kinds of men, just waiting for them, gamblers, crooks, all kinds, the saloons reaped a harvest."[93] Once the lumberjack was intoxicated, he was pretty easy pickings for a gambler working with an unethical saloon keeper. Philip Bowen, a young logger fresh from the woods with three weeks pay, found that out in a Sault Sainte Marie dive in 1888. He was out for "a great old time" and went into the Jerry O'Brien Saloon. After several drinks he went into the back room where Frank Parrish operated a gaming place. Roulette and several card games were under way. Bowen had another drink and toured the room. But there was something in the drink that made him suddenly lose control of himself. His next memory was waking up wretchedly sick at his boardinghouse where he lay ill for a week. When he recovered he found that all his money was gone. Bowen complained to the police, but he could not identify who took his money. Unable to locate the offender, the police were content with arresting Bowen—for gambling.[94]

Law enforcement was difficult in the boomtowns of the pineries. Local governments were dominated by lumber company officials who wanted a sober work environment but not the cost of paying for peace officers. Besides, saloons were businesses that were a base for local taxes. For the few underpaid police in the pineries, keeping drunken miners and lumberjacks in line was not easy. One of the best lawmen was Oarce Moore, a stocky French-Canadian with "sledgehammer" fists. He was the marshall of Stambaugh during its rugged youth. He refused to carry a gun and instead relied on his ability to give and take punches. A resident remembered: "In combating extreme lawlessness, Oarce never worried about methods. His idea was to settle fights, make arrests, chasten wife beaters on the spot or beat up a swindler. He took the law into his own hands. Few of his cases reached the justice of the peace."[95] The free-for-all lumberjack style of fighting meant that only the toughest lawmen could rely solely on their bare hands. The deputy sheriff of Mass City found this out one evening when he tried to arrest a drunk and disorderly reveler. The man turned on the deputy and the two fell into a rolling scuffle. The enraged drunk bit the deputy's right-hand fingers. When the man refused to loosen his bite, the deputy hit him in the head with his left hand, breaking several knuckles. The drunk still refused to let the man's fingers free, so the deputy was forced to painfully pull them free. But in drawing them out from the drunk's teeth, "he tore the skin and flesh all off so that the bone was exposed."[96]

The real danger to life and limb for pine country lawmen came from pimps and saloon keepers. They were more likely to resort to knives or guns than lumberjacks. This element usually kept its quarrels hidden from public view. Even when fighting became open, it did not draw legal attention unless innocent people were at risk. When two pimps fought for control of prostitution in the little hamlet of Kitchi, they openly did battle with knives and revolvers until "the place looked like a slaughter pen and the contestants like butchers." The only regret of respectable people in the county was that the two had not killed each other.[97] Violence in the bawdy houses eventually cost George Davidson, deputy sheriff of Trout Creek, his life.

The principal "sporting house" of Trout Creek was on the edge of town. On a fall evening in 1893, one of the girls working there tried to quit and leave town. When Alex Enos, the keeper of the bordello, found out, he was enraged. He pursued the girl and headed her off before she could reach the depot. Enos then drove the terrorized woman back through the town's main street, firing his pistol at her feet. His rage did not subside when they finally reached the bordello. Enos continued to fire his gun wildly, driving all three of his prostitutes upstairs where he intended to punish them. All this gunplay attracted Deputy Sheriff Davidson's attention. He reached the house just as Enos ascended the stairs, and he ordered the pimp to throw down his gun. Instead, Enos fired at the deputy, hitting him in the belly. Enos then deliberately walked up to the fallen lawman and put a second round in his head. By this time several citizens had gathered outside the house. Enos announced that he had killed Davidson and would do the same to anyone else who interfered with him. Nonetheless, two railroad workers entered the house. Enos shot one of them twice, but before he could reload, the other had overpowered him. Enos was eventually brought to trial, though there was much talk of lynching in Trout Creek that night.[98]

Vigilantism was a natural response to the lack of organized law enforcement on all early frontiers; the Upper Peninsula was no exception. An armed posse of vigilantes drove the gambling dens and brothels out of Florence, where the law officers were at first in the pay of the vice ring.[99] At Ford River, the brothel was closed by action of the town's married women. It was located a discreet distance outside town, but the women thought too many married men were taking the long way home from the mill. One night, two dozen angry wives, armed with brooms, rolling pins, and other domestic hardware, stormed the brothel. When they broke through the door, the married men were seen leaping from the windows to escape detection. The madam and her prostitutes were roughly treated, then packed onto a wagon and sent down the road to Escanaba.[100] In 1875 a group of "high-toned gentlemen" of Escanaba went on its own campaign of cleaning up the town. One morning, just after midnight, the men descended upon a group of sporting houses just outside the town. Armed with knives and firearms, they drove the prostitutes half-naked into the snowy street. They then fired the brothels, leaving the shivering women to seek shelter wherever they could.[101] A less self-righteous example of vigilantism took place at Marinette in 1894. Two lumberjacks who believed they had been cheated by a madam set fire to the brothel. The two men fled the city. The police refused to give chase, and the fire department did not lift a finger to put out the blaze.[102]

The most spectacular instance of vigilantism in northern Michigan took place in Menominee on September 19, 1881. The episode began and ended at a bordello in the "Frenchtown" district of Menominee. Two lumberjacks, Frank McDonald and John McDougal, fresh from a log drive on the Pine River, were intent on finishing a hard night of drinking in the soft arms of the local beauties. But before going off to a woman's room, they noticed an old enemy, Billy Kittson, drinking whiskey with a couple of prostitutes. Billy Kittson was the son of one of the town's earliest settlers, and a popular, if high-spirited, young man. McDonald had no love for Billy or his two brothers, George and Norman. The Kittsons had helped the county sheriff arrest McDonald and send him to a state prison.[103] Hard words between the two quickly led to a fight, which Billy brought a temporary halt to by breaking a bottle of whiskey on McDonald's head. Dizzy with drink, Billy Kittson staggered into the street, anxious to tell his brother about his latest victory over McDonald. But he was overtaken by McDougal and the now revived McDonald. They knocked Billy to his knees with a peavey and before he could rise, McDonald drove a six-inch dirk into his back. Norman Kittson saw the battle on the street and tried to help his brother. He was stabbed in the neck and probably would have been carved more had he not produced a pistol and wildly fired at his attackers. McDougal was grazed in the leg by one shot and he fled with McDonald. Billy Kittson then staggered into the nearest bar, ordered drinks for everyone, and promptly dropped dead.[104]

McDonald and McDougal were arrested as they tried to flee the town by train. Norman Kittson's ugly neck wound was treated and he survived. Billy Kittson was buried. However, the incident was not at an end. No sooner was Billy buried than the mourners began to gather in the saloons for a postmortem. Vows of vengeance were washed down with whiskey, and plans for lynching McDonald were hatched. County officials, nervous about their prisoners' safety, requested that the local Grand Army of the Republic chapter join the sheriff's deputies guarding the jail. That night a large mob did appear outside the jail and even the reinforcements could not hold them out. With a large log, they broke down the cells doors and roughly took control of the prisoners. Ropes were put around their necks and they were thrown through the windows of the jail. The mob then dragged the two men through the muddy streets, kicking, hitting, and otherwise abusing their bodies. At some point, the men died, although this did not prevent the mob from hanging the corpses from the railroad cross post. By this time the mob was completely out of control. Someone suggested that there was a better place to hang the dead men, so the bodies were again dragged through the mud. This time the bodies were hauled into the bordello where the incident began. The corpses were strung from the limb of a jack pine and left for the prostitutes to contemplate.[105]

Many legends grew up about the McDonald lynching. The most popular has the mob taking the bloody corpses into the brothel and forcing the prostitutes by turns to lie with them. All legends conclude with the observation that the ringleaders of the mob eventually "died with their boots on," most of them meeting violent and bizarre ends.[106]

Despite all the vice, violence, and dissipation that saloons engendered, they performed important services. Saloons functioned as informal labor exchanges. A lumberjack new to town would be assured that the bartender would know who was hiring; if a foreman was short of men, he would visit the local saloon and locate the jacks who had already blown their pay. Saloons were the only social centers for lumberjacks. In a saloon old friends could get together and tell lies about their prodigious feats during the past logging season. While the rank odor and shabby clothes of the lumberjack might make him unwelcome in the local church or even in a respectable hotel salon, the saloon owner greeted him enthusiastically. He did not need manners, etiquette, or even a knowledge of English to stand on equal footing at a bar. Most saloons provided their patrons with bar lunches, the most inexpensive, if not nourishing, meal available to a working man. The worst dives merely threw the drunken lumberjacks out into the snow or mud when his money was gone. However, most had a back room where they could spend the night.

Although most lumberjacks did visit saloons, it is not likely that they blew most of their pay within its precincts. Many jacks were farm boys from lower Michigan or Wisconsin and saved money to buy land or livestock. They would cash their checks as soon as they hit town and then buy a money order at the post office and mail it home, leaving only enough spending money for meals and a rail ticket home. As one lumberjack explained, "I cannot spend it and no one can rob me, and I need every cent I have earned."[107] After spending several months in a crude camp with little in the way of comfort, it is understandable that young lumberjacks did not trust themselves in the face of the tawdry pleasures of the town. Even if they intended to take the first train home, hunger and a place to wait might lure them into a saloon. A Seney merchant once had a man come into his store and ask if he could wait there for the train. He had three years pay in his pocket and wanted to avoid old friends who might lure him into a saloon. The lumberjack eventually made it home and used the money to pay the mortgage on the family farm. [108] In 1883 five Scandinavian employees of the N. Ludington Company cashed checks for four thousand dollars. They earned the money over several years and used it to make a return trip to Sweden and Norway. That same year the *Marinette Eagle* sought to clear the reputation of some wood-workers by pointing out that many men were "industrious, temperate and economical." There were those who blew paychecks in saloons, but others owned "nice comfortable homes" and saved money "for a rainy day."[109]

Lumberjacks had to be careful with their pay because they did not earn a large amount of money. During the late 1890s, at the height of pine logging, the average forest worker made between twenty-four and thirty dollars per month.[110] Wage rates varied because of several factors. Experienced teamsters or sawyers were paid more than a swamper, who merely cleared debris for roads. Men were offered a several-dollar bonus for staying with a camp an entire season. This was done to discourage men from drifting from operation to operation searching for the foreman and food they liked best.

The local labor situation had a great effect on wages. For example, in 1894 Menominee River lumbermen had no trouble filling their camps with experienced men. There was a labor surplus and wages dipped to eighteen dollars per month. But that same year Duluth, Minnesota, loggers desperately needed labor and paid between twenty-five and thirty dollars per month.[111] Such labor shortages could threaten an entire season's operations. In 1886 there was a labor shortage in the Upper Peninsula. Wages rose steadily. Lumbermen watched the trains daily "for incoming laborers who are hired at once and sent to the woods." Although the Ford River Lumber Company had a millpond full of logs it could not begin sawing for a lack of men.[112] When wages dropped because of a labor surplus, those lumberjacks not bound by family ties would often drift to other areas in search of better pay. The winter of 1896 was a particularly bad one for northern Michigan loggers. John Nelligan remembered: "Many of the lumberjacks were unable to get employment and they built shacks close to the lumber camps and stole provisions from the camps at night or during the day while the men were in the woods."[113]

Considering that their wages included room and board, lumberjacks were paid on a par with the immigrant laborers in the Upper Peninsula copper mines.[114] But woods workers were much less prone to collective job actions than were the mine workers. As early as 1872, copper mines were struck by prolonged labor disputes. By 1890 the Calumet and Hecla Company was forced to organize a company union in response to the activities of the Knights of Labor. The copper country faced strikes in 1890, 1892, 1894, 1896, 1897, and 1904 while the lumber industry was enjoying a much tamer labor environment.[115]

The most serious job action lumbermen faced during the Upper Peninsula's pine era happened in the summer of 1885. Sawmill workers on the Menominee River began to organize to reduce their working day from eleven and a half hours to ten hours. Organizers from the Knights of Labor led the formation of the Menominee River Laboring Man's Protective and Benevolent Union. The ranks of the union grew quickly to include about two thousand men. Recognition of the workers' new powers seemed to come as early as August 3, 1885. Mill owners unilaterally announced a half-hour reduction in the workday with no drop in wages. The union men were delighted and failed to detect the mill owners' true intention. The big lumbermen were seeking to avoid the provisions of a Michigan law that created a ten-hour workday. Before the law went into effect on September 20, 1885, the mill owners requested that their employees sign a contract waiving their rights under the new act. When most workers led by the union refused, the mills were closed. Negotiations between the union and the mill owners led to a reopening of the mill. The workers were not looking for a showdown; they knew the mills had a large stock of lumber in their yards. Laborers had their eye on next spring for a strike. But again mill owners forced them to respond. The Kirby-Carpenter Company, anxious to show it could not be bullied by a union, reopened with only nonunion workers. Samuel Stephenson, Isaac's brother and head man at the plant, bluntly asserted that he had run affairs on the Menominee River for twenty years and he had every intention to do so for another twenty years.[116]

At this point the dispute heated up. The union mobilized its membership and marched to the Kirby-Carpenter boarding house where the new nonunion members were housed. The union claimed the purpose of the march was to "enlighten the men whom the company brought in from the outside as to the true state of affairs." Union deputies warned the new workers that their members would not allow them to pass, and the sight of fifteen hundred angry men convinced them this was true.[117] With no workers the Kirby-Carpenter Company had to close its mill, and it refused to accept log deliveries from the Menominee River Boom Company that sorted all logs on the river. Because of the way the booms were arranged, when one company could not accept its logs, all sorting had to cease. So by closing down the Kirby-Carpenter plant, the union effectively starved all the mills. After an eleven-day shutdown, the strike ended with the mills and men going back to work at their old terms and the union not pressing for ten-hour workdays for the remainder of the 1885 season. On the face of it, the mill owners had won, but in reality the union demonstrated enough strength that next season the mill owners backed off and agreed to the ten-hour day.[118]

As part of the 1885 settlement, the union agreed not to concern itself with lumberjacks and that the ten-hour day did not apply to woods work. These provisions underline the strict control lumbermen maintained over logging labor conditions. Because camps were in isolated locations, the great pine era companies could control the flow of information and men into the men's shanties.[119] The success of the Knights of Labor in the mines and in Menominee did not really spread to lumberjacks elsewhere in the peninsula. Woods workers for the Nelson Ludington Company near Escanaba at first refused to sign a waiver of the ten-hour day law. But they were without organization or leadership, and after only a brief walkout, they signed the contract and headed up to camp.[120] In the Upper Peninsula organized job actions did not take place at the logging camps of the pine era.

A reporter visiting Delta County camps in the wake of the Menominee strike found no talk of "Henry Georgism," "the labor question," or "social problems." "The cry of ten hours pay," he observed, "for eight hours work is an absurdity which confirmed no lodgement in the mind of the outdoor workers of this simple region."[121] But that is not to say that lumberjacks could not assert what they took to be their rights in the workplace. Indeed, the aggressiveness with which aggrieved lumberjacks pressed their claims made the task of camp foreman formidable. In 1896 the foreman for Flannigan and Nelligan tried to make up for lost time by putting his crew to work on Christmas. Normally, the men had Christmas off. Those who lived in the area would take a couple of days off and visit their families. The others had a celebration in camp. Faced with the foreman's unusual order, the men mutinied. They quit the camp and marched to Iron Mountain where they retained a lawyer and pressed for prompt payment of their wages.[122] Sometimes the men were much less orderly in pressing their complaints. A group on the Ford River was broken up one winter by a rumor that wages were twice as high elsewhere. The men quit their work and marched to Metropolitan where the Flannigan and Nelligan office was located. They got gloriously drunk. When they registered their complaint, it was dominated by slurred threats to person and property. This did not sit well with either John Nelligan or Larry Flannigan, who were both "wild Irishmen." They treated the rebellious crew to a dose of corporal punishment. "Some of the men ran a bit too fast for us," Nelligan later remembered, "but with those few exceptions, we beat up the whole gang."

Because men were plentiful that season, they paid off the battered crew and hired a new group.[123]

Besides wages, the most common grounds for dispute between lumberjacks and their foreman were the length of the workday and the quality of the food. The workday was generally accepted to last from dawn to dusk, but that did not provide for a very precise time frame. An aggressive foreman could squeeze an extra day's worth of work each week out of a crew by pushing the morning and evening limits. To drive men that hard did entail some risks, as a foreman for Hamilton and Merryman found out in the spring of 1891. Anxious to impress his superiors, the foreman had his men up at four o'clock in the morning and working until after eight o'clock at night. The men endured this regimen for several months before rebelling. One February morning they were called to breakfast about half past three. They grumbled but went out to the dark forest with the foreman afterward. However, four or five men stayed behind, packed the foreman's personal belongings, and forced the camp clerk to work up his paycheck. Later that afternoon the foreman returned to camp and was confronted by a deputation of the lumberjacks. He was given his pack and his check and told to leave "or else." The men went to work the next day on their own, vowing "to do their duty toward their employer unless discharged." However, they adamantly contended that they would "not endure the persecutions of an overly ambitious foreman" and that from "eleven to twelve hours is sufficient for a days work in the woods."[124]

A good foreman, capable of developing esprit de corps among his men, could get both extra labor and respect out of them. One such foreman was Jim Spain of the Metropolitan Lumber Company. For several seasons he operated a handpicked crew at a camp on Perch Lake in Iron County. The men worked from before dawn to after dusk. When spring finally arrived and the lumberjacks were settling up their accounts with the camp clerk, one jack asked to have the foreman pointed out to him. Half jokingly, the lumberjack stated he recognized foreman Jim Spain's voice but not his face. He approached his boss of six months and said, "How do you do, Mr. Spain? I hardly know you. I never saw your face in daylight before."[125] One old logger observed, "Most men respect and admire a boss who drives them," but he also added, "as long as he isn't too hard a driver."[126]

Good food was one feature that kept even hard-driven lumberjacks happy. "They demanded it," John Nelligan recalled, "and it paid the camp operators to feed them well. The better they were fed, the better work they did."[127] Because of the importance of good food, cooks were often paid as well as the camp foreman. Their task was difficult. They worked seven days a week over wood-burning stoves. Besides three full meals, they also were constantly making bread, cookies, pies, and cakes. With such a formidable task, it is not surprising that good cooks were rare and their services were vied for.[128] Careless or incompetent cooks risked more than angry words. River drivers working on the Manistique River forcibly drove a cook from their camp after he served them pancakes made of flour, water, eggs, and nine mice. The cook ran a full seven miles to escape the crew, and he never returned for his belongings.[129]

The quality of camp food was variable. During the early pine days, when no farms and few towns were in the region, a monotonous and even meager fare was offered.[130] Somewhat more variety and considerably enhanced quality later became a standard of logging camp cook shanties. "We always had plenty to eat," a young woodsman recalled, "but it was not always well cooked." Salt pork was the standard meat at breakfast and dinner. "We would pile a lot of beans on our pan, then take a big chunk of fat pork, then pour about a cup full of molasses over it," Charles Schaible remembered, "and boy did that taste good when we were real hungry."[131] Quantity was important because, in the words of a camp choreboy, lumberjacks "inhaled" their first serving and went back for seconds and thirds. "Once out of town," the boy observed, "and away from liquor and women, the lumberjack lived to eat and ate to live."[132]

Camp living conditions during the pine era were spartan at best. Only the necessities were provided. An experienced crew could build an entire camp complex in three days. Charles Schaible witnessed the erection of a camp near the Whitefish River in 1899. When the crew arrived at the campsite, the men immediately built several temporary sheds for themselves and the cook, thereby keeping the rain and sleet off their bacon and blankets. The second day, skilled sawyers cut enough pine logs for four structures: a cook camp, men's camp, barn, and office. The third day, actual construction began. Two forty-foot logs were laid parallel on the ground, about twenty-five feet apart. Earth was shoveled around the logs to prevent them from rolling. Axmen cut notches into the ends of the logs and shorter logs were laid at right angles on the notches. This was repeated until the building stood about eight feet high. A ridgepole was then raised and cut boards brought from town were used for a roof. A door and window at opposite ends of the building were made by spiking the notched logs in place and cutting an opening out of the logs. "All of this work was very simple," Schaible recalled, "and required remarkable little time but [the camp] was strong and cost but little."[133]

Inside the camp buildings was little natural light, but because the men worked all the daylight hours but Sunday, this mattered little. Many men's camps had a skylight in the roof to allow smoke from the inefficient wood-burning stove to escape. But it was usually closed to conserve heat. The men dried their sweated socks and shirts over the stove, which resulted in "an indescribably atrocious odor which permeated the bunkhouse."[134] Bunks were densely stacked along the walls. Each bunk, upper and lower, was shared by two men. They slept on straw or wild marsh hay and were covered by several heavy blankets provided by the logging company. Bathing was rarely indulged in during the winter. By spring, according to a Huron Mountain logger, "bunks and blankets were stinky and very lousy. Trying to keep one's bunk deloused was useless—the pests migrated."[135] Bedbugs were another "bane of lumber camp life." A young man spending his first night in camp was awakened by their stings. "I opened my eyes in the dim lantern light, they seemed to drop from the roof onto my face and stung me in a dozen places at one time. I hid under the rough woolen blankets, but they crawled down in and attacked my tender skin in all its exposed places." When he complained that, despite great fatigue, he got little sleep, he was told that bedbugs had "to be endured like snow, ice and long hours of work."[136]

In the brief leisure time afforded lumberjacks, they sharpened their saws, smoked pipes, occasionally read an old newspaper or an issue of the then popular *Police Gazette*.[137] Some card playing took place. Poker was played for matches that could be redeemed for clothing credits to the loser's account at the camp store.[138] Occasionally someone would write a letter, though mostly they talked. "It was lots of fun to be with so many young fellows," recalled one first time lumberjack. "It was hard work and we got very tired, but when we got to camp after our day's work and had our supper, we all felt good and there always was something going on."[139] Another teenager, in his first camp, recalled many yarns of brothels and barroom brawls.[140] No eyewitness accounts of Upper Peninsula logging mention Paul Bunyan tales being told. One pine era logger categorically stated, "Long Paul Bunyan stories did not exist. There were only quips—those were exceedingly rare. They were always uttered by some freshie or youngster who brought them in from some city."[141]

Paul Bunyan stories might not have been popular with Upper Peninsula lumberjacks, but the region figured prominently in several Bunyan tales, notably the story of Paul's departure. The great lumberjack was scouting timber near the Pictured Rocks on Lake Superior's south shore. Attracted by the magnificent view, Paul leaned against a young maple tree and peered out over a two hundred-foot cliff. But the hardwood was not as trustworthy as a mighty white pine. The little maple cracked and broke. Paul Bunyan fell over the edge. The fall would have killed any other creature, but Paul managed to land on his feet. He was wearing a new pair of rubber boots. The tremendous impact of the fall and the new rubber caused Paul to bounce high into the air, eventually leaving the earth's atmosphere.[142]

It is appropriate that it was a hardwood tree that brought the mythological end to the mightiest lumberjack, because the evolution of the lumber industry from pine to hardwood spelled a very real end to the frontier phase of Upper Peninsula history. During the pine era, lumbermen and lumberjacks lived in a frontier environment. Resources were abundant and cheap. Economic opportunity was great. An impoverished boy like Isaac Stephenson could rise from the ranks of the woodsman to become a millionaire lumberman and eventually a United States senator. Social restraint and legal enforcement were lax. Violations of land, liquor, and vice laws were openly flaunted. The natural and human challenges to success were manifold, but so was the resourcefulness and energy of men like Robert Dollar, Thomas Nestor, and thousands of lumberjacks who labored in the forest camps. A combination of risk and prospect characterized the lumber industry in northern Michigan from 1835 to 1900.

But by the end of the nineteenth century, the pine forests, which had sustained the booming frontier, were gone. The Upper Peninsula still boasted deep dark woods, and fortunes were yet to be made by cutting, hauling, and milling timber. New methods, however, were required to exploit the abundant hardwood forest. Slowly the technology, business structure, and social environment of the Upper Peninsula changed as a new pattern began to appear in the woods. The way of the pine became legend and the hardwood era had begun.

Leading lumbermen of the Upper Peninsula awaiting the arrival of the directors of the Chicago and North Western Railroad at the mouth of the Menominee River in 1867. *Left to right:* John Spaulding, E. S. Ingalls, Jesse Spaulding, Nelson Ludington, Daniel Wells, Jr., Dr. J. C. Hall, Abner Kirby, Isaac Stephenson, and Chaney Simonds. (Courtesy of the Delta County Historical Society.)

Sawmill on the Escanaba River built in 1844. (Courtesy of the Delta County Historical Society.)

Maine lumber baron Jefferson Sinclair failed in pioneering the Upper Peninsula. (Courtesy of the Delta County Historical Society.)

Isaac Stephenson, a poor New Brunswick boy who carved a fortune out of the pineries of northern Michigan. (Courtesy of the Delta County Historical Society.)

Milwaukee hotel owner Daniel Wells invested heavily in early Upper Peninsula logging ventures. (Courtesy of the Delta County Historical Society.)

A gang saw in operation. The gang saw became popular with northern Michigan lumbermen during the mid-nineteenth century and remained in use in many mills well into the twentieth century despite the availability of the more efficient band saw. The gang saw produced a notorious amount of sawdust. (From the collection of the Marquette County Historical Society.)

River drivers clearing a small jam on the Menominee River. (From the collection of the Marquette County Historical Society.)

Logging near Escanaba. (Courtesy of the Delta County Historical Society.)

Log dam at the lower falls of the Salmon Trout River, 1890. (From the collection of the Marquette County Historical Society.)

Nestor Estate lumberjacks showing off the record load of fifty logs (thirty-six thousand board feet). The load was held in place by two thousand pounds of chain. At the 1893 Columbian Exposition the lumberjacks demonstrated their skill by loading the sleigh each day. (From the collection of the Marquette County Historical Society.)

Big Wheels used to transport logs over dry ground at a logging camp in 1912. (From the collection of the Marquette County Historical Society.)

Nahma in 1918. (Courtesy of the Delta County Historical Society.)

A vacation cottage at the Cleveland-Cliffs Iron Company's Grand Island
Game Preserve, 1907. (Courtesy of the Delta County Historical Society.)

Log drive on the Rapid River. (Courtesy of the Delta County Historical Society.)

The lumber town of Bryan. (Courtesy of the Delta County Historical Society.)

Crystal Falls circa 1900. (Courtesy of *The Diamond Drill*.)

Sawmill on the Paint River, about 1900. (Courtesy of *The Diamond Drill*.)

Processing pine at the mill in Sagola: logs on the conveyer from the mill pond, sharpening a band saw for cutting lumber, discarding culls and loading lumber to be graded. (Courtesy of *The Diamond Drill*.)

Tractor clearing snow off a logging spur. (Courtesy of the Delta County Historical Society.)

Tractor towing a train of log sleds. (Courtesy of the Delta County Historical Society.)

The office of Furlong's headquarters camp near Trout Lake, 1897. The baby is future logger Francis Furlong. (Courtesy of the Delta County Historical Society.)

Francis Furlong when interviewed by the author in 1982. (Photograph by David J. Keene.)

A lumberjacks' dive in Crystal Falls. (Courtesy of *The Diamond Drill*.)

A Ford truck being loaded by a gasoline-powered jammer at Ford Motor Company operations in 1941. (From the Collections of Henry Ford Museum & Greenfield Village.)

A hearty old shacker, 1935. (From the Collections of Henry Ford Museum & Greenfield Village.)

PART 2

THE HARDWOOD ERA

6

PERIOD OF ADJUSTMENT

Timothy Nestor was wistful yet optimistic as he sat in the bustling Detroit rail terminal chatting with a young business reporter. "They are still getting a few scattered trees," he said, referring to the Upper Peninsula logging industry, "but the end of a pine supply that was considered inexhaustible is almost at hand." Speaking with the experience of a veteran lumberman and the professional politician's relish for reporters, Nestor warmed to the gloomy subject at hand. "There are some good stretches of timber still standing in northern Wisconsin and Minnesota, but soon these too will have been laid low, marking the last of the grandest pine forests that ever grew." As he spoke Nestor reflected on his early years in the woods when he worked from dawn to dusk for little more than a dollar. In his mind's eye, he saw once more the tremendous wealth of the logging frontier's salad days. "I am not an old man," Nestor told the reporter, "and yet since I have been able to earn a man's wages, I have seen Black River . . . choked with big pine logs for a distance of fifteen miles." He thought also of the dark, deep forest with mammoth pine trees each able to produce four thousand board feet of lumber. "Now even the vast forests of the Upper Peninsula have gone into the country's tremendous maw," said Nestor. "What does it mean?"[1]

That was a common question among Upper Peninsula lumbermen during the late 1890s. Even lumbermen who had been foolish enough to think of the region's pine resources as inexhaustible were given ample warning during the 1890s that the new century would bring changes. The Menominee River, the region's mightiest production center, was shaken by several ominous signs. The average size of logs sent downriver to the mills declined steadily. In 1893 newspapers reported that log size had decreased by forty-one percent during the past ten years.[2] The decline in log size presaged a decline in the number of logs sent downstream. By 1897 the Menominee River Boom Company had reduced its number of river men from as many as a thousand, during the good years, to as few as three hundred. There were fewer and fewer pine for them to handle.[3] As the number of logs decreased, sawmills closed. The city of Menominee declined drastically from having twelve sawmills producing more than 280 million board feet in 1892 to a mere five mills cutting 35 million board feet ten years later.[4] Isaac Stephenson, who had ridden the pine boom from its beginning, tried to be optimistic, but he had to admit the region was amid a transition. He called for local capitalists to develop new industries and for people to wait patiently "until the change from the old to the new was brought about." [5]

While the people waited patiently, many lumbermen thought they knew exactly what the decline of pine meant: the region was finished as a lumber center. Russell Alger moved his operations to Minnesota's north shore and he also invested heavily in far western timberlands. The Diamond Match Company and the Nestor Estate, which was formed from Thomas Nestor's company, left northern Michigan for Minnesota.[6] One by one the pine barons of the Upper Peninsula liquidated their holdings and scattered to the timbered corners of the western frontier. At Trout Creek the owners of an old pine mill sold out and relocated in the mountains of Arizona.[7] The Metropolitan Lumber Company, which had fought homesteaders for control of its land, sold its cutover tracts and relocated in Eureka, California. The Sparrow-Kroll Company, which operated a substantial mill at Kenton, Michigan, cut pine until 1910 when it began operations in Idaho.[8] The great lumbermen of the Menominee were no less inclined to leave. A. C. Merryman bought pinelands in Washington, Frederick Carney invested in Ontario forests, and Isaac Stephenson invested extensively in Louisiana and Texas yellow pine.[9]

Nor was it only lumber barons who headed west. Smaller operators tried to get their share of the golden west's tall timber by forming partnerships and joining claim clubs. One such organization was the Oregon Club of Rockland, Michigan. The club pooled funds to send a pair of land-lookers to Oregon to scout public lands for potential logging sites. When the cruisers returned with favorable recommendations, the entire twenty-two-man club went west to enter Timber and Stone Act claims, under the public law that encouraged the disposal of nontillable public forest.[10] Some big mill towns such as Menominee began to experience population declines after decades of rapid growth. Workers went to where the mills were humming, not closing. Such gloomy statistics were generally met by brave talk of the area's "natural advantages" and appeals to sentiment: "Some of us have married here, our children were born and educated on this river; now we have our grandchildren with us.

This is our home where we expect to live here for many years to come."[11] Yet even optimistic community boosters had to admit by 1900 that the pine frontier had busted. Standing in the shadows of the closed mills and hearing the clamor for one way rail tickets in their ears, they too asked the sober question, "What does it mean?"

Timothy Nestor knew the answer to that question better than most men, perhaps because he and his brothers had pioneered the Lake Superior timber industry, perhaps because of his involvement in politics; but Timothy Nestor saw the significance of the decline of Michigan pine in the sharp relief of the expanding American economy. "People don't realize how this country of ours has been growing," Nestor said. The population had more than doubled since the Civil War began. Cities crowded with millions of factory workers were gradually becoming the focal point of the nation. The American economy was on the threshold of becoming the leading industrial power in the world. It was the combination of natural resources, transportation systems, and the emergence of the corporation that sparked this tremendous economic surge. Of increasing importance in the economy, were combinations of individual corporations into trusts, which would dominate all facets of an industry from raw materials to production to distribution. Many businessmen roundly criticized the trusts, but not Nestor. "I am going to say, even at the risk of being misinterpreted, that some of the trusts are a benefit." He went on to explain, "with their immense resources and facilities for economical production, they are able to steady the market." Although the lumber industry because of its overly competitive structure could not combine into a trust, Nestor knew the industry's future in northern Michigan was tied to modern, integrated industrial combines.[12]

In 1893 Nestor first became involved in the type of large-scale organization he believed the region's resources needed. He investigated a large tract of timberlands in Alger County. The land had been part of a grant given to the builders of the ill-conceived Lac LaBelle Ship Canal. The canal and its backers met little financial success, and by 1887 most of the grant was up for sale by the North of England Trustee, Debenture, and Assets Corporation. Many investors shied away from the land because it contained little pine, but because Nestor knew the sellers were eager to dispose of the tract, he investigated its potential. He employed three veteran timber cruisers to scout the land. Their report revealed that the hundred thousand acres were basically covered by hardwood, but even with the depressed price of that product on the market, the stumpage alone was worth $750,000, and the land for later agricultural purposes might fetch $1.25 per acre. Depending on the price it could be purchased for, it might make a good investment. Nestor assembled a pool of investors led by Emmet H. Scott, a LaPorte, Indiana, man who already had considerable northern Michigan holdings. In December 1894 they bought the entire land grant for a mere $1.30 per acre.[13]

The investors then formed two separate companies: the Munising Company, which was composed of a group of Cleveland businessmen who also owned much real estate in the area, and the Lac LaBelle Company, composed of those who bought the grant. Tim Nestor coordinated the joint activities of the two concerns. Their plan was to develop the infrastructure of the area to encourage industrial and agricultural settlement. A town was platted at the shore of Munising Bay, a fine natural harbor. Nestor directed the building of a commercial dock at the harbor and the laying out of industrial sites.[14]

The most ambitious aspect of the project was the building of a railroad from Munising Bay and Lake Superior to the Chicago and North Western Railway that touched Lake Michigan. Nestor realized that without a railroad operating through the heart of the extensive Lac LaBelle lands, it would be difficult to attract buyers. The railroad ran for a distance of thirty-eight miles. At one point there were three hundred men working on it. Nestor did not want a hastily built logging road but a stable full gauge, well-graded railway that could be used for general transport in the years to come.[15]

Such foresight paid off well in the long run. By the winter of 1895 the investors succeeded in attracting the first industries to their lands. Two lumber contractors founded mills on Munising Bay. More important was the decision of the Sutherland-Innes Company, based in Chatham, Ontario, to establish a mill to cut elm for cooperage (barrels). They were followed by the Munising Cedar Company, which exploited the scattered stands of swamp cedar in the area. But the most important industry that Nestor attracted to the area was the Cleveland-Cliffs Iron Company, one of the biggest iron miners in the Upper Peninsula.[16] In 1901 they purchased eighty-four thousand acres and the entire Munising Railway. Although Nestor's Indiana partners wanted to hold out for more money, the sale resulted in the liquidation of most of the Lac LaBelle Company's assets at a considerable profit.[17] With the kind of profit that Nestor made on the Lac LaBelle deal, he could afford to be optimistic about the future of the Upper Peninsula.

The Cleveland-Cliffs Iron Company was indicative of a new organized, efficient approach to logging that transformed the hardwood forests of the Upper Peninsula from a dubious investment to a valued asset. The company had gradually purchased extensive holdings throughout the peninsula. The Lac LaBelle purchase increased their Alger County holdings alone to three hundred thousand acres. The area became the basis for intensive forest operations using railroad transportation. The Munising Railway, which Nestor built, was merged with the company's Marquette & Southeastern Railway and another line that linked the ore fields with Lake Superior to form a network known as the Lake Superior & Ishpeming Railroad. With these facilities forest products could be shipped from the woods to locations on Lake Michigan or Lake Superior, from Alger County, Delta County, or Marquette County.[18]

The company's flexible transportation network was used to integrate woods operations with a diverse assortment of forest product industries. Lumberjacks clear-cut all holdings. They removed all trees and most tree limbs from the forest, regardless of tree size, type, or quality. The best hardwoods were shipped to the Munising Woodenware Company, a subsidiary of Cleveland-Cliffs, where they would be made into wooden bowls and plates. Later, a wood veneer plant was also included. Rotted woods, which pine loggers would have left on the forest floor, the company shipped to its Marquette chemical plant for processing into wood alcohol and other products. Pulpwood was sent to the Munising Paper Company, another subsidiary, for production into paper. Cordwood was sent south to the Lake Michigan town of Gladstone, where a charcoal iron furnace consumed massive amounts of fuel. Selected cedar, tamarack, and spruce were sent to Ishpeming for the mining division, the company's core unit, to use in shoring mine shafts.

Cleveland-Cliffs required detailed long-range planning for such comprehensive logging operations. Ten-year plans were developed to predict the wood needs of the company's diverse operations.[19] The land department then dispatched its land-lookers to assess the timber potential of an area. If the cruisers estimated that it held enough wood to meet production demands and operational costs, they would then map out right-of-ways for bringing logging railroads into the heart of the forest. The land-lookers, who were surveyors, always tried to avoid swamps and hills, never accepting grades more than four percent.[20] The company's lumber department would then take over by detailing a team of men to cut out the right-of-way. A gang of laborers followed with pick and shovel. They were aided by horse-pulled graders, which gradually built a smooth railroad bed. Once the grade was ready, the men laid down a standard-gauge track. The company never used cheaper narrow-gauge equipment because it wanted to easily transfer its forest railroad rolling stock onto the common carrying lines that would haul the wood to the production points. The cost of installing a standard-gauge railroad, including grading, surfacing, and laying down the steel rails, varied with conditions, but a cost of twelve hundred dollars per mile may be considered average.[21]

Upon completion of the railroad logging camp, construction began.

Preferably, camps could be placed adjacent to two or three sections of uncut forest. This reduced the necessity of moving the camp as nearby woods were cut. Although it was both a distraction and an expense to move camps, it was often necessary because of the rapid rate at which the Cleveland-Cliffs people clear-cut the forest. From one wooded acre in Alger County, the company lumberjacks cut five thousand board feet of saw logs, twenty-nine hundred feet of rail ties, and more than eleven hundred feet of chemical logs. When operating at full efficiency, under good conditions, a Cleveland-Cliffs camp of 100 men could clear as much as two acres of forest per day.[22]

The highly integrated, multifaceted approach to lumbering repre-sented by the Cleveland-Cliffs Iron Company required a degree of mana-gerial organization and capital investments that few of the old pine log-ging giants were prepared to match. Isaac Stephenson, however, was an exception. Having presided over the birth of the industry in the north-ern peninsula, he knew more about the forest resources of the region and the business of logging than any man alive. He began to prepare for the future in 1888 when he reorganized the old. N. Ludington Company into the I. Stephenson Company. Near the mouth of the Escanaba River, Stephenson built a new mill and founded the town of Wells. The town was named after Stephenson's partner, John W. Wells, who joined the firm in 1899. In that year the I. Stephenson Company began the expensive process of moving from a pine log base to becoming a sophisti-cated hardwood logging concern. New band saws were brought in, with blades strong enough to cut the denser hardwoods. An entirely new mill was built to manufacture hardwood flooring material. To supply those mills, a railroad was necessary. Stephenson organized the Escanaba & Lake Superior Railroad and laid out thirty-four miles of track the first year.[23]

Those expensive cash outlays could be justified only if the company controlled enough timber to sustain operations for several decades. Step-henson already controlled 140,000 acres of timber, but anxious to secure hardwood lands before the price rose, he purchased an additional 110,000 acres from the Ford River Lumber Company in 1903. The Ford River lands were denuded of white pine but boasted virgin stands of cedar, hemlock, and, of course, hardwood. The cream of the I. Stephen-son Company hardwood was its maple trees, which besides its attractive surface was well known for its strength and durability—well suited for the floor material marketed by the company. The vast forest controlled by Stephenson covered an area fifty miles in width and seventy miles in length.[24]

The center of Stephenson's hardwood empire was the bustling com-pany town of Wells. Stephenson had little direct involvement with the town; it was his partner and general manager, John W. Wells, who presided over the place. The company built and rented 100 workers' cottages and maintained a large boardinghouse for bachelor workers. Because the company owned every inch of ground in the town and controlled every building, it could impose temperance on its workers by not allowing a single saloon. By 1903 the mills at Wells were annually producing seventy-five million feet of lumber, twenty million feet of maple flooring, and millions more of shingles, lath, posts, and poles. That year, *American Lumberman* proclaimed Ike Stephenson's company "the largest lumber operation in the State of Michigan," and because of his smooth transition to hardwood logging dubbed him one of "the mental giants" of the Upper Peninsula—not bad for a seventy-four-year-old former chore boy.[25]

Another old pine logging concern to evolve successfully into a complex hardwood logger was the Wisconsin Land and Lumber Company, based in Hermansville, Michigan. Unlike Ike Stephenson, the owners of this company had a very rough transition. The firm was founded by Charles J. L. Meyer, a German-born cabinetmaker's son. In Fond du Lac, Wisconsin, he established a wooden sash, door, and blind factory. To make its products, his firm consumed more pine than the Winnebago Valley possessed. So in 1878 Meyer began to purchase lands in Menominee County, Michigan. A year later he founded the town of Hermansville where a single mill cut pine into roofing materials. Meyer was an engineer and an empire builder. In 1883 he tried to build a more efficient machine for sawing railroad ties. What he got was a machine that sent cedar ties hurtling through the air and workers scurrying for cover. Later he spent thousands more trying to perfect a mechanism to make hardwood flooring. At the same time, Meyer expanded his real estate holdings in the Upper Peninsula, buying close to one hundred thousand acres, spread out over eight counties.[26] Hermansville, named after his son, he made into the seat of the empire. He spent eleven thousand dollars on charcoal kilns, close to forty thousand on sawmills, twenty-three thousand on workers' cottage. In 1883 he founded the Hermansville & Western Railroad and spent forty-three thousand dollars on it during its first two years.[27] Together with plants in Fond Du Lac, Oshkosh, and Chicago, Meyer's lumber business looked like an impressive monument to an immigrant's success in the New World. It proved to be an edifice with a weak foundation.

For Meyer and his Hermansville empire, the ground began to shift in 1890. Across the nation the economy declined, credit tightened, and loans were called due. Meyer, who expanded on borrowed capital, was forced to assign all his corporate and personal assets to cover his debts. He sold his Chicago and Wisconsin properties, hoping to keep the

Michigan lumber operation intact. However, it was not enough and the timberlands went on sale. They fetched little on the market because most of the pine was cut and the remaining forests were hardwood. Meyer hung on for several years slowly selling land and hoping that his hardwood flooring mill might save the day. He proudly dubbed the product "IXL Maple Flooring" and rejoiced when it was installed in the Mormon Temple in Salt Lake City. But that was only one of a handful of orders.

As his company disintegrated, so did Meyer. After a riding accident in which he hit his head on a curb, Meyer suffered a brain hemorrhage. He at first lost physical control of himself and became delirious. It appeared he was going to die. But the hardy German recovered his health and freedom of movement. However, his mind never returned. For the rest of his life he was morose, confused, and uncertain—helpless to prevent the demise of his timber empire.[28]

At Charles Meyer's bedside, as he struggled to recover, was Dr. George Washington Earle, a hard-working general practitioner from upstate New York. In 1888 he had married Meyer's daughter and on his shoulders fell the task of saving Wisconsin Land and Lumber. He was no lumberman and only came to the north woods for the first time in 1889. But he was a hard worker. At the age of eight, with all his personal possessions tied into a bandanna, he began to make his way in the world. He worked at first to survive; later to afford a medical education; and then to succeed in a demanding profession. When he married Meyer's daughter, he decided to rest for the first time in his life. He invested his life savings in the lumber company and planned to spend a year in Hermansville relaxing before returning to his New York practice. Then came the financial panic that slowly consumed the company. Dr. Earle and the rest of the family closed ranks and tried to work through the crisis. His planned vacation stretched into two years as he became increasingly important in the effort to satisfy all creditors. When Meyer became unbalanced, Earle was the only family member who could take charge.[29]

Earle took over at a bleak time. By 1893 the economy settled into a prolonged depression, making it impossible for the lumber company to work its way free of debt. In frustration the creditors demanded foreclosure and sale of the company's assets. Earle labored mightily and behind the scenes to raise new loans. He negotiated with the original creditors to purchase their notes for $220,000—less than the amount of debt yet considerably more than the property would have fetched at a public auction. To raise money for the sale, Earle scrambled for large and small investors. He offered stock in the reorganized company to the workers, but few thought it a smart investment and passed by an opportunity that would later haunt them. Finally, in July 1910, Earle secured control of all outstanding bonds and reorganized the firm as the Wisconsin Land and Lumber Company of Michigan.[30]

One of the factors that helped the reorganized company pull into the black was the steady, if conservative, management of George Earle. He worked to keep expenses to a minimum and promoted the company's products, particularly the "IXL" maple flooring, which became the firm's mainstay. The "IXL" logo became famous in the industry. Architects wrote "IXL or equivalent" in building contracts. Carloads of flooring were regularly shipped to dealers around the country. A letter was once delivered to the Wisconsin Land and Lumber Company that was simply addressed: "IXL Lumber Company, U.S.A."[31]

As profits began to accumulate, Earle began the slow building up of the company's timber reserves. Profiting from the example of his father-in-law, he refused to build on a foundation of credit. When that tight-fisted policy threatened the mills with a shortage of wood, Earle instructed his superintendent, E. P. Radford, to purchase logs from small lumbermen who then acted as jobbers for the "IXL" Company.[32]

However, on at least one occasion, Earle's frugal approach to timber-lands ended up costing the company dearly. In 1902 the company was offered several thousand acres of hardwood in Schoolcraft County. The doctor looked over the stumpage and liked what he saw, but not for the price the owners were asking. He was outbid by the Buckeye Stave Company, which only held on to the tract long enough to sell it for a profit to William Mueller, a cedar post wholesaler. Mueller had been successful at marketing forest products and thought that he could make a fortune in the lumber business if he became involved in production as well. He was sadly mistaken.

Mueller knew nothing about forest operations; his head foreman, Neal Blaney, was a schooner captain and knew even less. But their inexperience did not prevent them from building a lumber operation on a grand scale. In the heart of their forest, they built a handsome company town, which they named Blaney. The only trouble with the town was that it lacked rail connections and therefore could not serve as a hardwood distribution center. Of course, that was nothing that money could not change, so Mueller invested in a steam engine, rolling stock, rails, and construction crews. Seven miles of track were laid between the town and the Soo Line Railroad. Mueller called his short spur the Blaney & Southern Railway. The only thing that interfered with Mueller's pleasure of looking over the fine new town and his shiny new railroad was his accumulation of unpaid bills. Before it ever cut down a single tree, William Mueller & Company was bankrupt. Either Mueller got a quick injection of capital or he would lose everything. In desperation he appealed to George Earle.[33]

It was not just sympathy for someone in a plight like that he had been in only five years before that motivated Earle to bail out William Mueller & Company. Mueller controlled an entire township of forest. Earle knew the quality of the timber, particularly the fine maple, that was found on the tract. He gave Mueller more than forty thousand dollars to pay the man's debts in exchange for hardwood logs of equal value. It would have been a good deal for both parties if Mueller ever delivered the logs. Instead of maple, Earle received excuses and further requests for money. Earle honored Mueller's request, and a trickle of logs arrived. However, they were followed by a new appeal for loans. This dreary drama was reprised until the fall of 1909 when it became clear that the Mueller Company was disastrously grounded on the rocks of bankruptcy. Mueller owed the "IXL" Company ninety-seven thousand dollars in lumber and loans. Thousands more were owed to the First National and Commercial National banks of Chicago and scores of other financial backers. These businessmen had enough of Mueller's excuses and they contacted Schoolcraft County officials to begin bankruptcy proceedings. Liquidation would never return to Earle anywhere near the money he had sunk into Mueller's firms; his only choice was to buy the lumberman out and take over the town of Blaney. Incredibly, for a year after the sale, Earle continued to let the incompetent Mueller manage the operation. Only when his debts began to mount again did he send the man packing. The Wisconsin Land and Lumber Company found itself owner of the thirty-three-thousand-acre tract at many times more money than Earle refused to pay for it seven years before.[34]

The company logged the Blaney tract for years, harvesting fine maple, basswood, and cedar from its forests. Yet there was something unlucky about the area. Dr. Earle was not the last member of his family to invest a fortune in Blaney. Years later, when hardwood logging was finished, Blaney would again charm thousands of dollars out of the Earle family, only to leave frustration in its wake.

The Bay De Noquet Company, like Wisconsin Land and Lumber, was a notable exception among the pine-logging giants, because it made the transition to hardwood production. Based at Nahma, on the shore of Big Bay De Noc, the company had relied on the Norway and white pine of the Sturgeon River Valley to keep its mills busy. During the 1890s the company operated from four to six logging camps each season. Every camp was expected to cut about three million feet of logs per year and was assigned thirty to forty men for the task. When camps fell below the three-million mark, they were closed and plans were made to move to a new location.[35] By the late 1890s camps began consistently to fail to meet their pine log production goals. Some residents of the town became anxious that the company might curtail operations at Nahma. Anxiety blossomed into alarm when the Bay De Noquet's main sawmill caught fire and burned in April 1899. There was not enough pine left in the Sturgeon Valley to justify rebuilding the plant. Many lumbermen would have taken the fire as a cue to liquidate their investment. But the Oconto Company, parent concern of the Bay De Noquet Company, operated a Wisconsin mill for the production of boxes and barrels. It was confident that the hemlock and elm of the Upper Pensinula would prove as profitable as Wisconsin hardwoods.[36] Fifty-one thousand dollars were invested in a new mill for Nahma.

Softwoods continued to be driven down the Sturgeon River each spring to the working shingle or post mills, but most hardwood species could not be so transported and the company was forced to construct a logging railway. Construction was not vigorously pursued until the dearth of pine and cedar became acute. Rail was first laid in 1901, southward from the Soo Line, yet it took two years for the track to reach the mill at Nahma, only four and a half miles south.[37] After 1903 construction was conducted at a quicker pace. Eventually sixty-five miles of track were laid from Bay De Noc deep into the interior of Delta County. The company purchased several locomotives, one of which originally operated on the Chicago elevated railway, more than 100 log cars, plus a handful of gondolas, gravel cars, boxcars, even a passenger car, which was used by the company to take its lumberjacks to camp each fall. The men who also rode the steel road to town and the company saloon each spring or on an occasional weekend bout, called the route the "whiskey northern." Company officials, more prosaic and less eloquent, insisted the logging line be called the Nahma & Northern Railway.[38]

Some lumberjacks did their best to keep the informal name, the "whiskey northern" alive. One was Bill Gingway, a hardy lumberjack and river man who often persuaded the engineer of the line to give him free trips into town on Sundays. Gingway usually spent the day in the town's only saloon. After one such spree, he headed back to the train with a jug for the boys in camp. Fred Good, the company's "walking boss," saw Gingway mount the train with his cargo. It was standard policy not to allow liquor into the camps. After a chewing out, Gingway brought the jug back to the saloon. Moments later, he again was about to board the train, this time with a kerosene can. Good was wise to what was in the can, but with a smile on his face, he turned to the engineer and said, "Let him on, if he's that smart." That was one night the "whiskey northern" lived up to its name.[39]

The railroad gave Nahma and its mill a new lease on life. More forestlands were purchased increasing the corporate total to more than 150,000 acres. The Bay De Noquet Company was among the elite dozen landholders in northern Michigan.[40] The Nahma milling operations were integrated with plants elsewhere in the region. Lumber and lath were shipped to Chicago or Buffalo. Maple logs were sent by water around the Garden Peninsula to Manistique where the Bay De Noquet directors operated the Brown Dimension Company, a hardwood flooring and furniture maker. Low-quality woods were sent down the lake to Oconto, where a box factory operated. Even during the depression the company maintained a regular payroll of six hundred employees. The hardwood era was a prosperous period for the Bay De Noquet Company.[41]

The original directors of the Bay De Noquet Company were based in Oconto, a Wisconsin lumber port that boomed during the pine era. The Oconto Company, parent to the Nahma firm, was rivaled in the Wisconsin town by the Holt & Balcom Lumber Company. When the Oconto Company looked to expand its operations during the 1880s, it moved north to Bay De Noc; the Holt & Balcom Company continued to concentrate its purchasers in the Badger State. By the early twentieth century, however, the Holt people began to doubt the ability of their Wisconsin forestlands to supply them with either softwood or hardwood in the quantity desired. Like the Oconto Company before them, the Holt timber cruisers went north to the Upper Peninsula to look for a lease on life.

Historically speaking, northern Michigan was not an entirely foreign area for the Holt concern. The founder of Holt & Balcom was Devillo Holt, who began in the logging business in 1847 as a partner with Richard Mason sawing timber on the Whitefish River. By 1863 Holt quit the Upper Peninsula and formed a new firm with Uri Balcom. They thrived in Wisconsin until 1893 when Balcom died. The firm was reorganized as the Holt Lumber Company and plans were made to expand farther north.[42] William A. Holt, Devillo's son, assumed control over the business. He led the old lumber company through a difficult series of transitions. The Chicago office of the company that previously had directed management was gradually downplayed and control was shifted to Oconto. As part of a northward shift in the operations, logging ventures around Rhinelander, Wisconsin, and in the Upper Peninsula became vital to the flow of forest products. Finally, William Holt shepherded his firm through the transition from pine to hardwood.[43]

Only by gradual stages did the Holt Company become an Upper Peninsula logger. During the late 1890s the company several times purchased a trainload of Ontonagon County pine and shipped it to its mill in

Wisconsin. In 1898 the firm also began to saw logs for the Diamond Match Company. At a cost of $2.75 per thousand feet, the Holt Lumber Company did not get rich by this contract, but it did keep its mill busy. The Diamond Match Company was, at that time, still cutting timber along the Ontonagon River and shipping the logs south to Wisconsin mills. However, the Michigan operations were becoming more and more burdensome to a company whose major holdings were in Minnesota and the western mountains. The Match King successfully lobbied to have the Holt Lumber Company take over the remaining pinelands in southern Ontonagon County.[44]

About one hundred million feet of pine was owned by the Diamond Match Company and other interests in the area. It was not the best pine the Holt timber cruisers ever saw. It was relatively small and in places it was scattered amid hardwood. But it was white pine and that was rare stumpage in the twentieth century. Beginning in 1901 the Holt Lumber Company bought Ontonagon lands. They met little competition. Because of the location of the lands, few lumbermen thought the operation could be made to pay, even with the high price of pine. Most of the timber was along a tributary of the Ontonagon called Baltimore Creek. It was a twisted and contorted waterway whose many falls and rapids made log driving a nightmare. The worst stretch of water was near the mouth of the creek where the Diamond Match Company had several giant jams. To avoid this spot and the troubled bends of the Ontonagon River itself, the Holt Lumber Company built a rail spur from the Duluth, South Shore & Atlantic Railway to the banks of Baltimore Creek. Logs coming down the creek would be pulled up and shipped to the Oconto mill.[45]

Despite the planning William Holt put into the Baltimore operation, it was a difficult chance for the Wisconsin logger. To haul sleighs of logs up the steep ravines of the Ontonagon valley, it was necessary to install steam-powered hoisting engines. Steel cables from the engines pulled the sleighs over the obstacle. On one occasion the cable snapped as a sleigh neared the top of the hill and the load of logs slid back down the hill as if "it has been shot out of a cannon." Another team of horses at the base of the hill could not be moved out of the way in time and were "crushed to a pulp." In attempting to bridge one ravine for the railroad, the Holt Lumber Company was forced to employ one hundred thousand feet of pine for a trestle. Nor was the Holt Lumber Company familiar with railroad logging. Experience came at the expense of efficiency. On one occasion an entire line of log cars was accidentally uncoupled and they rolled down a steep grade before crashing into Baltimore Creek.[46]

Even nature seemed to conspire against the Holt Lumber Company.

In the fall of 1903, just as they were putting in their first logging camps, a tornado tore through the forest. For more than ten miles the violent storm left a trail of fallen trees in its wake. If the pine was not harvested quickly it would begin to rot. Fortunately most of the damage was near the Holt logging railroad and could be easily harvested. There was, however, a considerably damaged tract that was inaccessible by river or by the existing rail. William Holt approved the building of a spur track to the damaged area. But no sooner was the expensive spur completed when a massive early snowstorm hit. Much of the fallen timber was buried and required considerable time to uncover. Some logs were never found; many that were found disappointed Holt as they had been badly splintered by the tornado.[47]

Most of the logs hauled out of the ravines of Baltimore Creek were pine, although the Holt lumberjacks also cut some cedar, spruce, and hemlock. Hardwood stood on some of the lands the company purchased in northern Michigan, but the old pine logging firm was unsure how to deal with this resource. William Holt and his brothers read with interest the articles on hardwoods that were beginning to appear regularly in the *American Lumberman.* They also talked with loggers experienced in dealing with the denser deciduous forest products. From such sources, they learned that basswood, if cut during the summer, has a tendency to spoil. Maple and birch had their special particularities as well. Although Holt had cut hardwoods in Wisconsin for several years and should have known better, in 1901 they could not resist trying to drive some hardwood logs a short distance. The logs floated to the boom in fine fashion, but then began to sink. The river drivers scrambled to save the bulk of the logs, but William Holt was forced to report "it is surprising how many logs . . . went to the bottom." Thereafter, he did not try to move hardwood by river.[48]

The Holt Lumber Company cut logs in Ontonagon County until 1919. When the pine was cut out, they suspended operations. Logging was renewed again in 1926. By that time hardwood and hemlock were the cream of the forest and the Holt Lumber Company committed itself to the intensive forest operations required to make hardwoods profitable.[49]

The pine loggers who managed to stay in business after the turn of the century found themselves facing logging changes as difficult or even worse than the Holts tackled on Baltimore Creek. The remaining pine stood on mountain slopes or in dismal swamps. The swampy terrain was the kingdom of one of the last colorful characters of Michigan's white pine kingdom, Con Culhane. He was a cutover land farmer in lower Michigan who entered the logging business in 1893. For ten years he took on difficult logging chances in the lowland between the Two Hearted and Tahquamenon rivers. Rather than struggle with long sleigh roads from the interior to the river, he operated his own logging railroad. When he finished one job and moved to another, he would transport his entire outfit by train, pulling the tracks up behind him, laying new rails in front.[50]

Culhane was no desk-bound lumber baron, but a two-fisted logger whose name is often heard in the folktales of northern Michigan lumberjacks. He tested men applying for work in his camps with the question: "Me bye, can you fight?"[51] Those who answered yes he tested himself in bare knuckle brawls. It was his opinion that "a man that can fight can work." Win or lose, a man who took up the challenge secured a job. Culhane's rough and tumble ways and homespun appearance belied his success as a logger. In 1902 he netted a thirty-five-thousand-dollar profit. Yet on the street he was easily mistaken for a common woodsman. On one trip to Chicago to purchase supplies for the coming year, he surprised the clerks of a wholesale house by demanding to see the owner. Instead, he was assigned a mere underling. Culhane exploded, "I won't talk to any walking boss. I'll do business with no one but the big boss. He's the man that can set the price." When the owner hustled forward, the logger said, "I'm Con Culhane. I want to buy around thirty-five thousand dollars worth of goods. I'm coming down every year, and if you treat me right, you'll get my business."[52]

Culhane did not own forestlands. He cut trees for the large corporations that were beginning to dominate stumpage in the region. One of his biggest jobs was for the Calumet and Hecla Company, which needed pine for mine timbers. While completing that contract Con Culhane came to his colorful end. He was riding on his logging train one morning. As usual he sat with the engineer, but before reaching camp he wanted to give some instruction to the brakeman. He walked back over the empty log cars. As he was stepping from one car to the next, the train gave a sudden jerk. "Instantly his feet were jerked from under him and he fell between the cars, two of them passing over him before the train was stopped." His men rushed to the accident site and found his broken and lifeless body.[53]

The end for the pine logging companies that could not adjust to the altered realities of the industry was much less dramatic but just as final. Like Culhane who died under the wheels of his own train, they were the engineers of their own destruction. The Kirby Carpenter Company might have profitably cut pine logs well into the twentieth century, if it had pursued a conservative policy. Instead, its directors insisted on a fast-paced production schedule that resulted in the closing of Menominee's biggest mill in 1901.[54] The Chicago Lumber Company in Manistique pursued a similar policy. One evening a young clerk presumed to question that company's aggressive cutting schedule. He approached George Orr, the corporate vice president, and said, "Mr. Orr, don't you think the company would make more money by saving more of the timber for the future instead of cutting so heavily now?" The old lumberman thought over the question and answered, "Yes, Will, that is probably true, but there are a lot of things we would like to do if we could only stop eating for ten years."[55] Many pine lumber men, like George Orr, could simply not conceive of running a logging business with restraint. When profits sagged, lumbermen wanted out; there were fortunes to be made in western or southern timberland. Why keep money locked in Michigan forests?

In 1911 the Chicago Lumber Company, which still had millions of feet of standing timber and owned 160,000 acres, began to look for a buyer to assume control of the company. Within a year a deal was completed that gave all the company's real estate and logging equipment to two former employees for $750,000. The directors sold out so cheaply because they individually had expanding operations on the Pacific shore, and because of declining lumber production from corporate lands. They did not consider a stand of pine that yielded less than four thousand feet per acre worth the trouble of cutting. The buyers organized the Consolidated Lumber Company, which agreed to sell much of the remaining pine it cut to the old owners and contracted to sell the hardwoods it harvested to the Edward Hines Lumber Company in Chicago. Through mismanagement, the new company bordered on bankruptcy for several years before selling out to hardwood loggers from lower Michigan, thus ending Manistique's days as a white pine port.[56]

RISE OF THE CUTOVER FARM

In the wake of the collapse of the pine kingdom, when hardwood logging was more promise and prospect than production, the hopes of many northern Michigan communities were directed to agriculture. It has been the tradition of America's retreating frontier that farmers succeeded loggers in settlement. Agricultural scientists, the large land companies that succeed the pine loggers, and the residents of abandoned mill towns all looked to farming as a source of hope. Ewen, which had thrived on the lumberjack trade, had seen half its population leave when the pine was gone. Ontonagon County's McMillan township, typical of the stricken pine country, declined from 868 people in 1900 to only 458 in

1910. As the cutover lands were converted to farming, the township again boomed. By 1920 its population grew to more than eighteen hundred.[57]

Enthusiasm ran high throughout the north country. Boosters proclaimed: "The Upper Peninsula of Michigan is destined to become the greatest fruit country in the world. It will also become great dairying country. There is no more productive land to be found anywhere for root crops." One promoter described the region as a veritable "cornucopia."[58] Journalists in the western Upper Peninsula and northern Wisconsin advertised the cutover land's dairy potential by describing it as "cloverland." Roger Andrews, editor of the *Menominee Herald-Leader*, used the burgeoning agricultural sector to justify the establishment of the Upper Peninsula as a separate state. In more sober moments, Andrews also published a monthly magazine, *Cloverland*, which advised cutover farmers on agricultural prospects and techniques.[59]

What especially recommended the Upper Peninsula to the farmer was the availability of cheap land. Government land was open for homesteading. Homestead claims were particularly important for the families that pioneered northern Michigan farming during the 1890s. In 1890 one observer at the General Land Office described the filing of claims as "fast and furious."[60] Railroad companies, which had been rewarded with generous land grants, also were anxious to attract farmers to their lands. Some companies sold their lands cheaply to encourage settlements that would then use the railroad to get crops to market. The Duluth, South Shore and Atlantic Railway gave half price rail fares to those who wanted to inspect farmlands. If a farmer agreed to settle on their lands, the company granted him forty free acres and half-price fares to transport family and belongings.[61] Several mining companies used their extensive holdings to attract settlers. In one case, farmers were sold land near the mine at a very low price with the provision that the farmers would sell excess wood on their lands to the company. This arrangement gave farmers a source of income while they improved their tracts, while the company was free of land taxes and rewarded with mine timbers.[62]

Despite all the optimism of boosters, cutover farming was often a difficult struggle. The severe work regimen demanded to successfully farm the undulating and rocky terrain of Iron County led farmers to joke: "Did you hear about the farmer up the road? He's dead, you know. He tripped and fell off one of his fields and was killed."[63] The five years of "proving up" required to get free government land was more than some homesteaders could take. Not unique was the case of a pioneer named Stone, who was found dead in his cabin in the fall of 1896. He had worked four years clearing five acres and building a farm. One morning he rose to work but was stricken, perhaps by a heart attack, and he died. It was days before he was found. No one really knew him. The home-steaders nearest to him found his nearest kin's name in a Bible, sent a letter, and buried Stone on the land he tried to claim.[64] A Chippewa County homesteader recalled her struggle to set up a backwoods farm:

> We started on a new farm with only enough cleared ground to make a site for our shanty, which was three logs high in the rear, and four in the front. We put on a lumber roof covered with tar paper, and we plastered the walls with mud. For lighting the shanty we had a half-window at one end. The door consisted of two rough boards joined together, and the floor was also of rough boards. During the first winter we had cleared 30 acres of land and built a log barn. We ploughed 30 acres in the fall but the ground was wet and we have very little crop off in the next year. . . . The second winter because our crop had been so poor, my husband went to work in a lumber camp. . . . When he returned to our pioneer home we had enough money to build a small farm home.[65]

Because thousands of families were willing to endure such a bleak life, the Upper Peninsula grew even as pine logging declined.

Much of the rural population growth stemmed from the immigration of northern, eastern, and southern Europeans into northern Michigan. Finns, Poles, Italians, and Yugoslavs flocked to the region. Although their languages and customs were different, their reasons for coming to the Upper Peninsula were the same: jobs. During the 1890s these groups swelled the ranks of underground miners and lumberjacks. Besides steady employment they were interested in owning land. A farm was a link to the peasant society they had left behind. Land ownership was also a source of pride, a measure of security, and a yardstick of progress in the New World. Even men who worked full time in the mines often took up homesteads in the forest.

Sometimes backwoods farms were grouped into ethnic enclaves. An Iron River resident recalled that

> these early settlers bought or homesteaded land along the winding dirt roads which radiated from town in all directions. Each nationality tended to settle in a territory where others of their nationality had taken up land. Up one road was a settlement of Germans, up another Swedes, another Scotch, another Polish, and another Finnish. Each settlement became a tight compact group with its own schools and its own customs. Each group was loyal to its own nationality and to a degree to its "old country."[66]

In the isolated rural areas, away from mining towns like Iron River and Stambough, ethnic settlements were much less common. Towns like

Matchwood and Bergland served mixed ethnic communities of farmers.[67] The cutover region, with its inexpensive homesteads, was an important part of what Progressive Era Americans liked to call their national "melting pot."[68]

The Finns were the immigrant group most successful in settling the cutover land. They left Finland at a transitional time, when the old agricultural life-style was giving way to a new industrial economy. The transformation was marked by political and religious persecution and the concentration of rural land into increasingly fewer hands. Northern Michigan first beckoned to Finns during the boom copper years of the Civil War. The Quincy Mining Company in Hancock was short on workers and long on copper orders, so it sent two agents to Norway where they eventually contracted for Finnish miners. During the next twenty years, labor agents sent eight hundred Finns to jobs in Upper Peninsula mines. The success that these pioneers had at their mine jobs, as well as at establishing farms, induced thousands of their countrymen to follow. By 1911 twenty-five percent of all miners on the Gogebic Range were Finnish.[69]

A late nineteenth-century journalist noted that the Finns were particularly suited to cutover farming because of their passion for dairy cows, the skill with which these ex-miners handled dynamite (needed to blast out tree stumps), and their deep rooted fear of debt.[70] The journalist should have added the inclination of Finns toward communal organization. Finns played a leading role in the organization of both miners and timber workers. Some Finns were forced to take up backwoods farms to escape from corporate blacklists. Others were attracted by the prospect of safer, healthier, out-of-doors work. Yet as much as the Finnish farmers relished owning their own land, some of the cooperative patterns that marked Finnish-American industrial life did carry over to rural living. The experience of Finnish farmers in Carp Lake Township of Ontonagon County is a case in point. They first began to establish farms in the area about 1903 when the C. V. McMillan Lumber Company began to sell its logged-over lands.[71] By 1918 the mostly Finnish farmers in the area had managed to clear fields and plant grain. To speed harvesting, the farmers formed a cooperative and bought a thresher. Each farmer in the district bought a ten-dollar share in the cooperative to pay for the purchase. Later, the cooperative purchased a portable sawmill so that its members could use their own timber for farm improvements. In 1926 the cooperative again showed its vigor by purchasing a hay baler, which allowed the farmers to market their surplus hay directly to local logging camps.[72] Similar joint ventures took place elsewhere, but they were most common among Finns and gave the hardy woodsmen an edge in settling the marginal lands of the Upper Peninsula.

A major threat to the pioneers of the cutover were forest fires. From 1891 through the 1920s forest fires were like an annual plague threatening the rural population. Even today, the pulse of gray and aged farmers quickens when they recall the cycle of flame and smoke that drove them from their homes to the protection of a creek or river.[73] In 1907 an Ontonagon County farmer named Nathan Stone could not escape to the shelter of water. He and his family were ringed by fire on their homestead. Three times the house caught fire, but each time the family could extinguish the flames. After battling the blaze for a day and a half, the Stone family was completely exhausted, desperately thirsty, and blinded by the constant glare of flames and engulfing waves of smoke. Only the timely arrival of the township supervisor, with a water wagon, saved the homesteader. It was popular to blame red-hot cinders from logging locomotives for starting these blazes. Some wry homesteaders, perhaps recalling the sales pitches they had heard, blamed real estate brokers who found it easier to sell land once the brush was already removed. Logging did create the conditions for fires, but farmers carelessly burning brush often began the conflagrations.[74]

Agriculture blossomed in the Upper Peninsula from 1900 to 1920. The number of farms doubled, growing from sixty-one hundred to well over twelve thousand. Although this boom can be explained partly by the decline of employment in pine logging and the copper mines, which may have forced workers on to the farm, national trends also played a role. The first two decades of the twentieth century were relatively prosperous for America's economy. World War I stimulated a worldwide rise in food prices, which made farming lucrative even in marginal areas like the northern Michigan cutovers.[75]

Although individual mill towns were left stricken by the decline of pine logging, most residents of the Upper Peninsula faced the twentieth century with confidence. The first shoots of progress were clearly evident from the infant hardwood logging industry. There was a clear prospect of an enduring forest products industry. While Michigan bemoaned the loss, by 1900, of national leadership in lumber production, loggers could take heart in the fact that by 1905 the Great Lakes State was one of the foremost hardwood producers in the country.[76] Further promise was held by a growing agricultural sector that seemed to help ease the region's transition from a pioneer lumber frontier to a modern economically diversified community. The period of adjustment seemed to have gone well; they looked with optimism to the future.

7

RISE OF INDUSTRIAL FORESTRY

When Henry Ford asked for something, he usually got it, particularly when he was talking to a Ford automobile dealer. He was, after all, the father of the Model T, which transformed American life, and he was the wealthiest man in the country. It is surprising, therefore, that Edward Kingsford hesitated to accommodate the industrialist's simple request that he join him and a few friends on a camping trip. Henry Ford knew Kingsford because of Kingsford's marriage to his cousin, Minnie Flagherty. Ford wanted a chance to pick Kingsford's brain on the lumber and iron industries of northern Michigan. Besides operating an auto dealership in Iron Mountain, Kingsford was a veteran timber and mineral land-looker. Yet he at first refused Ford's request to join the camping party because summer was his busiest time of year. Only later when friends warned him, "You are going to miss the chance of a lifetime," did Kingsford agree to Ford's request.[1]

Kingsford met Henry Ford in Buffalo, New York. The trip was a chance of a lifetime. Among the friends gathered for the vacation were Thomas Edison, Harvey Firestone, and nature writer John Burroughs. They were outfitted with several cars and a couple of trucks full of tents, tables, chairs, food, and a refrigerator. The caravan wound its way along the back roads of upstate New York, through Vermont, and into the hills of New Hampshire. There was no set itinerary; they traveled according to whim, stopping at picturesque streams and inspecting historical sites along the way. At night they sat around a campfire, sometimes swapping yarns, discussing the issues of the day, and sharing their plans for the future. Henry Ford talked much about northern Michigan. The industrialist was planning to bring under his control all the resources he needed to produce automobiles. He spoke of acquiring coal mines, rubber plantations, glass factories, limestone quarries, and a fleet of ships to convey the materials to Detroit. Kingsford was asked detailed questions about iron ore and hardwood in the Upper Peninsula. In Kingsford's answers and Ford's imaginative plans were the seeds of industrial forestry in the Upper Peninsula.[2]

Henry Ford was no lumberman. He was a manufacturer who would supply his own market for forest products. What he wanted out of lumber operations was an assured quality and quantity of hardwood. He was the world's leading automobile producer and he intended to stay in the business for many years to come. Yet each one of his famed Model T cars contained 100 board feet of hardwood. The frame of the car, although braced by steel, was basically made of wood. There was also a heavy demand for wood as boxing, pallets, and for pattern work. With the company selling more than one million vehicles in 1919, Ford clearly had need of much timber.[3]

Kingsford was given the task of locating a large block of forest in the Upper Peninsula. He was also told to keep alert for good iron ore properties. It was not a good time to purchase lands in bulk. World War I caused a boom in the northern hardwood market and forestlands jumped in value. But Ford would not be denied. Kingsford at first suggested that the company purchase a 140,000 acre tract, but Henry Ford rejected this as not enough. At the same time, Kingsford heard that the Michigan Iron and Land Company was willing to sell its extensive holdings. Since 1856, when it was granted several hundred thousand acres to try to complete two railroad lines, the Michigan Iron and Land Company was one of the Upper Peninsula's largest landowners. In March 1920 Ford bought 313,000 acres of their land for $2.5 million. Nor was this the end of the Ford acquisitions. The Michigan Iron and Land Company lands, like most railroad grants, had been divided into a checkerboard of alternate sections. For the sake of efficiency Ford wanted a solid block of ownership. During the next three years Kingsford negotiated with the lumber companies who owned the alternate sections of forest. The breakthrough came in January 1923 when the Stearns and Culver Lumber Company sold their holdings in the L'Anse area to Ford. The Charles Hebard and Sons Lumber Company was next to fall to Ford. Kingsford purchased their railroad, timberlands, and company town, Pequaming. A few odd sections of forest bought from the Cleveland-Cliffs Iron Company rounded out Ford's forest empire. It sprawled over four western Upper Peninsula counties and was composed of four hundred thousand acres.[4]

In the summer of 1920 the great man himself went north to inspect his expanding domains. He steamed up the lakes from Detroit on his yacht, the *Sialia*. The boat's arrival in Escanaba was greeted by a throng of enthusiastic citizens and curious reporters.[5] Ford officials had a motorcade waiting, and the procession of Ford cars drove west to Iron Mountain. Ford loved the Upper Peninsula. He loved its natural beauty, once telling friends, "It is one of the prettiest places in the world." He also reveled in the challenge of the remote and rugged region. As he drove through the wilderness terrain, he liked to talk about "improving the country, like building roads." A former Ford employee in the Upper Peninsula remembered, "He'd go here and there and build a road where there was no road. He'd open up a region so people could get in there. He liked to open up farmlands and give jobs to people."[6]

When Ford met Kingsford in Iron Mountain, he let these personal considerations influence his industrial decisions. The Iron Mountain area was hard hit by the postwar recession, employment in mining lagged, and the farm situation in Dickinson County deteriorated. Although hardwood logging helped sustain many communities, the forests near Iron Mountain were pretty well stripped by 1920. Even though logs had to be shipped 100 miles to sustain a mill in Iron Mountain, Kingsford persuaded Ford to build his principal forest products plant in Iron Mountain. The only factor that supported the decision was the ready labor force available in Iron Mountain.[7] People in the town were ecstatic when the rumors of Ford's coming were confirmed. One businessman recalled, "Everyone went crazy, and real estate doubled and tripled for a period of about four or five years. . . . There was an enormous influx of people."[8] Millions of dollars were spent in Iron Mountain. A new sawmill, capable of cutting one hundred thousand feet of logs every eight hours, was completed. Later dry kilns, an auto body parts mill, and a wood chemical distillation plant were installed.

Iron Mountain was the center of Ford activities in northern Michigan, but it was by no means their only production facility. The company renovated the mills it purchased in L'Anse and Pequaming. The L'Anse plant made some auto body parts, but both mills worked mainly to produce boxing and crating. In 1936 Ford established a fourth mill at the village of Alberta, but it operated only intermittently. The final piece in the Ford forest products operation was a completely redundant component. In 1941 Henry Ford, acting once again more on sentiment than savvy, bought a large hardwood mill at Big Bay, Michigan, just northwest of Marquette. Ford had driven past the mill many times when he visited his cabin at the elite Huron Mountain Club. The plant's production was not really needed, even during the booming production years of World War II.[9]

In a less spectacular way, Ford also invested in iron ore. He purchased twenty-two hundred acres of Menominee Range ore lands and one working mine, the Imperial, and used its ore at his massive Rouge factory. A second mine, the Blueberry, was opened on Ford lands in 1929. Neither mine produced more than a fraction of the Ford Motor Company's iron ore requirements. The Ford expansion program had nowhere near as big an effect on the mining industry of the Upper Peninsula as it did on logging.[10]

"Henry Ford," comic Will Rogers once remarked in a semiserious vein, "changed the habits of more people than Caesar, Mussolini, Charlie Chaplin, Clara Bow, Xerxes, Amos n' Andy, and Bernard Shaw."[11] It was therefore inevitable that if Ford got involved in logging he would put his personal stamp on the enterprise. He broke with tradition at the first logging camps established by the company. He paid his woods workers three to four dollars per day, at a time when $1.50 was the rule. Some lumbermen were enraged, thinking that Ford would ruin the labor market for all loggers. But Ford cared more about maintaining a wage scale comparable to his Detroit area workers than he did about following industry standards. The short-term effect of Ford's policy, one logger recalled, was to raise "the cost of operations of all people in the region somewhat."[12]

Ford dismayed fellow lumbermen and stunned the lumberjacks even further with the condition of his camps. Most logging camps during the 1920 were crude log or frame shanties, heated by wood stoves and lighted with a few kerosene lanterns. Washing facilities were limited and bunks were shared. Ford's camps replaced straw tick with iron frame mattresses. Steam heat and electric lighting made the rooms bright and warm. Showers, baths and a laundry service were added. After the evening meal, Ford lumberjacks had a recreation room to retire to where there were card tables for poker and magazines for reading.[13] Lumberjacks did not know how to respond to the bright paint and the "No spitting on the floor" signs. One Ford woodsman remembered, "I guess this cleanliness and showers took them off their feet for a while."[14] The lumberjacks were crazy about it," another recalled, "once they got used to it."[15]

Some old-time lumberjacks wanted nothing to do with this new-fangled type of camp. Nor did Ford want men who would not keep clean of lice or bedbugs. "It got so you got a better element of lumberjacks in the camps," a Ford foreman stated, "because these younger men who came liked that. They wanted to have a clean place to sleep and eat."[16] During the 1920s a few elite logging operations in Minnesota and Wisconsin, such as the Edward Hines Lumber Company, began to bring modern residential technology to the lumber camp.[17] But they were an exception. Most lumbermen in the Upper Peninsula resented Ford's camps. Even a Ford logger complained that "it caused all the other loggers up here a great deal of trouble." Lumberjacks became more assertive about working conditions. When this climaxed in 1937 with a timber workers strike, some forest foremen blamed Henry Ford's camps as planting the seeds of dissent.[18]

Yet the most controversial aspect of Ford's woods operations was his attempt to integrate aspects of scientific forestry with his logging program. Appreciation of the need to apply natural science to the management of timberlands grew slowly in the United States. A breakthrough was achieved between 1901 and 1908 when President Theodore Roosevelt and his chief forester, Gifford Pinchot, sold the general public on the need for the conservation of forests through national timber reserves. Large national forests were established in the western United States, but little was done to nurture or husband the remaining forests of the lake states. In the north country, lumbermen jealously guarded their right to cut trees when and how they wanted to. They feared forest fires but dismissed the advice of college-trained foresters to remove the rubbish left by logging, which was recognized as a principal cause of the blazes. When Ford announced his massive timberlands purchase in 1920, foresters around the country wondered if the motor magnate would pursue a traditional "cut and get out" policy or if he would adopt some of the conservation practices advocated by scientific foresters.

Ovid M. Butler of the American Forestry Association summed up the sentiments of many who were concerned about natural resource use by dismissing Ford's other accomplishments and asking, "But is Henry Ford actually practicing forestry?" To find out, Butler visited Ford's Upper Peninsula forests. Edward Kingsford escorted Butler through the Ford mill at Iron Mountain, and Hermann Hart showed him Ford's modern camps. Operations in the forest were just beginning. The Ford Motor Company in 1921 was still purchasing most of its lumber on the open market. But in the first logging procedures used by Ford lumberjacks on corporate lands, basic forestry was being introduced. Hart took Butler to an area that had recently been logged. "We are not cutting and logging much differently from the ordinary lumberman," Hart explained, "but we are looking out for our young trees and getting rid of the brush. We leave all thrifty trees twelve inches and under. . . . I try to make my men use their heads about cutting low stumps and we insist that they be mighty careful about falling big timber so as not to break up the small trees." Butler was so impressed by the Ford loggers that he told members of the American Forestry Association: "I found that in a very serious-minded way, he [Henry Ford] is harvesting his mature crop of trees, leaving his young, fast-growing trees for an oncoming crop and ridding this young forest of the hazards of fire by cleaning it of all brush resulting from logging. If that isn't forestry, what is?"[19]

The Ford Motor Company, already an industrial model of efficiency in the business-oriented 1920s, basked in the praise that foresters bestowed on their infant natural resource management program. But behind the favorable public relations was considerable division over the practice of forestry. Kingsford, for one, did not agree with the concept. He did want to see the land recycled for new growth, but he thought the best way to do that was to "clear cut"—remove all trees and brush.[20] Nor were the logging superintendents pleased with the policy, despite the forestry-conscious words of Hermann Hart to Butler. Disagreement over logging policy may have encouraged several superintendents in succession to quit the job. When Albert Olson took over the job in the mid-1920s selective cutting was not being practiced. However, efforts were made to clear out the debris of logging so as not to lay the foundation for forest fire.[21]

Ford Motor Company did not begin selective logging again until 1934. By that time there had been a revolution in the Ford forest. Kingsford was removed from any active hand in management. The Ford logging camps, with their lavish appointments and well-paid lumberjacks, were discontinued. When most of the corporation's timber needs were met by market purchase, which was so during the 1920s, the corporation could afford several model camps. But during the 1930s logging intensified on corporate lands and then began to contribute directly to the costs of producing an automobile; managers, therefore, wanted expenses held down. Contractors were brought onto Ford lands to handle all logging. This passed the costs of paying and accommodating the lumberjacks to the small logging jobber. Ford foresters would mark the timber to be taken out of a section of woods, indicating the young growth to be left for the future. But the contractors, in their haste to complete the job, would often ignore the markings. Even when it was practiced, Ford selective cutting was not very successful.[22]

The failure of the selective cutting program was probably due to the way the forest products division was managed. Beginning in 1935 logging operations were coordinated with production schedules at automobile plants. Instead of trying to develop a large inventory of wood, Ford managers wanted it shipped from the northern Michigan mills to the assembly line. This did not give the loggers adequate time to plan their harvest or properly prepare their forest roads. Selective logging called for taking the best trees over a large area, but pressure to meet Detroit's demands forced foresters to log smaller areas more intensively. The corporation officially continued to log selectively until 1946, when clear-cutting became the policy, but in reality production problems had undone much of the forestry scheme before that time.[23]

The most successful feature of the Ford forestry program was fire control. By clearing their logged-over areas of limbs and brush, the corporation did much to reduce the danger of fire. Corporate watchtowers gave early detection of a blaze, and timber patrols in the summer and fall quickly squashed what fires did occur. The effectiveness of these simple measures was demonstrated as early as 1923.[24] That October, fires raged across much of northern Michigan and Wisconsin. Heavy smoke closed the road between Ashland and Hurley, Wisconsin, while on Lake Superior dense banks of smoke forced the suspension of coastal navigation.[25] Millions of feet of timber were burned to the north, northeast, and west of Ford lands. The Sawyer-Goodman Lumber Company lost three million feet of hardwood logs.[26] Two hundred square miles of forest was reported burned in Ontonagon County.[27] Several small fires began on Ford land, but they were quickly extinguished. This was the type of payoff that Ford and other timber owners wanted from forestry techniques. They were not overly concerned about future forest growth—Ford never reseeded any of its lands—but the protection of the timber they had already paid for was a priority. This was a more modest approach to forest management than many conservationists had hoped for from Ford, but it was a more positive step than the pine loggers had ever taken.

The Ford Motor Company did not take its first timid steps toward corporate forestry alone. Several other lumber concerns experimented with sustained yield logging and forest fire control. These progressive companies were a minority in the lumber community, but they were among the most important timberland holders in the north country. The most significant of these, and the single largest landowner in the Upper Peninsula, was the Cleveland-Cliffs Iron Company.

By 1913 the Cleveland-Cliffs Iron Company had amassed land holdings that topped 1.5 million acres, all of it in the Upper Peninsula. Their forestlands were computed in billions of standing feet of timber. In fact, fourteen per cent of the entire land area in the Upper Peninsula was owned by the company and on thousands of acres more they claimed mineral rights. They became the largest timber holder in the lake states. Between 1900 and 1910 they acquired various land or logging concerns, which they then continued to operate as subsidiaries. One of these was the Upper Peninsula Land Company. This single subsidiary controlled most of the seven hundred thousand-acre grant the state gave to build the Detroit, Mackinac & Marquette Railroad in 1881.[28] Another significant subsidiary was the Bay Mills Land and Lumber Company, which was formed in 1905. In that year Cleveland-Cliffs purchased the Hall & Munson Company. Based in Bay Mills on Lake Superior, they had been one of the largest pine loggers in Chippewa County. But when the company's sawmill burned in 1904, it fell on financial hard times. Cleveland-Cliffs assumed their debts and acquired 105,000 acres of land and the entire town of Bay Mills for eighty cents on the dollar.[29] The massive real estate holdings of these and other component companies of the Cleveland-Cliffs empire were managed by a single Land Department located in Negaunee, Michigan.[30]

Just as the active ingredient in the Ford Motor Company's forestry program was Henry Ford, so too did the head of the Cleveland-Cliffs Iron Company inch his land managers toward industrial forestry. William Gwinn Mather was born in 1857, a descendent of the lofty Puritan dynasty of divines. In 1891 he presided over the merger of old Cleveland Iron Mining Company with the Iron Cliffs Company and served as president of the new concern. On the Marquette Range he pioneered social reforms that gave miners modest health care pensions, and a worker safety program. Mather nursed an interest in conservation. All company lands were open to public access, for hunting, fishing, or wild blueberry picking.[31] In 1901 Mather established the Grand Island Forest and Game Preserve. The private preserve was on a 13,500-acre island in Munising Bay. Mather enhanced the natural splendor of its sandstone-cliffed shore and rugged hills by stocking its streams with fish and the forests with exotic game. Elk, caribou, antelope, and a herd of albino deer were introduced to the Island. Later wild rice and celery were planted in a large lake on the island to support natural and exotic waterfowl. As the preserve thrived, it exported deer and elk to other wildlife refuges. Between 1909 and 1935 more than seventeen hundred animals were shipped from the island. No hunting was allowed, even for the guests of a hotel on the southern end of Grand Island.[32]

Although Cleveland-Cliffs was in the business of exploiting natural resources, Mather ensured that resource development was well thought out. In 1896, even before the company began to make its major real estate purchases, Mather allowed Henry S. Graves, future chief of the U.S. Forest Service, to inspect the company's thirty-six thousand acres of forest land in Marquette County. His report provided the company with a detailed description of the holdings and recommended varying management strategies for the virgin hardwood lands, the young growth stands, and cutover acreage. However, Graves's advice, which included selective logging, does not seem to have been acted on.[33] The most important effect of the report was intellectual. It influenced Mather to regard forestry as a profession that might enhance the profitability as well as the public image of his company.

By 1903 Mather came to the conclusion that he could forestall the rapid deforestation of corporate lands if he adopted a more vigorous system of management. Graves had argued that logging did not necessarily have to lead to tangled cutovers and forest fires. Mather therefore added a forester to the Cleveland-Cliffs land department. S. M. Higgins, a graduate of Cornell University's School of Forestry, became the first full-time corporate forester in Michigan. He took an academic approach to his job, spending most of his time doing research on corporate lands. His goal was to gather enough data about Cleveland-Cliffs lands to prepare a comprehensive forest management scheme. But he was frustrated in this by the continual expansion of company timberlands during the first decade of the twentieth century. Little was actually accomplished in the woods until February 1905 when Thomas B. Wyman was hired as Higgins's assistant.[34]

Wyman was destined to be important in the growth of forestry in the Upper Peninsula. He was a graduate of the one-year program offered at the Biltmore Forest School on the Vanderbilt estate in North Carolina. In a short time he became involved in several programs to actively improve the Cleveland-Cliffs lands. The most important of these was a reforestation program begun in the spring of 1905. Nurseries were established at Negaunee and Coalwood (a small town in Alger County) where young spruce and pine seedlings were raised. The actual reforestation took place near Munising where nineteen thousand spruce plants were set out. Wyman also planted a ten-acre cherry orchard.[35] So successful were his first years' effort that Wyman was given the job of resident forester for the Munising District. Under a new management plan, all Cleveland-Cliffs lands would be divided into a series of districts administered from a local control center by a professional forester. The first such center was at Munising. Besides continuing reforestation, Wyman was to advise logging operations and provide protection against fire. He was also given his own assistant forester, Marcus Schaaf, a former National Forest Service employee and a fellow alumnus of the Biltmore School.[36]

The creation of the Munising District of the Cleveland-Cliffs Land Department was supposed to be the first step in a "broad system" of forestry embracing the company's forest and cutover lands across the peninsula. Instead, the Munising District remained only a tentative and isolated first step for the company, one not pursued for another three decades. Yet Thomas Wyman, without strong corporate backing, made impressive gains for forestry through individual effort. He not only continued the replanting program in the Munising area, but with company permission began a forestry training program.

The "Wyman School of the Woods" was begun in Munising in 1908. Unlike most forestry training programs of the time, which were too theoretical, Wyman wanted to teach forestry by doing forest work. A student, Wyman promised, would not just hear of silviculture but get experience growing trees. "He hears of forest measurements and he makes them; he hears of forest fires, and he fights them; he hears of cruising and he cruises. . . . He goes into the field to perfect his knowledge; he asks the 'why' and is taught the 'because.' "[37] The program used Cleveland-Cliffs lands in the Munising area, allowing Wyman to accomplish more improvements than he otherwise could have tried. The school was popular with students. When it began, Wyman had between ten and fifteen students, though by 1915 there were thirty young men participating in its course of study. To assist in the instruction, Wyman lured Carl A. Schenck, his old professor, away from the Biltmore School. Schenck's participation lent considerable prestige to the school during the few terms he was involved with it. The school had a two-year full-time program, but few students were in Munising long enough to complete it. Job offers from around the country lured the fledgling foresters before graduation. Wyman's bold experiment ended in 1917 when the United States went to war with Germany. The faculty was involved in war work and the students enlisted en masse.[38]

Wyman achieved his most notable successes in industrial forestry in fire control. This was an issue that was bound to interest lumbermen who would not listen to discussions on reforestation or selective cutting. Throughout the early twentieth century, fires raged back and forth across the peninsula. In 1906 fires ravaged the Menominee Range. The towns of Cornell, Quinnesec, Ralph, and Talbot were destroyed. Munising was ringed by flames and was saved only by breezes off Lake Superior. Marquette County lost $200,000 worth of property. Refugees from the blaze swarmed into Escanaba and Marquette for relief.[39] In 1908 an autumn drought again brought widespread burning. As a spokesman for the Michigan Forestry Association, Wyman tried to use the blazes as a catalyst to organize lumbermen behind conservation. He was supported in this by Thornton Green of the Greenwood Lumber Company, C. H. Worcester of the Worcester Lumber Company, and C. V. Townsend, the head of the Cleveland-Cliffs Land Department. In November 1910 these men called a general meeting in Marquette of Upper Peninsula lumbermen and drew representatives mostly from companies operating in the western and central Upper Peninsula. At Wyman's suggestion, they agreed to form the Northern Forest Protective Association.[40]

The association immediately became one of the largest such groups in the country. Wyman was appointed Chief Forest Fire Warden with the task of making mutual protection work. He proposed to do this by forming squadron wardens to patrol the forests of member companies. Their salary and expenses would be paid by a penny per acre assessment on the member lumbermen. Within a year Wyman had nineteen men patrolling the forest. Besides watching for fires they posted signs, supervised controlled burning, and located potential fire hazards. But because these few men were scattered over eleven counties and access to the forest was hampered by poor roads, their efforts met with few successes. It often took the wardens as long as ten hours to reach a fire reported in their district.[41] Wyman tried to strengthen the association through cooperation with sportsmen and state conservation officers. He persuaded the founders of the association to refrain from barring fishermen and hunters from their lands. Although he conceded that these sportsmen had been guilty in the past of carelessly igniting fires, he also argued that they could increase the effectiveness of the wardens if the sportsmen were educated to their stake in forest conservation.[42] Wyman met with only mixed success dealing with local officials. Township governments were supposed to pay for the cost of fighting forest fires, and the state was bound to reimburse them one-third of the cost. But the state was often tardy in its repayment and townships were hesitant to be too aggressive in fire fighting. Such problems were only partly solved in 1914 when the state appointed its first full-time fire warden, William Pearson.[43]

In 1917 an attempt was made to resolve problems between the Northern Forest Protective Association and state officials by having Wyman appointed chief state fire fighter in the Upper Peninsula. The move recognized Wyman's and the association's pioneering in fire protection, but it was destined to fail. Wyman and Pearson, who retained control over lower Michigan, clashed over budgets, policy, and personalities. Wyman resigned in disgust in 1919.[44] He went to work for the Upper Peninsula Development Bureau, served for a time as mayor of Munising, and finally left the state, going to Ohio where he had a long career in civic administration.[45]

The Cleveland-Cliffs Iron Company began to retreat from its forestry program during the 1920s. When Wyman became head of the protective association in 1910, he left the company's employ. Reforestation languished. Clear-cutting became the standard logging practice. Once an area was logged, its future prospects were ignored and the land was marketed for farming. Iron production boomed during the 1920s and corporate officials looked for the most productive way to keep up with contemporary mine expansion. The future was left to tomorrow's care.[46]

Ironically, the Cleveland-Cliffs Iron Company retreated from forestry just as the Ford Motor Company began its experiments. Although neither firm had been entirely successful or persistent with applied forestry, they did help lay a foundation on which efforts could build. Nor were they alone in their efforts to organize logging on a more secure basis. Throughout the 1920s there were isolated examples of lumbermen experimenting with forestry. The Goodman Lumber Company of Wisconsin experimented with selective logging on its Upper Peninsula lands,[47] but it did not effect the company's long-term logging policy. In 1929 the Connor Land and Lumber Company, another Wisconsin-based logger, also experimented with selective cutting. They found it to be a workable system in some cases and gradually expanded its application.[48] The U.S. Forest Service tried to make the most of these meager buds of progress, but most hardwood loggers showed little more concern for the environment than the pine loggers did before them.[49]

A typical example of the self-destructiveness of many hardwood loggers is the Cadillac-Soo Company. The company was founded in 1923 when two established Upper Peninsula firms, the Richardson and Avery Company and the Cadillac-Lumber and Chemical Company, merged. The Richardson and Avery Company was worth one million dollars at the time of the merger and the combined holdings of the two companies topped fifty thousand acres. The Cadillac-Soo Lumber Company began life rich in cash, land, and logging experience.

Had the new company embarked on a sustained-yield program, it might still be producing forest products today. Instead, they adopted a clear-cutting strategy. From a short-term perspective this looked to be very efficient. Sawlogs from quality maple, birch, or basswood were used for lumber. The limbs of hardwood trees were used as cordwood for the company's chemical plant. Small trees not eligible for lumber production were sent to the chemical plant. The small branches and other slashings left in the wake of the clear-cut were left where they fell on the ground. Cadillac-Soo cut lumber in this fashion year-round. During the winter, sleighs carried the logs to the rail siding; during the summer "big wheels" did the job. As the years went by, the amount of devastated land produced by the company increased.[50] Even those areas not devastated by brushfires were practically worthless because of the accumulated slashings. As early as 1928 the company tried to relieve itself of the tax burden of these tracts by selling them to the U.S. Forest Service.[51]

Cadillac-Soo continued its logging operations until 1956 when the board of directors decided to close the company and sell its assets. The company survived as long as it did only because it had much land and because it had shut down completely during the worst years of the Depression. As it was, forty-eight thousand acres of land were devastated by their operations.[52] A forester, sadly looking over the lands, described their condition as desperate: "The area lay ravished and exhausted; great stretches had been logged. . . . Fires in the 1920s and early '30s had left extensive barrens over which the wind whistled. . . . "[53] Another land manager put it more succinctly: "A woodpecker would have to carry his lunch to fly over it."[54]

The hardwood era ended the same way the pine lumbermen had gone out, with large sections of forest lands devastated. Attempts were made at sustained-yield logging and timber farming, but the political and economic climate in the industry and society was not right to support such experiments. Stronger leadership by federal and state officials, as well as further conservation in the industry, was required before forestry could guide logging. Remarkably, the forests of the Upper Peninsula in 1940 had endured 100 years of logging and could still boast nine million acres of uncleared forest.[55] However, half of that land was formerly deforested land now covered with small trees, and the best pine and hardwoods were gone. Still, if this resource were managed, not merely exploited, the Upper Peninsula could still sustain a forest products industry. But to bring that about would take a reorientation of the logging industry. The first winds of that change began to blow across the peninsula in October 1929. The Great Depression was the catalyst that ushered in a new era in the history of logging in the north country.

8

THE PROCESS AND PATTERN OF
HARDWOOD LOGGING

On crisp autumn evenings, when deer hunters clad in flame-orange jackets and caps gather in the taverns of Munising or Grand Marais, tall tales, hunting stories, and bawdy jokes are mixed with pitchers of Wisconsin lager. The hunters recount in detail their successes and elaborate on the "ones that got away." They also speak of the forest, much less articulately, but with equal feeling. Some speculate what it must have been like before the tall timber had been cut, when the land belonged to the Chippewa. Others mention the abandoned logging camps and ghost towns that make good locations for a hunter's deer stand. Often conversation drifts to the subject of the old logging railroads. The grades still provide hunters with open access to the interior of the forest. On the sides of the old rights-of-way, hunters often find rotting ties, rusted spikes, perhaps even a coupling. These mementos fuel one of the north country's most enduring folk legends. For over beer are exchanged rumors of vintage locomotives stranded in cedar swamps, iron horses sidetracked a generation ago, forgotten and now left rusting in the forest. Like the Sasquatch and the hodag, these phantom locomotives are often discussed, occasionally sought out, but never found.

One writer who investigated the stories concluded that if any old railroad engines "are holding their rusty stacks aloft among the pines or tag alders on an abandoned grade in northeast Alger County, they might well be but shadows of an old Paul Bunyan tale." Despite a lack of proof, the stories of lost logging era locomotives linger, in part because of the desire of the people who live on the fringe of the forest to have a more direct contact with their community's golden past. The period 1900–1920 was a boom era for many forest towns. Hardwood logging was prosperous; even agriculture was expanding. There was talk of statehood for the Upper Peninsula. It was the railroad that wrought this prosperity out of the decline of pine. The railroad was the symbol of that age.[1]

Railroad logging was modern industrialization brought into the forest. But there was something about trains that softened their hard steel edges. Engineers often named their locomotives, but even when company bosses assigned iron horses numbers, there was a personal quality to the way men referred to reliable Number Nine, as "a great little teapot."[2] Lumberjacks affectionately named their lines "the Whiskey Northern," or "the Haywire Railroad," or "the Myrtle Navy Line." Yet these homey phrases obscure the technological revolution that railroads brought to logging.

THE TECHNOLOGY OF HARDWOOD LOGGING: FOREST OPERATIONS

Railroad technology was first applied to Upper Peninsula logging operations in 1879. In that year Wellington Burt and Henry Gamble, two lumbermen who made fortunes on the shores of Saginaw Bay, took over a pine mill in the little town of Grand Marais. The two men owned several million feet of timber on an eastward-flowing stream known as Sucker Creek. Because the creek, however, flowed in the opposite direction of their mill, Burt and Gamble built a seven-mile narrow gauge railroad line from Sucker Creek to another stream that did lead close to their mill. Their decision to build a railroad was considered daring. Only three years before, Winfield Scott Gerrish operated the first railroad logging venture in lower Michigan. It had proven spectacularly successful, but that was in the relatively settled Lower Peninsula; no one knew if the iron horse would prove practical in the remote forests of the Upper Peninsula. However, Burt and Gamble's seven-mile line operated for several years, opening up country otherwise isolated from the logger. After Burt and Gamble, the potential of railroad logging was not seriously doubted again.[3]

A predecessor of the logging railroad was the tramroad. The partnership of Beaufort and Martell, which logged on Delta County's Stonington Peninsula, used such a device to move logs from the interior to Lake Michigan. It was constructed of strap iron and powered by horses, its rolling stock was made up of wooden cars.[4] Similar outfits were used by Peter Mallmen, another Delta County pioneer logger, and by Russell Alger in lower Michigan.[5] Tramroads were necessary to move logs during the summer, when, of course, ice roads were impossible or where no rivers were near on which to drive logs. They could cost, however, as much as $125 per mile. Because they did not fare well with heavy loads, they were not practical for long hauls.[6]

Logging railroads began to be integrated with forest operations during the 1880s. In 1881 Holmes & Son, a logger under contract to Menominee's Kirby Carpenter Company, built a short rail line.[7] Two years later, Russell Alger's Manistique Lumber Company began to use a logging railway. The Wisconsin Land and Lumber Company began work on its private railroad the same year. Although, originally, the route of the Hermansville & Western Railroad was only ten miles, it became much longer in later years.[8] The pace quickened during the 1890s. The Chicago Lumber Company built the Manistique & Northwestern ("Haywire") Railroad in 1896. Isaac Stephenson invested in the first thirty-four miles of what became the Escanaba & Lake Superior Railroad in 1898.[9] By the beginning of the new century logging railroads were becoming a necessary part of almost all large Upper Peninsula lumber companies. Even the old pine logger, the Bay De Noquet Lumber Company, began work on a railroad in 1902. Across the bay from them, the Van's Harbor Land and Lumber Company also built a forest railroad. It never was much more than thirteen miles long, but its founders gave the line the grand name, the Van's Harbor & Northern Railroad.[10]

Railroads became essential to logging in the twentieth century because of the switch in emphasis from pine to hardwood. Unlike pine, it was difficult to float hardwood from the forest to the mill. Unlike river driving, railroad logging was efficient but expensive. Losses due to shrinkage or timber stealing were greatly reduced by logging railroads. Yet what made mill owners frown was the cost of building a rail line. The Wisconsin Land and Lumber Company paid out forty-two thousand dollars for its first few miles of track and rolling stock.[11] The Chicago Lumber Company spent a quarter of a million dollars building their logging line.[12]

One way to reduce the cost of railroad logging was to use narrow-gauge track and equipment. Narrow-gauge roads were cheaper to construct than the standard wide gauge used by trunk lines because they could be built with sharper curves, lighter rails, and less fill for grades. The engines and rolling stock for narrow gauge dominated forest railroads in many regions of the country. This was not, however, so in northern Michigan. Narrow gauge was used largely by poorly capitalized, short-term ventures. Most major logging firms went with standard gauge because such lines could carry heavier loads of logs and could transfer their rolling stock with trunk lines.[13] The Bay De Noquet Company, Cleveland-Cliffs, Cadillac-Soo, Chicago Lumber Company, even Ford Motor Company all went with standard gauge because they owned large blocks of forest and were planning on years of logging. For these giants of the region's industry, the long-term benefits were worth the start-up costs.

The building of logging railroads may have been expensive, but it was not necessarily very elaborate. Many companies eschewed the use of professional construction engineers and had the railroads laid out and built by loggers who learned railroading in the woods.[14] The equipment used in construction was minimal. Often horse-pulled graders would be used to help build a roadbed over low or swampy ground. However, an old logger recalls building up one grade solely with "three or four wash tubs" for holding dirt and the sweat of immigrant labor for hauling it. Brush and dirt were thrown on the soft spots and the men kept moving. Large trees were supposed to be cut and their stumps blasted out of the ground. But sometimes construction crews tried to save the cost of buying dynamite by cutting a tree down at ground level. The workers probably looked ridiculous kneeing at the base of a tree pulling on a crosscut saw. But the men were paid only a little more than a dollar a day, while dynamite cost over two dollars a crack.[15] Some logging roads looked pretty ragged. When the Ford Motor Company bought the Stearns and Culver Lumber Company railroad, it had to tear out the entire roadbed. This was partly because the old logging company had used narrow-gauge equipment, but also because it did not ballast its tracks. One of their lumberjacks told the Ford Motor Company: "The old company used to just throw in a few planks here and a few logs there and fix up a place to get by. . . . Half the time we were in the woods with locomotive off the track."[16]

The better lumbermen built their roads carefully. Some of these logging lines, such as the Manistique Railway of Russell Alger and the Chicago Lumber Company railroads, eventually became common carrying lines. Established railroad companies, such as the Chicago and North Western or the South Shore Line, often worked in conjunction with loggers. When the Holt Lumber Company began operations in Ontonagon County, it arranged to have the South Shore build a logging railroad six miles north from their main track. The South Shore Line operated this branch, but the Holt Lumber Company was required to build and operate the spurs that spread out into the forest and reached the actual logging areas.[17] The Chicago and North Western Railroad offered similar services. In 1906 the Mercer-DeLaittre Lumber company of Saint Paul, Minnesota, operated a hardwood flooring mill in the isolated hamlet of Calderwood. The company planned a spur line to link the mill with the North Western's main trunk. The logging company was given the task of clearing the right-of-way and preparing the grade.[18] Then the railroad came in and built the necessary bridges and laid the rail. Mercer-DeLaittre bought their own engine but paid rent for the use of North Western rolling stock, as well as for the rails and the fastenings that held them in place. When the spur was abandoned, this equipment was taken out and returned to the railroad company.[19] There was such a heavy demand from lumber companies for these sort of lend-lease agreements that in the Watersmeet, Michigan, area alone, the North Western employed several hundred workers.[20]

Railroads revolutionized forest operations. Clear-cutting—the cutting of all trees, large, small, sound, or rotten—not only became possible but necessary. Pine loggers, operating remote from their mills, could not afford to trim and transport cull (or rotten) trees. If lumberjacks cut down a white pine and found it was rotted by age or disease, they let it lie where it fell. However, once the iron horse came directly to the scene of the logging, it required little cost to load healthy as well as rotted logs. Indeed, the profit derived from the sale of cull logs to wood chemical distilleries helped offset the increased financial burden of building a railroad. Similarly, the limbs of trees, more pronounced on deciduous than on pine trees, were salvaged to sell as cordwood for charcoal or pulp production. Thus railroad logging ventures left a once forested landscape barren, save for bushes, stumps, and tangles of dried branches that were too small for cordwood.

Railroad logging also accelerated forest destruction in the north country. There had been a seasonal pattern to logging during the pine era. Woods operations were conducted in winter so that ice roads could be used to transport logs to the river bank. In the spring all logging stopped and attention was directed to the rivers whose spring freshets would carry the logs to the mill site. Railroads allowed for the year-round transportation of logs to market, which in turn allowed logging to continue year-round. There were types of hardwoods that lumbermen still preferred to cut during the winters. The Holt Lumber Company would not cut basswood during warm weather as they felt it would "spoil." They similarly avoided maple and birch during the summer.[21] But they and other lumbermen were active enough during the summer to exhaust timber reserves at an alarming rate.

Railroad technology gave lumbermen an opportunity to operate over a wider area, which helped compensate for the speed with which they exhausted an area. Delta County lumbermen, in the center of the peninsula near the hub of the rail network, could exploit forests throughout northern Michigan. The Stack Lumber Company, headquartered in Escanaba, had extensive operations in the Bryan and Germfask area of Schoolcraft County. By 1914 most of the company's eighty thousand acres were not in the same county as its main mill.[22] The Holt Lumber Company and the Diamond Match Company harvested logs more than two hundred miles and another state away from their mills.

Two basic types of locomotives were used in the northern Michigan logging industry. The first was the rod locomotive that excelled at high speed transport over long distances with easy grades and slow curves. Rod locomotives were favored by the trunk lines and by the lumber companies that operated on level ground over good track. The second type was the geared locomotive, first perfected in 1880 by Ephraim E. Shay, a lower Michigan lumberman. He wanted a locomotive that had greater pulling power on narrow gauge or poor track, and he built an engine that placed more of its weight over the wheels. Those wheels were also less likely to spin when pulling a heavy load or climbing a hill because a geared shaft linked each one. Because the Shay design was also smaller than most rod locomotives, it could operate over sharper curves and required rails secured by less ballast and fewer ties.[23] Small forest routes like the Van's Harbor and Northern Railroad used the slow but steady Shay engine.[24] This design became so popular among lumbermen that between 1881 and 1946 more than twenty-seven hundred Shay locomotives were sold by the Lima, Ohio, plant.[25] The Bay De Noquet company used the hard-working little Shay engine as well as another popular small locomotive built by the Baldwin Locomotive works. The Shays were better suited for work on spur tracks or in switching yards; the Baldwins worked well on the main track. The Manistique Railway of the Alger-Smith Company, the William Lumber Company of Chippewa County, and the I. Stephenson Company also used Baldwin locomotives.[26]

The most difficult area for railroad logging in northern Michigan was the rugged terrain of the western Upper Peninsula. Hills and mountains were the bane of a railroad engineer's life. The tractive force of a locomotive is greatly reduced by inclines. Professional engineers avoided grades greater than three percent (a three-foot rise over 100 feet of track). Railroad loggers who were not building for posterity but only to exploit a limited resource accepted steeper grades. Such decisions often came back to haunt loggers, for steep grades generally meant longer hauling times, larger construction costs, and greater chance of accident. One bold lumber concern, the Porterfield & Ellis Company, operated a logging spur that had grades as great as twenty percent! This seemingly impossible stretch of railroad track was in the Ontonagon River Valley. The fifteen-mile main track of the Porterfield & Ellis line had to cross both the Ontonagon River and a tributary, Rousseau Creek. The river crossing was complicated by two hundred-foot hills on both flanks of the mile-wide valley. To climb these hills and two slightly lower ones near Rousseau Creek Porterfield & Ellis adopted what might be termed the "roller coaster approach." When a log train approached the valley, the engineer would allow the train to glide down the first steep embankment; gravity and momentum gave the train terrific speed. As the train reached the bottom of the hill, he opened up the throttle to full speed,

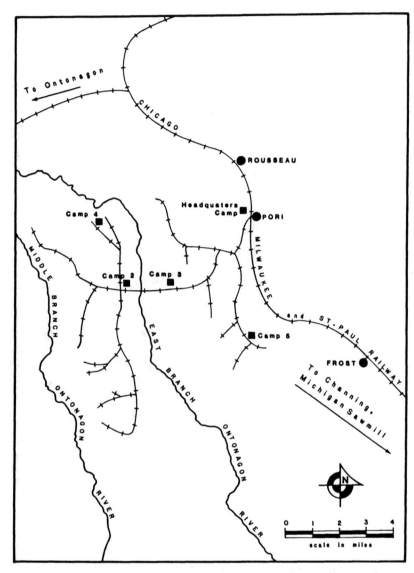

Spatial Arrangement of the Porterfield and Ellis Logging Rail Network near
Ontonagon, 1916–1928
Source: Clinton Jones, "World's Steepest Adhesion Railroad?", *Trains*, June
1969

calling forth the Baldwin engine's full strength. Usually the train had just enough speed built up to crest the second hill and carry it on its way. Occasionally a train could not make the second hill. To avoid being stranded in the valley, the crew would sidetrack one or two log cars before trying to climb out by rocking the train back and forth, full throttle, then reverse throttle, up the slopes until enough momentum was built up to seesaw out. Porterfield & Ellis operated a remarkable eight years over the river loop, as it was called, without a serious accident. Such a safety record was possible only because of the careful maintenance of the rail grade. To speed log trains down steep hills and across trestle bridges at a mile-a-minute speed would spell disaster on most logging railroads.[27]

The swampy terrain of the eastern Upper Peninsula also posed special challenges to the railroad logger. The Manistique Railway encountered soft ground and sinkholes when it was extended across the Seney Swamps. Sinkholes were expensive to build over. One such obstacle required thousands of feet of white pine and tons of gravel to fill. Years later, a string of flatcars left at the spot overnight sank into the hole, along with the entire roadbed. Local legend maintains there was no way to retrieve the cars, so the roadbed was filled in right over the sunken train.[28] The Worcester Lumber Company, which specialized in swamp cedar logging, compensated for the terrain in several ways. One strategy was logging in the winter when below-zero temperatures assured the logger of solid, frozen ground. Worcester also favored lightweight power equipment that did not put excess weight on the roadbed and allowed for quick harvesting of swamp cedar. Steam engines mounted on rail cars used eight hundred-foot steel cables to pull trees from the swamp to the train for loading.[29]

The use of steam engines in the forest area was not restricted to locomotives. Clear-cutting encouraged the adaptation of other labor-saving machines to handle the increased volume of logs and cordwood produced by logging operations. One such device was a steam hauler. A Pine Tree State manufacturer, Alvin Lombard, invented the first practical steam hauler. He adopted a Shay locomotive to operate without a track by replacing its wheels with a cleated tread. Without a track Lombard had to supply his machine with a steering mechanism. This he did by replacing the front wheels of the engine with a bobsled and securing a driver's seat and a steering wheel to the sled. Originally, Lombard manufactured his own haulers, but in 1903 his patent was taken over by the Phoenix Manufacturing Company of Eau Claire, Wisconsin.[30] The use of Phoenix haulers was never widespread in the industry. Yet several lumbermen in the Upper Peninsula found them useful. They were particularly popular with loggers operating in terrain unsuitable for railroads. Logger R. H. Jenny of Ishpeming and the Sawyer-Goodman

Company both used haulers in the Huron Mountains. Under good conditions, when a proper ice road was prepared, the hauler did yeoman service for Sawyer-Goodman, pulling as much wood in one haul as ten or twelve horse-powered sleighs combined. R. H. Jenny's hauler pulled only eight sleds, each carrying five thousand feet of logs. The hauler was particularly good for long hauls. Jenny's hauler pulled sleighs nine miles from the site of logging to the main track of the Chicago and North Western Railroad. Unlike horses, which tired out, the steam hauler could be worked twenty-four hours a day, so it made the eighteen-mile round-trip twice a day.[31]

Steam haulers proved their superiority on steep hills. Sawyer-Goodman's hauler pulled sleighs up a 250-foot hill near Champion, Michigan, in 1910. The grades on that ice road were between twenty-five and thirty-five percent, impossible for horse or train. Yet steam haulers were sensitive machines and were more prone to breakdowns than the old reliable horse sleighs. They were also less tolerant of poor weather conditions. They were at their best in below-zero weather; a warming trend could reduce their efficiency. The heavy weight of the Phoenix hauler caused it to bite deep into a soft road, ruining it for the sleighs in tow.[32] For these reasons, only about 100 Phoenix haulers were ever made.[33]

During the hardwood era loggers also experimented with equipment that would allow them to log during the summer. As logging became linked to expensive technology, such as railroads, and its products were used by manufacturers, such as barrel makers, chemical companies, paper producers, and automobile combines, there was considerable pressure to log year-round. Summer logging ensured that forest equipment was earning back its investment and ensured that the production schedules of district plants were not disrupted by a shortage of wood. Upper Peninsula lumbermen borrowed several devices from colleagues elsewhere to move logs the short distance from forest to trackside. One such device was the Big Wheel. It was invented by Iowa farmers during the 1850s and then introduced to Wisconsin and Michigan forests.[34] The Big Wheels, which were indeed large, twelve feet in diameter, were joined together by an axle. The wheels could easily move logs over dry ground by hitching a team to the device and slinging a log from the axle. The wheels held only one end of the log off the ground, but they did bear most of its weight. One set of Big Wheels and a team of horses could haul two or three large logs several hundred yards over partly cleared ground. Big Wheels were not popular in hilly or mountainous terrain, but on the level plain of the eastern Upper Peninsula they were often used.[35]

Instead of Big Wheels, some northern Michigan lumbermen experimented with cable logging. This approach was used by the Worcester

Lumber Company to cut quickly on swampy terrain. It was also the basic technique of far western lumbermen operating on the slopes of mountains. Originally the technique was pioneered by Horace Butters, a lower Michigan pine logger. During the 1880s he devised an overhead cable rig suspended over the logging ground from a large "spartree." A steam donkey engine pulled the logs up off the ground through the air along the cable and to the decking area.[36] Several Upper Peninsula loggers experimented with this system, most notably the Richardson, Avery Company in Chippewa County. But cable logging, because of the time and expense to install an overhead rig, did not take root in Michigan.[37]

One innovation that did take root and became essential for the modern logger was the steam loader. The loading of logs onto sleighs or railcars had long been one of the most dangerous and time-consuming phases of forest operations. An early method for loading logs onto railcars entailed a simple device known as a cross haul. It was merely two planks extended against the side of the railcar to form an inclined plane. A log would be rolled up the plane with the help of a horse on the opposite side of the track.[38] It was a simple and quick procedure for loading the first few logs, but as the car filled and logs were laid upon logs, it became time-consuming and dangerous. It also required the labor of five men and a team of horses. A better way was adopted by 1912 with the popularization of the Forest Loader. This method also used horsepower but was composed of a pole and a swinging boom, which actually lifted the log into the air and onto the car.[39] The steam loader replaced wooden poles with a steel derrick and horses with a coal-fired engine. However, the principal advantage of the best of the steam loaders was their ability to hoist the entire engine house fifteen feet so that the loaded car of logs could pass beneath them and an empty car moved into position. Once a steam loader was in position, it could load an entire train in a matter of hours. It was not unusual to have a steam loader service twenty-five to thirty cars per day.[40]

TECHNOLOGY OF HARDWOOD LOGGING: THE MILL

The complexity of mill activities greatly increased during the transition for the pine logging frontier to the hardwood era. Mid-nineteenth-century lumbermen principally concerned themselves with sawlogs or shingles; a few were devoted to charcoal iron production. By the early twentieth century, northern mills were producing many specialized forest products. Besides traditional sawmills producing board lumber, northern Michigan capitalists established plants for the production of woodenware, wood alcohol, flooring, veneer, cooperage, and furniture. Lumber companies were also involved in the production of fence posts, broom handles, lath, telephone poles, and tanning acid. No one company tried to produce all these potential products, but there was a marked increase in the size of industrial sites during this period as special plants were put into effect.

A good example of a hardwood era mill center is the I. Stephenson Company of Wells, Michigan. The company's lumberjacks harvested white pine, Norway pine, cedar, spruce, tamarack, balsam, maple, beech, elm, birch, basswood, and hemlock. The pine, cedar, and spruce were shipped to the company's softwood mill. There, gang saws and double band saws reduced the logs that were large enough into boards. Once cut, the boards were transferred to drying kilns. In early pine logging days, boards were dried at Chicago or Milwaukee lumberyards. However, dry kilns produced a better seasoned piece of lumber. From the kilns, some of the boards went to a planing mill attached directly to the softwood plant. At the planing mill, special saws reduced the large pine boards to the dimensions required for siding, molding, or paneling. Small softwood logs were dispatched to a nearby shingle mill or lath mill.[41]

I. Stephenson hardwood logs went through a similar, though separate, process. The large logs were made into boards and kiln-dried for shipment to lumberyards. A few boards went to a planing mill where they were cut into dimension lumber for the local market. Maple boards were sent to a giant hardwood flooring mill. The Wisconsin Land and Lumber Company had pioneered the production of maple flooring in the Upper Peninsula. I. Stephenson got into the business by hiring Edwin C. Shank, a foreman at the Hermansville plant. Shank took his knowledge of the Wisconsin Land and Lumber process with him and helped lay out one of the largest flooring plants in the country at Wells. The key to the flooring mill was the rapid cutting of narrow strips of defect-free maple so that the ends of pieces could be properly matched when actual construction began. Special machines were required for cutting, matching, and bundling the strips of wood.[42]

Shipping was complicated at large hardwood-era mills because of so many types, grades, and sizes of products. Massive warehouses, carefully inventoried, were necessary to store the lumber. The I. Stephenson Company maintained an extensive docking area for water commerce. Its mills were also serviced by a rail yard that offered connections with six common carriers. Like many of the later pine-era plants, the extensive I. Stephenson factories were powered by electricity produced from the company's dam across the Escanaba River.[43]

Most forest products reached the mill by rail, but log driving and log rafting still brought enough raw material to make most mill men continue to favor waterfront locations for their plants. Even loggers such as the Northwestern Cooperage Company or the Cleveland-Cliffs Iron Company, which operated their own logging railroads, used log drives to send cedar or pulpwood to their plants. Hemlock, an important timber type during the early twentieth century, could be floated if it was first debarked. Large rafts of hemlock were hauled along the Lake Superior shore through the 1920s.[44]

Rail transportation and production innovations were vital in making charcoal iron production an important facet of the hardwood era. By the late 1880s the industry was clearly in decline. Some of the largest plants, such as that at Fayette, were closing because of high operation costs and limited fuel supplies. Railroads gave charcoal iron producers an opportunity to tap a broader area of forest as well as the ability to exploit that forest more intensely. Equally as significant were changes in the production of charcoal. The sites of early charcoal iron plants were dotted with dozens of beehivelike rock kilns, loaded with cordwood transformed by fire into charcoal. The kilns, however, were extremely inefficient. It would take more than a month to produce a load of charcoal worth only forty-five cents a bushel.[45] However, more than time was lost in the kilns; the fuel burned unevenly resulting in the squandering of fine hardwood. Nor did the process retain the potentially valuable gasses produced by charcoal making.

The leader in charcoal making in the Upper Peninsula was the Charcoal Iron Company of America. This giant logger and iron smelter grew slowly in northern Michigan by incorporating several smaller producers. An early predecessor was the Burrell Chemical Company, which had combined Abijah Weston's Manistique Iron Company, founded in 1887, and the Weston Furnace Company. Later, Detroit capitalists became interested in a scheme to establish a network of modern charcoal iron facilities across the hardwood belt of northern Michigan and Wisconsin. With money from the Union Trust Company, the Manistique firm evolved into the Lake Superior Iron and Chemical Company. Additional plants were built or renovated at Newbury, Marquette, and Ashland. In 1917, with production scoaring, the company was reorganized and named the Charcoal Iron Company of America.[46]

By investing in new technology, the company made more money from chemical production than from iron smelting. A new charcoal producing process was made possible by installing retort plants, which were large iron ovens, externally heated and airtight. They did not burn off valuable wood, and succeeded in trapping all chemicals that were released. Each day the Newberry plant, the company's most modern, produced two hundred cords of charcoal. The chemicals trapped by the retort were taken to another plant where they were separated into wood alcohol and acetate.[47] Nor did the Charcoal Iron Company waste quality hardwood by converting it into charcoal. The best woods went to a large electric-powered sawmill attached to the plants. The lumber produced further contributed to the profitability of the venture. Tree limbs and lower-grade timber were used for charcoal production.[48] The production of charcoal for smelting became an increasingly less significant feature of the Charcoal Iron Company's operations. By the 1930s the entire emphasis of these works was on chemical and lumber production.[49]

FOREST RESOURCES OF THE HARDWOOD ERA

The Upper Peninsula was hardwood country. Perhaps as much of the region as 4.7 million acres was covered by forests composed of yellow birch, sugar maple, hemlock, elm, basswood, and beech. During the first decade of the century, the cutting of these lands and the forests of lower Michigan gave the Great Lake State the distinction of being the leading hardwood producer in North America.[50]

The nature of this vast hardwood forest greatly affected the way the logging industry patterned its exploitation. Lumberjacks moving into upland broad-leafed forests were struck by the size of individual trees, often growing more than 100 feet from the forest floor. Their green canopy branched outward, darkening the earth below. Such trees, magnificent in appearance, represented a mature forest. In some stands most of the trees were past their prime and weakened by rot. Less mature stands were very likely to contain many branches and limbs because of a lower forest canopy.[51] Therefore, lumbermen had to find a profitable use for cullwood and tree limbs if they were to fully exploit a hardwood forest.

Hardwood logging was further complicated because deciduous trees of northern Michigan were seldom found in pure stands. Unlike pine or cedar that occasionally could be found in dense, solid stands of a single species, northern hardwoods were usually found intermixed with other types. These timber associations were common because the environmental conditions found in most of the Upper Peninsula were conducive to the growth of several different kinds of hardwood and softwood species. One typical stand of hardwood might contain beech, birch, elm, and maple; another might contain maple, basswood, elm, and hemlock, perhaps even some pine.[52] Under such forest conditions, the coordination of mill production schedules with logging activities was made more difficult. Many different logs—suited for various products—were shipped from a single logging operation.

Maple, for example, might be made into lumber, furniture, or flooring. The Cleveland-Cliffs Iron Company selected its best bird's-eye maple for sale to other companies in the paneling business.[53] Basswood was one of the most important and versatile of the northern hardwoods. Among the many uses to which it was applied were house siding, cheap furniture, and woodenware. Basswood's soft, malleable texture and its ecru white color made it a popular species for veneer and woodenware producers. Before plastic and paper vessels took over the consumer-disposable industry, basswood was the favored material for containers holding butter, lard, fruits, and vegetables. Upper Peninsula basswood was known for its clear, defect-free texture.[54] Elm was favored for the making of cooperage, and birch found many uses from flooring to spools for thread. Hemlock was used for rail ties, mine timbers, lumber, and pulpwood. Hemlock bark spawned, for a time, an entire subsidiary industry for the region.

Hemlock bark contained tannic acid that was then used to treat cattle hides. During the late 1890s tanneries were established across northern Michigan and Wisconsin. One of the biggest companies was the United States Leather Company, which operated several plants in Wisconsin, near the Michigan line. Such plants allowed many logging companies to derive a profit from bark they had previously thrown away. Lumberjacks, paid on a piecework basis, were sent into hemlock forests during the summer. They cut down the trees and used a special tool known as a "bark spud" to pry the bark off the log. A former bark peeler remembered:

> They helped move the sheet of bark with one hand and used the spud with the other hand. They often wished they had two more hands to fight off flies and mosquitoes. I have honestly seen mosquitoes so bad that you could hardly tell if a man had a shirt on or not. Some people ask how the men stood it. It is a good question. You just had to become immune to them. Some homemade lotions helped, such as pine tar and lard. Skunk grease was good, too. . . . It took real men to peel bark successfully in those days.

Bark was scaled by the cord and shipped by rail to the tanneries. Although eastern tanneries used bark from other trees, only hemlock bark was harvested in the lake states.[55]

Hemlock bark harvesting ended during the 1920s. Quebraco, a forest product from South America, supplanted hemlock and the lake states tanneries closed within a few years.

The cutting and peeling of bark during the summer dovetailed nicely with the complex pattern of hardwood logging. Most hardwood species could not be cut during the summer, when the tree's sap was rising because the wood tended to stain. But lumbermen wanted to get year-round production out of their forest railroads. Fortunately, hemlock peeling needed to take place during the summer because the running of sap freely through the trees made the bark looser and therefore easier to peel.[56]

The diversity of products produced from a single area of hardwood forest gave railroad loggers fits. Birch, elm, and maple might all be cut together and hauled to the landing at the same time, but they would often have to be segregated for loading because they might be destined for different mills. Nor could hardwood logs be left stacked in the forest as long as pine. Fungi affected hardwood much quicker and could ruin the value of a log for veneer or paneling purposes.[57]

In response to the several northern hardwood associations, some lumber companies tried to enter into agreements for the exchange of specific timber types. For example, the Wisconsin Land and Lumber Company, renowned for its maple floors, agreed to send elm to the Northwestern Cooperage and Lumber Company. In return, the barrel maker sent its maple logs to the Wisconsin Land and Lumber Company's Hermansville flooring plant. Each company scaled the railcars of logs it received from the other and was given a credit up to the amount of their current market value. The arrangements was operative for many years, though it was marred by regular disputes over the correct scale of logs shipped or the quality of logs received.[58] Nor could the cooperage company buy as much elm from its partner as it would have liked. In 1909 the Northwestern Cooperage Company built its own flooring mill and began to use its maple in cooperation with the Hermansville concern.[59] Even big timberland owners such as the Cleveland-Cliffs Iron Company or the Ford Motor Company occasionally had to enter into cooperative agreements with other firms. The Cleveland-Cliffs lumber department leased or bought cutover lands from the Northwestern Cooperage Company and from the Charcoal Iron Company to supply its Gladstone, Michigan, chemical plant with cordwood.[60]

Although hardwood forests were exploited intensively, they were not as productive as the old pine stands. It was sometimes possible for a gang of pine sawyers to cut twenty thousand board feet of logs in a day. In contrast, a hardwood gang would usually average about five thousand feet per day. The difference was partly a result of hardwood's much more plentiful branches and limbs. Pine trees required little in the way of trimming, or, as lumberjacks referred to the task, swamping. But during the hardwood era swamping became a larger task. Also, pine trees in northern Michigan were much less likely to be defective than the often too mature hardwood forest.[61]

Hardwood's propensity of branches left more slash per tree in the forest than pine logging. Although it is true that Ford Motor Company and several others undertook experimental efforts to remove logging debris, most loggers salvaged the larger branches and let the rest lie where it fell. Forest fires plagued the region annually until 1940. These blazes destroyed thousands of dollars worth of property and ruined many acres of standing timber. Yet the scourge of forest fires affected hardwood cutovers differently than the old pine lands. Hardwood slash and stumps decomposed quickly so that such cutovers posed a fire threat for a much briefer time. Even when such fires hit, their destructiveness was nowhere near as great as on the pine plains because the loamier soils favored by the northern hardwoods proved more durable. Rapid forest recovery was common for hardwood stands. Regrettably, maple and birch forests were not generally replaced by similar species. Northern hardwoods represented the climax forest; in their wake came fast-growing, economically less valuable "weed trees."[62]

Although hardwoods dominated Upper Peninsula logging between 1900 and 1930, a considerable minority of lumbermen focused on the swampy wetlands to harvest cedar and swamp conifers. The ready market for cedar posts, poles, and ties made that species valued by all lumbermen, although several concerns, National Pole Company, Diamond Pole and Piling Company, Standard Post and Tie, and others specialized in cedar logging. Spruce and tamarack, trees of the conifer swamps, received serious exploitation for the first time during the early twentieth century. Tamarack and spruce were resorted to as mine timbers when pine and hemlock became short.[63] A less significant but nonetheless interesting use of swamp conifers was "ship knees." These were hockey stick-shaped sections of tamarack limbs, between five and fifteen inches thick, that were used for the ribbing of wooden hulled ships. However, the limited logging that took place on the poorly drained balsam and spruce forests in the early twentieth century was merely a prelude to the final phase of northern Michigan's logging frontier.

SPATIAL DIMENSIONS OF THE HARDWOOD ERA

The pine era's reliance on water transportation created a unique spatial arrangement on the landscape, one that stands in sharp relief to the hardwood era that followed. Although log drives still took place after 1900, waterways handled only a modest percentage of the logs moving from forest to mill. The dominance of the iron horse and the density of hardwood logs, which prevented them from floating, created a distinct land-use pattern, which in some ways was even more pervasive than that of the pine era.

Between 1900 and 1930 railroads went where the timber was. The rights-of-way of logging railroads and spur tracks were dotted with the locations of logging camps. Where formerly access to a driving water-way was vital to planning a logging venture, railroads opened up almost the entire forest to the lumberjack. In contrast to past years, hardwood-era lumbermen working for the Cleveland-Cliffs Iron Company and the Cadillac-Soo Company could not recall any corporate logging camps adjacent to a navigable waterway. Until the 1930s these firms were al-most exclusively involved with railroad logging. It was not unusual for logging railroads to pass directly through the center of the campsite—within a few feet of the buildings.[64]

Some companies bowed to the rapid pace of railroad logging by not building traditional logging shanties, but instead mounted the dwellings on rails. Car camps, as they were called, originated in northern Wiscon-sin during the early 1890s.[65] As early as 1891 mobile car camps were experimented with in the Upper Peninsula.[66] By the 1920s some of the area's most important loggers, such as Cleveland-Cliffs and the Charcoal Iron Company, adopted this system for at least some of their operations.

Car camps were composed of a kitchen car, dining car, several board-ing cars, and usually an office. The kitchen car usually required a long ventilator on the roof to dissipate the heat build-up in the car from the baking that was ongoing. The dining car was divided into ten to twelve tables of six men each. The sleeping cars offered single bunks stacked three high. One lumberjack remembered: "Straw or conifer boughs were used for mattresses, whichever the sleeper preferred. They were not bad. I slept in one bed for two months with no after effects. I used a sack partly filled with bran for a pillow." The only structures built on the ground at a car camp were the root cellar, outhouse, and well.[67]

Car camps were used during the spring through the autumn for hem-lock peelers, summer loggers, or railroad building crews. Because dwell-ing cars were elevated on rails and lacked insulation, they were less than desirable as year-round accommodations. They were used only by the lumber companies that owned large solid blocks of territory. Such car camps had to be specially built to the logger's own specifications and therefore were expensive. They paid for themselves in adaptability only over the long haul.[68] Like logging railroads, steam haulers, and other new technology, car camps were a useful innovation that helped to accel-erate the cost of logging and encouraged the concentration of timber-lands. Large lumber companies found it more practical to buy extensive holdings rather than have their forest railroads pass through land they did not own. This meant that a lease of right-of-way had to be negotiated, and more importantly, no profit could be derived from those sections of track.

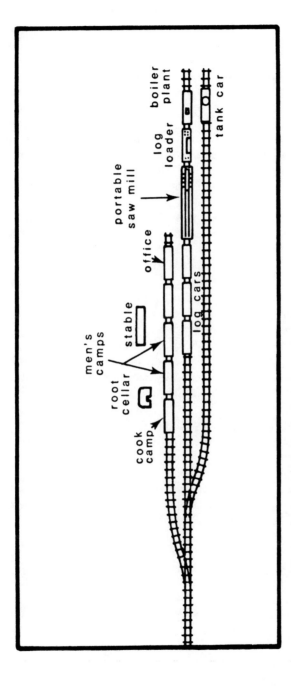

Spatial Arrangement of a Portable Railroad Logging Camp
Source: "Charcoal Iron Company," *American Lumberman*, February 3, 1916

The Hardwood Era

Not only could railroads rapidly move camp locations from cutover areas to the heart of the forest, but they also brought sawmills into the woods. Portable sawmills, which could be easily set up and taken down in a matter of days, began to appear in the forest after 1900, in the wake of the iron horse. Such portable mills often were used in conjunction with railroad building for they could be used to transform the trees that blocked the right-of-way into ties for the rails. The Charcoal Iron Company experimented with a rail mill in 1916. The mill was erected on a sidetrack and was powered by a separate boiler plant mounted on an adjacent railcar. This mill could be moved in a matter of hours. Most portable sawmills were used in conjunction with cordwood operations. Because the mills could produce only between five and seven thousand board feet per day, they were not serious rivals to the giant stationary mills.[69]

The railroad encouraged the establishment of highly mobile logging car camps, and they also abetted the maintenance of large stationary camps. During the pine era, a camp of 100 men was considered a very large crew. However, the crews of some hardwood loggers, such as the Cadillac-Soo Company or Cleveland-Cliffs, boasted more than 200 men. Such large camps often grew into temporary villages in the forest. The many dwellings, cook shacks, barns, root cellars, and warehouses were a costly investment—not eagerly abandoned or moved. Often quarters would also be provided for the railroad crews, and a roundhouse might be built for the train engine. When the Cleveland-Cliffs Iron Company built such a large camp, it was usually maintained in one location for five years.[70] Railroads made such camps possible by bringing large quantities of supplies regularly into the forest. Spur trains and rail speeders could relatively quickly bring crews of men from central camp locations to the scene of logging, thereby extending the life of a camp location.

Many times these large railroad camps existed side by side or were transformed into cordwood-choppers villages. Unlike the all-male lumber camps, these villages featured individual family dwellings for married men and a boardinghouse for bachelors. They worked chopping the large limbs and branches of hardwood trees into stacks of cordwood. The villages were supplied by logging railroads, which hauled the wood to distant chemical plants. An example of this type of settlement was the village of Half. It began life as a Charcoal Iron Company logging camp. When the sawlogs were taken out, the site was taken over by cordwood choppings. A handful of shacks and adjacent garden plots marked the town site, which, for a time, had enough children to support its own schoolhouse. But when the nearby cutover lands were cleared of cordwood, the residents moved on and the site went back to nature.[71]

Cordwood choppers' villages, large corporate camps, and mobile car camps were tied to the railroad; there were also logging activities that were started remote from the steel rail. These were sections of forest that could not be reached by either waterways or logging railroads, and they were very risky areas in which to undertake operations. Few corporations were willing to risk logging anywhere that required more than a short haul to their rails. Remote locations were left up to independent contractors, jobbers, who committed themselves to taking out the timber and return for a set price. In 1921, for example, Francis Furlong, a small-scale independent logger, assumed a contract to take out tamarack from difficult-to-reach sections of forest. His men had to carry all their equipment and supplies for three miles just to reach the campsite. The trail Furlong blazed to the site passed over largely swampy ground. In many places, poles had to be cut and placed on the trail to keep men and horses from sinking into the moss and muck. Working three miles from the rail over bad terrain made Furlong's task of road building and log hauling all the more difficult. Because jobbers camps were often more isolated and were moved more often, they tended to be more primitive than the larger corporate camps.[72]

Logging railroads tended to sustain and even increase the numbers of the small lumber processing centers of the interior of the Upper Peninsula. Towns such as Basswood, Elmwood, and Bergland were nurtured by hardwood logging, just as Seney, Ewen, and Trout Creek had grown up on pine. These towns not only acted as mill towns and supply depots for loggers, but also provided commerce and markets for the many backwoods farmers who settled in the forest. Hardwood cutovers had the rich loamy soil favored by Michigan farmers, and the logging railroads provided access from the small towns to the forest farms. During the hardwood era, the interior of the Upper Peninsula was more thickly settled than it would ever be again. For when the forest thinned, the railroads were closed, the towns decayed, and the backwoods farms, like a plant without roots, withered and died.

9

THE SOCIAL ENVIRONMENT OF
HARDWOOD LOGGING

In March 1919 lumbermen from eleven companies met in Marquette, Michigan. The quietly gathered, private affair was billed as a "Meeting of Representative Lumbermen of Upper Michigan." The purpose of the meeting was to discuss common problems. Herman Kunnert of the Charcoal Iron Company complained of the shortage of railcars for cordwood hauling. A report was made by one lumberman that demonstrated that United States Army cooks prepared meals cheaper than most lumber camp cooks, which spurred a Cleveland-Cliffs official to note: "The lumber industry has been cursed for years with inefficient and wasteful cooks." A motion was passed advocating the better training of camp cooks. The lumbermen present also polled each other concerning the wages they paid. The Lake Independence Lumber Company of Big Bay, Michigan, found to its chagrin that it paid considerably higher wages than any other operators. Before the meeting concluded, a report was made predicting an increase in Midwestern housing starts, which left lumbermen confident of the future and pleased with their afternoon meeting.[1]

The Marquette gathering of "representative lumbermen" was a sign of the growing sophistication of the logging industry during the first decades of the twentieth century. Trade or protective associations became popular with lumber manufacturers during the late nineteenth century. They proved an important vehicle for the establishment of standard grades and sizes of lumber. The competitiveness of pine era lumbermen and the primitive simplicity of their operations made industrial organization insignificant during the nineteenth century. However, hardwood lumbermen, who invested sizeable amounts of capital in an endeavor that harvested many timber types and was capable of a plethora of products, felt more inclined to seek cooperation over competition.

There were also national forces at work. American business under-

went a profound change during the years between the Panic of 1873 and
the beginning of the twentieth century. Small-scale, family-operated industries were reoriented from the local, often rural, market to the dynamic opportunities of national, urban markets. The railroad was behind this change. It not only provided the means for rapid commercial
circulation across American, but was the model for the new organizational structure of the business community: the large, vertically integrated corporation. Giant enterprises emerged, which controlled all
facets of the production of raw materials, finished products, by-products,
and sales. Major industries became dominated by a few corporations,
such as United States Steel Corporation or Standard Oil. However, the
hardwood era lumber industry, because of its poor competitive structure,
which allowed for the easy entry of competition, did not produce a handful of giants. Yet it did feel the tug of national currents of consolidation.
In the Upper Peninsula, this is best demonstrated by the concentration
of timberland ownership and the movement to effect regional trade
cooperation.

By 1913 ninety elite timberland holders controlled fifty-six percent of
the land in the Upper Peninsula. A mere thirteen of those accounted for
a full thirty-seven percent of the region. The Cleveland-Cliffs Iron
Company was the greatest of these. If its holdings had been merged into
a single unit, it would have covered sixty-six townships. Cleveland-Cliffs
stood with such behemoths as the Southern Pacific Company, Northern
Pacific Company, Weyerhaeuser Timber, and the Consolidated Land
Company as the five biggest forest owners in the United States. Other
northern Michigan firms owning more than one hundred thousand
acres were I. Stephenson, Bay De Noquet, Worcester, and the Charcoal
Iron Company.[2]

There were several factors encouraging forest consolidation. The
price of timberlands increased steadily between 1890 and 1910. Speculative investors as well as lumbermen fearing a timber famine competed
with one another to secure holdings. Several of the Upper Peninsula's
large forest owners were not logging companies at all, but natural resource investors. The prospect of securing a profit from the increasing
value of stumpage also appealed to lumbermen but they were more motivated by fear. The high cost of railroad building and the multiple mills
needed to produce hardwood products drove lumbermen to purchase
extensive timberlands. A twenty-year supply of timber was generally estimated as necessary to adequately offset the start-up costs of a major
hardwood manufacturing plant. An expensive mill sitting idle for lack of
logs was a lumberman's nightmare.[3]

It was not inevitable that timberland ownership would become dominant in the Upper Peninsula logging industry. It was true that most

early mills established in the Upper Peninsula controlled the timber-lands off which they cut, but this was by no means universal. On the Menominee River there were several mills, such as the McCarthy Mill and the R. W. Merrymen Company, that did not own forestlands. Instead, they purchased their logs on the open market.[4] This had been the tradition at early mills in Maine. Indeed, many independent loggers did not own mills but did purchase timberlands and cut logs. Flanigan and Nelligan were among the more prominent loggers who did not invest in sawmills. Even on Puget Sound, which had become the cockpit of the lumber industry during the early twentieth century, independent loggers cut trees and sold the logs to mills that operated without timber-lands.[5] In the Upper Peninsula, however, the logging industry polarized between the elite real estate–rich, capital-intense large operators and the small operators, whose access to timberlands became increasingly restricted.

What helped encourage timberland concentration in northern Michigan was the massive transfer of public lands to private hands that had taken place in the nineteenth century. Millions of acres, often in large checkerboardlike blocks, were granted to construction companies for transportation improvements. Lumbermen were therefore mostly able to purchase the solid blocks of territory necessary for successful railroad logging. The Cleveland-Cliffs Company acquired 48,000 acres from canal companies, the Bay De Noquet Company bought 13,480, and the Charcoal Iron Company ended up with more than 77,000 acres of former canal lands.[6]

During the early twentieth century, the lumbermen who made the massive investments necessary to build plants and secure timber began to work for greater control over the market. The example of the oil trust and steel trust demonstrated how control over competition could produce greater profits. Despite much speculation, no one could establish a similar timber trust; forestlands were still too numerous and the number of lumbermen too great. So it was to trade associations that lumbermen turned to achieve control over their industry through cooperation. As early as 1895 Michigan lumbermen had nascent hardwood trade associations. In 1910 two of these organizations joined to form the Northern Hemlock and Hardwood Manufacturers Association. It was headquartered in Oshkosh, Wisconsin, and represented about 100 lumbermen from that state and northern Michigan. Its basic program centered on the promotion and sale of general hardwood products.[7] Special associations devoted to particular hardwood products also were established. For example, there was the Veneer and Panel Manufacturers Association and the Maple Flooring Manufacturers Association.[8]

The latter organization reveals the problems hardwood lumbermen faced trying to control their trade. The association was born in 1897 at the initiative of J. E. Defebaugh, the editor of *The Timberman*. His basic reason for cooperation was price control. "The maple flooring producers are not many," he noted, "while the consumers are numbered by the thousands." If the maple floor makers agreed on a set price, they could avoid the losses many of them were suffering. The association was dominated by midwestern manufacturers, and George Washington Earle of the Wisconsin Land and Lumber Company took the lead. Despite the standard price set by the association, many members would quietly cut their prices to increase sales when faced with hard times. To maintain discipline, the association secretly made what amounted to trade agreements. By 1923 this practice had gone far enough to invite an antitrust suit for conspiracy to eliminate trade. A lower court judge ruled against the association and ordered it abolished. The members were forced to take their case to the United States Supreme Court, which was less harsh and allowed the association to continue to gather and dispense information on prices without forming fixed agreements.[9]

The Maple Flooring Manufacturers Association case revealed the limits to which associations could go to aid their members, but it did not restrain the growing importance of such organizations in the Upper Peninsula. Even logging, long the most competitive feature of the lumber industry, the facet where so many fortunes were won or lost, was influenced by the cooperative trend.[10] In December 1917 the Northeastern Wisconsin and Upper Peninsula Logger's Association was formed. Membership was open to any lumberman or logging jobber who handled more than a million feet of logs a year. The association's first action was to vote to support the war effort, and members reduced their expenses by sponsoring "meatless" and "wheatless" days in their camps.[11] Another organization that represented loggers in the region was the Upper Peninsula Loggers Association. Each year these organizations met together with other Wisconsin groups at a convention known as the Northern Logging Congress.

One of the biggest challenges to the new logging associations came from timber workers' similar attempt to organize. Behind this move was the Industrial Workers of the World (IWW). Known to friend and foe alike as "Wobblies" the IWW had been formed in Chicago in 1905. It soon made a reputation as one of the most radical labor groups in the country. Its most successful organizing efforts were among lumber and mine workers in the far west. However, in 1916 the Wobblies returned to the midwest and were leaders in a mill workers and lumberjack strike in northern Minnesota. The strike lasted a little more than a month and ended in failure for the one thousand men who walked off their jobs. But it was only the opening round in a regionwide fight to organize the lumber industry work force.[12]

The Wobblies were greeted with hostility by many workers but conditions favored their success. The lumber market was slow between 1914 and 1916; wages were low; labor was plentiful. However, by the spring of 1916 the World War I boom was spreading to the forest. The demand for labor increased but wages did not. Nor did conditions in the camps improve; they remained little different from during the pioneer pine days. When the United States entered the war in 1917, labor became even more dear as thousands of timber workers went to the armed services. Birch was a vital war supply, needed for the production of allied warplanes; hardwoods were also needed for gun stocks. Although wages did inch gradually upward, the men were asked to work hard and long for the war effort. Fear of the draft also may have held men in check.[13] When the war ended in November 1918, timber workers in northern Wisconsin and Michigan were restless.

Representatives of the IWW competed with the American Federation of Labor (AFL) organizers to sign up dissatisfied workers. The AFL's International Union of Timber Workers got a foothold first in Ashland, Wisconsin, and later spread throughout the north country. A district headquarters was established in Marinette. The Wobblies promoted a rival organization, the Lumber Workers Industrial Union (LWIU). Both groups met with enough success to frighten lumbermen. In Munising nine hundred workers were unionized. In 1919 the Charcoal Iron Company was alarmed to find about four hundred of its workers had been successfully recruited. The Forest Products Company of Strongs, Michigan, had its entire mill force unionized but kept recruiters out of their logging camps.[14] By the early spring of 1920 the LWIU circulated its list of demands, which included eight-hour days, a minimum wage of $100 per month (plus board), separate rooms in camp for washing themselves and laundering their clothes, hot water in camps, an end to hospital fees, and no discrimination against union men. There was also reference to the IWW's political agenda, which one lumberman said included "release of all class war prisoners, immediately, and the right of free speech, free press and free assemblage, also recognition of the Soviet Government of Russia."[15] The AFL's International Union of Timber Workers demanded the same reform agenda, save for the political rhetoric. It circulated its terms to all lumbermen in Wisconsin, Minnesota, and upper Michigan, along with the notice that it would seek to enforce the eight-hour day—where it was not granted—after May 3, 1920.[16]

On the regional level, the Northern Hemlock and Hardwood Association led the corporate counterattack. It sponsored several formal meetings at which information about the extent of organizing efforts was exchanged and opposition tactics were discussed. Contacts formed through the Northern Hemlock and Hardwood Association led to informal local groups, such as the Representative Lumbermen of Upper Michigan. Some lumbermen who did not belong to the association appealed for admission to these councils.[17] Most closed ranks with lumbermen in their area, even though they were often the most bitter of competitors. Manistique lumbermen overcame a tradition of competing recklessly with one another for labor to join together to oppose unionization. In Baraga County, loggers and lumbermen banded together and issued an announcement to the public, which sidestepped most worker's demands and made its stand on the principle of the open shop. The announcement was much publicized and "The Baraga County Policy" became the rallying point for antiunion sentiment.[18]

The willingness of lumbermen to unite in opposition to the union surprised many. William Chesbrough of the Willwin Company noted:

> For the past five years . . . there has never been an earnest attempt on the part of us lumbermen to stick together. There have been meetings at which we all expressed ourselves on the wage question, price of bark, etc., but any understanding that we ever reached at any of these were promptly discarded just as soon as each and every lumberman got back to his plant and nothing much has ever been gained by such meetings.[19]

But labor trouble proved to be a tonic for industrial cooperation and the action of Baraga County loggers led to similar declarations, such as the "Newberry Policy" and the "Cloverland Policy." However, there was little agreement among lumbermen beyond the open shop principle. Some believed wages should be increased, others believed that an eight-hour day was inevitable. A heavy demand for lumber in the spring of 1920 made them particularly anxious about anything that might curtail production.

The labor trouble came to a head in May 1920. Job actions were tried in various localities, but with little success. The IWW, which spearheaded the strike in Luce County, mustered 200 strikers. One hundred of those were brought out of the Charcoal Iron Company's lumber camps. By using white-collar staff and loyal workers, all of Newberry's facilities stayed open. In a matter of days, newspapers proclaimed the strike "near fizzle."[20] There were ugly moments during the trouble. A Trout Lake logging jobber, who was followed home one evening by a group of strikers, responded to their threats with counterthreats and when they attacked him, met their fists with his own counterpunches.[21]

Another logger in that town was confronted by strikers armed with knives, though verbal abuse was the limit of their harassment.[22] After the long build-up, no doubt heightened by the nationwide red scare, the job action was broken up easily.

Union busting and price agreements were not the only basis for cooperation among hardwood era lumbermen. There was also a considerable amount of sharing of timber resources. For example, the Worcester Lumber Company operation at Cusino specialized in softwood products—shingles, posts, and ties; the Lake Superior Iron & Chemical Company (a predecessor to the Charcoal Iron Company) used hardwood for lumber and charcoal making. It is only natural that they jointly exploited a tract of land that featured both timber types. Such an arrangement allowed for the resource to be used to its maximum potential and for the operations who also partly shared the cost of railroad building it assured maximum profitability.[23] The Cleveland-Cliffs Iron Company, despite its vast land holdings and many subsidiary firms, participated in many cooperative agreements. After the Big Bay Lumber Company was formed in 1901 Cleveland-Cliffs contracted to have the new firm send its cordwood to the latter company's Marquette charcoal mill. Cleveland-Cliffs also extended its railroad from Marquette west to Big Bay, linking the new settlement with the city.[24] The giant iron maker also had similar contracts with the Bay De Noquet Lumber Company and the Northwestern Cooperage Company.[25] Another type of timber sharing saw Cleveland-Cliffs send all the bird's-eye maple it cut to the Great Lakes Veneer & Pane Company of Grand Marais. Without such a contract, the veneer company would have quickly depleted its own lands and been forced to close.[26]

A similar form of cooperation was land exchanges. Solid blocks of territory were desirable for railroad logging. Land exchanges were often negotiated between the major timber owners to consolidate their holdings. Bay De Noquet, I. Stephenson, Northwestern Cooperage, and Cleveland-Cliffs—who between themselves shared most of Delta County—were particularly accommodating to one another.[27] Land purchases, which entailed hundreds of thousands of dollars in capital, marked another sphere of cooperation. When the Michigan Iron Land and Timber Company was formed, it made its first real estate purchases in conjunction with another newcomer, the Northern Peninsula Lumber Company. By thus pooling their assets, they secured close to 400,000 acres of timber and mineral lands.[28] When Von Platen-Fox Lumber bought 172,000 acres of land from the James C. Ayer Estate in 1923, it underwrote some of the massive cost by selling sections of the huge tract to other hardwood lumbermen in the area.[29]

Perhaps because of their involvement in trade associations, lumbermen were also willing to share detailed information about their logging and milling operations. Sawyer-Goodman of Marinette allowed U.S. Forest Service logging specialists to study their Upper Peninsula forest operations. They also allowed Cleveland-Cliffs lumber agents to undertake a detailed study of their mill and forest procedures. Cleveland-Cliffs regularly inspected logging operations of rival firms, sometimes visiting Upper Peninsula lumbermen, such as Chippewa County's Richardson & Avery Company, and on other occasions inspecting lower Michigan or Wisconsin concerns. The purpose of such visits was to compare logging costs, personnel procedures, and assess new applications of rail or gas-powered technology.[30]

Cooperation and comparative openness were features of the hardwood era because the complexity of mill operations and the sophistication of the technology involved presented comparatively stiffer barriers to new entrants in the field than had existed during the pine era. Lumbering was still an easier industry to enter than steel processing or many manufacturing sectors, but increasingly large amounts of capital were required to be a lumberman. When the Holt Lumber Company moved into the Upper Peninsula, it made a ninety thousand-dollar investment in forestlands, and then had to build a logging railroad at considerable cost.[31] When the Big Bay Lumber Company merely wanted to expand its timber reserve in 1901 it required a seventy thousand-dollar investment.[32] Ford Motor Company entered the industry with an investment of $2.5 million.[33] The high cost of being a lumberman made the industry more select and less competitive in its own ranks.

Yet it would be wrong to describe the early twentieth-century logging as one great love feast. Forest operations were still a competitive arena. On one occasion Gunlak Bergland clashed with the Holt Lumber Company over the purchase of timberlands near Sidnaw. The land was adjacent to Bergland's logging railroad but the wily Norwegian did not want to pay the owner of the tract the high price he asked. By waiting, Bergland hoped to bargain for a lower sale price. Besides, his logging crews were cutting the area, and there was little chance anyone would discover if they removed several thousand feet of logs from the tract in question. In the meantime, the Holt Lumber Company purchased the tract at the original asking price. Bergland was furious that the Oconto-based firm would infringe on what he regarded as his territory. He had a chance to avenge himself less than a month later when the Holt lumber crew wanted to use five hundred feet of Bergland's railroad to remove logs from the tract. He agreed but demanded twenty-five cents for every thousand feet transported. Holt was rightly upset by this astronomical fee for the use of a few hundred feet of track, and they in turn countered by charging that Bergland owed them several thousand dollars because of his trespass on the tract. The trespass fine would have made Bergland pay Holt the better part of what he was trying to charge them. Holt offered Bergland a simple agreement: the trespass would be forgotton for permission to use the track. However, Bergland was in a punitive mood. He knew that Holt would need months to get court action on a trespass charge; all the while the logs were in the forest ready to be transported. Every day of delay meant a further loss for the Holt people. Finally, they determined it was "useless to haggle with Bergland any longer" and they paid him the fee he demanded.[34]

A more clear-cut example of sharp tactics happened in the 1920s. Logging jobber Louis Anderson had recently moved from Mackinac County to the western Upper Peninsula where he hoped to be an independent operator. His limited capital forced him to buy an isolated tract of hardwood with no good access or egress. The only way to get the logs out was to use a logging spur built by a rival lumberman. Anderson received verbal permission to use the spur and he brought his own engine and log cars to haul the logs. But as the job neared completion, the lumberman, without notice, tore up his spur track, leaving Anderson's train and most of his logs stranded in the forest. Anderson was already in debt and he could not secure another loan until he sold his logs, yet they could not be removed until he rebuilt the spur track. In a hopeless position, Anderson was forced to abandon his entire outfit. For years it sat rusting in the forest until it was eventually salvaged.[35]

One of the toughest hardwood era lumbermen was William "Big Bill" Bonifas. He was a throwback to an earlier, more aggressive time. Born the son of a village blacksmith in Luxembourg, Bonifas immigrated to the United States as a young man. He originally intended to head west to the Dakota wheat fields but ended on a train bound for the north woods instead. He was given work in Delta County making rail ties. Bonifas was paid by the number of ties he produced each day. He sawed down the swamp cedar and then hewed out the tie with an axe. It was exhausting work that had to be done to specifications. Ties that were too narrow or improperly squared were disqualified. But that seldom happened to Big Bill who mastered the lumberjack's trade in short order. By saving his money and impressing the purchasing agent who bought the ties, Bonifas eventually set up his own logging operation. He brought his brother and sisters over from Luxembourg to help him run the business, and rounded out the family nature of the business by marrying the chore girl at one of his boardinghouses.[36] Originally, he concentrated his logging activities in Delta County's Garden Peninsula. But by 1910 he purchased several thousand acres of forest north of Watersmeet and transferred his operation to that rich hardwood country. There he founded the village of Bonifas, a typical company town of 200 people and about twenty-five buildings. In the outlying forest, Big Bill Bonifas employed 350 men in the five or six camps he operated each winter.[37]

By this time, Bonifas had made himself a substantial lumberman. His William Bonifas Lumber Company was no rival of the major loggers in the region, such as Bay De Noquet or I. Stephenson, but he was more than a struggling jobber. A chance to enter the elite circle of dominating concerns came when the Kimberly-Clark Paper Company looked for a secure source of plywood. Bonifas agreed to provide the company with part ownership of his concern in exchange for what was reported to be a quarter of a million dollars of Kimberly-Clark stock. Bonifas retained day-to-day control over the company, which expanded to several new production centers, the largest being in Marenisco.[38] Through his partnership with Kimberly-Clark and prudent investment in General Motors stock, Bonifas because a multimillionaire.

Yet as rich as Big Bill became, he still conducted business like a struggling immigrant. He refused to quit work and spend his money on relaxation. Instead, he kept his hand in the logging business and commented. "I just enjoy making money."[39] Author Edna Ferber was impressed by his aggressiveness, when she met him while researching *Come and Get It!*, her 1934 novel about the life of a lumber baron. She borrowed heavily from Bonifas to paint her picture of Barney Glasgow—a less than scrupulous, dynamic man who rose from camp chore boy to a millionaire status.[40]

Sometimes Bonifas's aggressive drive for a profit made him difficult to deal with. John Anguilm discovered this during the early 1920s. Anguilm was a successful small businessman in Trout Lake. He operated a livery stable, blacksmith shop, and hotel. Beginning in 1916 he did some independent logging in western Chippewa County. He at first prospered, but then came his deal with Bonifas. An agent for the William Bonifas Lumber Company agreed to purchase a large amount of cordwood from the logger at a set price the following spring. The deal was sealed with a handshake, not an unknown practice at the time and a common one during the pine era. Guaranteed the sale of a large amount of lumber at a good price, Anguilm invested heavily in forest operation that winter. He mortgaged his home and farm to operate two camps. But while forest operations were under way, the World War I boom lost momentum and a recession began. Bonifas had intended to buy up large quantities of cordwood and then sell at a dear price to the charcoal iron furnaces in the region. But with the recession those plants cut back production. When spring came, there was a glut of cordwood on the market and the price had fallen considerably. The Bonifas Company was chagrined by the high price they promised Anguilm and backed out of the deal. Anguilm was shocked by their breach of faith and protested to Bonifas, but to no avail. He was forced to sell his wood at a price far below his costs. To cover his debts, he sold the personal property he mortgaged. Anguilm remained in the forest products business for several more years but he never fully recovered, financially or emotionally, from the Bonifas deal.[41]

Small logging camp operators like John Anguilm became more common during the 1920s. They lacked the capital to operate processing plants or to make large land purchases. Independent loggers were often dependent on the large companies for their access to isolated timberlands, and frequently contracted with them for shipping logs on their railroads and for sawing logs in their mill. Without his own mill or transport, the small-scale logger was forced to take the prices offered by the big companies. Some of these loggers, like William Bonifas, eventually set up their own forest products companies, many others became more dependent on the great forest owners and functioned as jobbers. A jobber was a logger who cut logs on someone else's land. He was generally contracted to supply an amount of logs from a specified tract of forest. Out of the fee he received came the cost of his equipment, labor force, camp buildings, and if, anything was left, profit.[42] Jobbers and small loggers represented no competitive threat to the elite hardwood lumbermen; they became an increasingly popular alternative to the cost and problems of managing forest operations.

A much more serious form of competition was posed by the buyers of forest products. Unlike loggers, many buyers did possess the capital to establish a production capability. This gave buyers significant bargaining leverage—the threat of backward integration. Ford's decision to move into lumber production was prompted by rising market prices and his desire to protect his source of supply. Although Ford brought a vast expanse of forest, it was not merely for current use. Ford wanted to use his forest as a hedge for future needs and as leverage in negotiations with suppliers.[43] It is significant that at the same time Ford's competitior, General Motors Corporation, also bought extensive forest lands in northern Michigan. The Kimberly-Clark Corporation's relationship with the William Bonifas Lumber Company is another example of a major buyer moving into the logging business. Other buyers, such as the Edward Hines Lumber Company and the Marathon Corporation, were experienced enough in logging to deal sharply with their suppliers. Logging was made all the more difficult because loggers and lumbermen alike bargained with buyers who were well informed and well positioned to demand the best product at an advantageous price.

All lumbermen competed in both a regional and national marketplace. Regional production centers emerged in Wisconsin and Michigan that used hardwood products. For example, Grand Rapids, Michigan, and Sheboygan, Wisconsin, became national centers for the manufacture of hardwood furniture; Chicago, Milwaukee, and Detroit continued as important consumers of housing lumber and as national distribution centers. But the logging of hardwoods in the Upper Peninsula came when Wisconsin and lower Michigan forests were reaching their peak production. As lake states hardwood production fell off in the 1920s, lumber centers like Chicago began to import more and more lumber from the Appalachian highlands. Southern hardwoods, like southern pine before it, were a substitute source that helped hold down the price of northern forest products. Such competition held down profits in the Upper Peninsula, restrained conservation, and accelerated production. Southern manufacturing centers also began to cut into the national market of northern industries such as furniture production. By 1930, High Point, North Carolina, had replaced Grand Rapids as the leading furniture-making center.[44] As King Pine had been deposed before, hardwood logging in northern Michigan was near eclipse by the beginning of the Great Depression.

HARDWOOD ERA WOODWORKERS

"The subduing of the frontier," a journalist for *Harper's* noted, "must of necessity be the work of foreigners." This observation had been true in the nineteenth century when Canadian woodsmen, supported by Irish and German laborers, pioneered the pineries, and it was equally true during the hardwood era. Joining Canadians and northern Europeans in the logging camps were immigrants from southern and eastern Europe. Between 1890 and 1924 a new wave of immigration broke against the shores of the Great Lakes states. Polish, Italian, and Finnish workers joined Slovaks, Slovenes, and Croats in the mines, mills, and logging camps of the Upper Peninsula. The region was booming at the turn of the century. Another new iron range, the Gogebic, went into production in the 1880s and it was the source of new employment well into the twentieth century. The western Upper Peninsula's new mines and its underused hardwood uplands proved particularly attractive to immigrants. By 1890 the population of that region had grown by eighty percent. Ten years later, the census revealed another sixty-one percent gain. Through 1920 the Upper Peninsula kept gaining population, many of them immigrants.[45] By 1920 Mackinac County was the only Upper Peninsula county that had less than one-half of its population of foreign-born stock.[46]

Like nineteenth-century immigrants, some of the second wave came into the forest with logging skills in hand. Most Finns learned to use an ax on the forest farms of their fatherland. Slovenes (often referred to as Austrians) came from the mountainous region of what is now northern Yugoslavia. There they worked as woodcutters, spending their winters in bark-covered shacks. Others, such as Poles and Italians, usually had no special background for woods work, only a strong back and an empty stomach. They found jobs in the mills, mines, as well as in the forest.[47]

"You must remember," an old hardwood foreman said, "that we had ethnic tensions in those days also."[48] As was so during the pine era, there was not always a smooth intermingling of the various streams of immigration in the logging camps. Although the large camps of the big corporate loggers usually contained many different groups, it was not unusual to find smaller loggers or jobbers who favored certain ethnic groups. Some favored a particular ethnicity for the sake of harmony; others because they thought one group were better workers than others. Not surprisingly, Finnish foremen tended to favor Finnish lumberjacks, and a Croatian foreman's camp usually was filled with other Croats.[49] Occasionally, a group of conationals might share separate quarters, away from the other men of the crew. During the winter of 1918–19 a Chippewa County jobber built a separate cabin, away from the main complex, for a group of "Austrian" lumberjacks who wanted to be on their own.[50] In the late 1920s the Cadillac-Soo Lumber Company operated several camps composed almost solely of Finns.[51]

After World War I, some lumber companies encouraged migrant laborers from the mid-south to settle in the Upper Peninsula. A few blacks were among these workers. Most white "Kentuckians" worked in the forest, but blacks tended to concentrate in the charcoal processing towns. Manistique had a considerable number of black workers at its Charcoal Iron Company plant. However, when that facility burned in the early 1920s the black community broke up and most of its members moved downstate.[52] In 1926 two Marinette cordwood dealers tried to settle a group of Chicago black families on their cutover lands. Their plan was to have the blacks work as choppers for several years and eventually allow them to farm the land that they cleared. But the lumbermen failed to provide the families with the supplies they needed to survive the harsh Michigan winter. After a little more than a year, the thirty-two people were destitute and the county sheriff used this as a pretext to have the group transported back to Chicago.[53]

The variety of timber types and products produced by a hardwood logging operation made profitable the employment of a veteran sawyer as well as a novice to the north woods. By necessity, logging became more a set of specialized skills. Although Isaac Stephenson decried the specialization of hardwood lumberjacks, complaining that two-thirds of the men in a pine era camp could handle any job from top loading to river driving, hardwood operations were more structured on an industrial model.[54] Each man did his part to contribute to the final product. Stephenson's idea of a foreman was someone who worked alongside his men; hardwood era operations required supervisors who would coordinate the distinct work of different men.

Immigrants who came to the forest with no logging background were put to work making logging railroads or working as swampers. The latter task was more important for hardwood logging because of the many limbs on deciduous trees. Swampers used double bit axes to cut off the branches from hardwood logs. Short of avoiding your own feet or your fellow workers', there was no great skill required for swamping. It was a job given to inexperienced labor, and one that veteran lumberjacks resented because, being the low man on the camp pecking order, swampers were often recruited for any menial odd jobs that might arise. Yet because swampers composed about twenty percent of a hardwood camps' work force, there was usually work in the woods even for a novice.[55]

Most of the forest crew were sawyers. Sawyers always worked in teams (they were usually hired in teams) because the basic instrument for felling hardwood trees was a two-man crosscut saw. A pair of sawyers might work with each other for years, becoming closer than brothers. Illustrative of the relationships that might emerge from this system is the story of two Bay De Noquet lumberjacks, "Pat" and "Mike." One spring they were in Nahma taking a few weeks off and drinking heavily. In between trips to the tavern with his partner, Mike found time to form an acquaintance with a lady of the town. Up to now, the partners had shared everything equally, so Pat thought nothing of paying a visit to the lady. When Mike found Pat with his lady, he grabbed an ax and began swinging at his partner's head. After several drunken swings, he managed to graze Pat's head, cutting off part of his ear. Mike ended up with a one-year prison sentence; Pat was patched up and sent back to the woods. There he worked as a lowly swamper. Attempts were made by the Bay De Noquet Company to match him with another sawyer, but they all failed. He was a pathetic figure until Mike was released from jail. The two had a joyous reunion party and went back to working the woods as if nothing had ever happened.[56]

Log loaders were the best-paid men in a hardwood camp, which meant they had the most dangerous job. Steam or horse-powered loaders speeded up the loading of log railcars, but technology did not remove the need for quick-footed dexterity by the "top loader" who guided the logs into place. The loader's job was complicated because hardwood logs tended to be more crooked than the straight pine tree. Uneven logs, improperly loaded, might shift and crush the leg of one of the loading crew. Loaders were among the few hardwood era loggers to wear the caulked boots that were the pride of a lumberjack.[57]

Finnish woods workers were known for their skill as axmen and were sought by cedar loggers to cut railroad ties. The tie was trimmed right in the forest with a broadax. Railroads bought only ties made to strict specifications so that a skilled tie maker was needed to ensure that no logs were wasted.[58] Tie makers were among the first loggers to work on a "piece" basis; the number of railroad ties cut each day would determine their wage.[59]

Most loggers were paid a monthly wage at the beginning of the hardwood era. But gradually the piecework system took root. New forest work specialties, such as bark peeling and cordwood cutting, lent themselves to a pay system that rewarded the more productive worker. Soon the piece system spread to railroad-related work. Building grades and laying and lifting steel were tasks paid according to how much work was performed.[60] Later, many sawyers also asked to be paid on a piece basis. The logging companies resisted the trend toward piece labor. It became the rule for jobbers and cordwood cutters, but it was by no means universal at regular logging camps. Rather than pay men by the month, many companies would give them a daily wage. This was meant to be a concession to the men who wanted the freedom to come and go. Under the old monthly pay system, lumbermen would often try to withhold the salary of a worker until a full month of labor was performed. If they left before the month was out, they were given nothing.[61]

Both wage rates and the system of payment were sources of tension between labor and management during and just after World War I. There had been a labor surplus for so long before the war that the industry did not respond very quickly to a more assertive, ambitious work force. "The old camp foreman had been indoctrinated so long in paying wages for each job classification at one level," one lumberjack wrote, "regardless of the abilities of the workers, that there was no incentive for the men to be better workers, other than their pride."[62] The pride of many lumberjacks was insulted by the shabby conditions of their camps, as well as by their low pay.

Although the camp buildings changed, the conditions inside hardwood era camps were little improved from the nineteenth century. The old shanties of the pine era were replaced by frame strucures with tar paper–covered roofs. The walls were fastened together by bolts so that the building could be disassembled and moved if necesary. There was, however, nothing new about the smell or surroundings in the men's camp. The stench of sweaty clothes drying on haywire racks above the stove still floored the uninitiated visitor. Lice and bedbugs still bred in the straw-covered double-decked bunks. Henry Ford had a fumigating process for some people that came into his camps. Occasionally other companies would try to inspect transient lumberjacks before allowing them into the camp. "These lumberjacks wanted a clean camp," a woodsman recalled, "but as a rule it didn't last that way very long. . . . They'd have individuals that would bring lice—a variety of different lice and bedbugs and chiggers. . . . It was miserable then. You could hardly sleep at night.[63]

Immigrant workers from Europe were often appalled by the conditions in the camps. Finnish lumberjacks left a verse that captured their view of the deplorable shanties:

> A wretched home, this cheerless camp;
> And "finer people" sneer, make cracks:
> "You ruffians, bums,
> bearded lumberjacks!"
> Our wages are the rags we wear,
> Our scraps of food no one digests.
> Our bed are bunks
> And fleas our only guests.[64]

Finns often tried to mitigate the filth of the camps by building saunas. Distinct ethnic camps, where Finns or Slovenes lived apart from the main complex, may reflect the immigrant's disdain for the traditional camp.

Immigrant workers were part of the evolution of collective bargaining among lake states woodworkers. Unlike their American counterparts, some of the immigrants came to the north country with a tradition for cooperative endeavors. Finns and Scandinavians, for example, used this background to develop economic associations for cutover farmers as well as to support labor organizations.[65] Polish laborers were involved in one of the only two lockouts that the Federal Commissioners of Labor reported in the lake states between 1881 and 1905.[66] Dissatisfied Finnish workers at a Luce County logging camp were dispersed by discharges of buckshot and forced to flee when the sheriff's deputies turned on them.[67] In 1910 a group of Polish, Hungarian, and Finnish lumberjacks were denied employment at several camps in Michigan because they had a reputation for job actions.[68] Finns were prominent in Minnesota's 1916 strike, and Finnish socialist halls were the nerve centers of that job action and the Upper Peninsula strikes of 1920 and 1937.[69]

Although the 1920 strike proved to be a dud, it by no means quelled all worker protests in the Upper Peninsula. In December 1924 the J. W. Wells Company mill of Marinette was destroyed by a spectacular fire.

The Wells plant had been picketed by striking workers in 1920, but after the offer of a small raise, the workers' solidarity was shattered. An employee was arrested for arson after he loudly proclaimed that the sooner low-paying mills left the Menominee River area, the better. The case was eventually dropped but there was trouble again at the rebuilt plant in 1931. Fire destroyed most of the plant and arson was suspected. However, the full story did not come out until ten years later when an arsonist was arrested in Sault Sainte Marie. The man admitted to setting several mill fires in the Upper Peninsula, including the Wells Company plant in Marinette.[70] Another example of worker sabotage happened just over the Wisconsin border in 1917. An IWW agent took a job at a Foster-Latimer railcar camp. After working quietly for several days, the agent gradually started to promote the Wobbly message. He did not make much headway with his fellow lumberjacks, so after quarrelling with the foreman he was fired. He took his check and headed down the rail track to town. When he was out of the sight of the camp, he took a spike-pulling bar and began to unfasten the track. A heavily laden log train was due down the track in a matter of hours, and it surely would have been wrecked. Fortunately, a single engine came down the track shortly after the IWW man had left camp. It rounded a curve in the track and saw him pulling spikes. The crew gave chase and caught the culprit, who was given a five-year prison sentence.[71]

Woodworkers usually did not resort to violence nor did they seek out national labor organizations to assert their interests. Yet the labor force was much more protective of their precious rights and more prone to united action than the pine era lumberjack. Throughout the 1920s isolated actions occurred even among forest workers. For example, in 1923 Finnish sawyers used a labor shortage at the Cleveland-Cliffs lumbering department to organize and demand a two-cent per log increase in their piece labor wage.[72] A year later, cordwood operations were disrupted by men "full of Bolsheviki ideas." When the company told the men to cut wood to the company's specifications or leave, to the foreman's shock they left.[73]

A crosscurrent to the growing assertiveness of the woodworker was the enduring bond of paternalism between workers and the lumber company for which they worked. This paternalism was expressed in a variety of ways: paying men with nonnegotiable checks to keep them from cashing and blowing a check at a saloon; providing jobs as watchmen or swamper for aged lumberjacks; and perhaps most profoundly through the operation of company towns.

Company towns existed during the pine era but they became more important in the Upper Peninsula during the late nineteenth and early twentieth century because of changes in the work force. "A large proportion of the lumberjacks" a turn-of-the-century lumberjack recalled, "were older men who had families in neighborhood towns with whom they spent some Sundays."[74] The better companies, which offered camps that were clean and food well prepared, attracted the middle-aged married lumberjack. This was a distinct advantage because such a timber worker was more stable in his job and easier to supervise.[75] Company towns were operated because it was necessary to provide dwellings and stores for employees living in a remote location. An orderly, attractive town rewarded the lumberman with an efficient motivated work force consisting of more married men than drifting hobo workers.

When a town was founded, the mill, needless to say, received the greatest attention. But as work progressed on the mill, workers' dwellings were also built. This would entail a boardinghouse for single workers and cottages for the married men. Single-family homes were in high demand at a new company town. A journalist visiting the new Marquette County mill town of Birch found twenty families in the town, "and as fast as houses are completed, more families will move to the place." Other workers, he noted, kept their families in Marquette or neighboring towns, waiting for further residential construction at the town. When the nearby town of Big Bay was founded in 1901, the company could not meet the demand for homes by itself and tried to provide assistance for those willing to build their own homes. Building lots and construction materials were provided for town residences, and assistance was offered workers who wanted to settle on nearby farmlands.[76]

Some towns were carefully laid out; others grew like "Topsy." Birch and Big Bay were platted at an early date. Big Bay had electric streetlights, a church, and a school within a year; at Birch, a public park was laid out for residents.[77] Hermansville, on the other hand, was so short of housing in its early days that some workers were forced to live temporarily in abandoned charcoal ovens. However, that did not persist. Charles Meyer developed Hermansville into a proper town with a community center, recreation hall, and a one hundred-foot wide main thoroughfare, First Street.[78] Wells, the town of the I. Stephenson Company, was one of the largest sawmill communities. Besides the fine homes of corporate management and the bachelor worker's quarters, the town boasted close to 100 workers cottages. Each cottage sat on its own lot, with ample room for a garden. A visitor to the town in 1903 concluded that Wells gave "a decent and comfortable home life" to the woodworkers, and it guaranteed the company "a set of workmen of character and ability."[79]

It was not unusual for Upper Peninsula Company towns to be described (as Wells was) as "a law abiding and moral community."[80] Such descriptions stand in stark contrast with the moral condemnation that inevitably accompanied descriptions of Florence, Ewen, Trout Creek, or Seney during the pine era. The contrast reveals the heavy hand of paternalism. Liquor was kept out of many mill towns. The I. Stephenson Company allowed no saloons in Wells, though it would sell whiskey by the bottle in its drugstore. Saloons were kept out of Birch and Big Bay in the early days by the refusal of company officials either to lease or sell land to a liquor peddler. At Cusino, in Schoolcraft County, the Worcester Lumber Company went so far as to insist not only for a dry village but by political pressure kept the entire township dry.[81] Hermansville was not dry nor did it develop into a hell-roaring sin city. The Wisconsin Land and Lumber Company founded the town at an earlier date than most hardwood communities. In 1884 the company's superintendent described the sale of liquor as "a necessary evil." Although a saloon was allowed to open in town, it was forced to sign a strict lease and post a large bond. "While this will not prohibit the sale of liquor," company officials contended, "it will tend to shut out the lower grade of saloons kept by irresponsible parties."[82] The town of Simmons, which was operated at a later date by the owners of the Wisconsin Land and Lumber Company, refused to allow any saloons. Men were encouraged to save their money and keep their health by playing basketball or indoor baseball in the company gym.[83]

The political life of mill towns was dominated by the lumber company. The Worcester Lumber Company dominated Cusino Township in Schoolcraft County because nearly every citizen worked for it. The Wisconsin Land and Lumber Company, like most big lumber concerns, had a separate township created for the area around their town. Menominee County's Meyer Township was created in 1890, and although it was smaller than the other townships, it conveniently embraced most of the company's holdings. Superintendent Radford served as justice of the peace and was the top politician in the township.[84] Any attempt to challenge the company's political clout was regarded with hostility. One Upper Peninsula community was divided politically between an official company party and the Homesteader party, which advocated a populist agenda. The two parties clashed over the issue of tax support for schools and roads. The Homesteader party advocated generous public support; the company that was the chief taxpayer in the community advocated fiscal conservatism.[85]

Henry Ford was the most paternalistic of the Upper Peninsula's twentieth-century lumbermen. When the Ford Motor Company took over the town of Pequaming, there was an immediate change in the regimen of life. All the company-owned homes were renovated and painted. A corporate clean-up squad was organized to cut down weeds, improve fire protection, and, in general, spruce up the town. With these improvements, came a rent increase from one dollar per year to twelve dollars per year. Many residents kept cows or chickens, even pigs, in their yards. Ford ordered all animals out. "It was going to be a city," one townsman remembered, "it was no longer going to be a lumber town." At the same time, Henry Ford loved to visit the town. He would chat with old-timers, organize dances, and play with children. People in the town grew to look forward to his visits.[86]

Alberta was the centerpiece of Ford's string of Upper Peninsula communities. It was founded in 1936 as an attempt to integrate industrialization with rural living. Henry Ford had the vision of many small plants in rural areas, each making one part, which could be shipped to a central location for assembly. The small rural plants could shut down during slack periods, and the workers would still have an income from their farm plots adjacent to town. A small mill and model town were built at Alberta. Agricultural lands were cleared. During the winter, men participated in selective logging; in spring they planted their crops and during the summer they would work in the sawmill. By not pursuing any of the three economic niches intensively, it was believed that the operation would be safe from resource exhaustion or general depressions. But the company had little need for the Alberta mini-mill's production, so it was shut down more than it was operational. Nor was the land suitable for agriculture. Village residents who attempted farming failed.[87]

Ford also tried his mix of agriculture and industry in the Iron Mountain area. Workers whose schedules were reduced by the Depression were offered a garden plot. "We didn't have any choice in the matter," remembered Omar Martineau. "They just called you in and said, 'Here's your lot.' You'd take it. If you didn't take it, they'd take you off the roll." That program, like the Alberta village experiment, resulted in failure.[88]

The paternalism of hardwood era lumbermen could have a healthy effect on their community. Although most mill towns had schools supported indirectly by the lumbermen through township taxes, Henry Ford directly sponsored primary and secondary education at Pequaming. The schools were approved and credited by local authorities but Ford supplied the teachers and supplies. When there was a shortage of students, Ford had them bussed in, including children of non-Ford employees who lived in the area. Even Ford's wife took a direct interest in the Pequaming school. "Mrs. Ford was much interested in the manual training, dressmaking, and sewing," one resident remembered. The Ford bungalow in town was used as a home economics laboratory for the female students.[89] At Hermansville, Charles Meyer was so frustrated by the Spaulding Township school board's failure to provide a school for "his people" that he started his own school and later created his own township. Meyer also built and operated a dairy, at great expense, so that fresh milk was on hand for the children of the town.[90]

One of the most poignant moments for a company town was when the company was sold or its plants were closed. The constant threat of this for the towns of "cut and get out" lumbermen made many residents indifferent about projects to improve the town. It was seen as a temporary residence.[91] In other towns people put down roots. "I think you are correct in saying that two-thirds of the people in this town were born in it," wrote Daniel Hebard about the mill town he sold to Henry Ford. "My idea would be that we have to be very generous with all our men here when we sell out to Ford and take care of old people that Ford would let go." The Hebard pensions were enough to support many of the old workers of Pequaming for the rest of their days.[92] Henry Ford later went to great lengths to avoid closing the mills at Pequaming and Alberta even after their production was no longer needed. He was enraged at one point when company officials closed the mill and school without his direct permission. Ford was similarly motivated by sentiments when he purchased the mill and town of Big Bay. He had more than enough mill capacity in the region; he just did not want to see the mill quit and the town abandoned.[93] When the Bay De Noquet Company shut down its mills, it launched a nationwide campaign to find a buyer for Nahma who would provide jobs for the people.[94]

The line about owing one's soul to the company store presents a stark and not entirely accurate picture of life in northern Michigan's mill towns. Company stores and, in some cases, even company saloons existed and they were profitable. But besides the economic domination of the company, there was social cohesion among the residents. At Chassell, the company town of first the Sturgeon River Lumber Company and later the Worcester Lumber Company, community activities, such as picnics, involved the entire town. Every summer the company's tug pulled a huge, covered barge of townspeople to a picnic up the shore of Portage Lake. The town would be empty for the day. "We had just as good times then, and better than you folks have now," maintained a former picnicker. During the winter, activities, save for skating parties, would move indoors. Lodges, such as the Maccabees, Modern Women, and the Knights of Phythias, sponsored meetings and dances. In 1914 the Worcester Lumber Company helped the latter group build a new hall that served as a community center.[95]

Although the central activity of all these company towns was lumber production, trees and saws did not dominate the everyday life of the people who lived there. At Tula in Gogebic County people lived quiet, comfortable lives. According to one local historian:

Most of the small houses, although they were not constructed too well, became pleasant and homelike quarters. Gay curtains, geranium plants, and knick-knacks brightened the sparkling, small windows of many homes. During the day, Aunt Louise watched happy children play in the snow, or she took time out from her bookkeeping to enjoy a cup of coffee in the kitchen of a friend whose home smelled of fresh-baked bread or of sudsy water and fresh washed and frozen clothes. . . . The mill workers' families spent some of the long winter evenings visiting at their neighbors, singing, jigging, or story telling. More often, tasks to be done kept them home. In the soft light of old-fashioned lamps, women pieced and stitched quilts while they discussed in low voices the day's events with the men, busy greasing boots or hanging socks to dry by the stove.[96]

In the larger logging towns, social activity might be, at least partly, segregated along ethnic or class lines. It was not unusual to have a few homes on the outskirts of the settlement clustered together and referred to as "Finntown." In one mill town, there were about 250 Swedes, 175 Anglo-Americans, 70 Finns, and 24 French Canadians. These people were geographically divided into sections known as Swedetown, Frenchtown, Finntown, and a section of company homes known as "Redtown." The Swedes and Finns went to the village's Lutheran church; Anglo-Americans banded together for a Union Protestant church.[97] In Kenton, the town of the Sparrow-Kroll Lumber Company, the top employees lived in a string of frame houses known as "the Yellow Row." To live there, the local schoolteacher recalled, was to be someone "special" in the local community. In Wells, Croats were congregated near the "Red Houses," three multifamily dwellings near the railroad track. Better-off workers lived in nicer, single-family homes "on the hill."[98]

Not all hardwood logging concerns built company towns. Gunlak A. Bergland, a Norwegian immigrant who rose from the ranks of the mill hands to found his own lumber company, in particular disdained a corporately owned town. In 1900 he purchased seventeen thousand acres of timberland near Lake Gogebic.[99] On the north shore of the lake he built a mill. He did name the town site after himself, but he disdained controlling all property in the town. He did not even operate a company store. This saved Bergland considerable start-up costs, but it cost him much in potential profits and control over the town's development. Without the restraint of a paternalistic owner, the town's first two businesses were saloons. On the other hand, Bergland continued to thrive as a town after its founder had pulled out of logging. Most company towns withered and died after their main support was removed.[100]

During the first two decades of the twentieth century, the overall age of the Upper Peninsula's population increased substantially. Though males between the ages of twenty and thirty made up at least ten percent of the population between 1870 and 1910, this group underwent a marked decline between 1910 and 1920.[101] The maturation of the region reflected the transition from frontier to settlement, just as staid company towns or peaceful forest hamlets reflected an evolution away from the Seneys and Ewens of the pine era. George Corrigan, a former lumberjack and logging contractor, contended that about 1916 some seventy-five percent of the woods workers disdained the allurements of booze and brothels and lived sensible lives:

> Some were men who were making starts toward buying a small piece of farmland so they could marry and raise a family. Some wanted their children to have a better education; others wanted to start a little business. Some were immigrants who had left their families back in the countries they came from and wanted to bring them over here.[102]

These men were stable workers who worked for four to six months steady in the woods to save money for their homes.[103]

As the Upper Peninsula matured, it shed its gaudy frontier adornments. After 1900 the opportunities for vice in the region, often overstated anyway, decreased dramatically. In 1906 the Ontonagon County Sheriff's Office launched a series of raids on bordellos on the outskirts of several towns in the southern part of the county.[104] This action was followed by a crackdown on saloons, which often tried to operate without a license or in violation of their license.[105] Scores of establishments were closed by this crackdown. In the Dickinson County town of Channing, citizens forced their officials to act more vigorously. For several years "Dolly's Place" had been tolerated by local residents. It was located just outside the town so that what went on there was not a flagrant affront to the law. Supplies were taken out to the brothel; Dolly and her prostitutes never frequented the town. Yet, as the town grew, homes were built near the brothel. Those residents protested to township officials who pressured Dolly to cease her salacious activities or leave the area. Confronted with such a choice, Dolly and her employees packed their bags.[106]

Dolly's Place, like many other dives in the north country, were no longer needed because fewer lumberjacks were rootless bachelors, shifting from job to job. The imbalance between men and women in the Upper Peninsula, which during the pine era had been considerable in favor of the male population, was gradually redressed by the outward migration of workers, many of them lumberjacks from the region. Although emigration from Europe continued at a high rate between 1900 and 1920, the outward movement of young males from the region

tended to balance the previously disproportionate male-female population ratio. In such a setting, there was a decreasing demand for the services of prostitutes.[107]

For the old-time lumberjack who disdained company towns, forest
farms, and a wife, the hardwood era was an uncomfortable transitional
period. Many had come to the region as young vigorous men. When
pine production soared, they were affectionately referred to as "the
lumber ladies." But as visions of a mixed Upper Peninsula economy
based on agriculture, mining, and logging grew, so too did impatience
with men who wanted to live the unrestrained woodsmen's life of old.
Terms such as "timber beast" or "cedar savage" became more common.
Some woodsmen reveled in the macho flavor of such a description, but
the terms were also clearly derogatory. Even the name "lumberjack"
began to assume negative connotations. To many, it brought up images
of "unruly nomads," spendthrifts, "a large number who were itinerant
workers and were little better than hoboes."[108] Some former lumberjacks had to defend themselves and their mates. One wrote:

> The word "lumberjack" is considered by many to mean that he was an illiter-
> ate and shiftless man, but nothing is further from the truth. The true defini-
> tion of a "lumberjack" is a man handy at most all woods work, (a jack of all
> trades in the woods) and didn't depend on certain job classification.[109]

The authors of a Wisconsin Industrial Commission report were equally
defensive, though less generous. They said "lumberjacks are a higher
grade of laborers than hoboes." This dubious distinction was arrived at
because "they usually have some baggage, while 'boes' commonly have
none. They get high pay for their work and are a more independent lot of
men."[110]

Yet, there were enough woods workers in the Upper Peninsula,
nearly as many as during the pine era, that there remained a core of
itinerant lumberjacks who unashamedly pursued their unrestrained life-
style. If there were fewer local dives to resort to, there still were Hurley
and, to a lesser extent, Florence. Vice continued to be concentrated in
the Wisconsin border towns because they were meeting points of the
mining and logging industries and because several Michigan counties
acted on their local option to restrict liquor sales.

A visitor to Hurley in the early 1930s remembered "the whole damn
street was all whorehouses and barrooms and pretty rough, too."[111]
Silver Street was as tawdry and tinseled as ever during the hardwood era.
It was the mecca of the north country for the itinerant lumberjack, and it
drew men from across the Upper Peninsula. Rail transportation made it

easier for these men to leave camp, so it was not unusual to have a hobo logger work a few weeks, claim his check, and head for town. If the jack's stake was big enough, he would head for Hurley; if it was small, a day or two in a local dive was all he could afford. Yet so many woodsmen regularly made it to Hurley that the town became a reserve labor pool for lumbermen.

The term "man catchers" was used to describe the men who cruised the bars of Silver Street and rounded up men who were ready to return to the woods. Bartenders were sometimes helpful to man catchers by pointing out the lumberjacks who had pretty much blown their stake. This saved the saloon keeper from having to call the sheriff when the busted woodsman started to make a nuisance of himself by begging for drinks. The man catcher's task was unending because the hobo logger never stayed very long on the job. "I worked in 12 camps in one year," one old jack recalled. "You left when you wanted to. If the smoke wasn't coming out of the stove pipe just right that morning, you packed and quit." Another woodsman maintained "you never worried about a job, some camp would want you."[112]

The National Prohibition Act proved a considerable challenge to Hurley's Silver Street saloon owners. Legislation did nothing to affect the social habits of the northwoods logger, but it made operating a saloon illegal. There were eighty-nine licensed taverns in Hurley at the time of Prohibition; more than half of the main street businesses were given over to liquor sales and vice. For a town whose prospects as an iron mining community were not very likely, the effective cessation of liquor sales would have been economically debilitating. Local officials, therefore, moved very slowly to enforce the provisions of Prohibition. When they did take action, it was merely the leveling of fines, which were needed to keep the city government solvent.[113]

When tough action did come in Hurley, it was through the efforts of federal officials. On December 31, 1926, in an effort to dampen another blatant New Year's Eve of partying along Silver Street, federal officials served restraining orders to the owners of twenty-nine saloons. Two federal agents, dressed as lumberjacks, had been served liquor in each of the establishments. The order requested the saloon owners to give evidence of their innocence or face closure. There was no doubt the saloons were guilty and on March 30 they were padlocked shut. For close to a year, the worst of the town's bars were closed, but the town was never dry, and it was frequented by lumberjacks throughout Prohibition.[114]

One reason the Volstead Act did not shut down Hurley was that the dives offered woodsmen more than a stiff drink. Prostitution and gambling were part of any spree on Silver Street. Unlike the bordellos near outlying towns, whose whores operated discreetly, the Hurley women solicited openly in many of the saloons. They were said to work as waitresses or dishwashers but performed their real services when they were hustling drinks or escorting lumberjacks upstairs "for a nap." A pretty or otherwise talented woman could be an attraction to customers who otherwise might not distinguish among the many saloons. A naive woodsman remembered: "I wondered why there were so many young women going and coming out of the back room as they were not allowed to be hired as bartenders at this time. I was soon informed what they were there for, but I will also say I never saw one of them drag a man into the backroom or upstairs and just about every saloon had at least one or more."[115]

"Those gambling dens were humming," reminisced one old jack of a six-day spree in Hurley.[116] Gambling and prostitution made Hurley special. "They can buy drinks anywhere—Bessemer, Ironwood, Duluth, Ashland," maintained a roaring twenties denizen of Silver Street. "The girls and games brought them here."[117] Even after federal marshalls closed several Hurley saloons, their owners continued to operate gambling houses on the premises.

Women, liquor, and gambling provided the lumberjack with abundant opportunity to indulge in a traditional form of recreation, fighting. "If you didn't have five or six fights when you went to town, you didn't have a very good time."[118] A Gogebic County woodsman recalled: "They loved to fight. But they went according to rules, too, about fighting. They couldn't use a knife, or they couldn't pick up a stick or a pole or anything like that—it was just hand-to-hand fighting."[119] The itinerant lumberjack would let nothing get in the way of a good time. "They'd close the bar early," said Mel Frisk, "and you'd come in and saw the door down and drink. Other times we threw the bartender out and served ourselves."[120]

There was a code of behavior among the hobo lumberjacks that required a man to look after his camp mate if he became too drunk. Woodsmen feared being rolled by strangers. A more common danger was staggering out into the winter night and freezing to death. Newspapers were regularly dotted with accounts of drunken lumberjacks who tried to hike up the tracks to camp and, upon tiring, fell asleep on the rails. Seldom were their shredded bodies a warning to others. The old-time woodsmen were not inclined to think of tomorrow. If they were, it would have been clear that the rugged, no-holds-barred frontier life-style was coming to an end. Instead, they drank with gusto and fought with abandon. When they were drunk, broke, or triumphant, they would stagger into the street and shout to the stars that they were the toughest timber beast in the north. Yet, after each spree, their shouts became less loud, less defiant, and more poignant. The logging frontier, which had broken over the Upper Peninsula with the force of a Lake Superior gale, was clearly receding and the old-time lumberjack was trapped in the stagnating backwater.

PART 3

THE PULPWOOD ERA

10

RISE OF THE RUBBER TIRE LUMBERJACKS

"He's what you call a rubber tire lumberjack," teased Jim Stark, a former lumberjack, former logging jobber, and, at the time, operator of a set of tourist cabins. As he spoke, Stark smiled and looked at a friend who had lived only half of Jim's sixty-some years. The younger man erupted as if deeply offended. "Not me, I still log on steel." But Jim only laughed harder. When he went into the woods as a boy, "logging on steel" meant railroad logging, not the metal treads of the caterpillar tractor the younger man used in the cuttings. Jim was particularly amused by his friend's defensive reaction because the younger man did not seem to appreciate that in the eyes of the old-time woodsmen, to be a rubber tire lumberjack was not merely to ride to work in a car or operate a gas-powered truck or skidder; it further inferred a logger who carried a spare tire around his waist. To Jim Stark, most modern loggers were rubber tire lumberjacks. The way they lived their lives, the institutional environment in which they operated, the equipment they employed, and even the type of forest products they produced—all marked a major departure from the early twentieth century.

The heroic era of the northern Michigan forests ended with the rise of pulpwood logging. Mighty pine and stately hardwood were replaced by "weed trees"; lumberjacks were replaced by "employees"; lumbermen by corporations; and "cut and get out" by sustained-yield forestry. As with all change, something was lost and something was gained. The freedom and color of the frontier were exchanged for the security of a regulated environment. Paul Bunyan was replaced by a rubber tire lumberjack.

THE DEFLOWERING OF CLOVERLAND

The pulpwood era marks as distinct a phase of northern Michigan history as the hardwood era before it. Yet pulpwood came to dominate the forest products industry of the Upper Peninsula in the same way as pine had earlier yielded to hardwood, gradually over several decades. The use of northern Michigan logs to make pulp for paper began in 1880 when the Marinette Paper Company was founded on the banks of the Menominee River. But not until the twentieth century did the Upper Peninsula become an important source of pulpwood. In 1902 the Munising Paper Company was founded, and ten years later the Escanaba Pulp and Paper Company began operation. By 1921 three other northern Michigan towns, Manistique, Ontonagon, and Menominee, boasted paper mills.[1] The demand for pulpwood by these new mills and the growing appetite of the Wisconsin Fox River firms made paper companies an important growth area for the logging industry during the 1920s. Such growth was needed because hardwood production in the Upper Peninsula began to lag by 1925. Wisconsin's and Michigan's lumber statistics were feeble compared with the burgeoning output of Alabama, Louisiana, and Mississippi mills. By 1931 Alabama had nearly seven times the number of sawmills as Michigan.[2]

The reasons for Michigan's decline in lumber were simple: production and destruction. Between the mammoth logging operations and the vast forest fires, ninety-two percent of the state's available forest was decimated by 1929. Fortunately, most of the remaining woods were in the Upper Peninsula, but they could not last for long, especially if the combined attention of lumbermen and pulp producers were directed against them. The economic consequences of the forest destruction experienced by northern Michigan were so severe as to threaten the future of even pulpwood logging in the region. The U.S. Forest Service saw the "menace of ruin" hanging over the entire lake states area.[3]

Forest depletion had a direct effect on several northern Michigan wood-using industries. The cooperage industry, which at the turn of the century employed nearly fifteen hundred people in Michigan, could claim only 122 workers by 1919. Cedar production also began to decline from its turn-of-the century high of 350,000 poles to a 1920s figure of 54,000. The drop in cedar tie and shingle production was equally precipitous. By 1929 pulpwood was the only forest product that Michigan produced in enough quantity to exceed the demands of its local industries. Throughout most of the state, the number of men employed in logging camps declined, as did the wages of many of those who stayed in the forest.[4]

The deterioration of hardwood logging industries had a direct and severe effect on the plight of cutover farmers in the Upper Peninsula. The infant agricultural section could ill afford any jolt during the 1920s. Farmers throughout the lake states had expanded during World War I when agricultural prices were high. When the war ended, demand plummeted and prices remained low because of strong domestic competition. Farmers on marginal lands could not compete with the rich agricultural lands of the lower Midwest. Many had taken up backwoods farms as a part-time occupation and were only lured into full-time agriculture by the artificial wartime prosperity. Those who had given mortgages to purchase additional land or equipment were caught short by the agricultural recession. Loan foreclosures and land forfeiture for nonpayment of taxes became common. The disintegration of Upper Peninsula farming was accelerated because farmers had grown to count on the supplementary employment of woods work that was increasingly hard to find. As logging camps closed and mine output declined, farmers lost local outlets for products such as garden vegetables, oats, and timothy. The camps also furnished the farmer with extra income if he let a logger rent a horse over the winter.[5] As logging declined, freight rates on railroads rose, further threatening the viability of farming.

The deflowering of Cloverland had ecological as well as economic origins. Homesteaders who planted a patch of potatoes on new farms were generally rewarded with bumper crops, which they proudly credited to their farming prowess and to the richness of the soil. Few of them thought that the virgin forest soil would shortly require more nutrients if it were to remain productive. Timothy hay, a favorite crop for dairying or for sale to loggers, was also a "vicious soil exhauster." Commercial fertilizers, which might have prolonged productivity, were not used much until the 1930s, when few marginal farmers could afford to purchase or apply them.[6] Some farmers had been lured into settling on pine plains, whose sandy soil was submarginal at best. Years of hard work on such farms were doomed to frustration and debt. Only too late did agriculture officials realize that these lands should never have been adapted to agriculture and would have been better suited for reforestation.[7]

Clearing a forest farm, even one that had been cutover, proved formidable for homesteaders. Many farmers could never clear enough land to become successful agriculturalists. Even though cutover farmers increased between 1900 and 1920, the average amount of improved land on each farm declined. The average northern Michigan farm had fewer than forty acres of improved land. Although a farm of such size was adequate for the part-time farmer or for the farmer blessed with rich soil and warm weather, in the Upper Peninsula, forty acres could not return in income the hard work needed to maintain the establishment. Tragically, this became apparent only after many farmers had invested decades of effort and were nearing retirement age.[8] Aging pioneers made up an increasingly large percentage of the population as declining job prospects drove young people out of the area. Between 1900 and 1920 the vigorous age-group between eighteen- and forty-four year-olds declined from twenty-seven per cent of the population to only twenty-one per cent.[9] This decline continued even more precipitously during the 1930s and 1940s. When the Upper Peninsula's economy required imagination and energy, a high proportion of its people were in dependent age-groups, either too young or too old for full-time work.[10]

As deforestation and farm failure forced lumbermen and agriculturalists out of the region, the tax burden on those remaining grew heavier. Historically, taxes had been grossly undervalued in northern Michigan, particularly during the pine era when lumber barons dominated thousands of acres of forest and bore little of the local tax burden. It was not unusual for forest owners in the nineteenth century to get away with paying less than ten cents per acre for prime forest. Accessors usually caught up with the true value of forestlands only after scarcity became a problem. The trend throughout the forested region of Michigan was that once the remaining pine was cut, valuations declined slightly only to rise again as hardwood was perceived as a valued resource. Yet, even for hardwood forestlands, taxes lagged behind intensive logging. Only after most of the forest was cut did tax evaluations rise. But by then the resource that made the land valuable to begin with had been stripped. For the lumber companies holding cutover lands, increased taxes on devastated land constituted an uneconomical burden. Companies eagerly sold their holdings to agriculturalists, ranchers, or real estate firms. Sometimes they simply let the land revert to government control through tax delinquency.[11]

Yet local tax revenues were still needed to finance education, roads, and civil government, and accessed rates skyrocketed for those who remained on the tax rolls. A parcel of land in Iron County is an example. The track had been logged for pine during the late 1880s or early 1890s. Taxes on the property went down in 1895 and stayed low until 1904 when they began to climb steadily. By 1926 the property owners had experienced an eighty-five percent increase. Nor were these increases equitably distributed.[12] Tax rates for Wells, Michigan, which because of the I. Stephenson Company's large holdings still boasted a large timber reserve, increased by twenty-one percent between 1904 and 1920. During those same years, the town of Ford River, whose forest hinterland was cut, suffered a 145 percent real estate tax hike. Clearly the tax system was laying an increasingly heavy burden on those communities least able to bear the burden.[13]

Lumbermen also felt the pinch of the accelerating tax schedule and they did not care for it one bit. The Cleveland-Cliffs Iron Company abandoned thousands of acres of cutover land it held in Luce County. The Fisher Body Division of General Motors Corporation, which, like

Ford, had invested in forests for the future, also began to dispose of its cutover holdings. In 1930 alone, the Keweenaw Land Association, among the largest landholders in Michigan, abandoned sixty thousand acres.[14] Yet it was not the great corporations, the General Motors or Kimberly-Clarks, that were hit the hardest by rising taxation. Capital-rich corporations could endure high up-front costs for the long-term prospect of profit; the small lumberman could not.[15]

Some lumbermen lashed out at county officials. "Big Bill" Bonifas, never known for his reticence on any subject, was particularly outspoken concerning the school board taxes in Marenisco Township:

> Now, I say to you people, that if you think you can spend the taxpayer's money as you have in the past, you are very much mistaken. The Bonifas Lumber Company will not stand for your spending one cent that is not in accordance with the law of this great state. We paid in that township last year a little over $45,000.00 taxes. This year we paid $52,000.00 taxes and besides cut off about fifty forties of timberland. . . .

The incident that roused the logging baron's anger was the news that the high school had hired an assistant coach. "I don't know what you need him for, nor do I know what the coach is doing."[16] Bonifas was a well-known skinflint, but he was not alone in his demand for tax relief. As early as 1920 the individual calls for government action had swelled to a chorus heard both in Lansing and Washington.

BEGINNINGS OF GOVERNMENT FORESTRY

The "Solons" in the state legislature had struggled with the problem of the cutover lands for several years before the problem had become acute in the Upper Peninsula. By the turn of the century, the lumbering region of lower Michigan was mired in the morass of growing tax rates and mounting delinquency. A critical step in the establishment of an effective policy for north country public lands came in 1902 when the State Forestry Commission was born. The commission began to reverse Michigan's historical land policy of rapid transfer of real estate from public to private hands. Rather than offer all delinquent lands to homesteaders for the nominal fee of two dollars per acre, the commission convinced the legislature to reserve some of those lands as state forest preserves. The first preserves were in lower Michigan, but by 1917 the Lake Superior State Forest was established on the Upper Peninsula's unwanted land.

The establishment of state forests indicated Michigan's recognition that something had to be done for the northern part of the state. But, besides reserving several thousand acres for forestry, what should be the direction of state cutover policy? Controversy greeted most proposed programs. Lumbermen demanded tax relief; township officials cried for higher rates. Development bureau publicists and avaricious real estate agents contrived to seduce farmers on to marginal lands; academic agricultural specialists described the area as largely unsuited to farming. In the state legislature, representatives from the old lumbering regions proposed greater financial support; the wealthier southern counties opposed any transfer of payments. The public good was anything but apparent.

The Michigan Academy of Science, composed largely of university-based social and natural scientists, tried to bring order to the chaotic debate by advocating the development of a "comprehensive data base" on the region's resources. The academy's advocacy led to the establishment of the Land Economic Survey in 1921. Although it was under-funded and never properly organized, the survey was an important step in stabilizing the decline of the north country. Survey teams were directed by professional foresters and soil scientists and staffed by senior undergraduate or graduate students. Township by township, in methodical fashion, the survey team would classify all agricultural soils and estimate forest resources. At the end of each day's work, field data were discussed and then entered on a general county resource map. Some farmers objected to the survey as "the last word in government interference with private rights," but most local officials eventually came to support the survey's determinations.[17]

The Land Economic Survey began in the Lower Peninsula and did not move across the Straits of Mackinac until 1925 when Menominee County was studied. Later Alger, Chippewa, Schoolcraft, Iron, and Luce counties were visited by survey teams. Survey data paved the way not only for forestry in northern Michigan, but actual land-use planning. Local assessors used the survey findings to evaluate holdings. Survey data also formed the basic rationale for expanding the infant state forest preserves and helped nurture the growing recreational industry by identifying potential wildlife refuges and identifying potential resort locations. Yet there was no formal attempt to develop a comprehensive plan or even general guidelines to use the undigested survey data. The Great Depression cut into the survey's findings and robbed the state of the ability to pursue the program to its logical conclusion. Nonetheless, the Land Economic Survey succeeded in branding much of the previous conventional wisdom concerning cutover lands as "bunk and over-optisims [*sic*]" and provided the data and trained personnel to undertake more aggressive action in the years ahead.[18]

On the federal level, progress was also under way. Michigan's north country crisis was reflected in the land management problems of Wisconsin, Minnesota, and, to a lesser extent, the old lumbering regions of the Northeast, and the new logging frontier of the Deep South. Lumbermen and legislators from these regions advocated immediate action to encourage corporate and government reforestation programs. Without such an effort, Forest Service officials predicted that the United States would face a timber famine in the not-so-distant future. To stave off such a disaster, the Coolidge and Hoover administrations advocated an aggressive program of corporate cooperation and federal forest expansion. The centerpiece of the movement was the Clarke-McNary Act. Approved in June 1924 the act provided for local, federal, and private cooperation to combat forest fires. Significantly, the act broadened the Forest Service's mandate to purchase lands in the eastern United States from mere watershed protection to the vital task of timber production. With Clarke-McNary, the Forest Service directly entered the business of reforestation in the lake states. Money was authorized for government preserves and to enable forestry scientists to work with corporations on private reforestation programs.[19]

The Clarke-McNary Act indirectly contributed toward solving the tax delinquency problem. Two million acres of abandoned lands reverted to the State of Michigan between 1921 and 1932. During 1925 alone, almost 100 acres per day were going back to the state. The act authorized $2.5 million to study the general problem of tax reform. Lumbermen had long believed that corporate forestry was an impossibility if they were to be taxed each year for the full value of forests that could be harvested only once a generation.[20] Federal and state studies generally supported the lumberman's tax position. Legislators in Michigan wrestled with the problem throughout the 1920s. The Commercial Forest Reserve Act of 1925 promised lower taxes to corporations who practiced forestry. However, not until comprehensive action in 1933, when the state constitution was amended to limit real estate and personal property taxes to one and a half percent of their assessed value, did real tax relief come.[21]

The most significant federal action for the future of logging in the Upper Peninsula was the decision of the National Forest Reservation Commission to establish a national forest in the Upper Peninsula of Michigan. Federal forestry in the lake states began in 1908 when a national forest was created in northern Minnesota. A year later the Huron National Forest was created in lower Michigan. The Upper Peninsula had to wait until the Clarke-McNary Act to become the scene of federal forestry programs. By 1931 the commission approved three purchases for the area. These were later approved by President Herbert Hoover as the Ottawa, Hiawatha, and Marquette national forests. The Ottawa National Forest was in the western Upper Peninsula between Lake Superior and the Wisconsin border. The Hiawatha National Forest was composed of cutover lands, largely in Alger, Delta, and Schoolcraft counties. The easternmost forest was the Marquette, which was shared by Chippewa and Mackinac counties.[22]

The new national forests were composed of some of the most devastated lands in the peninsula. Twenty percent of the Ottawa National Forest area had been burned over three to four times.[23] In 1925 Schoolcraft County, in the Hiawatha forest, led the Upper Peninsula in value of lands lost on taxes.[24] The extensive pine plains of northern Alger, Schoolcraft, and Chippewa counties were also embraced by the forests. These lands were made into empty, stump-dotted barrens by the fires of the early twentieth century. Repeated burning or the planting of heavy grass cover by agriculturists prevented these areas from naturally returning to forest cover. Only aggressive forest management could make such lands profitable again.[25]

THE GREAT DEPRESSION AND UPPER PENINSULA LOGGING

The Great Depression had the effect of accelerating the changes in public-land management that had been under way throughout the 1920s, but the financial hard times of the 1930s also restrained the growth of corporate forestry by slowing technological change and instilling conservatism in the logging industry of northern Michigan. Nonetheless, the 1930s were a crucial decade when the pattern of hardwood logging grudgingly gave way to the pace of modern logging.

The stock market crash in October 1929 did not have an immediate effect on the lumbermen of the northern forests. The construction industry, a major user of northern hardwood products, had begun to experience a decline in demand as early as 1928; thus there was no sudden onslaught of hard times. By the summer of 1930 lumber prices began to decline further and mill yard inventories grew.[26] Lumberjacks, whose wages had been improving during the 1920s, found their pay slashed by corporate retrenchment programs. Many men worked merely to get board during 1931–32, the worst years of the Depression.[27] As the times became more difficult, the work regimen also tightened. "You had to work from daylight 'til dark," recalled an old pulpwood cutter, "or you didn't have a job, that's all."[28]

The large lumber companies did not themselves have an easy time of it. A Cleveland-Cliffs logger attending a Hardwood Association meeting in Marquette discerned "a distinct note of pessimism prevailing, which had not been noticeable at past meetings of lumbermen." Lumber was abundant in the market and its prices were low. The Bay De Noquet, Van Platen-Fox, and I. Stephenson companies all ceased summer logging operations. Wage cuts were common. The decline was sometimes dramatic. Although some lumbermen were paid between forty and forty-five dollars per month before the Depression, cutbacks to twenty-five to thirty dollars per month were instituted. For some firms, cutbacks were not enough.[29] The Weidman Lumber Company was forced to close some of its plants; the Greenwood Lumber Company of Ontonagon and several other small companies across the peninsula were forced out of business altogether.[30] Between 1925 and 1931 the number of sawmills in Michigan dropped by a staggering thirty-nine percent.[31]

The Cleveland-Cliffs Iron Company was particularly hard hit by the Depression. The iron business, the company's principal concern, was devastated by the hard times. In the past, the lumber department could run operations in the red to harvest wood, but with the Depression, every expenditure had to bring an immediate financial return. There was considerable speculation that the venerable mine company would be forced to close. Corporate officers had been caught short by the stock market crash. In 1929 the company had invested twenty-three million dollars to purchase the Corrigan-McKinney Steel Company. It was the first step in a bold plan to weld several large iron and steel interests into a giant combine that would rival United States Steel Corporation. But the Depression ended that dream and nearly the company. Only the good name of Cleveland-Cliffs and William G. Mather's personal fortune prevented bankers from liquidating the firm.[32]

The lumber department was challenged to squeeze every drop of profit out of their operations that the poor market would allow. Costs had to be cut; logging had to be efficient; everything was at risk. Camp cooks were admonished about waste and warned to be frugal. Lumberjacks were told to accept longer hours and less wages for their work. Log transportation and camp supply were investigated for cost-cutting options. This belt-tightening worked. The cost of feeding lumberjacks at Cleveland-Cliffs camps, aided in part by a drop in food prices, declined from twenty-seven cents per man per meal in 1929 to a mere fourteen cents in 1932.[33] General logging cost also dropped dramatically. By 1932 there was a nearly sixty percent drop in the cost of logging per thousand feet of timber from the 1929 levels.[34] Corporate liabilities were also reduced. The Munising Woodenware Plant was closed and land was sold to raise cash.

There was no uniform response among lumbermen to the Depression. The Cleveland-Cliffs Company increased production in 1933 by forty-three percent as the economic slump had begun to bottom out. The

Cadillac-Soo Lumber Company, on the other hand, completely ceased forest operations during the worst years of the Depression. Horses were placed with local farmers to take care of for a fee. The corporate railroad was mothballed and watchmen were brought in to mind the abandoned camps. Only after 1935, when the New Deal was in full swing, did the company resume forest operations.[35] The giant paper mills of the Fox River Valley did not suffer the same extreme cutbacks as the iron and steel industry. Their agents continued to purchase pulpwood throughout the 1930s, which kept many small loggers in business during the Depression.[36]

The growth of the national forests proved a boom for many of the landed lumber companies. Cutover lands, which had become increasingly burdensome to maintain, were offered to the new national forests for sale. William L. Baker, who supervised Forest Service purchases from his Munising headquarters, was not lavish with federal money. When the exact locations of the Upper Peninsula national forests were announced, he was flooded with letters from the region's most important lumbermen. Northwestern Cooperage and Bay De Noquet sold extensive holdings to the Hiawatha National Forest.[37] The Stearns Coal and Lumber Company sold sixteen thousand acres of the old Chicago Lumber Company empire to the government in 1933.[38] The Cadillac-Soo Company eagerly sold seventeen thousand acres of land, some of it still forested, to the Marquette National Forest. The average price paid for land purchases was a mere $1.50 per acre. But lumber companies were happy to have any buyer for real estate that had become an unprofitable liability.[39]

Federal money was forthcoming for these and other extensive purchases because of the aggressive conservation program of President Franklin D. Roosevelt. The creator of the New Deal was an avowed conservationist who saw forestry as a vital tool in the battle to bring agricultural and industrial recovery. National forests loomed large in FDR's plans for the Civilian Conservation Corps (CCC), a jobs program directed to natural resource management. The president had referred to his proposed conservation force many times during the 1932 election campaign, and it became one of his pet projects after inauguration. By the end of March 1933 the dream became reality when he signed the CCC's enabling legislation. Operated along military lines, but devoted to conservation work, the CCC brought thousands of young men to labor in the exhausted forests of northern Michigan.[40]

The CCC was implemented immediately after the president approved the legislation. By the summer of 1933, despite the lack of precedent for such a program, thousands of young men were on their way to the woods. The first enrollees, usually those whose families were on relief, often had to endure the most primitive conditions. "The trucks jolted to a stop at 10 o'clock at night after four hours of traveling," recalled a recruit "Everybody was tired and ready for bed, but where was the camp? There were trees to the right of us, trees to the left of us; in fact, trees all around us. We were organized into groups and given axes. At midnight, we were to start to build the homes in which we were to live."[41] The men carved out tent camps, which in time were replaced by army-style barracks. There was a heavy military flavor to the CCC. Enrollees were supervised by army personnel and outfitted with army surplus equipment. But the pay of thirty dollars per month was much higher than that of an army private.[42]

Among the most important tasks to which the conservation army was put to work was fire control. More than fifteen years of much talk and some effort by both lumbermen and the State Conservation Department had done little to reduce the danger of forest fires in the Upper Peninsula. The Michigan Conservation Department did succeed in establishing fire protection districts during the late 1920s. But these districts, short of staff, looked better on a wall map in Lansing than in the reality of the cutovers. When a fire did occur, the district fire supervisor was forced to recruit emergency fire fighters. The Depression solved the problem of finding men to do the unpleasant, low-pay work by making many people desperate for work. Yet, as the example of a fire near Williams Lake in Chippewa County reveals, that hardly solved the problem. The Conservation Department offered men fifty cents per hour to battle the blaze. For many men, this was the best wage they were offered for quite a while. Human nature being what it is, they were not too anxious for the fire to go out. "Nobody was working, hell, they were hauling brush from half a mile to keep the fire going," recalled Percy LaRock, a Cadillac-Soo Company lumberjack. "Then they cut them down to fifteen cents per hour and the men thought, 'the hell with it,' and let the fire go out."[43]

The CCC gave to fire control efforts a disciplined, fairly reliable labor supply that could be brought to bear not only fighting fires but also preparing the forest to better resist fires. There was a need for truck trails to give crews access to a fire. In 1936, when a fire began on Bay De Noquet Company land in the Hiawatha National Forest, there was no access to the area save for the Nahma and Northern Railway. All water and equipment had to be brought in by rail, which slowed the fire crew's effort. That year was one of the worst in the Upper Peninsula for fires. The Burrell Fire in Alger County destroyed thirty-two hundred acres before the men could put it out. Access also bedeviled efforts to fight a fire along the Slate River in Gogebic County. Some of the CCC men were brought in by flatcar; others had to be transported by boat across

Lake Gogebic. With supplies coming by such an awkward route, it took four full days and nights to extinguish the flames. The worst fire fighting took place on Isle Royale, the forty-five-mile long archipelago in Lake Superior. A 1936 fire burned large sections of the main island. "We spent every day fighting the blaze," remembered Roy Hancock, "with no transportation to and from the field; we carried our pumps, hoses, and other fire fighting equipment on our backs and in our hands, sometimes for ten or twelve miles. We then put in a good many hours fighting the fire." Because of the problem of access and early detection, it is little wonder that fighting fires was made an early priority of the CCC. Within the first seven months, the Michigan CCC built more than 500 miles of truck trails, 67 miles of fire breaks, and 543 acres of emergency landing fields for observation planes.[44]

Local woodsmen occasionally participated in training streetwise recruits from Detroit and the South Side of Chicago how to use the tools of the lumberjack—the ax and crosscut saw. The young men were also made expert in the backbreaking tools of the conservationist, the hoe and the planting bar, which were used to renew thousands of acres with new forest. The introduction of city young men to the forests of the north, however, did not go without a few hitches. On one occasion, several Chicago men, anxious to augment their army-style rations and proud of their ability to "live off the land," cornered and killed what they thought was a wild boar. They dramatically brought the trophy back to camp and all enjoyed a roast pork dinner. The next day, the cook at a nearby Cadillac-Soo Company camp complained that one of his pigs, which foraged in the forest, was missing.[45]

A veteran forester remembered that "open suspicion and ridicule" greeted the CCC recruits when they arrived in the Upper Peninsula. But in a short time social bonds were established between the young conservation workers and the local residents. Ball games were held; dances and educational programs took place at the camps. By the time the program was disbanded in 1942, the CCC had won over its local critics. The young men who made up the CCC are credited with having "transformed the area and left a living monument that will last forever."[46]

The CCC performed its greatest service developing the new national and state forests of the Upper Peninsula into productive timber-producing reserves. "Cutover and burned over pine lands covered more than half of the area," recalled George Ferrar, the Hiawatha National Forest's first ranger. "It was a pretty desolate picture." The CCC helped transform that devastated landscape by tree-planting and fire-protection programs. Thousands of acres were planted with pine seedlings. Tree nurseries were built with CCC labor in both the Hiawatha and Ottawa national forests. In the Ottawa forest, the CCC also undertook thinning and brush-clearing operations to maintain eight thousand acres of prized mature timber. To control fires, an impressive thirty-eight lookout towers were built in the Ottawa National Forest alone. After the emergency conservation tasks were under way, CCC crews devoted considerable attention to enhancing a new type of forest exploitation—tourism. The CCC pioneered many recreation-site development programs in the national forests. The outhouses, boat landings, bathhouses, and recreation areas built by the CCC may have been primitive but they helped prepare the national forest for what would become one of its most important economic functions.[47]

The CCC did little to address the employment problems of Upper Peninsula residents. Yet thirty-three percent of families there were on relief. With mines and forest products, the twin pillars of the local economy, slumping during the Depression, the Upper Peninsula was devastated. Only one out of Dickinson County's forty iron mines was in operation. In Keweenaw County, as many as three out of four families were on relief. In frustration, the State of Michigan's relief administrator stated "at least 50,000 persons must eventually move [out of the Upper Peninsula] . . . or remain permanently dependent."[48] Such a prognosis, no matter how true, was of little comfort to unemployed men who had no money for their next meal, let alone the resources to move. To aid these men, the U.S. Forest Service supervised several other short-term conservation work programs. In 1932, for example, the Emergency Relief Program put men to work in the Hiawatha National Forest. Foresters in northern Michigan also supervised several Civil Works Administration projects in the forest and operated two camps, for Munising and Manistique residents respectively, that employed men under the National Industrial Recovery Act. But these programs were temporary, stopgap efforts that ceased by 1934 when the Depression bottomed out.[49]

The Indians of the Upper Peninsula were particularly hard hit by the Depression. Many of them worked in the lumber industry as sawyers or woodsmen. When those jobs became scarce, many Indians were without employment. Most of the quality timber had been cut off the Upper Peninsula's major reservations during the late teens and early twenties. In the spring of 1933 the Bureau of Indian Affairs approved CCC programs for Indians.[50] At the L'Anse Reservation in Baraga County, the bureau tried to balance "the urgent need of furnishing employment to the local Indians" with the need to provide fire protection for the reservation by having the local chapter of the CCC-Indian Division work almost solely on the reservation.[51] In the eastern Upper Peninsula, however, a special Indian camp was set up in the Marquette National Forest near Ackerman, which operated under Forest Service control and employed Indians from the nearby Bay Mills Reservations as well as from across northern Michigan. One of the men working at this camp quipped: "The white man stole our land in the first place; cut off the timber, and now they are making us plant it again."[52]

The CCC worked both on the national forests and on state forest-lands. As early as April 1934 there were thirteen camps of two hundred men each operating on state lands in the Upper Peninsula. The most important area of state and federal forestry cooperation, however, was in the area of land exchanges. Both state and national forest purchase units were difficult to manage in the 1930s because their holdings were scattered. Legislative action established ambitious boundaries for these units but ownership came slowly only after private titles could be bought or were surrendered. Blocking up forest reservations was enhanced by cooperation between the State Department of Conservation and the U.S. Forest Service. Beginning in 1936 a mutually advantageous land-exchange program was adopted. Michigan gave to the Forest Service tax-delinquent lands in the three major Upper Peninsula purchases; in return the federal government purchased lands in state forests. In this way, the state forests in the Upper Peninsula became large, easy-to-manage units and the national forests expanded quickly. The program made a virtue out of the flood of tax delinquencies that broke over northern Michigan in the late 1930s.[53] The Ottawa National Forest increased its control over an additional 65,927 acres; the Marquette was the largest beneficiary, receiving close to 94,000 acres in exchanges.[54]

The aggressive forest expansion programs of the State Department of Conservation and the U.S. Forest Service during the late 1920s and through the 1930s had far-reaching implications for the logging industry. Throughout the nineteenth century, state and federal authorities sought to encourage economic development in the Upper Peninsula by transferring land and resources to private control. Conservation forces reversed this trend, and by returning cutover lands to government control secured the future of the northern Michigan forest products industry. However, never again would that industry be free to pursue its economic agenda without regard to the public interest, as represented by conservation bureaucrats.

Nor was land use the sole aspect of the logging industry effected by the New Deal. The cornerstone of Franklin D. Roosevelt's plan to put Americans back to work was the National Industrial Recovery Act (NRA). As part of a program of industrial organization, producers and workers were both encouraged to organize. The NRA provided a labor code, which indicated federal support for unions and collective bargaining. When the NRA was established in 1933, not a single labor organization was active in the Great Lakes logging industry. But with the encouragement of the NRA's Blue Eagle, socially conscious woodworkers were quick to fill the gap. In 1935 lumberjacks in Oregon struck for and won an eight-hour day and a forty-hour workweek. Two years later, Minnesota lumberjacks organized and walked off the job. They were supported in their job action by most of the woodworkers and by the governor of the state. When their effort was rewarded with success, lumberjacks in Michigan renewed their interest in collective bargaining.

On May 17, 1937, timber workers in Marenisco began a strike that would spread across the Upper Peninsula. Nominal leader of the job action was Joseph Liss, a veteran organizer who had already been active in the Minnesota strike. The foundation for the action was laid in March of that year when the Communist party in Ironwood forged a union of local woodworkers and received a charter from the American Federation of Labor. Liss acted as the catalyst for a situation ripe for agitation. Not a man to waste time, Liss called for a strike on the very day he arrived in town from Minnesota. The cause he exploited was the Bonifas Lumber Company's firing of a young mill worker who promoted unionization of the Marenisco mill. Liss drove out to the surrounding logging camps and persuaded most of the lumberjacks to walk out. In short order, most of the camps in Gogebic County were closed, and the Marenisco Mill was forced to close for want of logs.[55]

The lumberjacks did not require much encouragement to strike. Spring was a wet, miserable place in the cuttings, and the conditions in the camps were overdue for improvement. A week before Liss called the strike, half of the lumberjacks at Bonifas Lumber Camp No. 2 walked out over poor living and working conditions.[56] Lumber camps had improved little since the late nineteenth century. Despite a generation of technological change and increases in the quality of life in most sectors of society, lumberjacks still slept in bunks with straw bedding. The bunks were built so close together that they could only be entered from the foot and were therefore known among woodsmen as "muzzle loaders." Those bunks were then shared by two men in each bed. Some lumberjacks placed a "snort pole" down the center of the bed to keep their neighbor from rolling onto their side. Yet no piece of wood could prevent lice from spreading from one man to the next. Lice were a repulsive but irrepressible part of lumberjack life. "Some of those camps were lousy," recalled an old woodsman. "One at Gibbs City was so lousy that they used to pick lice off the bedding. . . . Then they'd let them out on the bed and see if they could race them across the blankets."[57] As unpleasant as the itching caused by lice was the stench caused by the closely packed bodies of unwashed men and their sweaty clothes drying on haywire suspended above the stove. "The odor was almost impossible to stand," recalled a camp visitor.[58] The Ford Motor Company was one of the few employers that provided hot water and cleaning facilities for its workers.

Nor was the food, contrary to north woods lore, universally good. Lumberjacks almost never left the table hungry, but they seldom enjoyed fresh foods. Their diet in many camps was a monotonous succession of high-starch, high-fat foods. A woodsman at a Cleveland-Cliffs camp complained: "In the three years that I have been employed by this company, I saw fresh fruit only once, and that was when they served apples." When this same man tried to clean his clothes, he was "bawled out for taking wood to heat water. . . ."[59]

To a considerable extent, the lumber companies were to blame for the strike. They had not improved conditions in the camps as much as they were able. Railroads and truck trails did much to remove the isolation that had made camp supply difficult. Yet the Depression forced many lumbermen, certainly Cleveland-Cliffs, to try to squeeze the maximum profit out of their forest operations. This worked well, for a time, but long after the company's emergency passed, Cleveland-Cliffs kept wages and food expenditures low. In 1937 the company was enjoying its best year ever, but the woodworkers still suffered under miserable conditions.[60] Even the normally pro-business Ironwood *Daily Globe* agreed that conditions at the striking camps "left much to be complained about."[61]

Besides better food, washing facilities, single bunks, and a fifty-five-cent per hour wage, the strikers revived their 1920 demand for an eight-hour day and recognition of the union. Some lumber companies tried to head off the strikers by improving conditions before they were faced with a walkout. On April 30, 1937, the Patten Timber Company, in Iron County, increased its wage rate by ten to fifteen percent.[62] When workers began to walk out of the Lake Superior Lumber Company camps, the superintendent suddenly announced that the company had already decided to increase lumberjacks' wages by two cents per hour. When this did not work, he threatened the men with permanent closure of the plant.[63] This tone was more in keeping with the angry response of most employers. They maintained that the whole job action was a result of outside agitators. Nor was there any attempt to negotiate with management before the walkout. Many lumbermen believed that if they could meet with their men, demands would be redressed. But to men who had endured conditions that had gone on too long already, the mixture of pleas and threats from management sounded less persuasive than the Communists' clever paraphrase of Karl Marx: "Lumberjacks, unite! All you've got to lose is your bedbugs!"[64]

From the Bonifas camps in Gogebic County, the strike spread east and north. Marathon Paper Company loggers were forced to suspend operations for want of workers. The Connor Land and Lumber Company was forced to close its mill at Wakefield. In Iron County, the Van Platen-Fox Company lost about 125 men to the strike.[65] In Ontonagon County, the Lake Superior Lumber Company shut down after losing 300 lumberjacks.[66] Baraga County lumberjacks struck Ford Motor Company loggers, while farther east, the I. Stephenson, Wisconsin Land and Lumber, and the Newberry Lumber and Chemical Company were also affected by the strike.

The Cleveland-Cliffs Company's extensive logging operations in Alger County were crippled by the strike. After the job action began in Marenisco, a carload of Liss's deputies drove all night across the peninsula to the Cleveland-Cliffs camps. They arrived at a railcar camp before dawn. "Should we wake the boys up or should we wait until morning?" the strikers wondered. Finally they decided to organize the walkout immediately and began to go from car to car shouting, "Wake up, you sons of bitches and lumberjacks!" The men were sick of the company's cost-cutting measures and greeted the strikers warmly. One man jumped down from his bunk and began to dance a jig saying happily, "I knew you guys would be around eventually." The strikers then began to sign up lumberjacks as members of the union. "By daylight, the camp was empty," one organizer remembered, "all of them had gone on strike." In a matter of days, the company lost more than 250 men from three camps, and the Munising mills of both Cleveland-Cliffs and Jackson & Tindle were forced to close.[67]

The strike did not fare well in the towns. Local sheriffs and most residents were decidedly against the job action. The strike brought hordes of the worst type of lumberjacks into towns like Munising and Marenisco—woodsmen without money. Strikers organized relief committees that solicited merchants for aid. Men camped on the outskirts of town or crowded into the local Finnish Workers' Hall to sleep at night. Many a middle-class townsman feared what the "timberbeasts" might do if the strike became desperate. It was, however, the heavy Communist involvement in the strike that proved most antagonistic to the townspeople.

Through radical Finnish workers Communism got a foothold in the north woods. As early as 1906 radical workers formed the Finnish Socialist Federation, a Marxist organization that was first allied to the Socialist party but later split over the question of support for the IWW. While one faction joined with the Wobblies, another allied with the Workers' Party of America, a Communist organization. Both factions worked, in their own way, for better conditions in the mines and mills. For many immigrant workers in the Upper Peninsula, they were the only support available in towns dominated by one or two large companies. Central to their success were the worker's halls that the Finns founded in towns across the peninsula. These halls were focal points for community gatherings and social events that often had nothing to do with socialist labor causes. In Newberry, the hall was used by the American Legion for its dances. Only after the strike began did residents excitedly view the halls as potential beachheads for a Communist invasion of their town.[68]

The high-water mark of the strike came at Newberry on June 4. Strikers had successfully closed several Newberry Lumber and Chemical Company camps. Those men and some of the strike organizers then converged on the town intending to organize the main plant's 325 workers. But they never had a chance to make their case. The strikers were met by a mob of townspeople and mill workers armed with bats and iron bars. The armed men charged the strikers. As the cudgels came down on the fleeing strikers, several men were injured; one, Joseph Kist, was killed. The mob pursued the union men to the Workers' Hall, which they then gutted. Wounded strikers were loaded onto a flatbed truck and moved out. The remaining men straggled back highway M-28 to Munising. In Newberry, the editor of the local newspaper exulted: "Newberry should get the credit for breaking the strike wide open and showing it up for what it was—a communistic movement."[69]

The situation was also becoming critical in Munising. There Liss had led several marches to demand food for the strikers. The union had spent more than two thousand dollars on food and had bankrupted its treasury. Liss wanted government relief funds released to the strikers, but Alger County had spent all its money for the month of June. Nonetheless, Liss proclaimed the lumberjack's willingness to "use violence if necessary to see that we and our families get food." Fear of just that type of talk led Munising officials to arrest Liss on the charge of inciting a riot. When union lawyer Henry Paull and his wife, Irene, tried to win Liss's release, they were driven out of the county by a mob snarling anti-Semitic and anti-Communist epithets. Munising justified its high-handed actions the same way Newberry had done: "What the hell are they doing sleeping in a hall where Stalin's picture hung on the wall."[70] After two weeks of excitement, the strike was being broken and in the eastern Upper Peninsula logging proceeded as usual.

With their grip slipping, strikers in Gogebic County petitioned Governor Frank Murphy to send a mediator. The liberal governor acted neither wisely nor decisively. Talks broke down because the strikers objected to the governor's representative and lumbermen refused to recognize the strike leaders as legitimate workers. Trapped in this crossfire were the scores of small logging jobbers who had already invested all their savings, cutting logs over the winter. Now as the strike dragged on, their logs sat decked on forest landings. Either those logs were shipped to market or they would begin to depreciate in value. When desperate jobbers tried to truck their logs out of the forest, they were met by brigades of strikers who abused drivers with threats, stones, and fists. In Baraga County lumberjacks ambushed the truck convoy of a Ford jobber, Peter Hiltonen. His logs were dumped from the trucks before police arrived and forced the strikers to back off. This tactic was repeated several times in Gogebic County, much to the detriment of the jobbers' pocketbooks and the strikers' image.[71]

As the strike wound down, it grew increasingly ugly. Vigilante committees were formed to protect the nonunion loggers' right to operate. In Ontonagon County this committee was headed by members of the American Legion, an organization that had opposed the 1920 strike as well.[72] In Bessemer the strikers' headquarters was sacked; in Ironwood, "patriots" struck leaders with clubs and forcibly transported them across the state line. Faced with this kind of opposition, the strikers could not hope to achieve their goal of an industrywide agreement. In August they settled with thirty-eight small operators, but the strikers were defeated in their attempt to win union recognition and concessions from the big lumber companies. Cleveland-Cliffs, Bonifas, Newberry Lumber and Chemical, and Connor Land and Lumber remained unbowed. The strike was basically a failure; it did not lay the foundation for a unionized work force in the Upper Peninsula. The sixteen-week struggle did, if only incrementally, bring improvement of camp conditions.

The 1937 strike hastened the withdrawal of the large lumber companies from active logging. The three Cleveland-Cliffs camps closed by strike action were never opened again.[73] The company had threatened to close all its logging camps if an industrywide agreement was obtained. As it was, the National Labor Relations Board investigated charges that the company harassed unionized employees. There also were economic forces at work. The strike did not adversely affect the company. In 1937 the number of logs cut rose by a modest one percent. Cleveland-Cliff's Operation #203, a major railroad logging venture near the Hiawatha National Forest, was able to increase deliveries from forest to mill throughout the strike.[74] However, the prospect of an aggressive labor force backed by an interventionist federal government may have caused management to pause. Railroad logging, despite cost-cutting measures, had always been a high overhead proposition requiring long-term planning. The erratic nature of the steel industry during the late 1930s made such planning difficult. Although 1937 was Cleveland-Cliff's best year, the following year was its second worst since 1900. With the company's management finding it "most difficult to make any prediction" for the future, railroad logging may have appeared to be an unnecessary risk.[75]

Cleveland-Cliffs turned to jobbers to do the logging for them. These independent loggers purchased stumpage rights from the company and then cut the timber and delivered the logs to a Lake Superior and Ishpeming Railroad siding from where it could be shipped to production points. The jobbers were left with providing the improved camp conditions demanded by lumberjacks. The jobbers also had the task of transporting logs from the forest to the trunk line rails, thus largely relieving the company of the cost of maintaining rail spurs. Instead of the iron horse, jobbers relied on trucks to handle that expensive task.[76]

The new jobber system went through a difficult period of adjustment. During the first two years, the Cleveland-Cliffs Company's total log sales dropped by sixty-two percent. The reason for this dramatic decline was clear. There were not enough small loggers willing to assume the heavy financial burden the company demanded. The cost of operating a camp and purchasing trucks was more than what many jobbers could handle. On top of that, Cleveland-Cliffs wanted these men to purchase stumpage rights. If these men had the capital to do that, they would not have needed to work with Cleveland-Cliffs. Beginning in 1940 the company eased the small jobbers' burden by removing the requirement that they purchase stumpage and entering into a sharecroplike agreement. Jobbers agreed to cut the timber in return for a share in the profits from log sales. Under this system, production quickly rebounded, and by 1942 (aided by the war boom) lumber production again reached its 1937 highwater mark.[77]

Cleveland-Cliff's move to jobbers and truck logging was not an isolated action. By the late 1930s the logging industry was amid a profound change. The big paternalistic lumber companies were retreating from forest operations and in the process abandoning their logging railroads. The largest operator in the eastern Upper Peninsula, the Cadillac-Soo Lumber Company, also abandoned its logging railroads in 1937. The company continued to operate camps, but all shipments to the mill were handled by independent truckers who owned vehicles and were paid for the number of loads taken from forest to mill.[78] The Bay De Noquet Company and the Connor Land and Lumber Company were railroad stalwarts. The Nahma and Northern Railroad operated at capacity through most of the war years. Fifteen-hour days were the rule for the railroaders. When the war ended however, even the Bay De Noquet Company began to purchase logging trucks. In 1947 the last haul was made on the logging line. Within a year even the track north of Nahma Junction was removed and the old right-of-way began to return to the forest.[79] The old iron horses were sold for scrap and the rubber tire lumberjacks assumed their ascendancy in the forest.

11

THE PROCESS AND PATTERN OF PULPWOOD LOGGING

Frances Furlong was a small-scale lumberman during the 1920s. Out of an office in Trout Lake, he supervised a variety of logging operations. One of his most difficult chances was a pulpwood contract he assumed for the Bonifas Lumber Company in Chippewa County. The timber in question was a full eight miles from the railroad siding where the logs had to be delivered. It was too long a haul for his horse-drawn sleighs to make a round-trip every day. Of course, he could not leave his teamsters or even the horses outside overnight; nor could he afford to build an extra bunkhouse and stable. Fortunately, he did have access to two trucks. So Furlong tested them on his ice roads and they worked fine. Elated, he put them to work—but not hauling timber. Each night the trucks were used to bring the teamsters, teams, and sleighs back to camp. "That is mentality working there," Furlong later recalled with a laugh. "We could not think of hauling timber in the truck; all we could think of was the horses."[1]

Furlong's experience underscores the problems attached to introducing new technology to any industrial process. The adaptation that takes place is part mechanical and part cognitive. Machinery must physically be integrated with the flow of products; yet equally significant is the mental preparation that is the precondition to change. Lumbermen in northern Michigan were slow to break with both genuine horse-power and the iron horse. The internal combustion engine did not become the dominant feature of forest operations and transportation until the 1940s, well after the technology became significant. The Great Depression and the decline of the north country from forest storehouse to lumber backwater slowed the rate of change in the region.

TECHNOLOGY OF PULPWOOD ERA LOGGING

Early attempts to apply gasoline-powered vehicles to forest operations often suffered from fragile technology and high costs. The Cleveland-Cliffs Iron Company experimented with crawler tractors in the early twenties. But these devices were less satisfactory than horses, except on long hauls of two miles or more.[2] Even the Ford Motor Company, which naturally was dedicated to the use of the internal combustion engine, experienced trouble with tractors in the 1920s. Ford loggers tried to use small tractors manufactured by the company to skid logs to the landing. But in heavy snow the Fordson tractors failed to pull as well as horses, and the loads often had to be reduced thereby slowing forest operations.[3] Ford's experimentation eventually paid off. By the late 1930s heavier tractors began to replace horses. Cleveland-Cliffs also experienced more success with tractors during the 1930s. Breakdowns became less common. Tractors employed by the company at that time, had 640 fewer moving parts than their predecessors a decade before. Cleveland-Cliffs and the Bonifas Lumber Company used heavy-duty tractors to haul loaded sleds out of terrain unsuited for railroad logging.[4] The Connor Land and Lumber Company waited until World War II, when efficient caterpillar tractors were available, to get rid of the "hay burners."[5]

Ford was also an innovator in using trucks to transport logs from the forest to the mill. Yet once again Ford's belief in the future of gas engines was at first stronger than the truck's produced in Detroit. A Ford logger recalled that the trucks "were not the type you could use for hauling logs. They were pretty lightweight." Breakdowns were common and deliveries were delayed.[6] Cleveland-Cliffs used trucks in the late 1920s more wisely. By 1928 all company camps were being supplied largely by Chevrolet trucks. Food, logging equipment, even ice, were brought in from the Lumber Department's central warehouse.[7] Only as heavy-duty trucks became available in the 1930s did trucks supplant the railroad as the best means of supplying the mill with logs.

Although the rise of trucks meant the end of logging railroads, it brought with it the new problem of road building. Cleveland-Cliffs merely pulled up the steel and ties on its forest rail network and allowed its jobbers to use the heavily ballasted bed as a truck trail. As they worked off the timber adjacent to the old spurs, new truck roads had to be built.[8] Poorly prepared truck beds were sensitive to weather conditions. Heavy rain, snow, or a premature thaw could close truck roads and delay the shipment of logs or bolts to the mill. The newer heavy trucks of the 1930s were particularly hard on poorly prepared roads. The Ford Motor Company was often plagued with delays caused by bad weather and inadequately prepared roads.[9] Ford's forest operations were too closely tied to automobile production demands whose fluctuations had no relationship with the logging industry. The problem could have been avoided had executives been willing to establish a substantial inventory of lumber that would fulfill immediate needs while loggers could then plan their forest work well in advance. Instead, large inventories were regarded as a luxury, and the loggers scrambled to fulfill factory requirements. "We were so close on log input that the contractors practically hauled logs over plowed fields," recalled a Ford woodsman, "the roads being about equal to plowed fields."[10]

Smart loggers paid careful attention to their truck roads. Howard Anderson, a small-scale logger who established a camp near Tula, Michigan, in the late 1930s, saw money spent on road building as an investment in the future. He planned to use the camp for three years, so he rented a bulldozer to pull up stumps and fill in gullies along the right-of-way. Gravel trucks were then brought in to cover the surface with stone. There were some low soft spots in the road where gravel could not do much good. For those trouble areas, Anderson spiked heavy wood planks to logs laid in the roadbed, thereby making a trestle for the trucks. Because of the expense of all this careful preparation, loggers tried to make maximum use of old railroad grades, farm roads, and public highways. When Anderson built Tula Camp, he actually negotiated the right of passage for his trucks on a farmer's road by promising to give all his cook shanty garbage to the farmer's pigs![11]

Ford's less deliberate logging program made it unpopular with loggers and legal authorities alike. Albert Olson, a Ford woods superintendent, received an anxious visit from his superiors at the Iron Mountain mill every time weather forced a halt in the hauling. On several occasions, Olson was pressured to have his teamsters haul at night, a suggestion he resisted because of the Fordson truck's tendency to jackknife.[12] When Olson or other loggers did haul under favorable conditions, they loaded their trucks to the maximum capacity. Over time, this raised trouble with motorists in Marquette and Baraga counties who blamed the deterioration of paved roads on overloaded trucks. The State Highway Department began to spot-check logging trucks and fine them as much as fifty dollars for overloading.[13] Such police actions proved particularly painful for independent teamsters who owned their trucks and were paid by the amount of logs they hauled, and for jobbers who were sometimes penalized for the tardy delivery of logs.

Despite such difficulties, trucks clearly were the wave of the future. The CCC helped smooth the transition from railroad logging to trucks by building many roads in state and national forests. Such roads served the dual purpose of providing access for fire-fighting crews as well as for loggers. Other New Deal agencies also pumped money into public works projects leading to major improvements in Upper Peninsula highways. Yet the most significant development in the improvement of logging roads came with the development, during World War II, of rugged road-building machinery.[14] Instead of horse-drawn wheeler-scrapers, there were diesel bulldozers, which in a matter of days could tear out a path for trucks. Such roads were less imposing than the old logging railroads, but they were cheaper and quicker to build.[15]

As gasoline engines were perfected, they were gradually adapted to all aspects of logging. Steam log loaders were still popular with the large companies or those that shipped by rail. The "haywire," or small-scale logger, could not afford such equipment until gasoline engines were readily available. George Corrigan, a logging jobber in the Ottawa National Forest area during the Depression, employed a jury-rigged power log hoist. He hired a blacksmith to convert a salvaged Buick engine and the ruins of an old steam loader, found at an abandoned camp, into a gas-powered device. The camp "wood butcher," who handled carpentry in the woods, joined with the blacksmith and inside a week they fashioned an efficient loader.[16] Devices such as these, although they were not pretty, helped increase productivity in the forest. After a fairly stable period from 1890 through 1920, the productivity per lumberjack began to increase steadily through the 1930s and 1940s. The Depression, wartime labor shortages, and new technology contributed to the rising efficiency of forest operations.[17]

Another contributing factor was the increase in piece-work. This system became widespread during the Depression as a means to draw the most out of labor expenditures.[18] Instead of men being paid a flat daily wage, pieceworkers were paid based on the amount of wood that was cut. The system was used in all types of logging situations. In 1939, for example, Howard Anderson employed his hardwood sawyers on such terms. The sawyers were interviewed by Anderson and the cutting price would be agreed upon. The sawyers would then go out and inspect the timber to see if it was of sufficient size before signing on for the winter.[19] Piecework, however, was most common on pulpwood jobs. Workers would cut the small logs or branches to specific lengths and they were paid based on the scale of their pile at the end of the day.[20]

Improved tools were important in the rise of productivity. During the late 1920s, Finnish woodsmen introduced the bucksaw to pulpwood operations. It was lighter than the traditional crosscut saw, and best of all it was lightweight and equipped with a wood frame so that it could be used by just one man. Cedar saws, which were shorter than the old crosscut and equipped with a handle for one man to use, also became popular.[21]

The dramatic breakthrough came with the perfection of the chain saw after World War II.

The chain saw was invented by Andreas Stihl in Germany in 1927. But the early models were heavy, unreliable, and awkward to operate. Even when the war made labor dear, few Upper Peninsula loggers tried to use chain saws. Connor Land and Lumber Company was one of the firms that experimented with the two-man, 150-pound Titan power saw. The giant wood eater did a good job cutting firewood for the cook shanty and the bunkhouses, which was no small task, but it was not brought into the woods. It was only after the war, when single-man, relatively lightweight chain saws were developed that the power tool became widely used. Chain saws proved an asset for the pulpwood cutter where speed was desirable, but it was among the lumber cutters, who had been limited to the crosscut saw for eighty years, that the biggest improvement was felt.[22]

The chain saw marked the beginning of automation for the forest work force. During the 1950s and 1960s, more and more gas-powered equipment was adopted. Giant rubber-tired skidders were brought to haul logs to the landing. Many of these were equipped with hydraulic claws, which eliminated the messy task of fastening tackle and cable. Log handling was made more efficient by the invention of the self-loading truck. The most widely used in the Upper Peninsula was the Prentice loader, a truck equipped with a hydraulic grapple that lifted logs off the ground and onto the truck bed. With such vehicles the job of the top loader, once one of the most prestigious and dangerous in the industry, was eliminated. By the 1970s even sawyers were being threatened with elimination. For a couple of hundred thousand dollars, a "feller butcher" could be bought. This mechanized monster lumbered through the forest crushing trees at their base, lifting them off the ground, and leaving the branchless trunks to be sent to the mill.[23]

Yet for all the technological innovations that have taken place since World War II, the forest operations of small jobbers (as recently as the 1960s) featured horsepower and manual labor. Resourcefully, these undercapitalized lumbermen often made their own tools out of the broken machines that rusted on the fringes of Upper Peninsula towns. From the springs of wrecked autos, woodsmen made spuds, a hand-held tool used to pry bark off a log. Loggers who could not afford hydraulic loaders could afford pickaroons. A pickaroon was made from a broken and discarded ax. The steel head was cut down until it was in the shape of a hook that was then sharpened so that it would cut into wood. Two men armed with pickaroons would wrestle an eight-foot long piece of cordwood onto the bed of a truck. It took longer to load a truck this way, but the men seldom broke down and they received all the fuel they needed at the cookhouse table.[24]

TECHNOLOGY OF PULPWOOD ERA: MILLING

The growing technological sophistication of wood processing has been of major importance in the continued viability of logging in the Upper Peninsula. Since 1930 new products and new processes have meant a fairly consistent demand for forest products. The pulp and paper industry, which dominated this phase of northern Michigan logging, was particularly aggressive in its expansion. Kimberly-Clark, for example, sponsored extensive research and development during the 1920s and 1930s, which resulted in new consumer products such as facial tissues, paper, and sanitary napkins. Between 1929 and 1959 production of paper products in the United States increased threefold, with the lake states leading the nation in output.[25]

To accommodate such expanded demand, new processing techniques were developed. Mechanized debarking machines, which quickly removed the bark from logs, multiknife chipping machines, and chip washers prepared amazing amounts of wood for pulping in a matter of minutes. In the 1970s whole tree-chippers were introduced. These machines reduced an entire tree from its leaves to its roots to wood chips without ever leaving the forest. This process produced almost no waste and yielded large amounts of wood chips for pulping or fuel.[26]

The industry's dynamic growth after World War II has been fueled by new and ever expanding variety of products. Among the most important of these are building products. Although they are short of quality lumber, Upper Peninsula mills began to flood the construction industry with pulp products that served as lumber substitutes. Wood fibre produced at the Celotex Corporation mill in L'Anse was used for making ceiling tiles, panels, and insulation. Fiberboard, in recent years, has grown to become a major use of cordwood. It fits into a niche in the building trades that was pioneered originally by plywood, another of the new forest products of the twentieth century.

Plywood was a term that came into use during World War I. It described layers of wood veneer glued together in such a way that the grain of each veneer layer is alternated. The resulting board is durable and inexpensive. During and after World War I, most plywood manufacturers used hardwood veneer. Not until the 1930s did softwood plywood begin to assume a large share of the market. In the Upper Peninsula, the Atlas Plywood Company and Roddis Plywood Corporation, major Midwest producers, operated logging camps. Plywood manufacturers were hard pressed to meet demand as total consumption in the United States increased by one billion square feet between 1952 and 1962. A major innovation in the 1970s was the introduction of plywood with wood fibre cores. This allowed lake state producers to make use of the abundant pulpwood in the forests of northern Michigan.[27]

Products such as plywood and paper became the mainstays for the forest products industry because they found profitable outlets for wood that was either wasted or ignored by early generations of lumbermen. Through economic pressure, the industry processed forest products more efficiently. Where pine lumbermen burned sawdust or dumped it into Lake Michigan, polluting the air and destroying schools of white-fish, modern manufacturers tried to make use of their waste wood. The giant paper maker, Champion International, recycled its waste wood to use as fuel for its Quinnesec, Michigan, plant. Despite these trends, paper mills in the Upper Peninsula were viewed critically by environmentalists during the late 1960s and 1970s.[28]

Nor did all technological innovations bring a boon to northern Michigan lumber towns. Synthetic chemicals developed in modern laboratories replaced most of the products of the Upper Peninsula's wood chemical industry. The Newberry Iron and Chemical Company, which along with its predecessor firms, the Lake Superior Iron and Chemical Company and the Charcoal Iron Company, had been major loggers, could not resist the forces that brought an end to the charcoal iron industry by the close of World War II. Wood chemical and charcoal iron operations in Escanaba, Marquette, and elsewhere were also liquidated.[29]

FOREST RESOURCES AND THE PULPWOOD ERA

The most influential factor in determining the forest resource situation in the twentieth-century Upper Peninsula has been the rise of public and industrial forestry. By the 1940s the generations of technical bulletins, public lectures, and experimental forest programs finally began to pay off. Many of the landowners who survived the high taxes of the 1920s and 1930s began to adopt the principles of forestry. The Cleveland-Cliffs Iron Company, for example, adopted the principle of sustained yield. The company divided its Land Department into three districts, each of which was supervised by a professional forester. This was something the company had started to implement twenty-five years before; now it was followed through. Selective logging began in 1942. The foresters chose which units were to be logged and identified the mature or diseased trees that needed to be harvested so that young growth could prosper.[30] Connor Land and Lumber Company and the

Longyear Realty Corporation, the latter of which controlled hundreds of thousands of Upper Peninsula acres, also adopted forestry after World War II.

It was, however, among the paper products that forestry first took root on a broad scale. In the early 1930s the Marathon Division of American Can Company, Consolidated Water Power and Paper Company, and Kimberly-Clark began their forestry programs. Later in the decade, they were joined by the Copper Range Company, Mosinee Paper Company, and the Northern Paper Company. By 1947 Kimberly-Clark alone was employing forty-seven foresters for its American and Canadian timber holdings. An American Pulpwood Association report showed that between 1937 and 1947, the number of foresters employed by pulp producers increased fivefold. This was necessary because during those same years the amount of land controlled by lake states paper producers nearly doubled. A handful of paper mills bought large blocks of forestland to secure their future source of supply. Because of Wisconsin's leadership in pulp production, the convenient forests of the Upper Peninsula were a valuable resource that papermakers were anxious to develop and nurture.[31]

Paper producers and wood products manufacturers proved to be very adaptable to the changing nature of the Upper Peninsula's forests. "Weed trees," which had been despised by earlier generations of loggers, were successfully processed into valuable products. Aspen, for example, was abundant on cutover lands. It was one of the first trees to sprout after a fire and could grow very quickly—sometimes as much as five feet per year. Papermakers found that it could be readily transformed into pulp for wallboard or writing paper. Ford and other auto manufacturers found aspen made good material for shipping pallets or it could be ground for excelsior, a packaging material. Similarly, jack pine's reputation was revised when Norway and white pine became scarce. It quickly became one of the most favored materials for the papermaker. Producers needed imagination and ever improving technology to exploit fully the declining quality of northern Michigan's forest.

Fortunately, the Upper Peninsula in the late 1930s was still rich enough in forest resources to bounce back under the guidance of scientific forestry. The region was the last outpost of the lake states logging frontier, and despite heavy exploitation in the past, it still boasted virgin timber. In 1936 the Upper Peninsula held forty percent of the saw timber in the lake states and fifty percent of the cedar poles.[32]

Planting programs further enhanced the region's future prospects. Corporate forestry programs made modest gains. By 1952 private owners in the lake states had replanted nearly forty-five thousand acres. Over time, the pace of private replanting increased so that by 1960 seven million trees were being planted annually.[33] Federal and state foresters were forced to replant more aggressively, partly because the lands under their control were those that had been the most abused by past logging practices. Forested lands were also considered more inviting to the tourist, so national forest lands adjacent to highways were replanted at an early date. The CCC was of major importance in assisting the Forest Service and the conservation department in their replanting efforts. By 1953 the Marquette and Hiawatha national forests had together replanted 98,500 acres of forest. The State Conservation Department's programs have been less successful because of a shortage of money and that agency's broader range of commitments.[34]

Nonetheless, federal and state forests have been vital in maintaining the Upper Peninsula's logging industry. By 1952 government agencies controlled forty-nine percent of all Upper Peninsula lands.[35] For small loggers struggling to make equipment payments or farmers desperate for some cash income, the national forests proved an important resource. During the 1930s, the Forest Service offered small sales of less than five hundred dollars to local loggers. These were generally mature stands of conifers that could be sold for pulpwood. Such sales gave business to the small loggers that were the backbone of local business and provided employment for farmers and townspeople hit hard by the Depression.[36] Forest Service programs also benefited the larger loggers. The most important of these was the Division of State and Private Forestry, whose purpose was to provide guidance to agencies or corporations interested in practicing forestry.

Many early efforts, despite good intentions, resulted in frustrating failure. For example, in 1936 the division began an experimental program with the Von Platen-Fox Company in Iron County. At first, the division drafted a sustained-yield program for the lumber company; later the two organizations agreed to pool resources and establish the Basswood Resettlement Project. M. J. Fox, head of the lumber company, was interested in forestry. A year earlier, he donated a ten-acre tract that included a large logging camp to the University of Michigan Forestry School. The Basswood Project was to be a model of rural relocation and cooperative forestry. A community would be established and sustained-yield forestry would provide a stable income for the residents. The whole plan was reminiscent of Henry Ford's Alberta Project, which was under way at the same time. But the plan fell into disfavor with Forest Service officials in Washington and was canceled. Von Platen-Fox Company went ahead with its own selective-cutting program, but cut over seventy percent of the timber out. This was too much to allow for sustained yield. Not enough young timber was left behind to provide another harvest in the near future.[37] The company, however, could not afford to take less timber and still meet costs levels and the profit margin. The Basswood Project failure revealed the unpleasant truth that good intentions were not enough to make forestry pay. A very large block of forestlands controlled by the logger were essential to allow selective cutting and still supply a mill. The cooperative project would have pooled federal and Von Platen lands to create such a block of land; without access to those lands, Von Platen-Fox had no choice but to log intensively.[38]

Other programs undertaken by the Division of State and Private Forestry were more successful. Sustained-yield plans were prepared for most of the large iron mining companies in the region. Federal foresters did their best to manage timber exchanged with loggers in a way that would encourage sustained-yield programs. Government timber sales, usually done through competitive bidding, also helped maintain the viability of many logging companies. On the other hand, federal and state actions taken after World War II raised the ire of northern loggers.

One of the most volatile issues was the tension between recreational and commercial forestry. Loggers experienced many of the advantages of multiple-use management. Under this system, land was managed for watershed protection, wildlife habitat, commercial forestry, and recreation. They received no benefits from such a single-use management as wilderness protection. The Forest Service's few recreation areas were unobjectionable, but the growth of state and national parks caused concern among many loggers. The establishment of Pictured Rocks National Lakeshore in Alger County increased to 592,000 acres the amount of federal land in Michigan. The number of acres in state parks more than doubled between 1948 and 1972. Unlike national forestlands, parks were managed according to the preservation ethic. Loggers were caught in a shift in land-management priorities. Just as they were being converted to forestry's multiple use, the public began to shift its attitude toward the northern forest from one of an economic storehouse to one of viewing the forests as a retreat from urban civilization.[39]

Typical of this problem was the controversy over Porcupine Mountains State Wilderness Park. Located west of Ontonagon, the Porcupine Mountains had one of the few undisturbed tracts of virgin hardwood forest left in northern Michigan. Since the copper hunters of the early nineteenth century, few men had tried to exploit the resources of this rugged and remote landscape. The mountains gave a magnificent view of Lake Superior's undeveloped south shore and near the summit they hid a beautiful blue jewel known as Lake of the Clouds. For the wilderness lover, as well as the logger, there was much to recommend the area. Agitation for a park in the Porcupine Mountains began in the late 1930s. The Connor Land and Lumber Company, which owned the five thousand acres of the land, planned to log the area according to sustained-yield guidelines and opposed the park movement. A bitter political and legal battle ensued. Recreationalists were buoyed by support not only in Lansing in the Department of Conservation, but from national environmental groups such as the Wilderness Society. In the end, the Michigan Supreme Court decided in favor of the park, and in 1944 Connor lost its five thousand acres. To add insult to injury, the compensation prices offered Connor were far below what the company thought fair.[40]

Lumbermen argued that forest areas required management that allowed for logging. Trees left undisturbed age, die, and fall to the ground. Creating parks did not save timber but it did create economic hardship. Connor blamed the fifty-eight thousand-acre Porcupine Mountains Park for putting three mills out of business and robbing western Upper Peninsula communities of their much needed tax base. Yet although these complaints had some validity, they were based on the faulty premise that forest products were the best use of the north country. The Porcupine Mountains dispute revealed the decline in logging status even in the Upper Peninsula. For many residents of the region, logging was viewed as a remnant of the past while recreation and tourism held out hope of a new, more stable pattern for the deep woods frontier.

THE SPATIAL PATTERN OF PULPWOOD LOGGING

Pulpwood era loggers developed a distinct pattern of relationships between the forest, mills, and systems of transportation. This pattern, as unique as those of the past hardwood and pine eras, gives an important perspective on the nature of logging in the recent past. The most important feature in the emergence of this new pattern was the truck, just as waterways and railroads had been critical elements in the emergence of past spatial patterns.

To an extent, it was the forest resource situation that dictated the adoption of the truck. Large stands of virgin timber were needed to justify the higher overhead of railroad logging. When those woods were no longer available, a change was required. Truck roads could be built much more cheaply than railroads and therefore truck trails became the favored technology for shipping lots from the forest to the mill. Those tracts of virgin hardwood that did exist were usually found in small, isolated pockets.[41] They could not support a logging venture long enough to justify building a rail spur. Trucks, with a bulldozer leading the way, could exploit a small tract in almost any logging environment on short notice. This was significant because by 1936 pulpwood had begun to rival lumber as the principal product of the forest.[42] Many pulpwood species, such as balsam fir, grew in poorly drained or downright swampy environments. Such areas could be reached by rail spur only with the greatest difficulty and expense (costs not justified by the scanty price of pulpwood). But truck trails could be easily cut out, and, with the help of cold weather, the swamp could be turned into a solid road surface. For this reason, many pulpwood operations took place in the winter.[43]

The new technology did not lead immediately to a new pattern on the landscape. Instead, between 1930 and 1940 loggers gradually integrated trucks and other gasoline-powered vehicles with operations built around the older technologies of horse-drawn sleighs and logging railroads. The Corrigan and Organist Camp No. 2, which operated from 1935 to 1936, is a good example of the spatial organization of logging during the transition period.

George Corrigan and Edward Organist were jobbers for the Marathon Paper Mills Corporation. The company owned large tracts of forest in southeastern Gogebic County. Each year the company engaged as many as eighteen jobbers to cut pulpwood. Because Corrigan and Organist were a newly formed partnership and had no track record with Marathon, the company started them off with a tough logging job—a tract of forest two and one-half miles from the nearest railroad. They completed this job successfully during the 1934–35 season and were rewarded with better assignments for the next year. This second contract covered several forty-acre plots in the Ottawa National Forest.[44]

The loggers built Camp No. 2 a short distance from a township road. While constructing the camp, the men slept in boarding cars of the Chicago and North Western Railroad, which were spotted on a side track about three miles from the campsite. Each day Corrigan trucked the men to the campsite where they built shanties and carved sleigh roads out of the woods. Corrigan himself lived in Watersmeet with his family and drove to work at camp each day. By the middle of May, the camp buildings were completed and hemlock bark peelers were brought into camp. The proximity of the township road persuaded Corrigan to experiment with hauling his logs by truck. The timber was cut and then skidded by horse to a woods landing where it was loaded onto the truck by a gas-powered hoist. The trucks then transported the logs to a Chicago and North Western Railroad siding known as Sylvania Landing. Here the logs were again decked to await rail transport to Marathon plants at Ironwood, Michigan, or Rothschild, Wisconsin. This process continued through the summer and fall of 1935. Corrigan and Organist did not own their trucks; instead, they subcontracted with two brothers who owned a fleet of trucks and regularly hauled for the Bonifas Lumber Company.[45]

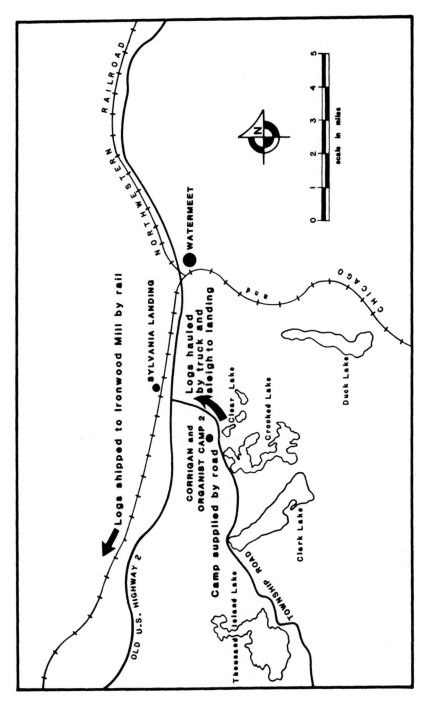

Spatial Arrangement of Pulpwood Era Logging

It may have been the force of tradition or the expense of renting trucks, but as soon as it was cold enough to build ice roads, Corrigan abandoned motorized transport and began to haul their timber to the rail landing by horse-drawn sleighs. Ironically, the most difficult section of their ice road was where they crossed U.S. Highway 2. The paved surface was well traveled and traffic played havoc with the iced crossing. By the time the snow melted, Corrigan and Organist had completed the hauling and were paid by Marathon. In May, Camp No. 2 was disassembled and loaded onto a truck so that it could be used at the next job.[46]

The Corrigan and Organist operation reveals the enduring significance of railways and sleigh roads to logging operations in the 1930s, but it also showed the potential of trucks and automobiles to transform the way logging was organized. The easy road communication that allowed George Corrigan to commute between Camp No. 2 and his Watersmeet home gradually undermined the centrality of the logging camp to forest operations. During the 1940s it became common for several of the lumberjacks in the camp to have their own cars. Many of these men could commute home to their families on weekends or sometimes even on weekdays. Vehicles also became a means of weekend relief for single lumberjacks who no longer had to stay in camp. The auto gave woodsmen easy access to the pleasure of the "Black Cat" or "Green Garage" bordellos of Florence or the even more "explosive" allurements of Hurley, Wisconsin.[47] The logging camp was further undermined by the tendency of many older lumberjacks to prefer living in nearby tar paper shacks rather than stay in the men's camps. Between the younger family men commuting and the old "timberbeasts" shacking, the logging camp began to disappear from the north woods. By 1960 it was little more than a memory.

The spatial relationship of forest operations to production centers was also altered during the pulpwood era. As the twentieth century wore on, there were fewer and fewer mills located in the Upper Peninsula. By 1936 there were only twenty-six mills in northern Michigan producing more than a thousand board feet annually. The statistic reflected the declining significance of sawlogs in the region. At the same time, pulpwood was on the rise. Yet in 1936 there were only six paper mills in the Upper Peninsula.[48] None of these could compare with the giant Wisconsin mills of the Kimberly-Clark Corporation, Marathon Paper Mills Corporation, Thelmany Pulp and Paper Company, Mosinee Paper Company, or the Rhinelander Paper Company. These mills had a tremendous appetite that required supplies of wood brought in from far afield. Over time, the number of pulp mills in the Upper Peninsula increased, but so did the consumption of the Wisconsin mills, thereby accelerating the trend of forest resources being processed in locations far removed from the seat of logging. Such a broad catchment made the old system of company towns unnecessary. The pulpwood era did not produce Hermansvilles or Nahmas to wither and die when the wood was gone.

12

THE SOCIAL ENVIRONMENT OF
PULPWOOD LOGGING

Charles E. Good crouched down and with a small brush put the finishing touches on a large sign that faced U.S. Highway 2, the main artery of the Upper Peninsula. Several photographers snapped pictures of the sixty-four-year-old lumberman. He was a lean, gray, worn-out man with a worried look on his face as he turned toward the cameras. He must have known how pathetic he looked as he stood in front of the sign, but that, after all, was the whole idea. As president of the Bay De Noquet Lumber Company, Good sought national publicity, so he played the deposed patriarch and posed with the sign that read: ENTIRE TOWN OF NAHMA, MICH.—FOR SALE.

After eighty years, the Bay De Noquet Company was closing its mill. The company had refused to adopt selective logging techniques during the 1920s when it was rich in timber resources; now its forests were gone and the company town faced extinction. Good sought a buyer for the old mill and the 100 homes, eight-bed hospital, golf course, barbershop, and tavern that made up Nahma. It was an awkward time when the company announced it would abandon the town it had created. Good himself had grown up with the town; his father had been superintendent before him. To ease the separation, Good persuaded the Board of Directors to set aside one hundred thousand dollars for severance pay. He also began the "sell Nahma" promotion campaign. The whole town and its mills were offered to anyone who would locate an industry there for a quarter of a million dollars. Nahma's uncertain future was typical of many Upper Peninsula towns in the post-World War II era. Unlike many others, the town did get a temporary reprieve when the American Playground Device Company accepted Charles Good's offer for the town. This, however, many younger residents saw as only a temporary reprieve; Nahma was on the long agonizing road to extinction.[1]

The pulpwood era has been a time of almost continual financial uncertainty for the residents of the Upper Peninsula. The agricultural hard times of the 1920s in the north country were followed by the Depression of the 1930s. World War II brought only temporary relief to the persistent economic problems brought on by the general decline of the region's farm, mineral, and lumber industries. After the war, young men and women wanted a secure economic future. From 1950 to 1960, sixty-one percent of all youths between twenty and twenty-four years of age left the upper Great Lakes region. They fled a persistent unemployment rate that in 1960 hovered over thirty percent, close to double the figure of the much lamented Appalachian region. In per capita income, housing, labor force participation, and other important indications, the Upper Peninsula was in many ways worse off than Appalachia.[2] These stark conditions only compounded the difficulty of adjusting to a logging industry based on small local operators instead of the giant metropolitan-based lumber companies.

Joining the Bay De Noquet Company in history's dustheap was the I. Stephenson Company that traced its roots to Jefferson Sinclair and the birth of northern Michigan logging. In 1942 the giant hardwood mill at Wells, once the busiest in Michigan, was closed. A year later, the old plants were bought by two Escanaba men, Hubert Shepeck and Charles Stoll. The Shepeck Dimension & Lumber Company operated at the site; the Stephenson Lumber Company assumed the task of selling off the hundreds of thousand of acres that old Ike Stephenson had amassed. It was a tribute to the scale of that pioneer logger's operations that not until 1962 were the final sixty acres of his empire sold and the Stephenson name passed from the Michigan logging scene.[3]

Sault Sainte Marie residents were distressed in May 1956 when it was announced that the Cadillac-Soo Lumber and Chemical Company would close. Like Bay De Noquet and I. Stephenson, the Cadillac-Soo Company owned enough timber to adopt selective logging; instead, its lower Michigan-based directors chose the route of immediate profit. A result was forty-eight thousand acres of cutover land. Although an additional six thousand forested acres remained, the directors decided to use those lands to attract a buyer for their entire property. No buyer could be found for the mill, so its equipment was sold and the buildings were demolished. One hundred and fifty-four mill workers and many more loggers and teamsters joined the ranks of the unemployed.[4]

The owners of the Wisconsin Land and Lumber Company tried to finesse the transition in the region's economy by embracing tourism. In 1927 the company completed logging operations on their thirty thousand-acre tract in Schoolcraft County. An attempt had been made to operate a cattle ranch on the cutover lands while logging still progressed, but it was unsuccessful. There seemed no choice but to shutter Blaney where operations had been headquartered. It was a shame because

Blaney was one of the more modern and better maintained company towns. To save the town, Stewart and Harold Earle, who controlled the lumber company, decided to transform the town into a modern resort for the "very best element of the tourist trade." In an early example of adaptive reuse, the brothers converted the former superintendent's house into a main hotel; workers homes were renovated into tourist cottages by adding electricity, running water, and fireplaces; the old general store was given a face-lift and a new stock of goods. They knew, however, that accommodations were not enough to attract tourists to remote Schoolcraft County; a resort needs recreation attractions. The Earles provided these by impounding a stream and creating a new lake; stump fields were transformed into a nine-hole golf course, and hiking trails were laid out. Blaney Park formally opened in July 1927 and was immediately the most extensive resort development in the Upper Peninsula.[5]

For a time the experiment flourished. But after World War II, although tourism expanded elsewhere in the Upper Peninsula, Blaney Park was eclipsed. Modern auto tourists, unlike elite visitors in the past, did not stay at Blaney for weeks at a time. Yet many long-term guests were needed to sustain the high overhead generated by Blaney's fifty-four square miles and 130 person staff. Nor did the Wisconsin Land and Lumber Company have the resources to adapt the park to more modern tourist practices. In 1965 Blaney was closed; by this time the parent company, headquartered at Hermansville, was also defunct. The giant flooring mill was closed in 1943, a casualty to wartime production priorities and the Wisconsin Land and Lumber Company's failure to modernize.[6]

Even Ford Motor Company, a comparative newcomer to the fraternity of giant Michigan lumber firms, left the business of logging and sold off its forests. Ironically, Ford, which had helped pioneer selective logging in northern Michigan, abandoned this practice in 1938 and clear-cut its tracts. The company began to retreat even more from its commitment to the Upper Peninsula after Henry Ford retired in 1945. He had always been the driving force behind integrating the company from forest to assembly line. He also had the emotional attachment to the Upper Peninsula. A new management team took charge of the auto company in 1947. Their attitude reflected Edsel Ford's remarks made in the late 1930s to a resident of Pequaming. "We don't need these anymore," he said as he pointed to the town's mill. "As for the lumber and stuff that we need, we can get it any other place. We can buy it in the South, the West or any place. . . . This is one of my father's hobbies."[7] Once Henry Ford was gone, the forest operations in the Upper Peninsula were slowly disassembled. In 1951 Pequaming was sold to a group that hoped to develop it into a resort; other properties followed. By the summer of 1954 Ford Motor Company closed out its northern Michigan operations.

The business structure of the pulpwood era was based on control of forest resources by a few large organizations. Federal and state forests controlled almost half of all forested lands, but large national or multinational companies such as Kimberly-Clark, Champion International, Diamond International, and Mead Paper also controlled large blocks of forest. By 1952 nine large companies controlled seventy-four percent of the industrial forestland in the Great Lakes region.[8] In the Upper Peninsula, a mere six companies controlled ten percent of all land in 1974. This trend did tend to reduce the tax base of local governments, and it has also proved healthy for the logging industry in northern Michigan. Only a handful of the old logging companies were able to engage in long-term planning; the rest were inclined to think only of the present, not of their future, profits. The larger the corporate investment in forests, the greater the concern of the manager over the well-being of that investment. Thus concentration of forest lands and the reform of the tax system have resulted in a much more stable forest products industry. Although mills still closed and the logging business ebbed and flowed, the boom-bust cycle of the hardwood and pine eras had been improved.[9]

The most striking feature of logging during the pulpwood era was the retreat of the large corporate landowners from forest operations. Although the hardwood era saw the emergence of jobbers and "haywire" loggers who operated independently in isolated woods or by cutting on corporate holdings on a contract basis, not until the modern logging era did this pattern become universal. Since the Great Depression, loggers have been largely small entrepreneurs who operate with low overhead and modest profit margins. These jobbers, however, are at least local men so that, unlike the old integrated firms, the profits accrued for logging, however small, do tend to remain in the local communities that need them so desperately.

During the 1930s and 1940s when logging began to be pursued by a pool of small operators, the entry barriers into the business were very low. "It didn't take any money," commented a former logger who was asked how he raised the start-up capital. "A single horse is all that I had. . . . You'd contract out the hauling, that's about the way it went."[10] Thomas Nordine of Bruce Crossing also began with a single horse. "Instead of me skidding wood for someone else for sixty cents a cord, if I could hire a couple of cutters, I'd come home with a dollar a cord instead and seen profit." To attract a couple of pulpwood cutters to work for him, he needed to be able to pay them wages regularly. Nordine solved this problem by getting a loan from a bank using his four-year-old Ford as collateral.[11]

The increasing technological sophistication of forest operations affected easy access to the logging business. "With the power saw," contended Gordon R. Connor, head of Connor Forest Industries, "whole armies of 'ma and pa' and family pulpwood cutters entered the woods."[12] But further equipment innovations raised the cost of logging considerably. A logger who entered the business after World War II with a few horses and a couple of power saws would eventually purchase a small crawler tractor, perhaps one with a cable jammer to ease landing and skidding. By 1960 an awesome array of equipment was available: rubber-tired skidders, automatic loading trucks, hydro-ax machines. A Mead Corporation jobber, during the 1970s, relied completely on automated equipment and made do with a crew of only two men, who, despite equipment breakdowns, could produce three hundred cords per month.[13] As one old logger noted: "You go in the woods today and you're talking in terms, to get automated, just reasonably well, of a half million dollars."[14] This sort of investment put logging beyond the means of many interested woodsmen. There was still the option of starting small and hiring out to another jobber; yet many young gung ho loggers chose instead to buy outright what they needed. If their first job went sour, as one forest manager observed, "the finance company ended up with the equipment."[15]

Even though logging during most of the pulpwood era had low entry barriers, there was not a great deal of competition among jobbers. The big corporations controlled both the forest resources and the market—and there was little a small logger could do about either. The only area of direct competition was over access to corporate or government timber and that was generally handled through invitation or sealed bids. Once a job was set up, cooperation was much more common than competition among jobbers. "Most loggers help each other out of tough spots if they can," said a Gogebic County logger. "They lend each other equipment and they use each other's roads and landings."[16] W. C. "Cedar Pole" Smith once ran short of food while operating a camp in the Ottawa National Forest. To help keep his camp running, another jobber in the area loaned him thirty bushels of potatoes.[17] It was in the logger's own best interests to be cooperative; as small operators they often had to pool resources to their mutual profit. For example, in 1934 George Corrigan found himself short of the horsepower necessary to haul his winter's cut to the rail landing. He had planned to hire several more teams of horses to speed up the sleigh hauling; then he heard that logger Thomas Ahonen had several trucks that were underused. Ahonen hauled out Corrigan's timber, saving the latter's contract with Marathon Paper and making a profit with vehicles that otherwise would have been idle.[18]

Loggers had little bargaining power with the paper and sawmills that functioned as the industries' buyers. Market prices were determined by forces outside their control. Loggers had no more success during the pulpwood era than there had been in earlier times of limiting production to control price. Loggers did not control the source of their raw material. The large corporations, through their extensive real estate purchases, held the high cards.[19] The Depression graphically demonstrated loggers' inability to control buyers' prices. In 1932–33 prices were understandably low for forest products. Yet instead of seeing a drop-off in production, lumber was readily available in the region because many farmers desperate for cash took up the saw and cut their woodlots.[20]

The great paper companies who bought most of the logs had the additional threat of backward integration, or entering logging for themselves, to help keep jobbers in line. This was less of a threat after World War II when company camps died out; nonetheless, it was an action taken earlier by the Kimberly-Clark Corporation through its control of the White River Logging Company in Bergland.[21] Most buyers realized that mere ownership of timber resources was enough leverage for them to control the cost of acquiring logs or pulpwood.

Lacking their own forest resources, loggers had to seek work from the large pulp or lumber producers on the best terms their limited leverage allowed. It was very attractive for a logger to become a regular jobber for a large corporation. Such a relationship would secure the logger access to timber, a major problem for the independent operator, and it guaranteed a market for the pulp or sawlogs cut during the job. This sort of arrangement was important in helping a logger upgrade the technological sophistication of his equipment. When Corrigan and Organist formed their logging partnership, they needed a twenty-five hundred-dollar loan to build and supply their camp. The Iron Exchange Bank in Hurley granted the loan only after it verified that the two men had a contract with Marathon Corporation. Without such a contract, the partners would have had to start at a much more modest level.[22]

The faith that banks had in national corporations rebounded to the jobber's favor in something called "Bill of Lading Financing." Once a logger completed his contract with a big outfit and delivered the last of the timber, he often had to wait several weeks for a check to be issued. His pieceworkers wanted to be paid immediately and his fuel oil bill had to be paid—which meant he needed cash immediately. Banks would advance loggers thirty or so percent of the contract price when they deposited the bill of lading showing that the timber had been delivered. Usually the buyer would then send his check directly to the bank, which would deduct the advance and give the balance to the logger.[23]

"The Marathon Corporation, who we were contracting for," recalled George Corrigan, "was always fair on their logging contracts." Many of the larger companies agreed to slightly higher logging costs in the wake of the 1937 timber strike so that camp conditions could be improved. Marathon had an escalator clause in its jobber contracts. If the cost of logging went up during the term of the contract, the amount of money involved would increase proportionately. Conversely, if costs fell, the amount would be reduced. This helped protect both parties from being locked into a bad deal.[24] Yet, here again, the company had the advantage. Jobbers were retained on short-term contracts. If, after a year, the company decided to cut back paper production, the land department merely decreased the number of jobbers who were offered a contract. Timber agents did try to maintain a long-term relationship with jobbers who could be relied on. These men could be rewarded not merely with new contracts but by being offered good logging chances where one camp might be used for three years. Unproven jobbers might be offered expensive jobs where road access was poor and timber scattered.[25]

"A logging contractor always had tough going," said veteran woodsman George Corrigan. "I can think of few logging contractors who were able to take annual vacations in California or Florida."[26] Life was especially difficult for the independent logger who bought his own stumpage and resisted becoming a jobber. Taylor Forest Products Company, founded in 1940, is a good example of this element of the business structure of twentieth-century logging. A family-run business, it contracted to supply Mead Corporation, the Escanaba-based paper producer, with pulpwood from scattered Chippewa County locations. Mead did not want to purchase small amounts of wood from a multitude of farmers or small loggers. It was simpler for Mead to place an order with a small logging company like Taylor Forest Products and have them do the local work. Taylor would conduct its own forest operations, building camps and truck trails on forest acreage the firm had purchased. The company would also advance money to farmers or jobbers. Many local farmers would supplement their meager returns from the soil by cutting pulpwood on their land. A farmer with good credit and some spruce or balsam on his land would approach Taylor Forest Products for an advance on his timber cut. The farmer would pay off the advance in the spring with the pulpwood he would sell to Taylor. In this way, Taylor Forest Products was guaranteed the farmer's pulpwood to fulfill its contract with Mead Corporation, and the farmer had the cash needed to hire several workers, usually other farmers, to help cut the trees.[27]

Many independent loggers also owned their own sawmills, but these differed substantially from the operations of the large integrated lumber concerns of the past. The mills were usually small, often portable, and produced for the local market or sold to retail brokers who operated across the upper Great Lakes region. The lot of the small logger was difficult. There was no corporate staff to whom responsibility could be delegated. The owner, with the aid of a partner—usually a family member—had to handle the full range of logging activities. Howard Anderson, for example, personally cruised every tract of forest before he bought. He then handled the bidding on the parcel and ran his own logging operations. Yet when cutting was completed, he still had to market the logs. From 1939 to 1942, when Anderson operated a logging camp near Tula, he sold logs to the Bonifas Mills at Marenisco. Pulpwood was sold to Kimberly-Clark and Marathon, and his veneer logs were marketed to Penokee Veneer Company. In each case, Anderson did not necessarily get the best price for his logs because he was so absorbed with scouting timberlands for his next job and completing the one at hand that he could not shop for prices.[28]

Decisions concerning equipment were particularly difficult for the independent logger. Too little or too much invested in chain saws, trucks, or skidders would mean an inefficient use of small capital reserves. More mechanized equipment would allow a logger to cut and haul a large volume of timber in a shorter time, but it also would increase his investment in logging, making it more difficult to pull out of the industry.

After bearing all these risks of being independent, the logger was still not completely liberated from the influence of the large pulp and lumber producers. They set the prices on the wood he produced. All the complaints in the world would not change the rates they offered. When dealing with these companies, the independent was always treated less favorably than their regular jobbers. Loggers who sold exclusively to one buyer would receive cash bonuses for their wood; loyal jobbers benefited by having roads built for them or by being given easily accessible tracts.[29] Despite these problems, men in the Upper Peninsula continued to be attracted to independent logging. A mother of one pulpwood era logger described his career choice: "All during his boyhood, he went to camp with his father. The lure of tall timber which kept my husband, Louis, engrossed in logging all his life also fascinated Howard. . . . He cut his teeth on a camp spoon."[30]

THE LAST OF THE LUMBERJACKS

The pulpwood era was marked by what one writer called a "thirty year transition from blood to oil-hydraulics" as the power that felled forests.[31] There are today no longer any of the old-time lumberjacks left in the forest; they have been replaced by the modern rubber tire lumberjacks. This change was brought about as much by social forces as by technological progress.

The ranks of the northern Michigan forest work force had always been replenished by recent immigrants. Canadians, Irish, Germans, Finns, and eastern Europeans took their place in the logging camp as time progressed. Open immigration helped keep camp conditions poor and woods work lowly paid; when one group was ready to graduate to better work, another wave of foreigners desperate for work could be counted on to take its place. But in 1921 and again in 1924 Congress acted to restrict the flow of foreign immigration into the United States. These actions eventually had a large effect on the status of unskilled labor in the United States.

The first response of Upper Peninsula lumbermen to the ebb of foreign immigration was to seek out a domestic source of cheap labor. As early as 1917, when immigration was temporarily restricted, the Charcoal Iron Company imported migrant laborers from Kentucky and Tennessee to cut cordwood. The Antrim Iron Company in lower Michigan had settled 150 "Kentuckians" on its cutover lands. These laborers were paid on a piece basis and produced about twenty cords per month per man from land that otherwise was worthless for lumber production.[32] It was among charcoal iron and pulp producers that Kentuckians—as these migrants were universally referred to—first found employment. They would inhabit abandoned logging camps or live with their families in earth-floored shacks of bonded tar paper.[33] Sometimes those huts would be grouped together in a little hamlet locally called Kentucky Town. The Cleveland-Cliffs Company practiced "strip logging" on its cutover lands. The company assigned a foreman to take charge of an area. This boss would then assign one or two families an area to live in and a strip of wood to cut. The system meant much less communication for the woodcutters and their families with other folks. One observer described the life-style of the Kentuckians in the cutovers as "desolate."[34]

The Kentuckians moved from place to place across the Upper Peninsula. Their families and personal belongings were bundled into rickety automobiles held together by haywire. They were disparaged by some town residents as "corn crackers," "ridge runners," or "hillbillies." Regardless, they accepted work in the cutovers that many other workers found unacceptable. Their ranks continued to swell into the 1930s, but the expansion of urban industries for war production after 1940 deflected the further movement of Kentuckians into the cities and away from the forests.

Kentuckians seem to have been favored by some lumber companies because they were a more docile work force than the Socialist-inclined

Finns who had preceded them into the cutovers.[35] Before the introduction of Kentuckians to Cleveland-Cliffs lands, company officials had a shortage of cordwood cutters and complained that those they had were "full of Bolshevik ideas" and agitating for more money.[36] Not enough Kentuckians, however, came to stem the increasing assertiveness of labor.

The 1937 timber workers' strike, though it enjoyed only mixed success, had broad-ranging implications for northern Michigan workers. As an attempt to organize forest workers, it was a failure largely because in the wake of the strike, the large timber-using companies withdrew from logging. Some companies did this only grudgingly, after failing to control the labor movement. Cleveland-Cliffs Iron Company was reprimanded by the National Labor Relations Board for blacklisting union employees. Connor Land and Lumber Company and the Newberry Lumber and Chemical Company tried to establish company unions.[37] When these attempts failed, the companies found it easier to turn over the handling of lumberjacks to jobbers and independent loggers. The jobbing system not only revolutionized the structure of the logging industry but also quieted the labor scene by giving the problem to the men who were most sympathetic to the demands of the lumberjack. Most jobbers had been woodsmen themselves. Their response to the demand for improved camp conditions were almost universally favorable. "It is a demand that should have been taken care of years ago. Without a doubt, it was the worst condition imaginable and the cost to remedy it was not excessive," said one veteran walking boss.[38] Those loggers slow to make changes found themselves facing sit-down strikes over food quality or living conditions. Most of these actions were justified, but occasionally there were frivolous job actions. Lumberman Gordon Connor arrived at one camp amid a sit-down strike over food. "What did you give these men for breakfast?" he asked. "Well, flapjacks, doughnuts, bacon, pies, beans, cake, cereal, coffee, cheese, and milk," replied the cook. "Yes," the men responded, "but there was no meat!"[39]

After the 1937 strike, the Communist party was of little importance in forest unionization. The American Federation of Labor took the lead organizing mill workers and lumberjacks. Considerable success was experienced unionizing mill workers, but lumberjacks continued to be a harder case. The union at first minimized wildcat strikes against conditions in a camp while it built a unified membership that might eventually negotiate an industrywide contract. However, the jobber system that replaced one large company with many camps, with many jobbers operating one or two camps, compounded the organizational problems of the union. The old-time lumberjack's unrepressed nature made him susceptible to sudden grievances that might bring a sit-down strike or a trip to Hurley. A sit-down strike tended to wear down the goodwill of the jobbers who wanted to cooperate with the union; a trip to town often cost the union a member because men were organized on a camp basis.[40]

The small loggers were also organized collectively. The Michigan-Wisconsin Timber Producer Association was formed on the eve of the 1937 strike to counteract the union effort. But as jobbing expanded in the region, the organization proved to be a valuable forum for those small businessmen constrained by economic and legal forces beyond their individual control. In June 1940 the association was formally incorporated.[41] Their principal concern was not so much the union, but the government. Activist federal and state labor departments brought new hour and wage standards that required adherence. Worker's compensation, which was something new to jobbers, became an increasingly heavy burden in the dangerous logging industry. The association was not strong enough to bring about legislative relief for its members, but it at least was a vehicle for expressing jobbers' concerns and disseminating information concerning adherence to the increasingly complex labor situation.[42]

The industrial revival brought by World War II temporarily strengthened labor's hand in the Upper Peninsula. Production was expanded in both the paper and lumber sectors at the very time that labor was becoming dear because of the draft. Jobbers competed with one another and with the mills for experienced workers. Instead of remaining stable, workman's compensation and wages accelerated. The Northern Hemlock and Hardwood Manufacturers Association vainly tried to stem the tide and keep wages within a few cents of the minimum wage. But this effort merely drove workers to waiting jobs in other industries and brought charges of "sabotage" from union officials.[43]

Despite wage advances, loggers encountered a severe labor shortage during World War II. To help ease the logger's problem and keep up the flow of forest products, the Department of the Army sent hundreds of German prisoners of war to the Upper Peninsula. Most were veterans of Gen. Erwin Rommel's famed Afrika Korps captured in Tunisia in 1942. Prisoners were based at former CCC camps, including camps Evelyn, Raco, Wetmore, Au Train, Pori, and Sidnaw. Administered from Fort Sheridan near Chicago, the camps were guarded by U.S. soldiers, although guard towers and wire fences were not used at all camps. The food afforded the POWs was standard army fare. At least once a week movies were available in the camps. English language magazines, German newspapers from Milwaukee and Cincinnati, and copies of *Die Post* (a weekly POW newsletter) were available to prisoners. Classes in English, U. S. geography and government, plus anti-Nazi lectures were offered regularly. All told, the conditions in these camps were not only much better than what U.S. prisoners experienced in Germany, but, ironically, were better than what some American lumberjacks enjoyed.[44]

Most of the POWs were employed in pulpwood logging operations. They were given thirty cents per day to spend on personal items; the remainder of their piece labor wage was put into a United States government account. The program at first had problems. "The POWs went through bucksaw blades—which are fragile—by the gross, partially from inexperience, and from deliberate destruction on the part of those who believed they shouldn't be working," recalled a Kimberly-Clark clerk. "They placed their bucksaws across stumps and whacked them with their axes." This problem was solved by adopting sturdier cedar saws.[45] There also were instances when zealous Nazis would sabotage the work of others. Cordwood needed to be cut to specifications for shipment. When close supervision was lacking, some piles of properly cut wood would be recut to make it unacceptable.[46] Over time, such malcontents were weeded out of the work camps and sent to high-security detention centers. Thomas Nordine won the goodwill of his POWs by giving little rewards of cigarettes or beer for the hard workers. "For gifts on the side, you got tremendous work out of them" he remembered.[47]

When World War II ended, lumberjacks did not flock back to the north country. The labor situation in the forest—the type of work, wages, and benefits—could not compete with the manufacturing industries. Young men returning from the war wanted a better life for themselves and their families. The high wages and suburban homes of metropolitan Chicago, Detroit, and Milwaukee seemed very attractive. Besides the relatively low pay of logging, it remained a fairly dangerous way to earn a living.

Some improvements were made in worker safety by pulpwood era loggers. Hard hats, for example, were bitterly resisted for many years before becoming a standard piece of equipment. Safety-consciousness programs and hard-toed boots were advocated with less success.[48] New automated technology did not measurably improve safety conditions. Some lumberjacks contended that technology quickened the pace of logging, making mistakes more common. One veteran of forty years of piece cutting said that "logging today with chain saws is much more dangerous than the old days."[49] Chain saws, for example, tended to kick back and injure their operators. Most serious accidents, however, continued to center in the difficulty of felling trees, each one individually unique. "Trees are living things which seem to fight for their lives, making it as difficult as possible for those who feel, buck, limb and load. They twist unexpectedly, bounce off other trees and seem possessed at times," wrote another lumberjack.

> Almost every night, while soaking in the tub, I find new nicks and bruises every possible place on my body. Although woods workers wear gloves for protection, fingers frequently get split or jammed. Bandages are as necessary in the woods as lunch and drinking water. Woods accidents and even death are part of the tree harvest, no matter what caution is exercised. . . . I have never known an old-timer who has not paid the toll of woods work, whether it be painful arthritis, a twisted back, gimp legs or reduced hearing caused by the whine of chainsaws. Each year in the Upper Peninsula, three or four loggers are seriously maimed or killed.[50]

In the post-World War II period, the rising costs of workman's compensation became an ever increasing burden for the logging contractor. These costs became part of the motivation to mechanize and thereby make do with fewer workers. It also was harder to find the "rugged individual" loggers of the past. Two such men were Eli and Vernon Miljevitch, Connor Land and Lumber Company jobbers. They entered the logging business as sawyers and were so good that on one occasion they were invited to New York to appear on national television. On the "I've Got a Secret" show, they crosscut timber faster than a competing chain saw.[51] They were as skillful and hardy as woodsmen of any era. Once Eli Miljevitch was pinned in his tractor by a fallen tree. Miles from professional assistance and with a broken back, he was in desperate straits. His brother Vernon, however, by brute strength lifted the tree and freed Eli. He then carried the stricken man several miles to their car, and thence to the hospital. Although doctors at first thought Eli Miljevitch would never walk again, he was back working in the woods within a year.[52] Many of the best of the old-time lumberjacks, like the Miljevitch brothers, became jobbers in the postwar period.

The veteran woodsmen who were unable or disinclined to become loggers found forest work increasingly burdensome as the years mounted. Piecework had no respect for seniority or experience. While most men in their fifties were entering their peak earning years, old woodcutters began to suffer declining paychecks when they began to slow down. This was a double penalty because social security retirement benefits were linked to a worker's salary in his latter years. The lumberjacks who spent their lives in the woods increasingly had less in common with the few younger men attracted to woodwork.[53] "Young shoots—as we call second-growth jacks," sneered one old veteran, "had little in common with real lumberjacks."[54] Even during the 1940s and 1950s many old-timers refused to live in camp with the other men, preferring to live in simple frame shacks made of lath and tar paper. These men became known as "shackers" and during the postwar period, they were an important part of logging operations.

Some shackers were expert axmen who specialized in hand-hewing cedar ties. They were referred to with a mixture of awe and contempt by the other lumberjacks, who seldom mixed with the shackers, as "cedar savages." But whether they cut cedar ties or pulpwood, shackers lived a pathetic lonely life. Julie Anderson, wife of a Gogebic County logger, described the inside of a shack:

> The pale winter sunlight slanting through the only window disclosed two up-ended orange crates filled with boxes, packages and cans of food. These crates served also as a stand for a granite washbasin and water bucket. Above these hung a grimy towel beside a kerosene lamp in a wall bracket. In the gloom beyond the window stood a gray-blanketed bed. From nails driven in the walls above the bed hung a lantern and clothes. A pot of coffee simmered on the small black cookstove. The smell of coffee along with that of sweaty clothes, cooking, old newspapers, stove wood, soap and kerosene produced a peculiar musty smell that hung thick in the poorly ventilated shack.[55]

Shacks were often built on skids and when logging was completed in one area, a jobber would pull the shack to a new location. Loggers were willing to do this or even build a new shack for an old-timer to get the benefit of their labor.

Woodsmen became shackers for many reasons. Before the wide use of the chain saw, when crosscut sawyers worked in teams, a shacker might be a veteran tree feller who lost a longtime partner. Like a widower, he would spurn the thought of another partner. Yet around camp the only jobs for an ex-sawyer were the comparatively demeaning tasks of swamper or barn boss. Rather than put up with these indignities, the old-timer might prefer shacking and cutting "short stuff." Later, many shackers were lumberjacks working for a jobber who could not afford to build a logging camp—or had too few old-time lumberjacks to justify the cost. There were shackers who were natural recluses, but most were merely old men without families or pensions who tried to live the life of a woodsman through the twilight of their years. Eventually their muscles failed and their step faltered. Shackers were often found frozen in their bunks or burned in the ashes of their cabin, or merely silently slumped over their woodpile.

The Upper Peninsula during the pulpwood era was a graying community that had largely lost the vigor of its frontier youth. A smaller rising generation of rubber tire lumberjacks gradually replaced the old woodsmen. Howard Anderson spoke for these younger, married men when he observed, "Saturdays, most loggers come home to play with their children, take a bath, take their wives to the show; and then on Sunday, they want to eat a so-good dinner and fall asleep listinin' to the radio."[56] The older, single lumberjacks took the bus to Hurley where tawdry Silver Street still echoed with their revelry. For many of them, drinking was keeping faith with the legacy of being a lumberjack. Customs were enshrined concerning the way it was to be done. It was, for example, mandatory that a jack fresh from camp buy drinks for others. "Come on, boys, belly up to the bar!" was the phrase for which down-and-out jacks waited. After fighting and squandering their money, the old-timers staggered back to the camp and the paternalistic camp foreman. "Alfred's drunk in the ditch down the road," a logger might be told on Sunday night, and he would go out and bring that inebriate in out of the cold. It was part of the logger's responsibility under the old code. Harry "Moonlight" Schmidt, a Luce County logger, once told the story:

> Two years ago that fellow [pointing to a woodsman] worked for me at a camp near Grand Marais, and spent one hundred and fifty dollars on a drunk. Another feller said to him, "That's too bad you spent all your money with winter coming on, you'll need some clothes. He just said, "That's Moonlight's worry."[57]

Each year, however, there were fewer and fewer men to prowl Silver Street, to be pulled out of the cold, or to work in the camps.

"Then all of a sudden it was all over," an old woods veteran recalled. "There weren't any more camps, as such." The old-style logging camp ended with the 1950s. "The true lumberjack just faded out of the picture," and with him went a way of life.[58] "No matter how much pulp a wood harvester produces, no machinery can compare with the flair and flamboyance of the lumberjacks I once knew," lamented Roy DeLongchamp, a fully automated modern logger. "And I feel a touch of sadness, for these men helped shape America."[59]

NOTES

INTRODUCTION

1 Walter Havighurst, *Upper Mississippi: A Wilderness Saga* (New York: Rinehart & Company, 1937), 99.

2 Lewis Mumford, *Technics and Civilization* (New York: Harcourt, Brace & Co., 1934). See also Evelyn M. Dinsdale, "Spatial Patterns of Technological Change: The Lumber Industry of Northern New York," *Economic Geography* 41 (1965), 252-274.

3 Stanley Bloom Shuman, "The Forest Resource Situation of the Eastern Part of the Upper Peninsula of Michigan" (Ph.D. diss., University of Illinois, 1957), 2-3.

4 R. N. Cunningham and H. G. White, *Forest Resources of the Upper Peninsula of Michigan*, U.S.D.A. Miscellaneous Publication No. 429 (Washington: U.S. Government Printing Office, 1941), 1.

5 Henry Rowe Schoolcraft, *Narrative Journal of Travels from Detroit Northwest through the Great Chain of American Lakes to the Sources of the Mississippi River in the Year 1820* (Albany, N.Y.: E. & F. Hosford, 1821), 178.

6 Charles Lanman, *Adventures in the Wilds of the United States*, quoted in Walter Havighurst (ed.), *The Great Lakes Reader* (New York: MacMillan Publishing Company, 1966), 89.

CHAPTER 1. THE PASSING OF THE FUR FRONTIER

1 Carl E. Krog, "Marinette: Biography of a Nineteenth Century Lumbering Town, 1850-1910" (Ph.D. diss., University of Wisconsin, 1971), 30-31.

2 Barbara Ellen Benson, "Logs and Lumber: The Development of the Lumber Industry in Michigan's Lower Peninsula, 1837-1870" (Ph.D. diss., Indiana University, 1976), 60, 66, 92.

3 Stephen H. Long, *The Northern Expeditions of Stephen H. Long*, ed. Lucile M. Kane, June D. Holmquist, and Carolyn Gilman (St. Paul, Minn.: Minnesota Historical Society, 1978), 240.

4 Otto Fowle, *Sault Ste. Marie and Its Great Waterway* (New York: A. P. Putnam's Sons, 1925), 376.

5 Ibid., 381.

6 Grace Lee Nute, "The American Fur Company's Fishing Enterprises on Lake Superior," *Mississippi Valley Historical Review* 12 (1925-26), 484-85.

7 Ramsay Crooks to Gabriel Franchere, July 12, 1835, American Fur Company (AFC) Papers.

8 Ibid.

9 John Livingston to William Brewster, April 3, 1839, AFC Papers.

10 Ibid., May 20, 1839.
11 Fowle, *Sault Ste. Marie*, 375–78.
12 Mary Beth Street, "Pierre B. Barbeau: Businessman—Land Speculator" (M.A. thesis, Central Michigan University, 1965), 18–24.
13 D. Webster to John Livingston, August 21, 1846, AFC Papers.
14 James B. Pendill to Pierre B. Barbeau, August 21, 1858, Pierre B. Barbeau Papers, Bayliss Public Library, Sault Ste. Marie, Mich.
15 James Anthony to Pierre B. Barbeau, September 16, 1856, Barbeau Papers.
16 Ibid., February 18, 1857.
17 Helen Longyear Paul, "Carp River Sawmill: A Compilation from the Correspondence (1857) of J. H. Anthony and Peter B. Barbeau," Marquette County Historical Society, J. M. Longyear Research Library, Marquette, Mich.
18 Street, "Pierre B. Barbeau," 76.
19 John Cumming, "The Timber Era," in *L'Anse Centennial*, ed. B. S. Lambert (Ishpeming, Mich.: Globe Publishing, 1971), 31.
20 James K. Jamison, *This Ontonagon Country*, (Ontonagon, Mich.: Ontonagon Herald, 1939), 194.
21 Krog, "Marinette," 34.
22 Ibid., 14–16.
23 Lewis S. Patrick, *Sketches of the Menominee River* (Menominee, Mich.: Herald Print, 1871), 11–12.
24 Krog, "Marinette," 27–29.

CHAPTER 2. MIGRATION OF THE LUMBERMEN

1 Krog, "Marinette," 27–29.
2 George W. Hotchkiss, *History of the Lumber and Forest Industry of the Northwest* (Chicago: George W. Hotchkiss & Co., 1898), 291–92.
3 Isaac Stephenson, *Recollections of a Long Life: 1829–1915* (Chicago: privately printed, 1915), 161–63.
4 Krog, "Marinette," 44.
5 Ibid., 63.
6 William Gerald Rector, *Log Transportation in the Lake States Lumber Industry, 1840–1918* (Glendale, Calif.: Arthur H. Clark Company, 1953), 68, 70, 74, 80.
7 Stephenson, *Recollections*, 47–51.
8 Ibid., 56–62.
9 Carl Sawyer, *History of Lumbering in Delta County* (Escanaba, Mich.: privately printed, 1949), 7.
10 Stephenson, *Recollections*, 74.
11 Ibid.
12 Ibid., 27, 48, 49.
13 Ibid., 77, 83–84.
14 Ibid., 85.
15 Sawyer, *Lumbering in Delta County*, 12, 17.
16 Stephenson, *Recollections*, 89–90.
17 James Willard Hurst, *Law and Economic Growth: The Legal History of the Lumber Industry in Wisconsin, 1836–1915* (Cambridge: Harvard University Press, 1964), 81, 87.
18 Stephenson, *Recollection*, 120.
19 Ibid., 131.
20 Sawyer, *Lumbering in Delta County*, 13.
21 Stephenson, *Recollections*, 136–37.
22 Krog, "Marinette," 47–48.
23 Stephenson, *Recollections*, 138–39.
24 Krog, "Marinette," 42.
25 Stephenson, *Recollections*, 147.

26 Ibid., 90.

27 Krog, "Marinette," 50.

28 Ibid., 42-44.

29 Hotchkiss, *History of the Lumber and Forest Industry*, 299.

30 Ibid., 430-34.

31 Krog, "Marinette," 65.

32 Frederick Merk, *Economic History of Wisconsin during the Civil War Decade* (Madison: State Historical Society of Wisconsin, 1916), 61.

33 Hotchkiss, *History of the Lumber and Forest Industry*, 672.

34 Merk, *Economic History of Wisconsin*, 81.

35 Arthur Charles Cole, *The Era of the Civil War, 1848-1870* (Springfield Illinois Centennial Commission, 1919), 348-50.

36 Merk, *Economic History of Wisconsin*, 61-62.

37 Harold Mayer and Richard Wade, *Chicago: Growth of a Metropolis* (Chicago: University of Chicago Press, 1969), 44.

38 *Northwestern Lumbermen*, April 1, 1876.

39 The organization of lumbermen on the river was named the Menominee River Manufacturing Company. However, the firm was commonly referred to as the "boom company" and its name was officially changed to Menominee River Boom Company in 1888. See Fred C. Burke, *Logs on the Menominee: The History of the Menominee River Boom Company* (Marinette, Wis.: privately printed, 1946), 21.

40 Stephenson, *Recollections*, 161-63.

41 Burke, *Logs on the Menominee*, 22.

42 Ibid., 40-62.

43 Hotchkiss, *History of the Lumber and Forest Industry*, 434.

44 William S. Crowe, *Lumberjack: Inside an Era in the Manistique, Michigan Region* (Manistique: Senger Publishing Company, 1977), 66.

45 Hotchkiss, *History of the Lumber and Forest Industry*, 321.

46 Ibid.

47 Crowe, *Lumberjack*, 18, 24.

48 Hotchkiss, *History of the Lumber and Forest Industry*, 318.

49 Ibid.

50 John Ira Bellaire, "Hiawatha-land: The Upper Peninsula of Michigan," unpublished MS, ca. 1942, Michigan Historical Collections, Bentley Historical Library, Ann Arbor, n.p.

51 Hotchkiss, *History of the Lumber and Forest Industry*, 321.

52 Bellaire, "Hiawatha-land," n.p.

53 Hotchkiss, *History of the Lumber and Forest Industry*, 418.

54 Ibid., 323-24.

55 Ibid.

56 Stephenson, *Recollections*, 8.

57 Willis Frederick Dunbar, *Michigan: A History of the Wolverine State* (Grand Rapids: William D. Eerdsmans, 1970), 371-72.

58 A. R. M. Lower, *The North American Assault on the Canadian Forest: A History of the Lumber Trade between Canada and the United States* (Toronto: Ryerson Press, 1938), 138-47.

59 Donald MacKay, *The Lumberjacks* (Toronto: McGraw-Hill Ryerson, 1978), 78.

60 Ibid.

61 State of Michigan, Supreme Court Record, Jonathan Nield vs. Martin Burton, James Burton, and Archibald C. Thompson (June 1882), 11.

62 D. D. Calvin, *A Saga of the St. Lawrence: Timber & Shipping through Three Generations* (Toronto: Ryerson Press, 1945), 51-52.

63 George Dawson to John Storey, July 15, 1873, Calvin Company Papers, Queen's University Archives, Kingston, Ontario.

64 George Dawson to D. D. Calvin, December 7, 1873, Calvin Company Papers.

65 George Dawson to Hiram A. Calvin, October 20, 1876, Calvin Company Papers.

66 Calvin, *A Saga of the St. Lawrence*, 53.
67 Ida M. Spring, "White Pine Portraits: Big Dave Ranson," *Michigan History Magazine* 31, (September 1947), 314–21.
68 Calvin, *A Saga of the St. Lawrence*, 53–54.
69 *Northwestern Lumberman*, November 4, 1876.
70 State of Michigan, Supreme Court Record, Jonathan Nield vs. Martin Burton et al., 40.
71 MacKay, *The Lumberjacks*, 78–80.

CHAPTER 3. THE IRON ROAD TO THE INTERIOR

1 *The Timberman*, August 3, 1889.
2 *Ontonagon Herald*, September 22, 1894.
3 Frank Bourke, "Trains to Everywhere," in *A Most Superior Land: Life in the Upper Peninsula of Michigan*, comp. David M. Frimodig (Lansing: Michigan Department of Natural Resources, 1983), 55–58.
4 Originally this line was built by the Milwaukee, Lake Shore and Western Railway Company, a Wisconsin corporation chartered in 1883. Personal communication, Robin Bourbecaris, Assistant Corporate Secretary, Chicago and Northwestern Transportation Company, to Theodore J. Karamanski, September 29, 1983.
5 *The Timberman*, August 3, 1889.
6 Ibid., November 28, 1891.
7 Ibid., May 4, 1889.
8 Robert Dollar, *Diary*, December 6, 1881 (typewritten MS), Bancroft Library, University of California, Berkley.
9 United States Department of Commerce, *The Lumber Industry: Standing Timber, Concentration of Timber Ownership in Important Selected Regions, and Land Holdings of Large Timber Owners* (Washington: U.S. Government Printing Office, 1913), part 3: 211.
10 Robert Dollar, *Memoirs of Robert Dollar* (San Francisco: Robert Dollar Company, 1918–28), vol. 1: 3.
11 Gregory Charles O'Brien, "The Life of Robert Dollar: 1844–1932" (Ph.D. diss., Claremont Graduate School and University Center, 1969), 19.
12 Dollar, *Memoirs*, 15–16.
13 Dollar, *Diary*, November 8–9, 1881.
14 Ibid., July 9, 1882.
15 Dollar, *Diary*.
16 Ibid., December 31, 1887.
17 Ibid., September 27, 1886.
18 Ibid., June 2, 1885.
19 *The Mining Journal* (Marquette, Mich.), March 19, 1927.
20 Dollar, *Diary*, July 14, 1884.
21 Ibid., July 31, 1883.
22 Ibid., August 8, 1885.
23 Dollar, *Memoirs*, 26–27.
24 O'Brien, "Life of Robert Dollar," 32–34.
25 Rodney Ellis Bell, "A Life of Russell Alexander Alger, 1826–1907" (Ph.D diss., University of Michigan, 1975), 126–34.
26 *The Timberman*, June 15, 1889.
27 James L. Carter, *Grand Marais: Voyageurs' Harbor* (Marquette, Mich.: Pilot Press, 1977), 22–31.
28 Bell, "A Life of Russell Alger," 8–24.
29 Ibid., 31–102.
30 Ibid., 107–21.
31 Carter, *Voyageur's Harbor*, 22–31.
32 Bell, "A Life of Russell Alger," 208–80.

33 Lewis C. Reimann, *Incredible Seney: The First Complete Story of Michigan's Fabulous Lumber Town* (Ann Arbor: Edwards Brothers, 1953), 170–71.

34 Carter, *Voyageur's Harbor*, 30.

35 Bell, "A Life of Russell Alger," 407–8.

36 Carter, *Voyageur's Harbor*, 50–51.

37 *Ontonagon Herald*, September 5, 1891. Also see Knox Jamison, *A History of Bergland, Ontonagon County, Michigan* (Ontonagon: by the author, 1965), 12–13.

38 William Franklin Fleming, *America's Match King: Ohio Columbus Barber, 1841–1920* (Barberton, Ohio: Barberton Historical Society, 1981), 18–25.

39 Ibid., 39–40.

40 State of Michigan, Supreme Court Record, the Diamond Match Company vs. Michael Powers, Register of Deeds (June 1983), 145–48.

41 Fleming, *America's Match King*, 40.

42 Alfred T. Andreas, *History of the Upper Peninsula of Michigan* (Chicago: Western Historical Company, 1883), 516.

43 Fleming, *America's Match King*, 110.

44 *The Timberman*, November 16, 1889.

45 *Ontonagon Herald*, May 5, 1891, and November 15, 1890.

46 Ibid., February 21, 1891.

47 Ibid., August 28, 1891.

48 Ibid., October 13, 1894.

49 Ibid.

50 Fleming, *America's Match King*, 40.

51 *Ontonagon Herald*, October 13, 1894, and January 19, 1895.

52 *The Timberman*, June 20, 1896.

53 *Ontonagon Miner*, February 22, 1890.

54 Krog, "Marinette," 171.

55 Jack Orr, *Lumberjacks & River Pearls: Memories of Manistique* (Manistique: Pioneer Tribune, 1979), 13.

56 Carter, *Voyageur's Harbor*, 26.

57 Jim Cooper, "The Great Ontonagon Fire," in Frimodig, comp., *A Most Superior Land*, 146.

58 *Ontonagon Herald*, August 29, 1896.

59 Fleming, *America's Match King*, 122, 137.

60 *Ontonagon Herald*, June 5, 1897.

61 Jamison, *This Ontonagon Country*, 206–8.

62 James O'Neil, "Ottawa National Forest, State of Michigan, Historical Appendix," unpublished report, 1938, prepared for the Ottawa National Forest, Ironwood, Mich., 22.

CHAPTER 4. THE PROCESS AND PATTERN OF PINE LOGGING

1 Crowe, *Lumberjack*, 9.

2 John Emmett Nelligan, *A White Pine Empire: The Life of a Lumberman* (St. Cloud, Minn.: North Star Press, 1969), 117.

3 Rector, *Log Transportation in the Lake States*, 71–75.

4 Stephenson, *Recollections*, 85.

5 Nelligan, *A White Pine Empire*, 70.

6 MacKay, *The Lumberjacks*, 80.

7 Nelligan, *A White Pine Empire*, 68–69.

8 Stephenson, *Recollections*, 84.

9 Nelligan, *A White Pine Empire*, 117.

10 Ibid., 119.

11 *Daily Mining Journal* (Marquette, Mich.), July 23, 1964.

12 Stephenson, *Recollections*, 81–82.

13 James H. Anthony to Peter Barbeau, February 18, 1857. Marquette County Historical Society.

14 Stephenson, *Recollections*, 109.

15 Sawyer, *Lumbering in Delta County*.

16 Rector, *Log Transportation in the Lake States*, 92.

17 Michael Williams, "Clearing the United States Forests: Pivotal Years 1810–1860," *Journal of Historical Geography* 8, no. 1 (1892), 24.

18 Ralph Clement Bryant, *Logging: The General Principles and General Methods of Operation in the United States* (New York: John Wiley & Son, 1914), 347–48.

19 Stewart Edward White, *Blazed Trail Stories and Other Stories of the Wild Life* (New York: Grosset & Dunlap, 1904), 58.

20 William D. Hulbert, *White Pine Days on the Tequamenon* (Lansing: Historical Society of Michigan, 1949), 46.

21 Stephenson, *Recollections*, 88.

22 Charles F. Schaible, *I Was Interested* (Cincinnati: privately printed, 1972), 75.

23 Stephenson, *Recollections*, 88.

24 Schaible, *I Was Interested*, 78.

25 Lewis C. Reimann, *Between the Iron and the Pine: A Biography of a Pioneer Family and a Pioneer Town* (Ann Arbor, Mich.: Edwards Brothers, 1951), 44.

26 Harvey Crookson Saunders, "Memories of Logging and River Driving," Manuscript Memoirs, 1878–1934. Michigan State University Archives, East Lansing.

27 Nelligan, *A White Pine Empire*, 143.

28 *Northwestern Lumberman*, June 23, 1888, quoted in Rector, *Log Transportation in the Lake States*, 96–97.

29 Saunders, "Memories of Camp Life & Logging Days," n.p., Manuscript Memoirs.

30 Ibid.

31 *Diamond Drill* (Crystal Falls, Mich.), June 6, 1896.

32 Ledgers, 1883–84, Bay De Noquet Company Papers, Bentley Historical Library, Ann Arbor, Mich.

33 Saunders, "How Grand Marais Became a Town, 5, Manuscript Memoirs.

34 *Diamond Drill* (Crystal Falls, Mich.), June 6, 1896.

35 Nelligan, *A White Pine Empire*, 112–13.

36 Rector, *Log Transportation in the United States*, 186.

37 Rector, *Log Transportation in the Lake States*, 186.

38 "J. J. Ramsey's Report," November 25, 1905, Holt Lumber Company Records.

39 Rector, *Log Transportation in the Lake States*, 187.

40 *The Timberman*, June 20, 1896.

41 Robert C. Johnson, "Logs for Saginaw: The Development of Raft-Towing on Lake Huron," *Inland Seas* 5 (Spring–Summer 1949), 39–40, 85.

42 Ibid., 166.

43 Ibid., 167.

44 *The Timberman*, July 23, 1887.

45 Ibid., May 18, 1889.

46 Ibid., September 14, 1889.

47 Ibid., October 15, 1887.

48 Ibid., October 16, 1896.

49 Johnson, "Logs for Saginaw," 84–90.

50 Hotchkiss, *History of the Lumber and Forest Industry*, 325.

51 Crowe, *Lumberjack*, 39.

52 Saunders, "Jamestown Account," n.p., Manuscript Memoirs.

53 McKay, *The Lumberjacks*, 172.

54 *Ontonagon Herald*, April 29, 1891.

55 Bryant, *Logging*, 230.

56 William Arthur Holt, *A Wisconsin Lumberman Looks Backward: An Intimate Glance into 100 Years of North Woods Lumbering by the Holt Family* (Oconto, Wis.: privately printed, 1948), 44.

57 Carter, *Voyageur's Harbor*, 26.
58 Merk, *Economic History of Wisconsin*, 377–79.
59 James Clary, *Ladies of the Lakes* (Lansing, Mich.: Department of Natural Resources), 97–98.
60 Henry Judkins—Father & Family, May 13, 1849. Henry Judkins Correspondence, State Historical Society of Wisconsin, Madison.
61 Stephenson, *Recollections*, 92–96.
62 Krog, "Marinette," 139–40.
63 Stephenson, *Recollections*, 169.
64 Merk, *Economic History of Wisconsin*, 377.
65 Krog, "Marinette," 147.
66 Sawyer, *Lumbering in Delta County*, 14.
67 Stephenson, *Recollections*, 102.
68 Ibid.
69 Rodney C. Loehr, "Saving the Kerf: The Introduction of the Band Saw Mill," *Agricultural History* 23, no. 3 (July 1949), 168.
70 Robert E. Pike, *Tall Trees, Tough Men* (New York: W. W. Norton, 1967), 179.
71 Benson, "Logs and Lumber," 158.
72 Loehr, "Saving the Kerf," 172.
73 Crowe, *Lumberjack*, 22–23.
74 *The Timberman*, August 27, 1887.
75 Hotchkiss, *History of the Lumber and Forest Industry*, 322.
76 Crowe, *Lumberjack*, 69.
77 John Bartlow Martin, *Call It North Country: The Story of Upper Michigan* (New York: Alfred Knopf, 1945), 125.
78 James Marston Fitch, *American Building: The Historical Forces That Shaped It* (New York: Shocken Books, 1973), 121.
79 *The Timberman*, October 2, 1886.
80 Ibid., May 4, 1889.
81 Ibid., July 17, 1886.
82 Shuman, "The Forest Resource Situation," 24–39.
83 Hugh Cuthbert Davis, "Demographic Changes and Resource Use in the Western Counties of Michigan's Upper Peninsula, 1860–1880" (Ph.D. diss., University of Michigan, 1962), 170–73.
84 Shuman, "The Forest Resource Situation," 71–72.
85 Stephenson, *Recollections*, 172.
86 Shuman, "The Forest Resource Situation," 72.
87 Reimann, *Between the Iron and the Pine*, 42.
88 *Diamond Drill* (Crystal Falls, Mich.), September 8, 1894.
89 *Ontonagon Herald*, September 8, 1894.
90 *Diamond Drill* (Crystal Falls, Mich.), May 16, 1896.
91 Ibid., September 8, 1894.
92 *The Timberman*, July 2, 1887, and September 24, 1887.
93 Ibid., July 18, 1891.
94 O'Neil, "Ottawa National Forest," 38.
95 Shuman, "The Forest Resource Situation," 75–76.
96 Sawyer, *Lumbering in Delta County*, 2.
97 *Ontonagon Herald*, March 1, 1890.
98 Ibid.
99 R. A. Brotherton, "The Jackson Mine and Nagaunee, Michigan," *Inland Seas* 2 (October 1946), 26–32.
100 Kenneth O. LaFayette, *Flaming Brands: Fifty Years of Iron Making in the Upper Peninsula of Michigan, 1848–1898* (Marquette, Mich.: Northern Michigan University Press, 1977), 39–40.
101 Davis, "Demographic Changes and Resource Use," 186.
102 *The Timberman*, February 21, 1891.
103 Davis, "Demographic Changes and Resource Use," 186–87.

104 Sawyer, *Lumbering in Delta County*, 11–14.
105 J. William Trygg, *Composite Map of United States Land Surveyor's Original Plats and Field Notes* (Ely, Minn.: J. William Trygg, 1969).
106 Schaible, *I Was Interested*, 50–55.
107 Ibid.

CHAPTER 5. THE SOCIAL ENVIRONMENT OF PINE LOGGING

1 Stephenson, *Recollections*, 91.
2 Nelligan, *A White Pine Empire*, 177, 193–94.
3 *Ontonagon Herald*, June 1, 1892.
4 Hotchkiss, *History of the Lumber and Forest Industry*, 325.
5 Lewis Publishing Company, *Memorial Record of the Northern Peninsula of Michigan* (Chicago, 1895), 580–81.
6 Hotchkiss, *History of the Lumber and Forest Industry*, 326.
7 Thomas Nestor to B. J. Stevens, December 23, 1884. Michigan Land and Iron Company Papers, John M. Longyear Research Library, Marquette County Historical Society, Marquette.
8 Hotchkiss, *History of the Lumber and Forest Industry*, 326.
9 Thomas Nestor to B. J. Stevens, November 28, 1884, Michigan Land and Iron Company Papers.
10 Horatio Seymour to B. J. Stevens, November 18, 1889, Michigan Land and Iron Company Papers.
11 *The Timberman*, November 16, 1889.
12 Horatio Seymour to B. J. Stevens, November 18, 1889, Michigan Land and Iron Company Papers.
13 Isaac Marston to B. J. Stevens, March 17, 1890, Michigan Land and Iron Company Papers.
14 Nelligan, *A White Pine Empire*, 160.
15 *Gladstone Delta*, April 30, 1886.
16 Reimann, *Between the Iron and the Pine*, 33.
17 Nelligan, *A White Pine Empire*, 139.
18 James Willard Hurst, "The Institutional Environment of the Logging Era in Wisconsin," in *The Great Lakes Forest: An Environmental and Social History*, ed. Susan B. Flader (Minneapolis: University of Minnesota Press, 1983), 152.
19 U.S. Department of Commerce, *The Lumber Industry: Standing Timber, Concentration of Timber Holdings in Important Selected Regions, and Land Holdings of Large Timber Owners* (Washington, D.C.: U.S. Government Printing Office, 1913), 188–216.
20 *Lake Superior Journal* (Marquette, Mich.), June 13, 1857.
21 Stephenson, *Recollections*, 120.
22 Reimann, *Between the Iron and the Pine*, 48.
23 *Escanaba Iron Port*, February 20, 1886.
24 *Gladstone Delta*, August 27, 1886.
25 *Lake Superior Journal* (Marquette, Mich.), December 18, 1891.
26 Horatio Seymour to B. J. Stevens, January 16, 1885, Michigan Land and Iron Company Papers.
27 *The Timberman*, March 16, 1889.
28 *Diamond Drill* (Crystal Falls, Mich.), December 18, 1891.
29 Marcia Bernhardt (ed.), *Frames for the Future: Iron River Area* (Caspian, Mich.: Iron County Historical and Museum Society, 1980), 53.
30 Reimann, *Between the Iron and the Pine*, 51.
31 *Diamond Drill* (Crystal Falls, Mich.), December 5, 1891.
32 Reimann, *Between the Iron and the Pine*, 210.
33 *Diamond Drill* (Crystal Falls, Mich.), December 5, 1891.
34 Bernhardt, *Frames for the Future*, 57.

35 John M. Longyear, "Reminiscences of John M. Longyear," n.d. (unpublished). Longyear Realty Corporation vault, Marquette, Mich.

36 *Diamond Drill* (Crystal Falls, Mich.), January 25, 1896; Bernhardt, *Frames for the Future*, 55.

37 *Daily Mining Journal* (Marquette, Mich.), February 13, 1954.

38 Martin, *Call It North Country*, 124.

39 Roy L. Dodge, *Ticket to Hell: A Saga of Michigan's Bad Men* (Tawas City, Mich.: Northeastern Printers, Inc., 1975), i.

40 Stanley Newton, *Paul Bunyan of the Great Lakes* (Au Train, Mich.: Avery Color Studios, 1985), 17–18.

41 Herbert G. Gutman, *Work, Culture, and Society in Industrializing America* (New York: Alfred A. Knopf, 1976), 74.

42 Stephenson, *Recollections*, 105–6.

43 Henry Judkins to Father and Family, May 13, 1849, Henry Judkins Correspondence, State Historical Society of Wisconsin, Madison.

44 Ibid.

45 Stephenson, *Recollections*, 106.

46 George B. Engberg, "Who Were the Lumberjacks?" *The Old Northwest: A Study in Regional History*, ed. Harry N. Scheiber (Lincoln, Nebr.: University of Nebraska Press, 1969), 276–77.

47 Ibid., 274; U.S. Bureau of the Census, *Population Schedule for Schoolcraft County, Michigan, 1870, 1880, 1900; Population Schedule for Delta County, Michigan, 1880, 1900.*

48 Russell M. Magnaghi, *An Outline History of Michigan's Upper Peninsula* (Marquette, Mich.: Belle Fontaine Press, 1979), 39.

49 Schaible, *I Was Interested*, 50.

50 Stephenson, *Recollections*, 87.

51 Nelligan, *A White Pine Empire*, 134.

52 Carl Addison Leech, notes on "Superstitions," Carl Addison Leech Papers, Bentley Historical Library, Ann Arbor, Mich., n.p.

53 Schaible, *I Was Interested*, 67.

54 Nelligan, *A White Pine Empire*, 96–97.

55 Wilfred Nevue, "Logging in the Huron Mountains," Wilfred Nevue Papers, Bentley Historical Library, Ann Arbor, Mich., 29.

56 Lewis C. Reimann, *When Pine Was King* (Ann Arbor, Mich.: Edwards Brothers, 1952), 63.

57 Schaible, *I Was Interested*, 59.

58 Crowe, *Lumberjack*, 58.

59 Walter Licht, *Working for the Railroad: The Organization of Work in the Nineteenth Century* (Princeton: Princeton University Press, 1983), 238.

60 Gutman, *Work, Culture, and Society in Industrializing America*, 36.

61 Ibid., 36–37.

62 Nelligan, *A White Pine Empire*, 113.

63 R. A. Brotherton, "Early Logging Days," MS in the Delta County Historical Society, Escanaba, Mich.

64 Schaible, *I Was Interested*, 73.

65 John Ira Bellaire, "Memoir," John Ira Bellaire Papers, Bentley Historical Library, Ann Arbor, Mich., n.p.

66 Ibid.

67 Ibid.

68 Ibid.

69 Reimann, *Incredible Seney*, 134–36.

70 *Ontonagon Herald*, March 28, 1891.

71 Ibid., January 8, 1891.

72 Ibid., November 14, 1891.

73 Ibid., April 2, 1892.

74 Ibid., April 27, 1895.

75 *Gogebic Iron Tribune* (Hurley, Wis.), December 17, 1890.
76 Walter R. Nursey, *The Menominee Iron Range: Its Cities, Their Industries and Resources* (Florence, Wis.: Board of Supervisors, 1891), 118.
77 Chase S. Osborn, *The Iron Hunter* (New York: Macmillan Company, 1919), 2.
78 Nelligan, *A White Pine Empire*, 185.
79 *Daily Mining Journal* (Marquette, Mich.), May 2, 1883.
80 Osborn, *The Iron Hunter*, 2.
81 Nelligan, *A White Pine Empire*, 85.
82 Ibid.
83 Osborn, *The Iron Hunter*, 3.
84 Herbert R. Larson, *Be-Wa-Bic Country: The Story of the Menominee Iron Range in the Upper Peninsula of Michigan* (New York: Carlton Press, 1963), 106.
85 Ibid.
86 Martin, *Call It North Country*, 180–81.
87 Ibid., 182.
88 *Ontonagon Herald*, October 11, 1890.
89 Arthur T. Bolt, "Escanaba, Michigan: Its Transition from a Lumbering and Iron Ore Shipping Center to a Tourist Haven with Particular Reference to the Press" (M.A. thesis, Medill School of Journalism, Northwestern University, 1937), 144.
90 *Ontonagon Herald*, December 19, 1891.
91 *Escanaba Iron Port*, September 5, 1885.
92 *Ontonagon Herald*, April 13, 1895.
93 Schaible, *I Was Interested*, 73.
94 *Sault Ste. Marie News*, March 24, 1888.
95 Reimann, *Between the Iron and the Pine*, 177.
96 Alma W. Swinton, *I Married a Doctor: Life in Ontonagon, Michigan from 1900 to 1910* (Marquette, Mich.: privately printed, 1964), 133.
97 *Ontonagon Herald*, February 3, 1894.
98 Ibid., November 25, 1893.
99 Osborn, *The Iron Hunter*, 8–13.
100 Marie Rademacher, "Reminiscences of Ford River," Michigan Historical Collections, Bentley Historical Library, Ann Arbor, 9–10.
101 *Escanaba Tribune*, May 15, 1875.
102 Krog, "Marinette," 300.
103 Ibid., 301.
104 Richard M. Dorson, *Bloodstoppers and Bearwalkers: Folk Traditions of the Upper Peninsula* (Cambridge: Harvard University Press, 1952), 170.
105 Krog, "Marinette," 302.
106 Dorson, *Bloodstoppers and Bearwalkers*, 174–76.
107 John Ira Bellaire, "Seney, Michigan," unpublished MS in the Floyd Ames Papers, Bentley Historical Library, Ann Arbor, Mich., 7–8.
108 Ibid., 11.
109 *Escanaba Iron Port*, November 7, 1885.
110 Payroll Records 1898, Sparrow-Kroll Lumber Company, Kenton, Mich. Bentley Historical Library, Ann Arbor, Mich., and George Barker Engberg, "Labor in the Lake States Lumber Industry, 1830–1930" (Ph.D. thesis, University of Minnesota, 1949), 300–1.
111 Engberg, "Labor in the Lake States Lumber Industry," 300.
112 *Escanaba Delta*, October 21, 1886.
113 Nelligan, *A White Pine Empire*, 162–63.
114 Joan Underhill Hannon, "Ethnic Discrimination in a 19th Century Mining District: Michigan Copper Mines, 1888," *Explorations in Economic History* 19 (1982), 33.
115 William Gates, *Michigan Copper and Boston Dollars* (Cambridge: Harvard University Press, 1954), 113–15.
116 Krog, "Marinette," 222–24.
117 *Escanaba Iron Port*, October 31, 1885.
118 Ibid., October 10, 1885.

119 Ibid., September 19, 1885.

120 Ibid., November 7, 1885.

121 *Escanaba Delta*, November 12, 1885.

122 Nelligan, *A White Pine Empire*, 129; Engberg, "Labor in the Lake States Lumber Industry," 399.

123 Nelligan, *A White Pine Empire*, 113-14.

124 *Diamond Drill* (Crystal Falls, Mich.), February 7, 1891.

125 Larson, *Be-Wa-Bic Country*, 217.

126 Nelligan, *A White Pine Empire*, 114.

127 Ibid., 123.

128 Engberg, "Labor in the Lake States Lumber Industry," 305.

129 Bellaire, "Seney, Michigan," 18.

130 Stephenson, *Recollections*, 85.

131 Schaible, *I Was Interested*, 73.

132 Reimann, *Between the Iron and the Pine*, 20.

133 Schaible, *I Was Interested*, 62-63.

134 Nelligan, *A White Pine Empire*, 126.

135 Nevue, "Logging in the Huron Mountains," Bentley Historical Library, 20.

136 Reimann, *Between the Iron and the Pine*, 22.

137 Nelligan, *A White Pine Empire*, 124.

138 Schaible, *I Was Interested*, 124.

139 Ibid., 65.

140 Reimann, *Between the Iron and the Pine*, 21.

141 Wilfred Nevue, "Lumberjack Ballads and Stories: An Evaluation" (unpublished MS), Wilfred Nevue Papers, Bentley Historical Library, Ann Arbor, Mich.

142 Newton, *Paul Bunyan of the Great Lakes*, 180-81.

CHAPTER 6. PERIOD OF ADJUSTMENT

1 *Weekly Mining Journal* (Marquette, Mich.), March 12, 1902.

2 Krog, "Marinette," 71.

3 *Northwestern Lumberman*, June 12, 1897.

4 Krog, "Marinette," 171.

5 *Northwestern Lumberman*, June 12, 1897.

6 *Ontonagon Herald*, March 27, 1901.

7 Ibid., October 6, 1900.

8 O'Neil, "Ottawa National Forest," 18-20.

9 Krog, "Marinette," 212-13.

10 *Ontonagon Herald*, May 4, 1906.

11 Krog, "Marinette," 209.

12 *Weekly Mining Journal* (Marquette, Mich.), March 12, 1902.

13 LeRoy Barnett, "Lac LaBelle Waterway: Keweenaw's Other Ship Canal," *Michigan History* 69 (January-February 1985): 40-46.

14 Lewis Pub. Co., *Memorial Record of the Northern Penninsula*, 580-82.

15 Roscoe C. Young, "The Lake Superior & Ishpeming Railway Company," Manuscript File, John M. Longyear Library, Marquette County Historical Society, Marquette, Mich., 1-6.

16 Ibid.

17 *Munising News*, November 8, 1914.

18 Young, "The Lake Superior & Ishpeming Railway," 7-8.

19 Superintendent to E. J. Judson, January 16, 1930. Records of Cleveland-Cliffs Iron Company, State Archives of Michigan, Lansing.

20 John Brotherton, oral history interview, July 1982.

21 Superintendent to William G. Mather, March 1, 1917. Cleveland-Cliffs Records, State Archives of Michigan, Lansing.

22 R. A. Brotherton, "Forest Materials Cut from One Acre of Section 35, T46, Camp S, Job 154 in 1933," Cleveland-Cliffs Records, State Archives of Michigan, Lansing.

23 *American Lumberman*, July 25, 1903.

24 Ibid.

25 Ibid.

26 Martin, *Call It North Country*, 158–62.

27 Charles M. Case, "Selected Excerpts or Historiette of Hermansville, Michigan," MS in Charles M. Case Collection, Bentley Historical Library, Ann Arbor, Mich., 11.

28 Ibid., 23.

29 Ibid., 25.

30 Ibid., 37–39.

31 Ibid.

32 *Escanaba Daily Press*, October 12, 1974.

33 Case, "Historiette of Hermansville, Michigan," 58.

34 Ibid., 59.

35 Jack Schwartz, "Memoir of Nahma," unpublished MS, 1932, Delta County Historical Society, Escanaba, Mich.

36 Hotchkiss, *History of the Lumber and Forest Industry*, 420.

37 Schwartz, "Memoir of Nahma."

38 George Springer, "Old Forest Railroads: Namha & Northern Railway & the Garden Bay Railway Company," *Soo Line* (July-August-September 1959), 15, 25, 29.

39 Reimann, *When Pine Was King*, 63.

40 U.S. Department of Commerce, *The Lumber Industry*, 195.

41 "Nahma Clipping File," Delta County Historical Society, Escanaba, Mich.

42 Hotchkiss, *History of the Lumber and Forest Industry*, 421.

43 Division of Archives and Manuscripts, "Inventory—Holt Lumber Company," State Historical Society of Wisconsin, Green Bay, 4–6.

44 Holt, *A Wisconsin Lumberman Looks Backward*, 40.

45 Ibid., 41–42.

46 Ibid., 40–43.

47 Ibid., 41–42.

48 William Holt to Chicago Office, June 14, 1901. Holt Lumber Company Papers.

49 Holt, *A Wisconsin Lumberman Looks Backward*, 46.

50 Ida M. Spring, "White Pine Portraits: Con Culhane," *Michigan History* 31 (1947), 437–42.

51 Dorson, *Bloodstoppers and Bearwalkers*, 197–99.

52 Spring, "Con Culhane," 441–42.

53 Ibid.

54 Krog, "Marinette," 172.

55 Crowe, *Lumberjack*, 61.

56 Ibid., 66–69.

57 Jamison, *This Ontonagon Country*, 122.

58 Upper Peninsula Development Bureau, *Seven Million Fertile Acres in the Upper Peninsula of Michigan* (Chicago: Poole Brothers, 1911), 1–3.

59 James L. Carter, Superior: *A State for the North Country* (Marquette, Mich.: The Pilot Press, 1980), 39–41.

60 *Ontonagon Herald*, March 29, 1890.

61 Ibid., July 4, 1896.

62 J. Russell Whitaker, "The Relation of Agriculture to Mining in the Upper Peninsula of Michigan," *Journal of Geography* 25 (January 1926), 23–24.

63 Marcia Bernhardt, *They Came to Iron County, Michigan* (Caspian, Mich.: Iron County Historical Museum, 1975), 55.

64 *Ontonagon Herald*, November 28, 1896.

65 Rena Thompson, *History of Kinross Township* (Sault Ste. Marie, Mich.: privately printed, 1981), 97–98.

66 Reimann, *Between the Iron and the Pine*, 82.

67 Rudolph Stindt, "Early History of Matchwood and Bergland Townships in the

County of Ontonagon," unpublished MS in the Ontanagon County Historical Society, Ontonagon, Mich., 1951.

68 Walter A. Rowlands, "The Great Lakes Cutover Region," in *Regionalism in America*, ed. Merrill Jensen (Madison: University of Wisconsin Press, 1965), 334.

69 C. Warren Vander Hill, *Settling the Great Lakes Frontier: Immigration to Michigan, 1837–1924* (Lansing: Michigan Historical Commission, 1970), 58–59.

70 Arnold R. Alanen and William H. Tishler, "Finnish Farmstead Organization in Old and New World Settings," *Journal of Cultural Geography* no. 1 (fall/winter 1980), 78.

71 *Ontonagon Herald*, June 17, 1905.

72 Arvo Karttunen et al., *Pioneers of Green* (Ontonagon, Mich.: Ontonagon Herald Company, 1976), 53–54.

73 Bess Elliot, oral history interview, July 1983.

74 Karttunen et al., *Pioneers of Green*, 12.

75 Henry Heimonen, "Agricultural Trends in the Upper Peninsula," *Michigan History* 41 (1957), 48.

76 *Hardwood Record*, March 10, 1905.

CHAPTER 7. RISE OF INDUSTRIAL FORESTRY

1 Allan Nevins and Frank Ernest Hill, *Ford: Expansion and Challenge, 1915–1933* (New York: Charles Scribner's Sons, 1957), 217.

2 Nevins and Hill, *Ford*, 486–87.

3 Charles F. Sutherland, "Consumption and Marketing of Forest Products in the Automobile Industry: A Case Study of the Ford Motor Company" (Ph.D. diss., University of Michigan, 1961), 24.

4 Nevins and Hill, *Ford*, 218–19.

5 Ibid., 219.

6 Charles Larsen, *Reminiscences*. Ford Archives, Edison Institute, Dearborn, Mich.

7 Sutherland, "Consumption and Marketing," 16–17.

8 Abbott Fox, *Reminiscences*. Ford Archives, Edison Institute, Dearborn, Mich.

9 Sutherland, "Consumption and Marketing," 12–15.

10 Nevins and Hill, *Ford*, 219–20.

11 Reynolds M. Wik, *Henry Ford and Grass-roots America* (Ann Arbor: University of Michigan Press, 1972), 5.

12 Fox, *Reminiscences*.

13 Ovid M. Butler, "Henry Ford's Forest," *American Forests* (December 1922), 725–31.

14 R. G. Steinke, *Reminiscences*. Ford Archives, Edison Institute, Dearborn, Mich.

15 Albert Olson, *Reminiscences*. Ford Archives, Edison Institute, Dearborn, Mich.

16 Robert Edwards, *Reminiscences*. Ford Archives, Edison Institute, Dearborn, Mich.

17 Randall E. Rohe, "The Evolution of the Great Lakes Logging Camp, 1830–1930," *Journal of Forest History* (January 1986), 28.

18 Carl Miller, *Reminiscences*. Ford Archives, Edison Institute, Dearborn, Mich.

19 Butler, "Henry Ford's Forest," 725–31.

20 Charles S. Sutherland, "Ford's Forest," *American Forests* (September 1963), 50–51.

21 Olson, *Reminiscences*.

22 Sutherland, "Consumption and Marketing," 27.

23 Ibid., 27–28.

24 *Daily Mining Journal* (Marquette, Mich.), October 25, 1923.

25 Ibid., October 10, 1923.

26 Ibid., October 11, 1923.

27 Ibid., October 27, 1923.

28 U.S. Department of Commerce, *The Lumber Industry*, 207–13.

29 *Hardwood Record*, March 10, 1905.

30 Michigan State Archives, "Inventory of the Records of the Cleveland-Cliffs Iron Company," Lansing.
31 Marquette County Historical Society, *A Bond of Interest* (Marquette: By the Historical Society, 1978), 8-11.
32 Beatrice Hanscom Castle, *The Grand Island Story* (Marquette: John M. Longyear Research Library, 1974), 70-74.
33 Henry S. Graves, "Report on the Forestry of Certain Lands of the Cleveland-Cliffs Iron Company," Michigan Technological University Library Archives, Houghton, Mich.
34 *Weekly Mining Journal* (Marquette, Mich.), January 20, 1906.
35 *Ontonagon Herald*, May 12, 1906.
36 *Weekly Mining Journal* (Marquette, Mich.), January 20, 1906.
37 Norman John Schmaltz, "Cutover Land Crusade: The Michigan Forest Conservation Movement, 1899-1931" (Ph.D. diss., University of Michigan, 1972), 334.
38 Charles Symon, "The Wyman School of the Woods—Pioneer in Conservation," in *Peninsula Portraits: People and Places in Michigan's Upper Peninsula* (Iron Mountain, Mich.: Mid-Peninsula Library Cooperative, 1980), 135-40.
39 *The Munising News*, May 25, 1906.
40 Ibid., November 11, 1910.
41 J. A. Mitchell and D. Robson, *Forest Fires and Forest Fire Control in Michigan* (Lansing: Michigan Department of Conservation, 1950), 24-26.
42 *The Munising News*, November 18, 1910.
43 Mitchell and Robson, *Forest Fires and Forest Fire Control*, 26-27.
44 Ibid.
45 Symon, "The Wyman School of the Woods," 140.
46 Marquette County Historical Society, *A Bond of Interest*, 17-18.
47 Raphael Zon and E. D. Graves *Selective Logging in the Northern Hardwoods of the Lake States*, U.S. Department of Agriculture Bulletin No. 164 (Washington, D.C.: Government Printing Office, 1930), 38.
48 Conner Forest Industries, *The First Hundred Years* (Wausau, Wis.: privately printed, 1972), 38.
49 Zon and Graves, *Selective Logging*, 40-46.
50 Percy LaRock, oral history interview, 1982.
51 C. A. Saunders to R. G. Schreck, April 13, 1928. Lands Files, U.S.D.A. Forest Service, Hiawatha National Forest, Escanaba, Mich.
52 *The Evening News* (Sault Ste. Marie, Mich.), June 1, 1956.
53 Malcolm McIver, "History of the Whitefish Bay Country," MS, n.d., in Cultural Resource Management File, Hiawatha National Forest, Escanaba, Mich.
54 Stewart Sunblad, oral history interview, 1982.
55 Cunningham and White, *Forest Resources of the Upper Peninsula of Michigan*, 9.

CHAPTER 8. THE PROCESS AND PATTERN OF HARDWOOD LOGGING

1 James Carter, "Logging Era Locomotives Exist Only in Alger's 'Bunyan' Tales." *Mining Journal* (Marquette, Mich.), February 22, 1965.
2 Nels Plude, "Record of the N & N Railroad," MS, September 1952, Delta County Historical Society, Escanaba, Mich.
3 Carter, *Voyageur's Harbor*, 18.
4 Sawyer, *Lumbering in Delta County*, 18.
5 Kenneth Mallmenn, oral history interview, August 1982.
6 Rector, *Log Transportation in the Lake States*, 198-99.
7 Larson, *Be-Wa-Bic*, 257.
8 Martin, *Call It North Country*, 162.
9 *American Lumberman*, July 25, 1903.
10 George Springer, "The Garden Bay Railway Company," *Soo Line* (July-August-September 1959), 15-25.

11 Case, "Historiette of Hermansville, Michigan," 11.

12 Crowe, *Lumberjack*, 50.

13 Bryant, *Logging*, 245–50.

14 Louis Verch, oral history interview, July 1983.

15 James Stark, oral history interview, July 1983.

16 Edwards, *Reminiscences*.

17 Holt, *A Wisconsin Lumberman Looks Backward*, 41.

18 W. S. Towne to D. Rounseville, April 2, 1907. Personal collection of James P. Kayson, Cedarburg, Wis.

19 D. Rounseville to E. Packard, April 4, 1907. Kaysen Collection.

20 Stark, oral history interview.

21 William Holt to Chicago Office, June 14, 1901, Holt Lumber Company Papers, State Historical Society of Wisconsin, Green Bay.

22 Stack Lumber Company, Annual Report, 1914. Delta County Historical Society, Escanaba, Mich.

23 Bryant, *Logging*, 304–8.

24 Springer, "The Garden Bay Railway Company," 25.

25 Malcolm Rosholt, *The Wisconsin Logging Book, 1839–1939* (Rosholt, Wis.: Rosholt House, 1980), 59.

26 John A. Anguilm, *Tales and Trails of Tro-La-Oz-Ken* (Trout Lake, Mich.: Trout Lake Women's Club, 1976), 137.

27 Clinton Jones, "World's Steepest Adhesion Railroad?" *Trains* (June 1969), 426–32.

28 Bourke, "Trains to Everywhere," 59.

29 *Munising News*, June 19, 1908.

30 *Mining Journal* (Marquette, Mich.), December 26, 1908.

31 *Weekly Mining Journal* (Marquette, Mich.), December 12, 1908.

32 Ibid., April 5, 1910.

33 Rosholt, *The Wisconsin Logging Book*, 60.

34 Rector, *Log Transportation in the Lake States*, 300.

35 LaRock, oral history interview.

36 MacKay, *Lumberjacks*, 172.

37 McIver, "Whitefish Bay Country," n.p.

38 Bryant, *Logging*, 322.

39 J. C. Ryan, *Early Loggers in Minnesota* (Duluth: Minnesota Timber Producers Association, 1975), 9–10.

40 LaRock, oral history interview.

41 *American Lumberman*, July 25, 1903.

42 Ibid.

43 Ibid.

44 Charles Hebard to Hulbert Brennant, July 1, 1984. Charles Hebard & Sons Company Papers. John M. Longyear Research Library, Marquette County Historical Society, Marquette, Mich.

45 Symon, *Peninsula Portraits*, 125–26.

46 Crowe, *Lumberjack*, 67.

47 Sawyer, *History of the Northern Peninsula of Michigan*, 402–3.

48 Ibid.

49 Richard H. Schallenberg, "Charcoal Iron: The Coal Mines of the Forest," in *Material Culture of the Wooden Age*, ed. Brooke Hindle (Tarrytown, N.Y.: Sleepy Hollow Press, 1981), 297–99.

50 Henry R. Steer, *Lumber Production in the United States, 1799–1946*, U.S. Department of Agriculture Miscellaneous Publication No. 669 (Washington, D.C.: U.S. Government Printing Office, 1948), 44.

51 Shuman, "The Forest Resource Situation," 39.

52 Ibid., 36, 56.

53 Brotherton, oral history interview.

54 *Hardwood Record*, May 10, 1905.

55 George Corrigan, *Calked Boots and Cant Hooks* (Park Falls, Wis.: MacGregor Litho, 1976), 19.
56 O'Neil, "Ottawa National Forest," 39.
57 Ibid.
58 Northwestern Cooperage and Lumber Company to Wisconsin Land and Lumber Company, May 7, 1907. Bentley Historical Library, Ann Arbor, Mich.
59 *Escanaba Daily Press*, October 12, 1974.
60 Brotherton, oral history interview.
61 O'Neil, "Ottawa National Forest," 39.
62 Shuman, "The Forest Resource Situation," 89.
63 Francis Furlong, oral history interview, October 1982.
64 Radcliffe, oral history interview; LaRock, oral history interview.
65 Randall E. Rohe, "The Evolution of the Great Lakes Logging Camp, 1830–1930," *Journal of Forest History* (January 1986), 28.
66 *Ontonagon Herald*, August 29, 1891.
67 Corrigan, *Calked Boots and Cant Hooks*, 3.
68 Ibid., 3–4.
69 *American Lumberman*, February 3, 1916.
70 Assistant Superintendent to William G. Mather, March 20, 1917. Cleveland-Cliffs Iron Company Records, Lansing, Mich.
71 John Anguilm, oral history interview, July 1982.
72 Furlong, oral history interview.

CHAPTER 9. THE SOCIAL ENVIRONMENT OF HARDWOOD LOGGING

1 Minutes of Meeting of Representative Lumbermen of Upper Michigan, March 1, 1919. Cleveland-Cliffs Records, Lansing, Mich. (hereafter referred to as Minutes).
2 U.S. Department of Commerce, *Lumber Industry*, 173–90.
3 Ibid., 179.
4 Krog, "Marinette," 63.
5 Rector, *Log Transportation in the Lake States*, 86.
6 U.S. Department of Commerce, *Lumber Industry*, 204.
7 Nelson Courtlandt Brown, *The American Lumber Industry* (New York: John Wiley & Sons, 1923), 242–43.
8 *Hardwood Record*, December 12, 1917.
9 Jean Worth, "Using the Hardwood Forest," MS in the Delta County Historical Society, Escanaba, Mich.
10 Stephenson, *Recollections*, 85.
11 *Hardwood Record*, December 25, 1917.
12 George Baker Engberg, "Labor in the Lake States Lumber Industry, 1830–1930," (Ph.D. diss., University of Minnesota, 1949), 208–9.
13 Corrigan, *Calked Boots and Cant Hooks*, 44, 52, 62–64.
14 Minutes, March 16, 1920.
15 Daniel N. McLeod to G. W. Ackerman, March 16, 1920. Cleveland-Cliffs Records, Lansing, Mich.
16 L. M. Richardson to G. W. Ackerman, April 5, 1920. Cleveland-Cliffs Records, Lansing, Mich.
17 Ibid.
18 Minutes, March 16, 1920.
19 William J. Chesbrough to G. W. Ackerman, April 8, 1920. Cleveland-Cliffs Records, Lansing, Mich.
20 Hilja Pekkarinen and Minnie Ida Mattson, *The History of Luce County: "Past Years"* (Newberry, Mich.: Luce County Historical Society, 1981), 323.
21 Furlong, oral history interview.
22 Anguilm, oral history interview.

23 *Weekly Mining Journal* (Marquette, Mich.), May 18, 1901.
24 Ibid., December 12, 1908.
25 General Superintendent to Austin Farrell, July 31, 1917. Cleveland-Cliffs Iron Company Records, Lansing, Mich.
26 *Hardwood Record*, March 10, 1905.
27 Memorandum from William G. Mather, August 24, 1917. Cleveland-Cliffs Iron Company Records, Lansing, Mich.
28 *Ontonagon Herald*, February 17, 1906.
29 *Daily Mining Journal* (Marquette, Mich.), February 28, 1921.
30 Assistant Superintendent to William G. Mather, March 1, 1917, and Assistant Auditor to Austin Farrell, January 29, 1923. Cleveland-Cliffs Iron Company Records, Lansing, Mich.
31 *Ontonagon Herald*, June 2, 1900.
32 *Weekly Mining Journal* (Marquette, Mich), October 5, 1901.
33 Nevins and Hill, *Ford*, 219.
34 William Holt to Chicago Office, January 3, 1896, and January 7, 1896. Holt Lumber Company Records, Green Bay, Wis.
35 Julie Anderson, *I Married a Logger: Life in Michigan's Tall Timber* (New York: Exposition Press, 1951), 90. For another version of what may be the same incident see Mary Roddis Conner, *A Century with Conner Timber: Conner Forest Industries, 1872-1972* (Stevens Point, Wis.: Worzalla Publishing Company, 1972), 112-13.
36 Reimann, *When Pine Was King*, 25-27.
37 O'Neil, "Ottawa National Forest," 24.
38 Reimann, *When Pine Was King*, 28.
39 Ibid.
40 Edna Ferber, *Come and Get It!* (New York: Doubleday, Doran & Co., 1934); also see Edna Ferber, *A Peculiar Treasure* (New York: Doubleday, 1938).
41 Anguilm, oral history interview.
42 Charles Taylor, oral history interview, August 1982.
43 Nevins and Hill, *Ford*, 219.
44 Harold W. Wisdom and Carmen D. Wisdom, "Furniture Industry," in *Encyclopedia of American Forest and Conservation History*, ed. Richard C. Davis (New York: MacMillan Publishing Company, 1983), 260.
45 Davis, "Demographic Changes and Resource Use," 18.
46 J. F. Thaden, "Ethnic Settlements in Rural Michigan," *Michigan Quarterly Bulletin* 29, no. 2 (1946), 102.
47 Charles A. Symon, *Who Were Those People: The Ethnic Beginnings of Alger County, Michigan* (Munising, Mich.: Alger County Historical Society, 1982), 53, 149.
48 Corrigan, *Calked Boots and Cant Hooks*, 49.
49 Tony Andreski, oral history interview, July 1983.
50 Anguilm, oral history interview.
51 LaRock, oral history interview.
52 Bertha Harding, oral history interview, July 1982.
53 *Iron River Reporter*, January 11, 1929.
54 Stephenson, *Recollections*, 81.
55 Stark, oral history interview.
56 R. R. Jehn, *Memoir of the Bay DeNoquet Company, Nahma, Michigan*, September 1952, Delta County Historical Society, Escanaba, Mich.
57 LaRock, oral history interview.
58 Ibid.
59 Ryan, *Early Loggers in Minnesota*, 39-41.
60 Jehn, *Memoir of the Bay DeNoquet Company*.
61 LaRock, oral history interview.
62 Corrigan, *Calked Boots and Cant Hooks*, 44.
63 Andreski, oral history interview.
64 John Ilmari Kolehmainen, "In Praise of the Finnish Backwoods Farmer," *Agriculture History* 24, no. 1 (January 1950), 2.

65 J. F. Thaden, "Finnish Farmers in Michigan," *Michigan Quarterly Bulletin* 28, no. 2 (1945) 92.
66 Engberg, "Labor in the Lake States Lumber Industry," 399.
67 *Newberry News*, January 1, 1904.
68 *Newberry News*, July 1, 1910.
69 John Haynes, "Revolt of the 'Timber Beasts': JWW Lumber Strike in Minnesota," *Minnesota History* (Spring 1971), 164.
70 *Hardwood Record*, May 10, 1920; Krog, "Marinette," 187–88.
71 Corrigan, *Calked Boots and Cant Hooks*, 62.
72 General Superintendent to Austin Farrell, October 1, 1923. Cleveland-Cliffs Iron Company Records, Lansing, Mich.
73 Ibid., July 22, 1924.
74 *Daily Mining Journal* (Marquette, Mich.), February 13, 1954.
75 Andreski, oral history interview.
76 *Weekly Mining Journal* (Marquette, Mich.), November 18, 1905.
77 Ibid., March 1, 1902.
78 Ibid.
79 Martin, *Call It North Country*, 159.
80 *American Lumberman*, July 25, 1903.
81 Ibid.
82 *Weekly Mining Journal* (Marquette, Mich.), December 26, 1908.
83 E. P. Radford to George Haggerson, April 29, 1884. Wisconsin Land and Lumber Company Records, Bentley Historical Library, Ann Arbor, Mich.
84 *Hardwood Record*, August 25, 1905.
85 Case, "Historiette of Hermansville, Michigan," 21.
86 Engberg, "Labor in the Lake States Lumber Industry," 218.
87 Alfred Johnson, *Reminiscences*. Ford Archives, Edison Institute, Dearborn, Mich.
88 Sutherland, "Consumption and Marketing," 13.
89 Omar Martineau, *Reminiscences*. Ford Archives, Edison Institute, Dearborn, Mich.
90 Joseph Francois, *Reminiscences*. Ford Archives, Edison Institute, Dearborn, Mich.
91 Martin, *Call It North Country*, 159–62.
92 Engberg, "Labor in the Lake States Lumber Industry," 218.
93 Daniel Hebard to Charles Hebard, February 8, 1923. Charles Hebard and Son Company Records, Marquette, Mich.
94 Sutherland, "Consumption and Marketing," 12–14.
95 *Escanaba Daily Press*, May 3, 1951.
96 Jesse Hamar, "Chassell, Michigan" (September 1934), Hamar Collection, Michigan Technological University Archives, Houghton, Mich.
97 Anderson, *I Married a Logger*, 80–81; Engberg, "Labor in the Lakes States Lumber Industry," 217.
98 Bess Elliot, oral history interview, August 1983.
99 *Ontonagon Herald*, September 29, 1910.
100 Knox Jamison, *A History of Bergland, Ontonagon County, Michigan* (Ontonagon, Mich.: Herald Press, 1965), 12–13.
101 Davis, "Demographic Changes and Resource Use," 28.
102 Corrigan, *Calked Boots and Cant Hooks*, 43.
103 Andreski, oral history interview.
104 *Ontonagon Herald*, June 23, 1906.
105 Ibid., April 28, 1906, June 15, 1907, and May 2, 1908.
106 Viola Stevens, *A History of Channing, Michigan* (Chicago: Adams Press, 1977), 43–44.
107 Davis, "Demographic Changes and Resource Use," 80.
108 Engberg, "Labor in the Lake States Lumber Industry, 73.
109 Corrigan *Calked Boots and Cant Hooks*, 43.
110 Engberg, "Labor in the Lake States Lumber Industry," 73.

111 Edward Glocke, oral history interview, July 1983.

112 Chris Chabot, *Tales of White Pine* (Ontonagon, Mich.: Ontonagon Herald, 1979), 136.

113 Lewis C. Reimann, *Hurley—Still No Angel* (Ann Arbor, Mich.: Northwood Publisher, 1954), 92.

114 Ibid., 78.

115 Corrigan, *Calked Boots and Cant Hooks*, 59.

116 Chabot, *Tales of White Pine*, 127.

117 Reimann, *Hurley—Still No Angel*, 76.

118 Chabot, *Tales of White Pine*, 134.

119 George Ferrar, oral history interview, July 1983, conducted by Jane Willan, U.S.D.A. Forest Service, Hiawatha National Forest, Escanaba, Mich.

120 Chabot, *Tales of White Pine*, 134.

CHAPTER 10. RISE OF THE RUBBER TIRE LUMBERJACKS

1 Jean Worth, "Paper Joins Upper Peninsula's Product Line in 1880," news bulletin from Mead Paper, Escanaba, Mich., May 1985.

2 Henry B. Steer, *Lumber Production in the United States, 1799–1946.* United States Department of Agriculture Miscellaneous Publication, no. 669, (Washington: United States Government Printing Office, 1948), 75, 84.

3 William N. Sparhawk and Warren D. Brush, *The Economic Aspects of Forest Destruction in Northern Michigan*, U.S. Department of Agriculture Bulletin No. 92 (Washington, D.C.: U.S. Government Printing Office, 1929), 3–9.

4 Ibid., 22–31.

5 Ibid.

6 Jamison, *This Ontonagon Country*, 242.

7 Sparhawk and Brush, *Economic Aspects of Forest Destruction*, 87.

8 Ibid., 79.

9 Ibid., 88.

10 Hazel H. Reinhardt, "Social Adjustments to a Changing Environment," in *The Great Lakes Forest: An Environmental and Social History* ed. Susan L. Flader (Minneapolis: University of Minnesota Press, 1983), 213.

11 Sparhawk and Brush, *Economic Aspects of Forest Destruction*, 49–52.

12 Iron County, Michigan, tax records, 1873–1936, Crystal Falls, Mich.

13 Sparhawk and Brush, *Economic Aspects of Forest Destruction*, 52.

14 E. R. McPhee to R. E. Brown, January 14, 1931. Bonifas Family Papers, Ann Arbor, Mich.

15 William Bonifas to R. E. Brown, April 13, 1931. Bonifas Family Papers, Ann Arbor, Mich.

16 William Bonifas to Dr. M. M. Hansen, January 13, 1931. Bonifas Family Papers, Ann Arbor, Mich.

17 Norman John Schmaltz, "Cutover Land Crusade: The Michigan Forest Conservation Movement, 1899–1931" (Ph.D. diss., University of Michigan, 1972), 290–93.

18 Ibid., 304–10.

19 Harold K. Steen, *The U.S. Forest Service: A History* (Seattle: University of Washington Press, 1976), 188.

20 Ibid., 190.

21 Dunbar, *Michigan*, 636.

22 O'Neil, "Ottawa National Forest," 15.

23 Ibid., 69.

24 Kenneth C. McMurray and Mary Greenshields, "Tax Delinquency in Michigan," in *Papers of the Michigan Academy of Science* 14 (1931), 382.

25 Shuman, "The Forest Resource Situation," 96.

26 Corrigan, *Calked Boots and Cant Hooks*, 181.

27 Andreski, oral history interview.

28 Glocke, oral history interview.

29 Superintendent to E. J. Hudson, June 13, 1930. Cleveland-Cliffs Records, Lansing, Mich.

30 U.S.D.A. Forest Service, *Ottawa National Forest Basic Data and Policy Section: Timber Management Plan, Fiscal Years 1950-1960* (Ironwood, Mich.: Ottawa National Forest, ca. 1960), 84.

31 Steer, *Lumber Production in the United States*, 84.

32 Marquette County Historical Society, *A Bond of Interest*, 22.

33 "CCI Feeding Men—Cost per Meal Chart," 1927-36, Cleveland-Cliffs Records, Lansing, Mich.

34 "Chart of Logging Costs per Thousand Feet, Average All Operations," 1926-35, Cleveland-Cliffs Records, Lansing, Mich.

35 LaRock, oral history interview.

36 Corrigan, *Calked Boots and Cant Hooks*, 191.

37 P. Staple to R. B. McKennan, February 11, 1935. Lands Files, Hiawatha National Forest, Escanaba, Mich.

38 Stearns Coal and Lumber Company to Solicitor, U.S.D.A., n.d. Lands Files, Hiawatha National Forest, Escanaba, Mich.

39 C. A. Saunders to R. G. Shreck, April 21, 1928. Lands Files, Hiawatha National Forest, Escanaba, Mich.

40 Steen, *The U.S. Forest Service*, 210-14.

41 Charles A. Symon, *We Can Do It! A History of the Civilian Conservation Corps in Michigan—1933-1942* (Escanaba, Mich.: Richards Printing, 1983), 9.

42 Ibid., 12-13.

43 LaRock, oral history interview.

44 Symon, *We Can Do It!*, 182, 90, 5-8.

45 LaRock, oral history interview.

46 McIver, "Whitefish Bay Country," n.p.

47 Symon, *We Can Do It!*, 69.

48 Philip C. Bellfy, "Michigan's Upper Peninsula, an Internal Colony: The Sault Sainte Marie Experience" (M.A. thesis, Michigan State University, 1981), 22-23.

49 Symon, *We Can Do It!*, 69.

50 Calvin W. Gower, "The CCC Indian Division: Aid for Depressed Americans, 1933-1942," *Minnesota History* (spring 1972), 5.

51 J. C. Cavill to John Collier, October 24, 1939. Great Lakes Indian Agency Records, Department of the Interior, Federal Records Center, Chicago, Ill.

52 Symon, *We Can Do It!*, 78.

53 Harold Titus, *The Land Nobody Wanted*, Michigan Agricultural Experimentation Station, Special Bulletin 332 (Lansing, Mich.: Department of Conservation, 1945), 3.

54 U.S. Forest Service, "Historical Summary of Land Adjustment and Land Classification, Ottawa National Forest, 1931-1962," Forest Supervisor's Office, Ironwood, Mich.

55 Debra E. Bernhardt, *We Knew Different: The Michigan Timber Workers' Strike of 1937* (Iron Mountain, Mich.: Mid-Peninsula Library Cooperative, 1979), 10-18.

56 Ibid., 16.

57 Erickson, oral history interview.

58 Anguilm, oral history interview.

59 Bernhardt, *We Knew Different*, 14.

60 Cleveland-Cliffs Iron Company, *Annual Report of the President* (Cleveland: By the Company, 1937).

61 Bernhardt, *We Knew Different*, 16.

62 *Diamond Drill* (Crystal Falls, Mich.), April 30, 1937.

63 Bernhardt, *We Knew Different*, 25.

64 Ibid., 15.

65 Ibid., 24.

66 *Ontonagon Herald*, June 5, 1937.

67 Bernhardt, *We Knew Different*, 22-26.

68 Ibid., 7–11.
69 Debra Bernhardt, "Ballad of a Lumber Strike," *Michigan History* (January/February 1982), 40.
70 Bernhardt, *We Knew Different*, 29.
71 *Diamond Drill* (Crystal Falls, Mich.), June 11, 1937.
72 *Ontonagon Herald*, June 19, 1937.
73 Brotherton, oral history interview.
74 "Distribution of Wood Cut in Operations #196 and #203 for the Period 1936–1938," Cleveland-Cliffs Records, Lansing, Mich.
75 Cleveland-Cliffs Iron Company, *Annual Report of the President*, 1939.
76 Brotherton, oral history interview.
77 Cleveland-Cliffs Iron Company, *Annual Report of the President*, 1942.
78 LaRock, oral history interview.
79 Plude, "Record of the N & N Railroad," n.p.

CHAPTER 11. THE PROCESS AND PATTERN OF PULPWOOD LOGGING

1 Furlong, oral history interview.
2 General Superintendent to Austin Farrell, May 1, 1923.
3 Olson, *Reminiscences*.
4 Superintendent to E. J. Hudson, September 3, 1930. Cleveland-Cliffs Records, Lansing, Mich.
5 Connor, *A Century with Connor Timber*, 109–10.
6 R. G. Steinke, *Reminiscences*, oral history transcript. Ford Archives, Edison Institute, Dearborn, Mich.
7 General Superintendent to Austin Farrell, November 3, 1928.
8 Brotherton, oral history interview.
9 Rogge, *Reminiscences*.
10 Ibid.
11 Anderson, *I Married a Logger*, 88–95.
12 Olson, *Reminiscences*.
13 Rogge, *Reminiscences*.
14 Connor, *A Century with Connor Timber*, 109.
15 Brotherton, oral history interview.
16 Corrigan, *Calked Boots and Cant Hooks*, 203.
17 Davis, "Demographic Changes and Resource Use," 178.
18 Superintendent to E. J. Hudson, June 13, 1930.
19 Anderson, *I Married a Logger*, 99.
20 Simon Brozoznowski, oral history interview, July 1983.
21 Thomas Nordine, oral history interview, July 1984.
22 Gordon R. Connor, "Logging Methods in the River Era, the Railroad Era, and in Today's Gasoline Era," in *Proceedings of the Sixth Annual Meeting of the Forest History Association of Wisconsin* (September 1981), 17.
23 Ibid.
24 Nordine, oral history interview.
25 David C. Smith, "Pulp and Paper Industry," in *Encyclopedia of American Forest and Conservation History*, ed. Richard C. Davis (New York: Macmillan Publishing Co., 1983), 554–56.
26 Ibid.
27 Herbert O. Fleischer, "Plywood and Veneer Industries," in *Encyclopedia of American Forest and Conservation History*, ed. Richard C. Davis (New York: Macmillan Publishing Co., 1983), 538–539.
28 Connor, "Logging Methods," 19.
29 *Escanaba Daily Press*, November 26, 1962.
30 Brotherton, oral history interview. See also Willard S. Bromley, "Selective Logging in Upper Michigan: A Case History," *Timber Cruiser* 10, no. 2 (Summer 1987), 4–8.

31 George B. Amidon, *The Development of Industrial Forestry in the Lake States* (Seattle: University of Washington College of Forestry, 1961), 32–33.
32 Cunningham and White, *Forest Resources of the Upper Peninsula of Michigan*, 25.
33 Amidon, *Development of Industrial Forestry*, 35.
34 Schuman, "The Forest Resource Situation," 106.
35 Ibid., 20.
36 Nordine, oral history interview.
37 O'Neil, "Ottawa National Forest," 59.
38 Schuman, "The Forest Resource Situation," 107.
39 Samuel P. Hays, "Human Choices in the Great Lakes Wild Lands," in *The Great Lakes Forest: An Environmental and Social History*, ed. Susan L. Flader (Minneapolis: University of Minnesota Press, 1983), 297–300.
40 Connor, *A Century with Connor Timber*, 117–18.
41 Anderson, *I Married a Logger*, 70.
42 Cunningham and White, *Forest Resources of the Upper Peninsula of Michigan*, 17.
43 Brotherton, oral history interview.
44 Corrigan, *Calked Boots and Cant Hooks*, 196–211.
45 Ibid., 211–14.
46 Ibid., 214–20.
47 Andreski, oral history interview.
48 H. F. Noske, "Map Showing Possible Sustained Yield Units, Upper Michigan," U.S.D.A. Forest Service, Ottawa National Forest, Ironwood, Mich.

CHAPTER 12. THE SOCIAL ENVIRONMENT OF PULPWOOD LOGGING

1 *Escanaba Daily Press*, May 3, 1951.
2 Bellfy, "Michigan's Upper Peninsula," 23–24.
3 *Escanaba Daily Press*, November 26, 1962.
4 *Evening News* (Sault Ste. Marie, Mich.), May 1, 1956.
5 *Daily Mining Journal* (Marquette, Mich.), August 9, 1927.
6 *The Timber Producer*, July 1977.
7 Anderson, *Reminiscences*.
8 Amidon, *Development of Industrial Forestry*, 35.
9 Schuman, "The Forest Resource Situation," 190.
10 Andreski, oral history interview.
11 Nordine, oral history interview.
12 Connor, "Logging Methods," 17.
13 *The Timber Producer*, August 1980.
14 Andreski, oral history interview.
15 Walter Mayo, "A History of Logging in Vilas County, 1856–1982," in *Proceedings of the Seventh Annual Meeting of the Forest History Association of Wisconsin* (August 1982), 28.
16 Anderson, *I Married a Logger*, 66.
17 Corrigan, *Calked Boots and Cant Hooks*, 223.
18 Ibid., 208.
19 Schuman, "The Forest Resource Situation," 190.
20 Corrigan, *Calked Boots and Cant Hooks*, 189.
21 Jamison, *A History of Bergland*, 17.
22 Corrigan, *Calked Boots and Cant Hooks*, 189.
23 Nordine, oral history interview.
24 Corrigan, *Calked Boots and Cant Hooks*, 233.
25 Ibid., 219.
26 Ibid., 223.
27 Charles Taylor, oral history interview, July 1980.
28 Anderson, *I Married a Logger*, 204–19.
29 *Northern Logger and Timber Processor*, August 1979.
30 Anderson, *I Married a Logger*, 26.

31 Shirley DeLongchamp, "The DeLongchamp Brothers—A Completely Mechanized Crew of Two," *Northern Logger and Timber Processor* (August 1980), 18.

32 Assistant Superintendent to William G. Mather, March 20, 1917.

33 Robert Radcliffe, oral history interview, July 1982.

34 Fred Cannon, oral history interview, conducted by Faye Swanberg, Munising, Mich.

35 LaRock, oral history interview.

36 General Superintendent to Austin Farrell, July 22, 1924.

37 Bernhardt, *We Knew Different*, 71.

38 Corrigan, *Calked Boots and Cant Hooks*, 232.

39 Connor, *A Century with Connor Timber*, 96. For another version of this anecdote see Anderson, *I Married a Logger*, 233.

40 *Daily Mining Journal* (Marquette, Mich.), February 10, 1941.

41 Ibid., June 15, 1940.

42 Ibid., January 15, 1941.

43 Ibid., August 26, 1942.

44 U.S. Department of State, "Special War Problems Division Report Concerning Red Cross Inspection of Fort Sheridan, POW Camps," Modern Military Branch, Military Archives Division, National Archives, Washington, D.C.

45 Shirley DeLongchamp, "World War II Prisoners Provided Woods Labor," *The Timber Producer* (December 1977), 30–31.

46 Brotherton, oral history interview.

47 Nordine, oral history interview.

48 Connor, *A Century with Connor Timber*, 98.

49 George D. Fowler, "The Last of a Dying Breed?" *Northern Logger and Timber Processor* (January 1980), 13.

50 Alex Bucephalus, "U.P. Woodsmen: Making a Living, Enjoying the Life," *The Timber Producer* (November 1979), 39.

51 Connor, "Logging Methods," 17.

52 Connor, *A Century with Connor Timber*, 99.

53 Fowler, "The Last of a Dying Breed?" 13.

54 Dorson, *Bloodstoppers and Bearwalkers*, 186.

55 Anderson, *I Married a Logger*, 155.

56 Ibid., 72.

57 Dorson, *Bloodstoppers and Bearwalkers*, 188–89.

58 Elmer Anderson, oral history interview, July 1983.

59 DeLongchamp, "The DeLongchamp Brothers," 51.

INDEX

Upper Peninsula Land Company, 167
Upper Peninsula Logger's Association, 197

Van's Harbor & Northern Railroad, 176, 179
Van's Harbor Land and Lumber Company, 176
Veneer and Paneling Manufacturers Association, 196
Volstead Act. *See* National Prohibition Act
Von Platen-Fox Lumber, 200, 231, 239, 251–52

Wakefield, Mich., 239
Warner, W. Wallace, 60
Watersmeet, Mich., 51, 178, 254, 256
Weidman Lumber Company, 231
Wells, Daniel, 31, 33–36, 39, 125
Wells, Daniel, Jr., 39, 124
Wells, John W., 146–47
Wells, Mich., 146–47, 184, 211–12, 215, 226, 259
West Bay, Mich., 76
Weston, Abijah, 42–43, 46, 81–82, 185
Weston Furnace Company, 185
Weston Lumber Company, 43, 81
Wetmore, Mich., 268
Weyerhauser Timber, 195
White, Stewart Edward, 70, 96

Whitefish Bay, 26, 47–48, 65, 69, 88
Whitefish River, 33, 36, 69–70, 80, 88–89, 92, 97, 121, 152
White River Logging Company, 263
Wilderness Society, 253
William Bonifas Lumber Company, 203–4, 227, 237–38, 241, 243–44, 254, 265
William Lumber Company, 179
William Mueller & Company, 150
Williams, Ephraim, 23
Williams, Gardner, 23
Williams Lake, 233
Willwin Company, 199
Winnebago Valley, 147
Wisconsin Land and Lumber Company (also known as the "IXL" Company), 147–50, 176, 184, 188, 197, 212, 239, 259–60
Wisconsin River, 71, 83
Witbeck, John H., 39
Wolf River, 38
Worcester, C. H., 170
Worcester Lumber Company, 170, 181–83, 195, 199, 212, 214
Workers' Party of America, 239
World War I, 160, 198, 203, 206, 208, 224, 248
World War II, 163, 244, 246–50, 252, 258–60, 262–63, 268–70
Wyman, Thomas B., 169–71
Wyman School of the Woods, 170

Titles in the Great Lakes Books Series

Orvie, The Dictator of Dearborn, by David L. Good, 1989

Seasons of Grace: A History of the Catholic Archdiocese of Detroit, by Leslie Woodcock Tentler, 1990

The Pottery of John Foster: Form and Meaning, by Gordon and Elizabeth Orear, 1990

The Diary of Bishop Frederic Baraga: First Bishop of Marquette, Michigan, edited by Regis M. Walling and Rev. N. Daniel Rupp, 1990

Walnut Pickles and Watermelon Cake: A Century of Michigan Cooking, by Larry B. Massie and Priscilla Massie, 1990

The Making of Michigan, 1820–1860: A Pioneer Anthology, edited by Justin L. Kestenbaum, 1990

America's Favorite Homes: A Guide to Popular Early Twentieth-Century Homes, by Robert Schweitzer and Michael W. R. Davis, 1990

Beyond the Model T: The Other Ventures of Henry Ford, by Ford R. Bryan, 1990

Life after the Line, by Josie Kearns, 1990

Michigan Lumbertowns: Lumbermen and Laborers in Saginaw, Bay City, and Muskegon, 1870–1905, by Jeremy W. Kilar, 1990

Detroit Kids Catalog: The Hometown Tourist, by Ellyce Field, 1990

Waiting for the News, by Leo Litwak, 1990 (reprint)

Detroit Perspectives, edited by Wilma Wood Henrickson, 1991

Life on the Great Lakes: A Wheelsman's Story, by Fred W. Dutton, edited by William Donohue Ellis, 1991

Copper Country Journal: The Diary of Schoolmaster Henry Hobart, 1863–1864, by Henry Hobart, edited by Philip P. Mason, 1991

John Jacob Astor: Business and Finance in the Early Republic, by John Denis Haeger, 1991

Survival and Regeneration: Detroit's American Indian Community, by Edmund J. Danziger, Jr., 1991

Steamboats and Sailors of the Great Lakes, by Mark L. Thompson, 1991

Cobb Would Have Caught It: The Golden Age of Baseball in Detroit, by Richard Bak, 1991

Michigan in Literature, by Clarence Andrews, 1992

Under the Influence of Water: Poems, Essays, and Stories, by Michael Delp, 1992

The Country Kitchen, by Della T. Lutes, 1992 (reprint)

The Making of a Mining District: Keweenaw Native Copper 1500–1870, by David J. Krause, 1992

Kids Catalog of Michigan Adventures, by Ellyce Field, 1993

Henry's Lieutenants, by Ford R. Bryan, 1993

Historic Highway Bridges of Michigan, by Charles K. Hyde, 1993

Lake Erie and Lake St. Clair Handbook, by Stanley J. Bolsenga and Charles E. Herndendorf, 1993

Queen of the Lakes, by Mark Thompson, 1994

Iron Fleet: The Great Lakes in World War II, by George J. Joachim, 1994

Turkey Stearnes and the Detroit Stars: The Negro Leagues in Detroit, 1919–1933, by Richard Bak, 1994

Pontiac and the Indian Uprising, by Howard H. Peckham, 1994 (reprint)

Charting the Inland Seas: A History of the U.S. Lake Survey, by Arthur M. Woodford, 1994 (reprint)

Ojibwa Narratives of Charles and Charlotte Kawbawgam and Jacques LePique, 1893–1895. Recorded with Notes by Homer H. Kidder, edited by Arthur P. Bourgeois, 1994, co-published with the Marquette County Historical Society

Strangers and Sojourners: A History of Michigan's Keweenaw Peninsula, by Arthur W. Thurner, 1994

Win Some, Lose Some: G. Mennen Williams and the New Democrats, by Helen Washburn Berthelot, 1995

Sarkis, by Gordon and Elizabeth Orear, 1995

The Northern Lights: Lighthouses of the Upper Great Lakes, by Charles K. Hyde, 1995 (reprint)

Kids Catalog of Michigan Adventures, second edition, by Ellyce Field, 1995

Rumrunning and the Roaring Twenties: Prohibition on the Michigan-Ontario Waterway, by Philip P. Mason, 1995

In the Wilderness with the Red Indians, by E. R. Baierlein, translated by Anita Z. Boldt, edited by Harold W. Moll, 1996

Elmwood Endures: History of a Detroit Cemetery, by Michael Franck, 1996

Master of Precision: Henry M. Leland, by Mrs. Wilfred C. Leland with Minnie Dubbs Millbrook, 1996 (reprint)

Haul-Out: New and Selected Poems, by Stephen Tudor, 1996

Kids Catalog of Michigan Adventures, third edition, by Ellyce Field, 1997

Beyond the Model T: The Other Ventures of Henry Ford, revised edition, by Ford R. Bryan, 1997

Young Henry Ford: A Picture History of the First Forty Years, by Sidney Olson, 1997 (reprint)

The Coast of Nowhere: Meditations on Rivers, Lakes and Streams, by Michael Delp, 1997

From Saginaw Valley to Tin Pan Alley: Saginaw's Contribution to American Popular Music, 1890–1955, by R. Grant Smith, 1998

The Long Winter Ends, by Newton G. Thomas, 1998 (reprint)

Bridging the River of Hatred: The Pioneering Efforts of Detroit Police Commissioner George Edwards, 1962–1963, by Mary M. Stolberg, 1998

Toast of the Town: The Life and Times of Sunnie Wilson, by Sunnie Wilson with John Cohassey, 1998

These Men Have Seen Hard Service: The First Michigan Sharpshooters in the Civil War, by Raymond J. Herek, 1998

A Place for Summer: One Hundred Years at Michigan and Trumbull, by Richard Bak, 1998

Early Midwestern Travel Narratives: An Annotated Bibliography, 1634–1850, by Robert R. Hubach, 1998 (reprint)

All-American Anarchist: Joseph A. Labadie and the Labor Movement, by Carlotta R. Anderson, 1998

Michigan in the Novel, 1816–1996: An Annotated Bibliography, by Robert Beasecker, 1998

"Time by Moments Steals Away": The 1848 Journal of Ruth Douglass, by Robert L. Root, Jr., 1998

The Detroit Tigers: A Pictorial Celebration of the Greatest Players and Moments in Tigers' History, updated edition, by William M. Anderson, 1999

Father Abraham's Children: Michigan Episodes in the Civil War, by Frank B. Woodford, 1999 (reprint)

Letter from Washington, 1863–1865, by Lois Bryan Adams, edited and with an introduction by Evelyn Leasher, 1999

Wonderful Power: The Story of Ancient Copper Working in the Lake Superior Basin, by Susan R. Martin, 1999

A Sailor's Logbook: A Season aboard Great Lakes Freighters, by Mark L. Thompson, 1999

Huron: The Seasons of a Great Lake, by Napier Shelton, 1999

Tin Stackers: The History of the Pittsburgh Steamship Company, by Al Miller, 1999

Art in Detroit Public Places, revised edition, text by Dennis Nawrocki, photographs by David Clements, 1999

Brewed in Detroit: Breweries and Beers Since 1830, by Peter H. Blum, 1999

For an updated listing of books in this series, please visit our Web site at http://wsupress/wayne.edu